The Everyday Internet All-in-One Desk Reference For Dummies®

Cheat Sheet

Search Engine Superstars

To Search For . . .	. . . Use This Search Engine	Address
Topics you are researching	Google Advanced Search	www.google.com/advanced_search
Topics arranged by category	Open Directory Project	http://directory.google.com
News	Google News	http://news.google.com
International news	World News Network	www.wn.com
An item you want to buy	Froogle	www.google.com/froogle
Same item at different stores	Price Grabber	www.pricegrabber.com
Airline tickets and hotel rooms	Mobissimo	www.mobissimo.com
A person	Yahoo! People Search	http://people.yahoo.com
A phone number	Phone Number.com	www.phonenumber.com
An address	White Pages	www.whitepages.com
Images	Google Image Search	www.google.com/imghp
MP3 files	Alta Vista Audio Search	www.altavista.com/audio
Magazine articles	LookSmart Find Articles	www.findarticles.com
Scholarly papers	Google Scholar	http://scholar.google.com/
Information about a company	Hoovers Online	www.hoovers.com
Newsgroups	Google Groups	http://groups.google.com
Mailing lists	Catalists	www.lsoft.com/lists/listref.html
Message boards	EZBoard	www.ezboard.com
Topics of interest to kids 7–12	Yahooligans!	www.yahooligans.com
Topics of interest to kids of all ages	Kids Click!	www.kidsclick.org

Copyright © 2005 Wiley Publishing, Inc. All rights reserved.
Item 8875-3.
For more information about Wiley Publishing, call 1-800-762-2974.

D0731230

For Dummies: Bestselling Book Series for Beginners

The Everyday Internet All-in-One Desk Reference For Dummies®

Cheat Sheet

Free Computer Security Tests

Online virus test at Panda ActiveScan (www.pandasoftware.com/activescan)

Online virus test at McAfee (http://us.mcafee.com/root/mfs)

Firewall and service-port tests at Shields UP! (https://www.grc.com/x/ne.dll?bh0bkyd2)

Take the Windows XP up-to-date test:

1. **Click the Start button and choose Control Panel.**
2. **Under "See Also" on the left side of the Control Panel window, click the Windows Update link.**

   Your Web browser opens a page at microsoft.com that tells you whether your copy of windows needs updating and instructs you how to download the latest updates.

Web Sites and Services

Use this convenient place to write down the user ID/names and passwords of Web sites and services on the Internet that you subscribe to. Please be careful to cross out or erase this information if you discard this book.

Web Site/Service/E-Mail Account	User ID/Name	Password

Wiley, the Wiley Publishing logo, For Dummies, the Dummies Man logo, the For Dummies Bestselling Book Series logo and all related trade dress are trademarks or registered trademarks of John Wiley & Sons, Inc. and/or its affiliates. All other trademarks are property of their respective owners.

For Dummies: Bestselling Book Series for Beginners

The Everyday

Internet

ALL-IN-ONE DESK REFERENCE

FOR

DUMMIES®

The Everyday Internet
ALL-IN-ONE DESK REFERENCE
FOR DUMMIES®

by Peter Weverka

Wiley Publishing, Inc.

The Everyday Internet All-In-One Desk Reference For Dummies®

Published by
Wiley Publishing, Inc.
111 River Street
Hoboken, NJ 07030-5774
www.wiley.com

Copyright © 2005 by Wiley Publishing, Inc., Indianapolis, Indiana

Published by Wiley Publishing, Inc., Indianapolis, Indiana

Published simultaneously in Canada

No part of this publication may be reproduced, stored in a retrieval system or transmitted in any form or by any means, electronic, mechanical, photocopying, recording, scanning or otherwise, except as permitted under Sections 107 or 108 of the 1976 United States Copyright Act, without either the prior written permission of the Publisher, or authorization through payment of the appropriate per-copy fee to the Copyright Clearance Center, 222 Rosewood Drive, Danvers, MA 01923, (978) 750-8400, fax (978) 646-8600. Requests to the Publisher for permission should be addressed to the Legal Department, Wiley Publishing, Inc., 10475 Crosspoint Blvd., Indianapolis, IN 46256, (317) 572-3447, fax (317) 572-4355, or online at http://www.wiley.com/go/permissions.

Trademarks: Wiley, the Wiley Publishing logo, For Dummies, the Dummies Man logo, A Reference for the Rest of Us!, The Dummies Way, Dummies Daily, The Fun and Easy Way, Dummies.com, and related trade dress are trademarks or registered trademarks of John Wiley & Sons, Inc. and/or its affiliates in the United States and other countries, and may not be used without written permission. [Insert third party trademarks from book title or included logos here.] All other trademarks are the property of their respective owners. Wiley Publishing, Inc., is not associated with any product or vendor mentioned in this book.

LIMIT OF LIABILITY/DISCLAIMER OF WARRANTY: THE PUBLISHER AND THE AUTHOR MAKE NO REPRESENTATIONS OR WARRANTIES WITH RESPECT TO THE ACCURACY OR COMPLETENESS OF THE CONTENTS OF THIS WORK AND SPECIFICALLY DISCLAIM ALL WARRANTIES, INCLUDING WITHOUT LIMITATION WARRANTIES OF FITNESS FOR A PARTICULAR PURPOSE. NO WARRANTY MAY BE CREATED OR EXTENDED BY SALES OR PROMOTIONAL MATERIALS. THE ADVICE AND STRATEGIES CONTAINED HEREIN MAY NOT BE SUITABLE FOR EVERY SITUATION. THIS WORK IS SOLD WITH THE UNDERSTANDING THAT THE PUBLISHER IS NOT ENGAGED IN RENDERING LEGAL, ACCOUNTING, OR OTHER PROFESSIONAL SERVICES. IF PROFESSIONAL ASSISTANCE IS REQUIRED, THE SERVICES OF A COMPETENT PROFESSIONAL PERSON SHOULD BE SOUGHT. NEITHER THE PUBLISHER NOR THE AUTHOR SHALL BE LIABLE FOR DAMAGES ARISING HEREFROM. THE FACT THAT AN ORGANIZATION OR WEBSITE IS REFERRED TO IN THIS WORK AS A CITATION AND/OR A POTENTIAL SOURCE OF FURTHER INFORMATION DOES NOT MEAN THAT THE AUTHOR OR THE PUBLISHER ENDORSES THE INFORMATION THE ORGANIZATION OR WEBSITE MAY PROVIDE OR RECOMMENDATIONS IT MAY MAKE. FURTHER, READERS SHOULD BE AWARE THAT INTERNET WEBSITES LISTED IN THIS WORK MAY HAVE CHANGED OR DISAPPEARED BETWEEN WHEN THIS WORK WAS WRITTEN AND WHEN IT IS READ. FULFILLMENT OF EACH COUPON OFFER IS THE SOLE RESPONSIBILITY OF THE OFFEROR.

For general information on our other products and services, please contact our Customer Care Department within the U.S. at 800-762-2974, outside the U.S. at 317-572-3993, or fax 317-572-4002.

For technical support, please visit www.wiley.com/techsupport.

Wiley also publishes its books in a variety of electronic formats. Some content that appears in print may not be available in electronic books.

Library of Congress Control Number: 2005923066

ISBN-13: 978-0-7645-8875-4

ISBN-10: 0-7645-8875-3

Manufactured in the United States of America

10 9 8 7 6 5 4 3 2

10/RY/QU/QV/IN

WILEY

About the Author

Peter Weverka is the bestselling author of several *For Dummies* books, including *Microsoft Office 2003 All-in-One Desk Reference For Dummies* and *Microsoft Money 2005 For Dummies*. He has written a grand total of 25 computer books. His humorous articles and stories — none related to computers, thankfully — have appeared in *Harper's, SPY,* and other magazines for grownups.

Dedication

For Aiko Sofia and Henry Gabriel.

Author's Acknowledgments

This book owes a lot to many hard-working people at the offices of John Wiley & Sons in Indiana. I would especially like to thank Steve Hayes for his good advice and for giving me the opportunity to write this and other books for Wiley.

The Internet is a big subject. I called on many friends and acquaintances to help me illuminate the far corners of the Internet. Thank you very much Jack Arnoux, John Boit, John Calder, Mona Dahl, Phil Gough, Kenneth Howard, Rob Rummel-Hudson, Michael Taylor, and Valentine Wannop.

Many thanks as well go to Beth Taylor, this book's project editor, for her diligence and grace under pressure, and John Edwards for copyediting the manuscript with so much care and attention. I would also like to thank Lee Musick, the technical editor, for following in my footsteps and making sure this book is indeed accurate. The witty cartoons on the pages of this book were drawn and captioned by Rich Tennant, and I thank him for it. I would also like to thank Anne Leach for writing the index.

Finally, thanks go to my family — Sofia, Henry, and Addie — for tolerating my odd working hours and my vampire demeanor at daybreak.

Publisher's Acknowledgments

We're proud of this book; please send us your comments through our online registration form located at www.dummies.com/register/.

Some of the people who helped bring this book to market include the following:

Acquisitions, Editorial, and Media Development

Project Editor: Beth Taylor

Acquisitions Editor: Steven Hayes

Copy Editor: John Edwards

Technical Editor: Lee Musick

Editorial Manager: Leah Cameron

Media Development Supervisor: Richard Graves

Editorial Assistant: Amanda Foxworth

Cartoons: Rich Tennant (www.the5thwave.com)

Composition Services

Project Coordinator: Nancee Reeves

Layout and Graphics: Andrea Dahl, Denny Hager, Stephanie D. Jumper, Barry Offringa, Melanee Prendergast, Heather Ryan

Proofreaders: John Greenough, Leeann Harney

Indexer: Anne Leach

Publishing and Editorial for Technology Dummies

    Richard Swadley, Vice President and Executive Group Publisher

    Andy Cummings, Vice President and Publisher

    Mary Bednarek, Executive Acquisitions Director

    Mary C. Corder, Editorial Director

Publishing for Consumer Dummies

    Diane Graves Steele, Vice President and Publisher

    Joyce Pepple, Acquisitions Director

Composition Services

    Gerry Fahey, Vice President of Production Services

    Debbie Stailey, Director of Composition Services

Contents at a Glance

Table of Contents

Introduction

These are exciting times for the Internet. Peer-to-peer file sharing, news aggregators, and other advances in technology have inspired a new generation of Web sites and services. Never before have this many Web sites and services been available on the Internet.

The idea behind this book is to present everything on the Internet that's worth doing because it's useful, it's a lot of fun, or it's innovative and therefore worth checking out. Close to a thousand different Web sites are described in this book, but this book isn't a directory of Web sites on the Internet. The focus is on doing things — researching, online banking, communicating, making new friends, playing games, talking over the Internet telephone, online shopping, online selling, and blogging. In the course of describing these and other activities — *everyday* activities that can be part of your Internet repertoire — I introduce you to the Internet's best Web sites and services.

What's in This Book, Anyway?

You are invited to dip into this book wherever you please or consult the Table of Contents or Index to find a topic that interests you. Either way, you will discover things about the Internet that you didn't know. This book was written in the spirit of the Internet itself. It is meant to be an adventure for the people who read it. Here is a bare outline of what you'll find in this book.

Book 1: Getting Started

Book I is meant to help you get going on the Internet.

In case you're curious about the technical aspects of the Internet, Chapter 1 explains in layman's terms how the Internet works, what an IP address is, how to read a Web-page address, and what goes on behind the scenes when you open a Web page. In Chapter 2, you find out how to select an Internet service provider and what the different modems are, and in Chapter 3, you get instructions for connecting your computer to the Internet.

Chapter 4 looks at a subject that seems to be on everyone's mind these days: how to protect your privacy and security while you're on the Internet. It explains how to protect your computer from viruses and spyware, what a firewall is, how to update Windows XP, and how to keep yourself from being a victim of identity theft. Chapter 5 detours into America Online and explains to AOL subscribers how to use that program on the Internet. Chapter 6 explains how to use plug-ins — companion programs such as Acrobat Reader, Flash Player, and Windows Media Player — that you need to make the most out of the Internet experience. In Chapter 7, I tell you how to make exploring the Internet a safe and rewarding experience for children. This chapter describes many Web sites for children, as well as Web sites for moms and dads looking for advice about parenting.

Book II: Exploring the Internet

Book II shows you how to use a Web browser and how to be an Internet researcher, or better yet, an Internet detective. It explains how you can reach into all corners of the Internet to find the information you need.

Chapter 1 describes the basics of browsing, how to bookmark Web sites so that you can revisit them, and how to engage in "social bookmarking" (sharing bookmarks with others). Chapter 2 explains how to customize the Internet Explorer browser as well as another browser, Mozilla, which I strongly suggest you check out.

Chapter 3 is the first of three chapters that explain how to conduct research over the Internet. It explains how search engines work and compares different search engines, their strengths, and their weaknesses. It also advises you on choosing a search engine and explains how to craft a thorough but penetrating search of the Internet. Chapter 4 looks at some specialty search engines designed for searching different areas of the Internet. It also explains how to search for images, audio, and video and tells you how to get help on the Internet from other researchers — you know, the human kind. In Chapter 5, I point you to online encyclopedias and other references and show you how to look up people, addresses, and telephone numbers on the Internet.

Chapter 6 examines how to get the latest news, where the online newspapers are, and how to get the news from abroad. It introduces an exciting new technology for staying on the top of the news — aggregators, which are software programs that gather news from different sources, including blogs, in one place so that you have all your favorite news sources at your fingertips.

Book III: E-Mailing

Book III explains more than a mere mortal needs to know about e-mailing, as well as how to protect yourself against spam, the junk e-mail that infests so many mailboxes.

Chapter 1 compares the merits of software and Web-based e-mail programs. It looks behind the scenes at how e-mailing works and tells you how to compress files to make sending them easier. Chapters 2, 3, and 4, respectively, describe how to handle e-mail with Outlook 2003, Outlook Express, and Yahoo! Mail. Not only do you find out how to send and receive e-mail and files, but you also discover how to organize e-mail so that you can always find the message you are looking for. To keep your inbox from getting too crowded, I show you how to send e-mail straight to different folders as soon as it arrives.

Chapter 5 explains strategies for stopping spam once and for all. It looks at how spammers get e-mail addresses, the preventative measures you can take against spam, and antispam software.

Book IV: Quick Communicating

Book IV examines all the different ways that you can communicate quickly with friends and strangers on the Internet.

Chapter 1 delves into AOL Instant Messenger, MSN Messenger, Yahoo! Messenger, and ICQ. It explains how to use these programs and maintain your privacy at the same time. Chapter 2 explains what blogs are, what makes for a good blog, and how to create a blog of your own. In Chapter 3, I look at two ways to exercise your ideas and obsessions on the Internet — mailing lists and message boards.

Chapter 4 looks at a much-neglected tool for researchers. It explains how to conduct research in newsgroups and subscribe to newsgroups with Outlook Express. Chapter 5 delves into the easiest way to connect and manage a group of likeminded people on the Internet — create a Yahoo! group. In Chapter 6, I explain how to chat on the IRC with people all around the world and how to create your own chat room.

Chapter 7 explains how you, too, can be a Web-site developer, and how you can do it on the cheap with online Web-site–creation tools. You also find out how to submit your Web site to search engines and make it more likely to appear in Internet searches. Chapter 8 explores the new online phenomenon of social networking. It describes Meetup.com, Upcoming.org, and other Web sites and services where you can make new friends and reunite with old ones.

Chapter 9 looks at what I think is the best deal on the Internet — free telephone calling anywhere in the world with Skype.

Book V: Your Personal Finances

Book V is all about improving your personal finances and making the banking chores go more smoothly.

Chapter 1 explains how to research different types of investments, get the latest financial news, and choose a broker. In Chapter 2, I describe how to maintain an online investment portfolio and be able to tell minute by minute how well or poorly your investments are doing. Chapter 3 looks at online banking — getting checking account balances online, paying bills online, and shopping for credit cards online.

Book VI: Bargain Shopping

Book VI is devoted to the idea that if you want it, you can find it on the Internet at a good price. For that matter, if you want it but can't afford it, you can at least find it on the Internet and dream about purchasing it one of these days.

Chapter 1 points you to some shopping search engines and Web sites that specialize in comparison shopping, as well as online catalogs, stores for bargain hunters, and consumer-report Web sites. In Chapter 2, I briefly take you to some online auction houses, and then you go to the granddaddy of auction houses, eBay, where you discover how to search for, bid on, and buy items. Chapter 3 looks into using PayPal, an excellent service for paying for items you purchased over the Internet. Finally, Chapter 4 presents a huge shopping bazaar of Web sites that sell items online. The Web sites are categorized so that you can find stores that interest you.

Book VII: Selling on the Internet

Book VII looks at how you can be the first on your block to be an online seller.

Chapter 1 explains everything you need to know to sell items successfully on eBay. It shows how to price items, make them attractive to buyers, manage an online auction, and close out a sale. Chapter 2 offers guidance for people who are thinking of selling items or services on the Internet. It explores how to find a market and set up an online store. Chapter 3 is a hands-on chapter with advice for packing the items you sold and buying postal services over the Internet.

Book VIII: Hobbies and Pastimes

Book VIII explains how to pursue different hobbies and exercise different pastimes on the Internet. I'm warning you: Some of the Web sites listed in Book VIII are addicting.

Chapter 1 is for people who like to play games — online video games, card games, and arcade-style games. You discover fantasy sports Web sites, as well as some unusual games begat by the Internet, such as the Geocaching. Chapter 2 is for travelers, armchair travelers, and adventurers of all stripes and varieties. It looks at how to plan a vacation and book airline tickets, hotels, and rental cars. You also find out where to go on the Internet to get travel advice.

Chapter 4 describes how to turn your lowly computer into an entertainment console. You find out how to view Internet movies, rent a DVD online, get your local television listings, play Internet radio, and find a book online. In Chapter 5, the focus is on music. You discover some Web sites for music lovers, look at online music stores, and survey services for sharing music files with others over the Internet. Chapter 6 takes you on a tour of iTunes, as you find out how to buy music from this online store, play and organize your music with iTunes software, and burn CDs. Chapter 6 shows amateur genealogists some of the many different Web sites and services they can use to search for their ancestors online.

Appendixes

Just when you thought you'd had enough torture, I tacked on three appendices and a glossary to the end of this book.

Appendix A explains how to register with and sign in to Yahoo! so that you can take advantage of Yahoo!'s many online services. Appendix B describes how to get a .NET passport so that you can play games online at the MSN Game Zone or open a Hotmail account. Appendix C explains how to sign up for a Google account.

Turn to the glossary at the end of this book whenever you are stumped by Internet terminology. I've done my best to define every Internet term, no matter how strange or obscure. Do you know what *airsnarf* means? How about *Googlewhacking?*

How I Selected Web Sites for This Book

You find descriptions and addresses of about a thousand Web sites in this book. Some people collect stamps. Some people collect butterflies. I collect Web sites. I am intrigued by the idea that a Web site is a creative endeavor in and of itself — that a Web site is a clickable piece of artwork. For this book, I chose not only Web sites that are useful for finding information or buying things but also Web sites that I consider intriguing, wonderful, astonishing, bizarre, or entertaining.

I stay away from the big corporate Web sites. Most Internet adventurers can find them on their own for one thing, and for another, those Web sites are too easy to get lost in. For shopping on the Internet, I prefer specialty stores to megastores that offer everything under the sun. It's easier to find interesting things at the specialty stores, and they're more fun. For the news, I prefer Web sites that specialize in one area to Web sites that blanket the earth, because the earth is too big to blanket. I still believe that the Internet is a democratic medium where the little guy has as much of a chance as the deep-pockets crowd to attract visitors to a Web site. I'm inclined to favor little-guy Web sites for that reason.

I also try to steer clear of Web sites and Web services that you have to pay for. Some Web sites are worth paying for. Ancestry.com, for example, is a bargain at $20 per month if you are doing genealogical research. I describe Ancestry.com and Web sites like it that are a bargain. Otherwise — and you can call me a cheapskate if you want — if I could find a way to get a service without paying, I did it. I'm trying to save you and me a buck.

Foolish Assumptions

Please forgive me, but I made one or two foolish assumptions about you, the reader of this book. I assumed that:

+ You have a computer and modem.
+ A Web browser — software for exploring the Internet — is installed on your computer.
+ You are kind to small animals.

Most of the computer instructions in this book are aimed at Windows users running the Windows XP operating system. My apologies to users of the Macintosh and to people running older versions of Windows. But take consolation: Except for instructions about setting up an Internet connection in Book II and instructions for using a Web browser in Book III, it doesn't matter which operating system or kind of computer you have. This book does you right anyway.

Conventions Used in This Book

I want you to understand all the instructions in this book, and in that spirit, I've adopted a few conventions.

To show you how to step through command sequences, I use the ⇨ symbol. For example, to create a playlist in iTunes, you choose File⇨New Playlist. This is just a shorthand method of saying "Choose New Playlist on the File menu."

Besides pressing hot keys to give commands, you can press combinations of keys. For example, pressing Ctrl+N is another way to create a new playlist in iTunes. In other words, you can hold down the Ctrl key and press the N key. Where you see Ctrl+, Alt+, or Shift+ and a key name or key names, press the keys simultaneously.

Where you see boldface letters or numbers in this book, it means that you should type the letters or numbers. For example, "Enter **125** in the Zoom box" means to do exactly that: Enter the number 125.

Icons Used in This Book

To help you get the most out of this book, I've placed icons here and there. Here's what the icons mean:

 All things being equal, nearly every Web site listed in this book deserves a Cool Web site icon. I wouldn't put a Web site in this book unless there was something special about it. Still, where you see the Cool Web site icon, I describe Web sites that are especially good, entertaining, intriguing, or useful.

 Next to the Tip icon, you can find shortcuts and tricks of the trade to make your travels on the Internet more enjoyable.

 Where you see the Warning icon, tread softly and carefully. It means that you are about to do something that you may regret later.

 When I explain a juicy little fact that bears remembering, I mark it with a Remember icon. When you see this icon, prick up your ears. You will discover something that you need to remember throughout your adventures on the Internet.

 When I am forced to describe high-tech stuff, a Technical Stuff icon appears in the margin. You don't have to read what's beside the Technical Stuff icons if you don't want to, although these technical descriptions often help you understand how a software feature works.

Good Luck, Reader!

If you have a comment about this book, a question, or a Web site you would like to share with me, send an e-mail message to me at this address: weverka@sbcglobal.net. Be advised that I usually can't answer e-mail right away because I'm too darned busy. I do appreciate comments and questions, however, because they help me pass my dreary days in captivity.

Book I

Getting Started

The 5th Wave   By Rich Tennant

"I think you're just jealous that I found a community of people on MSN.com that worship the yam as I do, and you haven't."

Contents at a Glance

Chapter 1: Getting Acquainted with the Internet

This chapter is devoted to people who aren't sure what the Internet is and people who are sure what it is but don't know how it works. How does a Web page that was created by someone on the other side of the planet take only a second or two to arrive on your computer screen? What is a Web address, anyway? How are Web pages constructed? These and other inscrutable mysteries are unscrewed in this chapter.

What Is the Internet?

The Internet is many things to many people. Erik-Lars Nelson, a *New York Daily News* columnist, famously called it ". . . a vanity press for the demented, the conspiratorial or the merely self-important." A newspaperman, Nelson lamented the fact that information presented on the Internet does not have to undergo a rigorous examination as to its accuracy. Whereas newspapers hold themselves to standards of truth and employ editors and fact-checkers to make sure what they print is accurate, fools can say whatever they want on the Internet — and they do so with complete confidence that somebody, somewhere will believe them.

In contrast to Nelson's dim view of the Internet, others describe the Internet in utopian terms. To these people, the Internet is a vast town meeting in which everyone can participate and everyone's voice is heard. The utopians see the Internet as a valuable tool for democracy and knowledge, a sort of international conversation for the greater good.

So what is the Internet? By the time you finish reading this book, you will decide for yourself. Meanwhile, here are some activities you can do on the Internet:

✦ **Research a topic:** If you know how to conduct a meaningful search, you can nearly always find the information you need on the Internet. Book II explains researching on the Internet. Figure 1-1 shows the home page of Alta Vista, a search engine.

✦ **Get the mail:** *E-mail,* or *electronic mail,* travels much faster than conventional mail. An e-mail message you send this instant can take as little as three seconds to reach its recipient, although you can't enclose a lock of hair or scent your e-mail message with evocative perfume. Book III explains e-mailing.

✦ **Connect to other researchers:** By joining newsgroups, mailing lists, and Yahoo! groups, you can get information about many different topics from other Internet researchers. Book IV looks into this subject.

✦ **Trade instant messages:** If you have teenagers, I bet you already know about instant messaging. Instant messaging permits a dozen or more people to gossip with one another while exercising their fingers on the keyboard. Book IV, Chapter 1 looks into instant messaging.

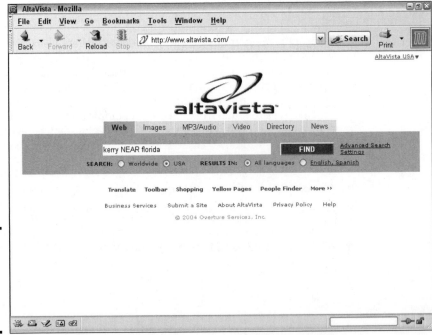

Figure 1-1:
The home page of Alta Vista, a search engine.

✦ **Turn your PC into a telephone:** Besides trading text messages, you can trade voice messages, and you can do it in real time such that your computer behaves like a telephone. Book IV, Chapter 9 shows how a PC can be made to act like a telephone.

✦ **Share your thoughts in a blog or online diary:** A *blog,* or Web log, is a journal, sometimes written anonymously, that anyone exploring the Internet can find and read. Book IV, Chapter 2 explains blogs, the latest Internet fad.

✦ **Join a social networking group:** You can make friends and connections online with people who share your passions and interests. Book IV, Chapter 8 explores this topic.

✦ **Improve your financial picture:** The Internet offers a thousand different ways to research financial opportunities, and you can also track your finances and bank online, as Book V explains.

✦ **Go shopping:** On the Internet, you can shop till you drop without leaving your own home. The Internet offers discount houses, auction houses, and better yet, Web sites where you can compare prices and find out whether an item is really worth buying. Book VI looks into shopping on the Internet.

✦ **Hold a rummage sale:** You can be a seller as well as a buyer. Selling your treasures and trinkets over the Internet is easier than you think, as you find out in Book VII.

✦ **Play games:** You can always find a card game on the Internet, not to mention a chess game and a poker game. Book VIII, Chapter 1 tells how to find a game for you.

✦ **Plan your next vacation:** For the sake of mental health, everyone needs to look forward to his or her next vacation. Book VIII, Chapter 2 explains how to plan and book ahead for your next trip to an exotic place.

✦ **Watch a movie:** Now that computers have more storage capacity and downloading files over the Internet is faster, you can watch movies on your computer. Just make sure that the boss doesn't see you do it. Book VIII, Chapter 3 shows how to temporarily turn your computer into a movie theater.

✦ **Turn your computer into a jukebox:** Downloading songs from the Internet is easier than ever, as Book VIII, Chapter 5 explains.

✦ **Trace your genealogy:** You can find many online databases with information about the dead, and many of them are free to explore. See Book VIII, Chapter 6.

How the Internet Works

In my experience, there are two kinds of people: the curious, who look under the hood of the car to figure out how the car runs, and the others, whose blind faith in machinery makes them indifferent. Even if you fall in the second category, knowing a little about the workings of the Internet is worthwhile. Someday you may decide to create a Web site. Or, you may wonder why your Internet connection isn't working. In times like those, it pays to know something about the Internet.

These pages explain in simple terms how the Internet works. And to help you understand the workings of the Internet, I start with a history lesson.

A mercifully brief history of the Internet

Most historians trace the beginning of the Internet to Sputnik, the first satellite to successfully orbit the earth. After Russia launched Sputnik in 1957, the United States embarked on an ambitious national project to bridge what was called the "technology gap" and catch up to the Russians in science and technology. As part of that effort, the Department of Defense established the Advanced Research Projects Agency, or ARPA, in 1958. The agency's job was to oversee the research and development of new technology for military use.

ARPA employed scientists and engineers in universities and laboratories throughout the United States. These scientists and engineers needed a way to exchange information and collaborate with one another. To this end, ARPA developed the first computer network, called ARPANET, in 1969. The network permitted researchers throughout the United States to dial in to and access four host computers — three in California and one in Utah — over the telephone lines.

To speed the transmission of data, ARPANET employed a novel means of sending information over the telephone lines called *packet switching*. Instead of data being sent in a continuous stream, it was divided into smaller units called *packets* and sent all at once over available telephone lines. Arriving at their destination, the packets were recompiled — in other words, the data were reassembled so that it could be read or interpreted. Like ARPANET, the Internet is a packet-switching network. Packet switching makes it possible for data to travel very quickly, because the packets can arrive out of order, withstand delays in transmission, and travel by many different routes to their destination. By the strictest definition, the Internet is simply a packet-delivery system. It can deliver information packets anywhere in the world in less than a second.

ARPANET was the forerunner of the Internet. In ARPANET, data did not pass through a central hub; instead, all the host computers were connected to all the other host computers. This revolutionary decentralized design permitted data to take many different routes from one computer to another because the computers were interconnected. And if one part of the network failed, the network's interconnectedness made it possible for other parts to pick up the slack and continue transmitting data by a different route. Moreover, the decentralized structure of ARPANET made it easier to add computers to the network.

In the beginning, only four host computers — computers that other computers can connect to, similar to what we call Web servers — were available on ARPANET, but universities and research centers soon understood the value of being able to collaborate over a network, and more host computers were added. By 1971, there were 23 host computers on ARPANET. In 1972, e-mail was invented so that researchers could quickly exchange messages, and network traffic increased dramatically. In 1977, ARPANET featured 111 host computers. By 1989, ARPANET had become a "network of networks," with some 100,000 host computers.

ARPANET had turned into the Gargantua that we call the Internet. ARPANET's designers envisioned an interconnected network with no central authority to which new networks could be added. ARPANET succeeded beyond its designers' wildest dreams. Estimates of how many people worldwide use the Internet range from 600 to 730 million. In 2001, for the first time, the number of hours that Americans watch television shrank because the Internet had become an alternative to television watching. Today, no single organization controls the Internet. Each organization with a host computer is responsible for maintaining its part of the Internet so that data packets can speed merrily along to their destinations.

The Open Directory Project, a Web directory maintained by volunteers, offers a Web page with links where you can get statistics about Internet use. The Web page is located at this address: `http://dmoz.org/Computers/Internet/Statistics_and_Demographics`.

The World Wide Web

The early Internet was strictly for academics and researchers. To retrieve documents, you had to know advanced programming commands. You had to remember arcane numerical Internet addresses. Each host computer had a different command set for accessing files.

Starting in the late 1980s, however, innovations in computer science made the Internet available to everyone. In 1989, a protocol called http, or *hypertext transfer protocol,* made it easy to transfer files over the Internet. In computer terminology, a *protocol* is set of rules by which computers communicate with one another. You no longer had to learn a different set of commands to transfer a file from a host computer to your computer because each host computer stuck to the http standard. The letters *http* at the start of Web addresses refer to the hypertext transfer protocol (see Figure 1-2).

The late 1980s also saw the invention of the World Wide Web, also known simply as "the Web." The letters *www* in Web addresses stand for World Wide Web (refer to Figure 1-2). The man who coined this term, a computer scientist named Tim Berners-Lee, called the Web "the universe of network-accessible information, an embodiment of human knowledge." Berners-Lee was one of those utopians I mention at the start of this chapter. In prosaic terms, the World Wide Web is just the sum of all the files — the Web pages, audio files, movie files, and computer programs — that you can bring into your computer from the Internet by way of the hypertext transfer protocol.

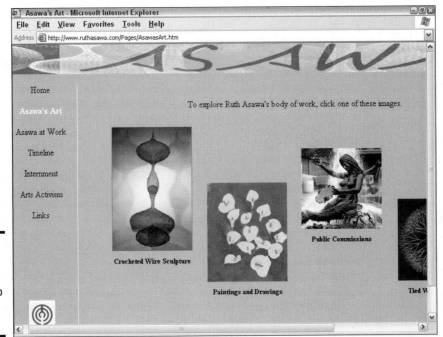

Figure 1-2:
Ever wondered what a Web address is all about?

Web addresses

Besides inventing the term *World Wide Web,* Tim Berners-Lee invented the addressing system for locating files on the Web. Previous to this system, you had to enter a hard-to-remember IP address number to visit a Web site, but the system replaced numbers with descriptive domain names. In the system, file addresses are designated by a domain name and then by a folder name within the domain. To see how Web addresses work, consider the address of the Web page shown in Figure 1-2:

```
http://www.ruthasawa.com/Pages/AsawasArt.htm
```

A computer reads this address like so:

✦ `http://`: The file at this address can be transferred using the hypertext transfer protocol.

✦ `www`: The file is located on the World Wide Web.

✦ `ruthasawa.com`: The domain name of the Web site to connect to is `ruthasawa.com`. The next section in this chapter explains what domain names are and how computers use them to locate computers on the Internet. The `.com` ending on the domain name tells you that the site is commercial (for-profit) in nature.

✦ `/Pages`: Within the ruthasawa.com Web site, the file is found in a folder called `Pages`. Files on Web sites are stored in folders, just as files are stored in folders on your computer.

✦ `/AsawasArt.htm`: The file to be transferred is called `AsawasArt.htm`. The `.htm` file extension means that the file is written in hypertext markup language.

The addressing convention that Tim Berners-Lee invented made it possible for computers to quickly locate and download files from the World Wide Web. His addressing convention also made the Web more weblike. Now that everyone agreed on how to address Web pages, linking Web pages became much easier. Hyperlinks began appearing on Web pages. For the first time, you could point to and click a hyperlink on one Web page and go straight to another page. (By the way, Berners-Lee called Web addresses *uniform resource locators,* or URLs, a term that is thankfully falling out of favor. I only mention URLs here in case someone mentions them to you and you want to nod your head wisely because you know what URLs are. In this book, I refer to URLs as Web addresses.)

More computer science innovations brought the Internet even closer to home. Faster modems decreased the amount of time you had to wait for Web pages to arrive on your computer. In the early 1990s, the first Web browser, Mosaic, appeared. Now a program made especially for exploring the Internet was available. Also in the mid-1990s, the Java computer language made it possible to incorporate video and sound on Web pages. And don't forget the mouse! All hail the mouse! Where would we be without it? You can explore the Internet for hours at a time without touching the keyboard thanks to this furry little animal. And it's amazing that the mouse didn't become a computer apparatus on Macs until 1986 and on PCs until 1987.

IP addresses

Every computer that's connected to the Internet has an *Internet Protocol address,* better known as an *IP address.* Computers use these addresses to locate data and to send data over the Internet.

Want to know your computer's IP address?

Follow these steps to find out your computer's IP address:

1. **Choose Start⇨Programs⇨Accessories⇨ Command Prompt (choose MS-DOS instead of Command Prompt if you are running Windows 98 or Windows Me).**

   The Command Prompt window opens.

2. **Enter** ipconfig **and press Enter.**

   The window shows you information about your computer, including its IP address.

   Here's an even faster way to find out your IP address. Open your Web browser, enter this address in the Address bar, and press Enter:

   www.whatismyip.com

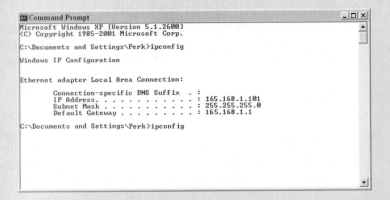

```
Command Prompt                                                          _ |□| x|
Microsoft Windows XP [Version 5.1.2600]
(C) Copyright 1985-2001 Microsoft Corp.

C:\Documents and Settings\Perk>ipconfig

Windows IP Configuration

Ethernet adapter Local Area Connection:

        Connection-specific DNS Suffix  . :
        IP Address. . . . . . . . . . . . : 165.168.1.101
        Subnet Mask . . . . . . . . . . . : 255.255.255.0
        Default Gateway . . . . . . . . . : 165.168.1.1

C:\Documents and Settings\Perk>ipconfig
```

If yours is a DSL Internet connection or cable modem connection, your IP address is permanent and unchanging. If yours is a dialup Internet connection, your Internet provider assigns you a new IP address each time you connect to the Internet.

An IP address is a 32-bit (4-byte) binary number, which needn't concern you very much. The point is that the number identifies a computer on the Internet. Here is an example of an IP address:

`216.239.39.99`

Each domain name — `google.com`, `yahoo.com`, and `microsoft.com`, for example — is assigned an IP address. The IP address just listed, for example, belongs to the domain name `google.com`. When you enter a Web address in your browser to view a Web page, your computer takes note of the domain name part of the address (`google.com`, `yahoo.com`, or `microsoft.com`, for example) and sends a query to a *domain name server* asking for the IP address that's assigned to the domain name. The domain name server, in turn, sends the IP address of the domain name back to your computer. Your computer then sends a request for Web-page files from the IP address in question, and in less than a second, if you have a fast Internet connection, a Web page appears on your computer screen.

Something similar happens when you send an e-mail message. Your computer sends a query asking for the IP address of the domain name, the part of the e-mail address after the at (@) symbol. When the IP number is returned, the e-mail message is sent.

To see how IP addresses work, try this simple exercise:

1. **Open your Web browser.**

2. **In the Address bar, type** www.google.com **and press Enter.**

Your browser opens to the Google home page, as shown at the top of Figure 1-3.

3. **Delete the** www.google.com **in the Address bar and enter the following:**

`216.239.39.99`

4. **Press Enter.**

You see the Google home page again, as shown at the bottom of Figure 1-3, because the number you entered in Step 3 is the IP address of `google.com`.

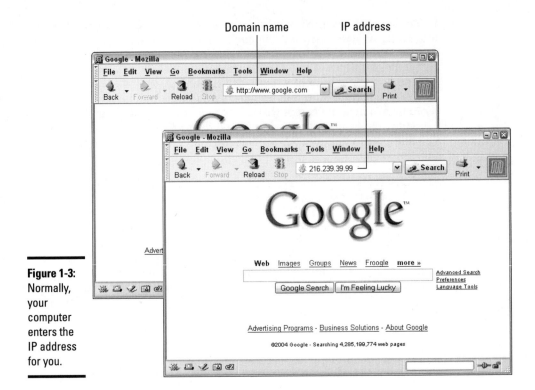

Domain name   IP address

Figure 1-3:
Normally,
your
computer
enters the
IP address
for you.

In the old days, before the domain-name addressing system for locating files on the Web, you had to enter IP addresses. Aren't you glad you don't live in the old days? Entering descriptive Web addresses sure beats entering 32-bit binary numbers.

Finding a Web site's IP address

If you are called on to play Internet detective and find the IP address of a Web site, you can follow these steps to find it:

1. **Choose Start⇨Programs⇨Accessories⇨Command Prompt.**

If you are running the Windows 98 or Windows Me operating system, choose MS-DOS instead of Command Prompt. You see the Command Prompt window.

2. **Enter** ping **and a blank space.**

3. **Enter the domain name of the Web site whose IP address you need.**

For example, to find the IP address of `google.com`, enter **google.com,** as shown in Figure 1-4.

4. Press Enter.

The Command Prompt window tells you the Web site's IP address (refer to Figure 1-4). Notice the "approximate round trip times in milli-seconds" in the Command Prompt window. It took my computer only 76 milliseconds to ask for and receive the IP address of `google.com`. That's less than a tenth of a second. Information travels fast on the Internet.

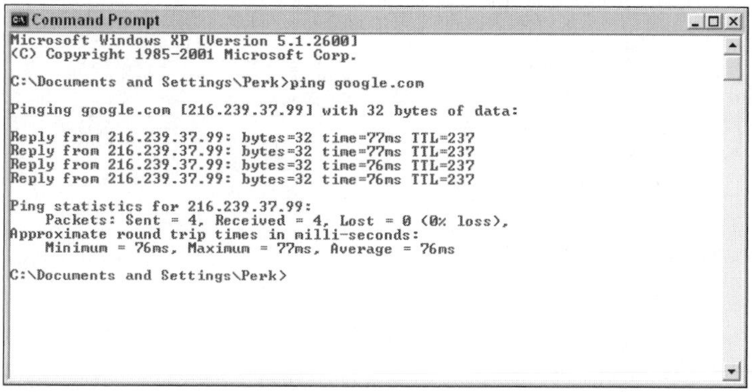

Book I
Chapter 1

Getting Acquainted
with the Internet

Figure 1-4:
You can "ping" to find IP addresses on the Internet.

```
Command Prompt                                                    _□×
Microsoft Windows XP [Version 5.1.2600]
(C) Copyright 1985-2001 Microsoft Corp.

C:\Documents and Settings\Perk>ping google.com

Pinging google.com [216.239.37.99] with 32 bytes of data:

Reply from 216.239.37.99: bytes=32 time=77ms TTL=237
Reply from 216.239.37.99: bytes=32 time=77ms TTL=237
Reply from 216.239.37.99: bytes=32 time=76ms TTL=237
Reply from 216.239.37.99: bytes=32 time=76ms TTL=237

Ping statistics for 216.239.37.99:
    Packets: Sent = 4, Received = 4, Lost = 0 (0% loss),
Approximate round trip times in milli-seconds:
    Minimum = 76ms, Maximum = 77ms, Average = 76ms

C:\Documents and Settings\Perk>
```

How Web Pages Work

If a friend tells you to go to the such-and-such Web page because it is entertaining, thought provoking, or funny, and you go there, you aren't really going anywhere. Really, the Web page is coming to you. The files with which the Web page is composed come to your computer so that you can view them.

All but the simplest Web page consists of many different files — text files, graphic files, and sometimes animation, video, and sound files. To see what I mean, take a look at Figure 1-5, a Web page from `amazon.com`. The top half of the figure shows the Web page without the graphic images; in the bottom half of the figure, you can see where the graphic image files have been plugged into the Web page. This Web page consists of a dozen or more files.

When you bring a Web page like this to your computer, the image files tag along behind the Web page. Hypertext markup language in the Web page tells your Web browser where to plug in each tag-along file, and the result is a full-fledged Web page.

Missing image files

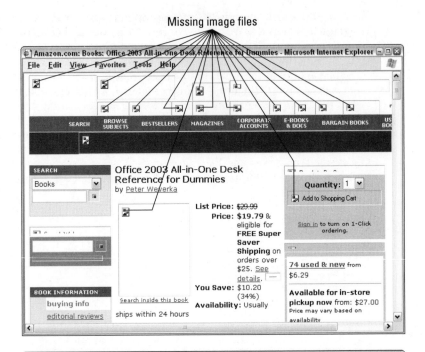

Figure 1-5:
Most Web
pages
consist of
many
different
files.

Web pages are written in *hypertext markup language,* or HTML, the computer language that tells the Web browser how to lay out and construct Web pages from the different files with which they are made. Want to see something scary? In your browser, choose View⇨Source (in Internet Explorer) or View⇨Page Source (in Mozilla) to see the HTML codes with which a Web page is constructed. Figure 1-6 shows some of the HTML code used to construct part of the page shown in Figure 1-5.

These codes are scary, but don't be discouraged if you want to create a Web site of your own. Thanks to the miracle of modern computer science, you can create Web pages and Web sites without having to know or write HTML codes, as Book IV, Chapter 7 explains. Keep your chin up. All is not lost.

Figure 1-6: HTML codes for the Web page shown in Figure 1-5.

```
103-9514531-5095842[1] - Notepad
File  Edit  Format  View  Help
<a
href=/exec/obidos/subst/home/home.html/ref%3Dtab%5Fb%5Fgw%5F1/103-95145
31-5095842><img
src="http://g-images.amazon.com/images/G/01/nav/personalized/tabs/welco
me-off-whole.gif" width=60 height=26 border=0 id=tb_gateway></a><a
href=/exec/obidos/tg/stores/your/store-home/-/0/ref%3Dpd%5Fysl%5Fb%5Ffr
%5F2/103-9514531-5095842><img
src="http://g-images.amazon.com/images/G/01/nav/personalized/tabs/yours
tore-off-sliced._ZCRABBLE%27S,0,2,0,0,verdenab,7,90,90,80_.gif"
width=81 height=26 border=0></a><a
href=/exec/obidos/tg/browse/-/283155/ref%3Dtab%5Fb%5Fb%5F3/103-9514531-
5095842><img
src="http://g-images.amazon.com/images/G/01/nav/personalized/tabs/books
-on-sliced.gif" width=39 height=26 border=0
id=tb_books></a></nobr></td><td colspan=2><nobr><a
href=/exec/obidos/tg/browse/-/1036592/ref%3Dtab%5Fb%5Fap%5F4/103-951453
1-5095842><img
src="http://g-images.amazon.com/images/G/01/apparel/apparel-tab-btm.gif
" width=70 height=26 border=0></a><a
href=/exec/obidos/tg/browse/-/172282/ref%3Dtab%5Fb%5Fe%5F5/103-9514531-
5095842><img
src="http://g-images.amazon.com/images/G/01/nav/personalized/tabs/elect
```

Chapter 2: Choosing an Internet Service

In This Chapter

✔ Looking at the equipment you need

✔ Comparing broadband and dialup connections

✔ Comparing the types of Internet connections

✔ Asking the right questions when you choose an Internet service provider

This short chapter is for people who want to jump aboard the Internet but haven't chosen an ISP yet. ISP stands for *Internet service provider*. You need to sign up with an ISP to explore the Internet and send and receive e-mail. This chapter gets you up to speed on speedy broadband connections and slower dialup connections. It compares the types of Internet connections and explains what to look for as you choose an ISP.

The Equipment and Software You Need

As nice as it is to connect to the Internet and view Web pages by relying on your psychic powers alone, most people can't do that. Besides a computer, most people need a Web browser and a modem.

A *Web browser* is a software program for exploring the Internet. Popular browsers include Internet Explorer and Mozilla. If your computer runs Windows, the Internet Explorer browser is already loaded on your computer. (Book II, Chapter 2 describes and compares the different Web browsers.)

A *modem* is a hardware device for linking a computer through the telephone lines to the Internet. Modems convert digital data (electronic signals representing binary numbers) to analog data (signals that can have many variations) so that the data can travel over the telephone lines. After the analog signal arrives, the modem on the receiving end converts the analog data back into digital data that computers can understand. Modem stands for *modulator/demodulator*.

Data transmission rates for Internet dialup modems are measured in kilobits per second (Kbps). Faster broadband modem rates are given in megabits per second (Mbps). Table 2-1 describes the different speeds at which modems operate. The first two entries in the table are dialup connections; the others are broadband (more about that in a minute).

Table 2-1		Modem Types
Modem	*Connection Speed*	*Description*
Dialup Connections		
Internal	56 Kbps	The modem is plugged into the motherboard of the computer — in other words, it's inside the computer. To connect to the Internet, you plug the phone line into a port on the back or side of your computer.
External	56 Kbps	The modem is attached to your computer through a parallel, serial, or USB (Universal Serial Bus) port. An external modem is separate from your computer. You plug the modem into your computer and the telephone line into your modem.
Broadband Connections		
ISDN	128 Kbps	This requires installing ISDN (Integrated Services Digital Network) adapters in your computer. The connection is made through high-speed digital cables installed by the phone computer or a service provider.
Cable	384 Mbps	This type of modem can be an external or internal type. Through a cable wall outlet, the computer is connected to the cable TV line.
DSL	384 Mbps	This type of modem can also be internal or external. It requires a network adapter.

Want to test the speed of your modem? Go to the Test Your Internet Speed Web page at this address: `http://modem.4mg.com`. Click the Test Your Internet Speed link, and you go to a page with a graph that plainly shows how fast or slow your Internet connection is.

Broadband versus Dialup Connections

Connections between a computer and the Internet fall in two categories: broadband and dialup. A *broadband connection* is an Internet connection that is always on and is capable of transmitting data very quickly. Broadband services can be delivered over the telephone lines, by way of a private network, by way of a cable modem, or in a wireless network. A broadband connection is much faster than a dialup connection. If you plan to spend more than an hour a day on the Internet and do sophisticated stuff like play video games online or download music, you owe it to yourself to spend the extra money for a broadband connection.

A *dialup connection* is one in which the computer literally dials a telephone number whenever you connect with the Internet. The only advantage of a dialup connection over a broadband connection is the cost. At $10–$25 per month, dialup service costs a third as much as broadband service, which is $40–$60 per month. If you've explored the Internet using a broadband service, it's hard to go back to the slower dialup method. What's more, if you have broadband service, you can simultaneously talk on the telephone while you explore the Internet. With a dialup connection, the phone line is occupied, so you can't make a phone call while you're online — nor can anyone call you. (The next chapter in this mini-book explains how to connect a computer to the Internet.)

Types of Connections

Table 2-2 compares the types of Internet connections. Apart from dialup connections, not all ISPs offer the connection types listed in the table. Before you can install a DSL connection, the telephone company must verify that the lines in your area can support DSL. With a cable connection, data are delivered over the same line that carries the television signal.

Table 2-2		Types of Internet Connections	
Connection	*Speed**	*Equipment*	*Cost*
Dialup	50 Kbps	Internal or external modem, telephone line	$10–25
DSL	384 Mbps	Ethernet card, external cable modem, Cat-5 cable	$40–60
Cable	384 Mbps	Ethernet card, external cable modem, Cat-5 cable	$40–60
Satellite	400 Mbps	Ethernet card, dialup modem	$50–110 plus installation

Upload average speed; download speeds are typically five to ten times higher.

Choosing an Internet Service Provider

If you intend to explore the Internet, send and receive e-mail, or create a Web site for the Internet, your first task is to choose an ISP. An *ISP* is a company that provides customers access to the Internet, e-mail services, and in some cases, the opportunity to post Web sites. You've probably heard of popular ISPs such as America Online (AOL), MSN, and EarthLink. Some 7,000 ISPs can be found in the United States. How do you choose which one is right for you? Following are some considerations to make as you choose an ISP.

Monthly service charge

Monthly service charges range from $10 to $30 (for people who use dialup modems) to $30 or more per month for a fast digital subscriber line (DSL), cable modem, or T1 connection.

The setup fee

Most ISPs charge a one-time setup or enrollment fee. Depending on how many ISPs are located in your area and how stiff the competition among ISPs is, fees vary from no charge to $40.

Long-distance dialup

If you connect to the Internet by dialup modem, the modem in your computer calls the ISP's computers. If that telephone call is a long-distance call, going on the Internet becomes an expensive proposition because you have to pay long-distance rates for each connection time. National ISPs, such as those run by the major telephone companies, offer regional phone numbers that you can call no matter where you travel. If you travel a lot and have to connect a laptop computer to the Internet from various cities and regions, consider signing on with an ISP that offers *points of presence* (or simply POPs), which are the regional telephone numbers that you can dial to connect to an ISP.

Online time

Nowadays, nearly every ISP charges a flat monthly rate to go online for as many hours as you want. Still, find out whether the ISP that you're considering charges a flat rate or a by-the-hour rate. That way, you know what to expect from your first bill.

Server space for your Web pages

Some ISPs offer their subscribers the opportunity to post Web sites at no extra charge on their company servers; others charge an additional fee to subscribers who want to put their Web sites on the Internet. Most ISPs allow 1–2MB to as much as 50MB of server space. If you are new to the Internet, the prospect of creating Web pages probably seems foreign to you, but believe me, you may well consider creating a Web site down the road, and you will need a place to put it on the Internet. If you can get free server space for your Web pages, more power to you.

Spam blocking and virus protection

Some ISPs have built-in software that screens out *spam,* which is the Internet equivalent of junk mail. Some ISPs screen all files for viruses as well. On the face of it, virus screening seems like a good deal, but some virus screeners aren't sophisticated and merely block certain kinds of files, such as .exe (executable) files or files that are larger than a certain number of megabytes. You may legitimately receive these kinds of files from coworkers, in which case virus screening isn't for you. Besides, you can rely on your own antivirus software to block viruses. (Book I, Chapter 4 looks into viruses and other security considerations; Book III, Chapter 5 explains how to prevent spam.)

Length-of-service contracts

Anybody who has a cell phone knows that length-of-service contracts can be a real burden. Under these contracts, you have to sign on for a year (and sometimes longer). If the service doesn't suit you, you can't quit the service during the contract period without paying a fee. If an ISP that you're considering requires you to sign a length-of-service contract, make sure that you investigate the ISP — especially its billing policies — before you sign your name on the dotted line.

Technical help

Typically, the big corporate ISPs such as SBC and Earthlink don't offer very good technical assistance to customers. Try to get assistance from them, and you have to negotiate a phone tree and be very patient. Small, local ISPs do a much better job of providing assistance. You can get a real, live human on the phone very quickly. However, local ISPs sometimes charge a higher monthly rate for service than the corporate behemoths.

Try to get an idea of how long the company takes to reply to e-mail queries for technical assistance. Find out as well whether the ISP maintains a 24-hour telephone line that you can call if you need technical assistance. (By the way, queries as to what to do about smoke coming from a modem should be directed to the local fire department, which is obliged to respond faster than an ISP.)

Chapter 3: Setting Up Your Internet Connections

In This Chapter

✔ Connecting to the Internet with a dialup modem

✔ Connecting to the Internet with a DSL or cable modem

✔ Setting up an e-mail account for an e-mail program

*B*efore you can climb aboard the Internet, you have to take care of all the Internet connections. You need to configure your software so that it knows how to connect to your Internet service provider (ISP). You need to set up an e-mail account.

Fortunately, the people who sell and set up Internet connections have made this business considerably easier than it used to be. You were probably sent a kit with a CD and other material that explains and takes you step by step through the setup procedures. This chapter explains those procedures and describes how to set up an e-mail account so that you can send and receive e-mail. (If you haven't chosen an ISP yet, refer to the previous chapter.)

Making a successful connection to the Internet for the first time is more your ISP's responsibility than yours. Do not hesitate to ask for help from your ISP to complete this task! This chapter gives general instructions for connecting, but every ISP is different. If you have any questions, call your ISP.

Connecting with a Dialup Modem

As the previous chapter explains, a dialup connection is one in which the computer literally dials a telephone number to connect to the Internet. To connect, you use a dialup modem. These modems can either be located inside the computer or be a separate device that sits on the desk or floor (where they collect dust and inevitably get kicked around a little). If you're lucky, your ISP has provided you with an automated program on a CD to help with the setup. But even if you're not lucky, setting up isn't that hard, especially if you're running Windows XP, which offers the New Connection Wizard for setup purposes. These pages explain — for Windows users of either XP or an earlier version — how to connect to the Internet with a dialup modem.

Before you begin

Before you tell Windows how to connect your computer to the Internet, you need this information:

✦ **ISP name:** Your ISP's domain name. The domain name is the part of a Web address after the www. It ends with the letters .com or .net. Example: sbcglobal.net

✦ **Telephone number:** The phone number to call your ISP. (See the following Tip for advice about entering the telephone number.) In some areas, you must dial the area code, even when making a local call. Example: 301-555-9753

✦ **Username:** The name on your account. If you have an e-mail address, your username is the part of the address before the at (@) symbol. Your ISP gives you the opportunity to choose this name. Example: KennyNYC

✦ **Password:** The combination of letters and numbers that you must enter when you connect to the Internet. Example: 4kings

How you enter your telephone number depends on whether you are dialing outside your area code, whether you are dialing from an office or other place where you have to dial 9 or another number to get an outside line, and whether call waiting is installed on your telephone:

✦ **Area code:** If the ISP telephone number that you call is outside your area code, include 1 and the area code in the telephone number with which you call your ISP. (I respectfully suggest that you find another way to reach your ISP or think of changing ISPs if you are dialing a different area code. Dialing outside your area code can cost you dearly if you spend a lot of time on the Internet.)

✦ **Outside line:** Enter the number, probably 9, that you need to get an outside line before entering the telephone number. Enter commas as well after the 9; each comma tells your computer to pause for three seconds before continuing to dial the outside line. For example, enter these numbers and commas to dial an outside line, pause six seconds to wait to get the outside line, and then dial an ISP:

    9,,555-9753

✦ **Call waiting:** If you have call waiting, you have to disable it while you are exploring the Internet, because if someone calls, your connection to the Internet will be disrupted. Most setup programs have a Disable Call Waiting option. If yours doesn't, you can disable call waiting by entering *70 or 1170 before the telephone number you dial to connect to your ISP. For example, these numbers disable call waiting and dial an ISP:

    1170 555-9753

Dialup connections for Windows XP users

Use one of these techniques to set up a dialup connection on a computer that runs Windows XP:

✦ Click the Connect to the Internet Icon on your desktop.

✦ Choose Start⇨All Programs⇨Accessories⇨Communications⇨Internet Connection Wizard.

You see the Internet Connection Wizard dialog box. Follow these steps to tell the Wizard what kind of connection you want:

1. **Click the Next button to bring up the Network Connection Type dialog box, shown in Figure 3-1.**

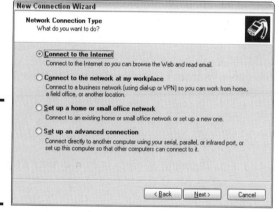

Figure 3-1: The Network Connection Type dialog box.

2. **Select the first option, Connect to the Internet; then click the Next button.**

3. **Select the second option, Set Up My Connection Manually; then click the Next button.**

4. **Select the first option, Connect Using a Dial-Up Modem.**

5. **Keep clicking the Next button and answering the Wizard's questions.**

You are asked for your ISP's name, its phone number, and your username and password (see the previous section in this chapter). You are also asked whether to "Use the name and password you enter when anyone connects to the Internet from this computer." Select this check box if you don't mind others who share your computer connecting to the Internet with your ISP.

If your connection needs adjusting, go to the Internet Properties dialog box. To get there, choose Start➪Control Panel. In the Control Panel window, switch the Control Panel to Category view, if necessary, click the Network and Internet Connection Settings link, and then click the Set Up or Change Your Internet Connection link. In the dialog box, select the name of your dialup connection and then click the Settings button.

Dialup connections for Windows 98, 2000, and Me users

If you don't have the latest version of Windows — Windows XP — don't despair. People with Windows 98, 2000, or Me on their computers can establish a dialup Internet connection by following these steps:

1. **Choose Start➪Programs➪Accessories➪Communications➪Internet Connection Wizard.**

   The Internet Connection Wizard appears.

2. **Select the third option button, I Want to Set Up My Internet Connection Manually; then click the Next button.**

3. **Select the first option button, I Connect through a Phone Line and a Modem; then click the Next button.**

4. **In the remaining dialog boxes, enter your phone number, username, password, and a connection name (so that you can identify the connection if you need to alter it).**

   Earlier in this chapter, "Before you begin" explains what this stuff is.

5. **Select Yes to create the connection.**

If your connection needs changing, open the Control Panel and click the Internet Options link. The Internet Properties dialog box appears. Click the Connections tab, select a connection, and click the Settings button. Then change the connection settings in the Settings dialog box.

Connecting with a DSL or Cable Modem

As the previous chapter explains, DSL and cable-modem connections are the fastest way to travel the Internet. Besides the price, which is two to three times higher with cable-modem or DSL service, the only drawback to DSL and cable-modem connections is having to wait for the ISP to come to your home and install your DSL or cable modem. It can take several weeks, depending on the ISP.

Before you begin

Gather this information before you tell Windows how to connect your computer to the Internet:

✦ **ISP name:** Your ISP's domain name. This is the part of a Web address after the `www`. It ends with the letters `.com` or `.net`. Example: `sbcglobal.net`

✦ **Username:** The name on your account. If you have an e-mail address, your username is the part of the address before the at (@) symbol. Your ISP gives you the opportunity to choose this name. Example: BillyNYC

✦ **Password:** The combination of letters and numbers that you must enter when you connect to the Internet. Example: king444

Making the connection

With a little luck, the person who installed your DSL or cable modem left behind a CD that handles connecting the modem for you. Better yet, the kind installer did the connection setup work for you. If that wasn't the case, however, making the connection is your job. To set up a DSL or cable-modem connection, start by doing one of the following:

✦ Click the Connect to the Internet icon on your desktop.

✦ Choose Start⇨All Programs⇨Accessories⇨Communications⇨Internet Connection Wizard.

The Internet Connection Wizard dialog box appears. Follow these steps to set up your Internet connection with the wizard:

1. **Click the Next button to see the Network Connection Type dialog box (refer to Figure 3-1).**

2. **Click the first option, Connect to the Internet; then click the Next button.**

3. **Select the second option, Set Up My Connection Manually; then click the Next button.**

4. **Select the second or the third option.**

Which option you choose depends on whether your connection is made automatically when you start your computer or whether you have to enter your username and password each time you connect to the Internet.

5. **Keep clicking the Next button and answering the wizard's questions.**

   You're done if your connection is always on. If a username and password are required, you are asked for your ISP's name, a username, and a password. You are also asked whether to "Use the name and password you enter when anyone connects to the Internet from this computer." Select this check box if you don't mind others who share your computer connecting to the Internet with your ISP.

If your connection needs adjusting, choose Start⇨Control Panel. Switch the Control Panel to Category view, if necessary, click the Network and Internet Connection Settings link, and then click the Set Up or Change Your Internet Connection link. In the dialog box, select the name of your connection and then click the Settings button to change your connection settings.

Setting Up an E-Mail Account

Before you can send and receive e-mail with an e-mail program, you need to set up an e-mail account. By setting up an account, you identify yourself to your ISP and make it possible for others to send you e-mail. By the way, Book III, Chapter 1 explains how e-mail is sent and delivered, in case you're interested in what goes on backstage.

The particulars of setting up an e-mail account differ from program to program, but no matter which e-mail program you use, you provide this information to set up your account:

✦ **Incoming mail server type:** Find out whether your ISP operates a POP3 or IMAP incoming mail server. It probably operates a POP3 server.

✦ **Incoming mail address (POP3):** E-mail addressed to you is kept on your ISP's incoming mail server until you go online to collect it, which is why you need this address. The address begins with the letters *pop* and looks something like this:

```
pop.sbcglobal.net
```

✦ **Outgoing mail address (SMTP):** This address begins with the letters *smtp* and looks something like this:

```
smtp.sbglobal.net
```

✦ **Account name:** Your account name is the same as your e-mail address.

✦ **Password:** Enter the password you recorded with your ISP when you set up your Internet connection.

Figure 3-2 shows a dialog box for setting up an e-mail account in Outlook Express. Here is how to create an e-mail account in different software programs:

✦ **Eudora:** Choose Tools⇔Personalities, and right-click and choose Account Settings. Then click the Next button and provide the account information.

✦ **Netscape Mail:** Choose Edit⇔Mail/News Account Settings, click New Account, and negotiate the New Account Wizard.

✦ **Outlook Express:** Choose Tools⇔Accounts, and in the Internet Accounts dialog box, select the Mail tab and click the Add button.

✦ **Outlook:** Choose Tools⇔E-mail Accounts, select Add a New E-Mail Account in the E-Mail Accounts dialog box, and click the Next button. Then negotiate the wizard dialog boxes.

✦ **Pegasus:** Choose File⇔Network Configuration, and in the Pegasus Mail Options dialog box, select the Network tab and enter the information.

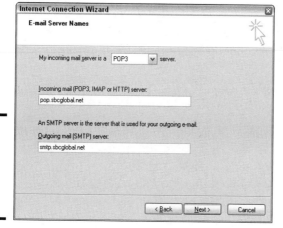

Figure 3-2:
Setting up
an e-mail
account in
Outlook
Express.

Chapter 4: Protecting Your Privacy and Security

In This Chapter

✔ **Protecting your computer from viruses**

✔ **Updating your copy of Windows**

✔ **Using a firewall to protect your computer**

✔ **Taking on spyware and adware**

✔ **Preventing identification theft**

The Internet brings the world to your doorstep, but it also brings hoaxters, scam artists, and phishers (this chapter explains who they are). Without the right protection, your computer is subject to getting sick from a virus. Spyware and adware, as this chapter explains, have probably already made their way into your computer. How's your firewall doing, anyway?

This chapter looks into how you can enjoy all the benefits of exploring the Internet without any of the hassles or catastrophes that come from not being properly protected. You discover how viruses work and how to protect your computer from viruses, how to throw a protective firewall around your computer, and what to do about spyware and adware. This chapter details how scam artists are stealing identifications on the Internet and why keeping your copy of Windows up to date can do a world of good where Internet security is concerned.

Preventing a Virus Attack

A *virus* is a software program that hides inside other software without anyone knowing it. Viruses are created with malicious intent, either to damage computers or to call attention to themselves and their anonymous creators. About 200 new viruses are introduced to the Internet each month. What makes some viruses dangerous is the speed with which they spread. In 2004, a virus called Mydoom infected a quarter-million computers worldwide in a single day. In 1999, the Melissa virus caused such havoc on the Internet that many companies, Microsoft included, shut down their e-mail systems. Viruses range in virulence from the docile Hank virus, which simply wished a happy birthday to someone named Hank, to the Michelangelo virus, which attempted to reformat computers' hard drives.

These pages explain how to prevent viruses from spreading, the different kinds of viruses, and how viruses spread. They also look at how to choose antivirus software and different antivirus programs.

Virus Bulletin (`www.virusbtn.com`) reviews and tests antivirus software. When you want to compare features and shop for antivirus software, it's the place to go. Next time somebody sends you a panicky e-mail claiming that you may have been hit with a virus, look up the virus's name at Vmyths (`http://vmyths.com`). This Web site catalogs virus hoaxes for the benefit of nervous Nellies.

Only you can prevent viruses from spreading

Ninety percent of viruses are spread in e-mail attachments sent over the Internet. The only way to prevent viruses from spreading is to use antivirus software, be careful which files you download from the Internet, only open files sent to you by e-mail if you know and trust the sender, and apply the same vigilance to files given to you on floppy disks and CDs as you do to files sent to you by e-mail.

It's generally understood that if a stranger sneezes near you in a crowded bus, you may get the stranger's germs. Why, then, do some people not think twice about opening files sent to them by strangers over the Internet? These files, like the stranger's germs, could well be infected. If you get an e-mail attachment from an address and person you don't recognize, start by assuming the worst. Assume you've been sent a file infected with a virus. Then study the file's three-letter extension to find out which kind of file was sent in the attachment. The file types listed in Table 4-1 are capable of carrying viruses.

Table 4-1	**File Types That Can Carry Viruses**	
Extension	*File Type*	*Notes*
`.bas`	BASIC program file	These are executable files.
`.bat`	Batch	Batch files are MS-DOS program files.
`.class`	Java program	As executiable files, these can carry viruses.
`.cmd`	Windows Batch	These can include viruses.
`.com`	Executable	Computers can read and execute commands in these files.
`.doc`	Word	Word files can contain macros, and macros can contain viruses.
`.dot`	Word template	Word templates can also contain macros.

Extension	File Type	Notes
.exe	Executable	A very dangerous kind of file. Many computer programs are executable files.
.hta	HTML application	A computer program that can contain viruses.
.jv	Java	Java code can include executable commands.
.mdb	Access	These files can contain macros, and macros can contain viruses.
.msi	Windows Installer	These program files tell Windows how to install other programs.
.ocx	ActiveX module	This is an executable file.
.pif	Program Information	These programs tell Windows how to run DOS programs.
.ppt	PowerPoint	PowerPoint presentations may contain viruses if they contain macros.
.scr	Screen saver file	This is an executable file.
vbe, .vbs, .vg	Visual Basic Script	Viruses can be written in Visual Basic, a computer language.
.vsd	Visio template file	This file type can contain macros.
.ws, .wsc, .wsf	Windows Script Host	These scripts can include executable commands.
.xls	Excel	Excel spreadsheets can contain viruses if they also contain macros.
.xlt	Excel template	Excel template files can contain viruses, too.

If the file sent to you is one listed in Table 4-1, don't open the file. Either delete the file immediately or, if you think the file may be legitimate, ask the person who sent it what is in the file and why it was sent. By the way, don't be fooled because the return address looks legitimate. Attaching a convincing-looking return address to an e-mail message is easy. There's even a word for it — *e-mail spoofing*.

Windows hides some kinds of file extensions. To be able to see all file extensions on your computer and adequately judge whether they may be carrying viruses, follow these steps:

1. **Open Windows Explorer or My Computer.**

2. **Choose Tools⇨Folder Options.**

The Options dialog box opens.

3. **Select the View tab.**

4. Deselect the Hide Extensions for Known File Types check box.

5. Click the OK button.

As Book III, Chapter 1 explains, you can roll several files into one file, called a *Zip file,* to make sending the files easier. Normally, antivirus software detects viruses in incoming mail, but that isn't so of Zip files. Because the files have been zipped, or compressed, antivirus software can't read them to tell whether they contain viruses. The moral of the story is to examine files carefully after you unzip them. Unzipped files can contain viruses.

Differentiating types of viruses

Viruses come in these different shapes and forms:

+ **E-mail virus:** This kind of virus reproduces itself by going into the recipient's Address Book, taking down names, and e-mailing itself to tens or hundreds of people at once. It's important to remember that no virus can spread inside an e-mail message. Viruses travel by e-mail, but not inside messages — they travel in files attached to e-mail messages.

+ **Time bomb:** This is a virus that is programmed to lie quietly in wait on a computer until the appointed hour, when it "explodes" and causes damage.

+ **Trojan horse:** This virus masquerades as one kind of program but is really another. The game you thought you downloaded turns out not to be a game at all, but a virus. Trojan horses travel on the Internet by stealth, not by reproducing themselves quickly like other viruses.

+ **Worm:** This is a virus that quickly makes copies of itself on many computers. Worms infect a security hole in a network, and when they are inside the network, quickly copy themselves from computer to computer. Code Red, the most notorious worm, copied itself to a quarter-million computers during one day in July 2001.

Viruses slow Internet traffic. They clog computer networks. They make computers run more slowly by tying up a computer's processor. They destroy important files. Always be on the alert for viruses, and make sure that antivirus software is installed on your computer.

How virus infections spread

When you open a program or file that contains a virus, the virus scans your computer for programs or files that it can attach to, and before it opens, it infects those programs or files. Now several programs or files on your computer are infected with the virus. In this way, the virus reproduces itself. Eventually, some activity — the arrival of a certain date, for example — triggers the virus to go into action.

Protecting your computer from viruses in macros

Files made with these Microsoft Office programs can contain viruses: Access, Excel, PowerPoint, and Word. They can contain viruses because they are capable of running macros. A *macro* is a set of command instructions recorded under one name. When you execute a macro, the program carries out the instructions. Macros are written in Visual Basic, a computer language. As such, they can contain viruses.

To protect your computer from macro viruses in Access, Excel, PowerPoint, and Word files, you can tell your computer to run macros only if the file to which they belong originated with a trusted source. If you try to run a macro from an untrusted source, either the macro doesn't run or you are warned beforehand that the macro may contain a virus.

Follow these steps in Access, Excel, PowerPoint, or Word to tell the program how to handle the virus-macro problem:

1. **Choose Tools⇨Options.**

   The Options dialog box opens.

2. **Select the Security tab.**

3. **Click the Macro Security button.**

   You see the Security dialog box.

4. **Choose a security setting — Very High, High, Medium, or Low.**

With the Very High and High settings, only macros from files containing a digital signature can be run. Choose the Medium setting to display a warning whenever you run a macro. Choose the Low setting if you trust your antivirus software to detect viruses in all macros. With the Low rating, all macros are run without a warning.

To disable all macros, select the Trusted Publishers tab and deselect the Trust All Installed Add-Ins and Templates check box.

5. **Click the OK button in the Security dialog box.**

6. **Click the OK button in the Options dialog box.**

Other viruses appropriate e-mail addresses from the receiver's address book and send e-mail with infected files to those addresses. Still others take advantage of the intimate relationships between computers on the same network to spread from computer to computer.

Looking at antivirus software

I know what you're thinking: "I'm already shelling out $10 to $40 a month for an Internet connection with an ISP. Do I have to shell out another $40 to $80 a year for antivirus software?" The answer is "Yes." Antivirus software is a bit like car insurance. You may not need it, but if you get in an accident, you're very glad you have it. Figure 4-1 shows an antivirus program called Norton AntiVirus at work.

Every antivirus software program keeps up-to-date virus definitions. To see whether files are infected on a computer, these programs scan the computer, comparing their virus definitions against each file. If a match is found, it means that the file is infected, and the file is cleaned of the virus. An antivirus software worthy of the name should have these features:

✦ **Disk scanning and cleaning:** You can choose a disk drive on your computer to be scanned for and cleaned of viruses. The software should tell you whether any viruses were found and whether they were successfully eradicated.

✦ **Automatic updates:** You can go on the Internet and download virus definitions into the software. This way, the software is always cognizant of the latest viruses and can delete them from your computer. The software should tell you when your virus definitions are out of date and need updating.

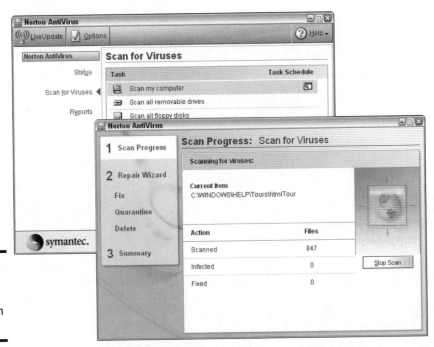

Figure 4-1:
Scanning
for viruses
with Norton
AntiVirus.

✦ **Scanning of incoming e-mail:** Incoming e-mail messages with attached files are scanned automatically for viruses. If a virus is found, it is removed from the e-mail attachment. Some antivirus software also scans outgoing e-mail to prevent viruses from spreading.

All the antivirus software listed in Table 4-2 meets these requirements. These are the most popular and best-known antivirus software programs, and for good reason. They are all reliable, easy to install, and easy to use. Table 4-3 lists free antivirus software programs. These programs can scan your hard disk for viruses, but they don't offer all the services you get when you pay for antivirus software.

Table 4-2	Antivirus Software		
Software	*Web Address*	*Price*	*Notes*
F-Secure Internet Security	www.f-secure.com	$80	Includes anti-spam and spyware features. For parents, comes with Web-site–blocking tools. No phone support.
McAfee Virus Scan Home	http://us.mcafee.com	$40	Includes anti-spyware features. Phone support costs extra.
Norton AntiVirus	www.symantec.com	$50	No anti-spyware features. No phone support. Easy-to-use program.
Trend Micro PC-cillin Internet Security	www.trendmicro.com	$45	Includes a firewall and anti-spam and -spyware features. Tech support by phone is free.

Table 4-3	Free Antivirus Software	
Software	*Web Address*	*Notes*
AntiVir Personal Edition	www.free-av.com	Does not scan incoming e-mail
Avast 4 Home Edition	www.avast.com/eng/avast_4_home.html	Scans all e-mail services
BitDefender Free Edition	www.bitdefender.com	Does not scan e-mail

TIP

Another way to scan your hard drive for viruses without paying is to go to Panda ActiveScan (www.pandasoftware.com/activescan). Access this antivirus utility by way of your Web browser without downloading any software. It works using ActiveX technology. McAfee, the antivirus software maker, also offers free antivirus scanning from a Web site at this address: http://us.mcafee.com/root/mfs. Because three's the charm, Trend Micro Housecall (http://housecall.trendmicro.com) also offers the service.

Making Sure Your Copy of Windows Is Up to Date

One way to thwart hackers and viruses is to make sure that your copy of Windows is up to date. As security holes are discovered in the Windows software, Microsoft issues updates to Windows. These updates patch the security holes. My copy of Windows has been patched so many times it's starting to resemble a ragamuffin, but that's another story.

If you want, Microsoft can update your copy of Windows automatically. It can also alert you when updates to its Windows software are available for downloading from the Internet so that you can download them yourself. You'll know when an update is available because a balloon caption with these words will appear in the notification area by the clock on your desktop: "Stay current with automatic updates/Click here to keep your computer up-to-date automatically with downloads from Windows Update." Clicking the balloon takes you to a Web page where you can download a Windows update patch.

Checking whether Windows is up to date — and updating

To find out whether your copy of Windows is up to date and, if it's not up to date, how to update it, choose Start⇨All Programs⇨Windows Update (you can find this command near the top of the All Programs menu).

Windows Service Pack 2

In October 2004, Microsoft issued an upgrade to its Windows XP software called *Service Pack 2*. The upgrade is designed to make Windows XP computers less susceptible to attacks from viruses and hackers. If you bought your computer in or after October 2004, you probably don't need to concern yourself with Service Pack 2, because your Windows XP software is up to date. But if your computer is older than October 2004 and it runs Windows XP, you owe it to yourself to load the Service Pack 2 software on your computer.

Unfortunately, at 50–250MB, depending on how much updating your software needs, Service Pack 2 is a big chunk of software code.

Downloading and installing it on my computer took two hours, and I have a fast Internet connection. You can follow the instructions "Checking whether Windows is up to date — and updating," earlier in this chapter, to find out whether Service Pack 2 is installed on your computer, and download the software if need be. If yours is a slow Internet connection and you don't have the patience to wait all day while Service Pack 2 downloads, you can ask Microsoft to send the software to you on a CD by going to this Web address:

```
www.microsoft.com/windowsxp/
downloads/updates/sp2/cd
order/en_us/default.mspx
```

Your Web browser opens a page at microsoft.com. The page tells you whether your copy of windows needs updating and instructs you how to download the latest updates, as shown in Figure 4-2.

Choosing how to update your copy of Windows

When it comes to updating your copy of Windows, you have the choice of updating automatically, updating when you give the order, or not updating automatically. If you opt for automatic updates, your computer queries Microsoft when you are online to find out whether any Windows updates are available. To tell your computer when and how to update your copy of Windows, follow these steps:

1. **Choose Start⇨Control Panel.**

The Control Panel window opens.

2. **Click the Security Center link.**

The Windows Security Center window appears (as long as Service Pack 2 is installed). This window tells you whether a firewall is installed and working on your computer, whether you are updating your copy of Windows automatically, and whether your computer is protected from viruses.

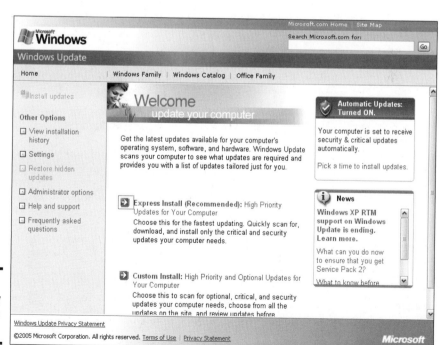

Figure 4-2:
Is your copy
of Windows
up to date?

3. **Click the Automatic Updates link.**

   You can find this link at the bottom of the window. You see the Automatic Updates tab of the Automatic Updates dialog box, as shown in Figure 4-3.

4. **Choose an Update option:**

   - **Automatic:** Update files are sent to your computer and installed automatically. You can schedule updates in the drop-down menus. If your computer is turned off at the scheduled time, the update files are downloaded at the next opportunity when you connect to the Internet.

   - **Download Updates for Me:** Updates are downloaded in the background without your noticing. To inform you that update files have arrived, the balloon caption and the Windows Update icon appear in the notification area. Click the icon or the caption to install the updates.

   - **Notify Me but Don't Automatically Download:** If updates are available, the balloon caption and the Windows Update icon appear in the notification area. Click either one to go on the Internet and download the updates and install them on your computer.

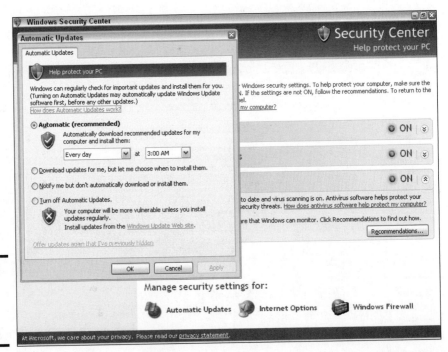

Figure 4-3: Choosing how to update Windows.

- **Turn Off Automatic Updates:** You are not notified or given the opportunity to download update files. Choose this option if you want to update your copy of Windows on your own (see the previous section in this chapter).

5. **Click the OK button.**

Protecting Your Computer with a Firewall

In the real world, a firewall is a wall between buildings that is designed to prevent a fire from spreading from one building to the next. A computer firewall does much the same thing — only digitally. A *firewall* is a software program or hardware device that serves as a gateway between a computer and the Internet. The firewall scans data as it arrives from the Internet and slams the door on unwanted intruders. To be specific, a firewall blocks ports on your computer to certain kinds of data. For example, data from certain domains and IP addresses may be blocked. A firewall may block data requests made using the Telnet or ftp protocol because those protocols can be used to commandeer others' computers. In short, a firewall protects a computer from unauthorized access and virus threats. It also hides a computer's IP address so that hackers can't target a computer.

Not so long ago, firewalls were deemed necessary only for computers connected to a company network, but because security threats from the Internet are on the rise and because people with DSL and cable-modem connections stay online for hours at a time, the current thinking is that all computers should be protected by a firewall. Microsoft as much as acknowledged how necessary firewalls have become when it began including a firewall with its Windows XP operating system software. If you have a copy of Windows XP issued after October 2004 or if you installed Service Pack 2, a firewall is already installed on your computer (see the sidebar "Windows Service Pack 2").

Want to test how strong your firewall is and whether your computer is susceptible to threats from the Internet? Take the Shields UP! test at the following address. The test looks at your computer's service ports and file-sharing vulnerabilities, among other things. (Notice in this Web address the letters *https,* not *http.* The *s* indicates that you are on a secure Web site.)

```
https://www.grc.com/x/ne.dll?bh0bkyd2
```

A look at third-party firewalls

The firewall that comes with Windows XP is not the best, but it is more than adequate if you use it along with antivirus software. The Windows XP firewall doesn't scan outgoing files sent over the Internet for viruses. Some firewalls do that to keep viruses from spreading. It also doesn't offer spoofing protection to keep hackers from commandeering your computer. Table 4-4 describes some firewalls that are worth looking into if your computer doesn't already have a firewall.

Table 4-4	Firewalls		
Firewall Software	*Web Address*	*Notes*	*Price*
Kerio Personal Firewall	www.kerio.com/us/kpf_home.html	Very configurable software; not for novices.	$45
Outpost Firewall	www.agnitum.com	Blocks cookies and conceals your surfing history, among other features.	$30
Sygate Personal Firewall	http://smb.sygate.com/products/spf_standard.htm	Very customizable with a friendly interface.	$48
ZoneAlarm	www.zonelabs.com	Can quarantine e-mail.	$70

Turning the Windows XP firewall on or off

Sometimes it's necessary to turn the Windows XP firewall off for a minute or turn it off altogether. Sometimes you have to turn the firewall off temporarily to upload Web-site pages to a Web server. Sometimes you have to turn it off permanently in favor of using a different firewall. Follow these steps to turn the Windows XP firewall on or off:

1. **Choose Start⇨Control Panel to open the Control Panel window.**

2. **Click the Network and Internet Connections link.**

   If you don't see this link, switch to Category View in the Control Panel.

3. **Click the Windows Firewall link.**

   The Windows Firewall dialog box appears.

4. **On the General tab, select the On or Off option button to turn the firewall on or off.**

5. **Click the OK button to close the dialog box.**

Some software programs have to breach the firewall to go on the Internet and do what they're supposed to do. When that is the case, you see a Windows Security Alert dialog box like the one shown on the right side of Figure 4-4. Click the Unblock button to open a port on your computer so that the program can go on the Internet. Programs that you unblock this way are added to an Exceptions list, a list of programs that can disregard the firewall, as shown on the left side of Figure 4-4. To remove a program from the Exceptions list, go to the Exceptions tab of the Windows Firewall dialog box, select the program, and click the Delete button. The step-by-step instructions previous to this paragraph explain how to open the Windows Firewall dialog box.

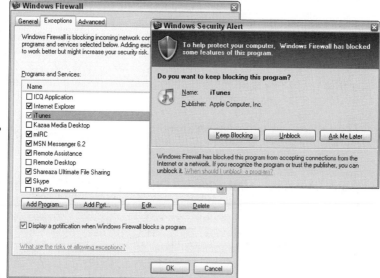

Figure 4-4:
Clicking the Unblock button exempts a program so that it can bypass the firewall.

What to Do about Spyware and Adware

According to the National Cyber Security Alliance, eight of ten computers are infected with spyware and adware. *Spyware* is a kind of software that is installed surreptitiously on a computer. It gathers information about the computer's owner without his or her knowledge. Some spyware programs can obtain personal information and send it to marketers or, worse, identity thieves. *Adware* is a variety of spyware. It, too, is installed without anyone knowing. Adware programs gather information about a user's browsing habits and send it to marketers. Adware programs display pop-up advertisements in the browser window tailored to the user's tastes and browsing patterns.

These programs are a nuisance at best and a menace at worst. Spyware programs called *keyloggers* can record keystrokes, including 16-digit credit card numbers and eight-digit Social Security numbers, and send them to a remote computer. Spyware slows computers. To use the terminology of the people who monitor spyware, spyware has a large "clot factor" — it loads down the computer with unnecessary folders and registry entries. Spyware can turn an adventure on the Internet into a frustrating misadventure of pop-up windows and screaming advertisements. Does this sound familiar? If your computer is anything close to typical, it is already infected with spyware. The first time I ran Webroot Spy Sweeper, my anti-spyware program of choice, I discovered 17 spyware programs on my computer.

Spyware finds its way onto computers on the back of shareware programs and file-sharing programs. The most notorious example of spyware piggy-backing on another program was Kazaa, a program for sharing MP3 files on the Internet. Kazaa was a sort of Typhoid Mary of the World Wide Web. According to its manufacturer, 214 million computers downloaded Kazaa. And every single one of them ran a bit slower because of it.

The only way to remove spyware is to employ the services of an anti-spyware program. Experts recommend using at least two anti-spyware programs because no single program can find and eradicate all varieties of spyware. Table 4-5 describes the leading anti-spyware programs. These programs scan computer files, comparing the programs' spyware definitions against the files. When a match is found, the spyware is quarantined. Anti-spyware programs give you the chance to examine the spyware before you delete it. You can download the anti-spyware programs listed in Table 4-5 at Cnet.com (`www.cnet.com`) and TUCOWS (`www.tucows.com`). Figure 4-5 shows the Webroot Spy Sweeper anti-spyware program at work.

Table 4-5	Anti-Spyware Programs		
Program	*Web Address*	*Notes*	*Price*
Ad-Aware SE Personal Edition	`http://www.lava soft.de`	One of the first anti-spyware programs.	Free
Spybot Search & Destroy	`www.safer-net working.org`	Removes cookies as well as spyware. Don't be put off by the unprofessional-looking interface — it works well.	Free
Spy-Subtract	`www.intermute. com/products/ spysubtract.html`	Tells you when spyware was installed and rates virulence of found spyware programs.	$30
Webroot Spy Sweeper	`www.webroot.com`	Besides removing spyware, prevents bookmarks from being added and the home page from being changed without permission.	$30

Program	Web Address	Notes	Price
Windows Anti-Spyware	`www.microsoft.com/athome/security/spyware/software`	Formerly Giant AntiSpyware, an award-winning program; it was purchased by Microsoft in January 2005.	Free to Windows users

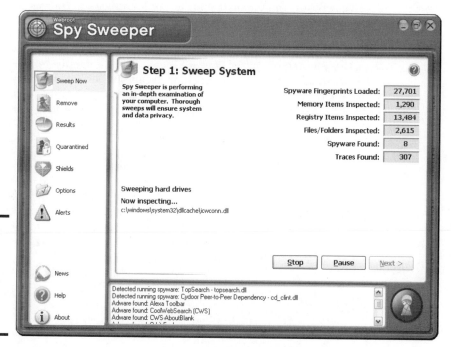

Figure 4-5:
Webroot
Spy
Sweeper,
an anti-
spyware
program.

Do not, I repeat, do not buy anti-spyware programs on the recommendation of pop-up advertisements in your Web browser. Ironically, some programs that profess to be anti-spyware are themselves spyware!

Preventing Identification Theft

Identification theft occurs when someone steals your credit card number, PayPal account number, Social Security number, checking account number, password to a Web site, or other valuable piece of information and pretends to be you. The thief makes purchases in your name — purchases that show up a month later on your credit card statement. Worse yet, the thief buys a cell phone or takes out a credit card or loan in your name. You can find your-self in the difficult and slightly schizophrenic position of having to convince creditors and the telephone company that you are you and not the person who has been spending so lavishly in your name.

According to a Federal Trade Commission report, nearly 10 million Americans were probably victims of some form of identification theft in 2003. Is the Internet making it easier for identification thieves to operate? No question about it. The anonymity of the Internet makes it that much easier for the thieves to pose as people and institutions they aren't. A term has even been coined for masquerading as someone else with fraudulent intent on the Internet: phishing. *Phishing* means to fraudulently solicit credit card information, identifications, usernames, and passwords by means of realis-tic-looking Web pages or e-mail messages that appear to come from genuine institutions. The word comes from the expression "going on a fishing expedi-tion," which means to vaguely and unhurriedly look into others' affairs with the hope of finding something damaging.

Figure 4-6 shows an example of phishing. This e-mail message appears to have come from a real bank, but it's a sham. If you click the link in the mes-sage, you go to a Web page with all the official trappings of the bank, where you are asked to enter your bank account numbers and other personal infor-mation. The Address bar on the Web page even appears to show the bank's Web address, but the real Address bar is hidden, something that can be done with the Java computer language.

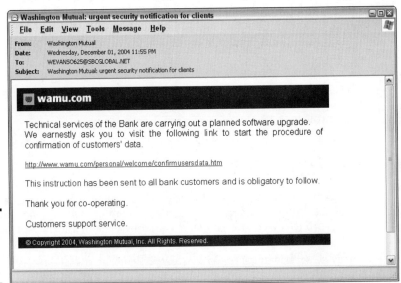

Figure 4-6:
Phishing for
suckers on
the Internet.

Phishers are good at creating the illusion that they are real. They dress up Web pages with all the tell-tale signs — the logos and graphics — of the institution that they are pretending to represent. A false request for usernames and passwords appears to have really come from eBay, for example, because it is dressed in the eBay colors. A request for Social Security numbers is accompanied by the American flag and appears to have really come from the United States government. Even the return address looks real. But faking an e-mail address, or e-mail spoofing, is just part of the illusion.

No legitimate institution will ever solicit personal information or ask you to update your account by e-mail. Nor will they ask you to enter personal information online, except for the first time you provide the information. Except for the first time, any attempt to get personal information from you is fraudulent. You can do everyone a favor by reporting these solicitations to the institution that the phishers are pretending to represent.

The Anti-Phishing Working Group maintains an archive of phishing examples at this Web address: www.antiphishing.org/phishing_archive.htm. Take a look at some of these examples to see just how sophisticated phishers can be.

Chapter 5: Using America Online

In This Chapter

✔ Installing and signing on to AOL

✔ Reading e-mail and receiving files

✔ Organizing and storing e-mail messages

✔ Sending e-mail and files

✔ Tracking addresses in the Address Book

✔ Surfing the Internet with AOL

*A*merica Online (AOL) is an online service for surfing the Internet, sending and receiving e-mail, storing addresses, and doing a few other things besides. As of this writing, the cost of the service is $24 per month (AOL usually offers free service for the first month or two). If you bought your computer at a big-time electronics store, it probably comes with the AOL icon on the desktop. Having that icon doesn't mean that you have to subscribe to AOL, but lots of people do. AOL has many fans and many detractors. In general, people who fall on the novice side of computing favor AOL over the hardier, more sophisticated programs for handling the Internet because AOL is easy to use. Starting from one place, you can surf the Internet and trade e-mail messages. AOL's keywords (you find out more about them shortly) make it possible to visit Web sites without having to enter cumbersome Web-site addresses. This chapter explains how to handle e-mail and surf the Internet with America Online.

Installing AOL

If AOL isn't installed on your computer, you can either install it from a CD or download the program from this address on the Internet: www.aol.com. As part of the installation, you are asked for a screen name and a password. You need this name and password each time you log on to AOL.

If you have trouble with the installation or trouble connecting to the Internet with AOL, call 800-827-6364. If you get frustrated and want to cancel the service, call 888-265-8008. You can find out more about AOL's cancellation policy by entering **Cancel** in the Keyword dialog box.

Signing on to AOL

You must sign on to AOL each time you run the program. To sign on, either double-click the America Online icon on your desktop or choose Start⇨ Programs⇨America Online⇨America Online. You see the Sign On window shown in Figure 5-1. Choose your screen name if you have more than one, enter your password, and click the Sign On button.

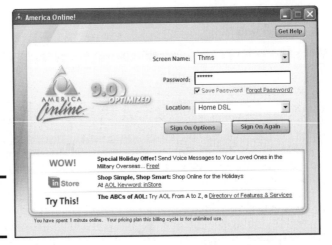

Figure 5-1:
Signing on
to AOL.

Changing and deleting passwords and screen names

AOL makes it easy to change and delete screen names and passwords. (Who doesn't need another Internet personality now and then?) AOL permits you to have as many as seven different screen names. Follow these steps to manage passwords and screen names:

1. **Press Ctrl+K or click the Keyword button on the Quick Start toolbar.**

   The Keyword dialog box appears.

2. **Enter this keyword:** screen names.

3. **Click the Go button.**

   A dialog box for changing and deleting passwords and screen names appears.

4. **Click the appropriate link, and answer the questions in the dialog boxes as they appear.**

   Don't worry — this is real simple stuff.

A Short Geography Lesson

When you start AOL, you see a window screen like the one in Figure 5-2. I wager that the menu bar and row of buttons along the top of the screen are not foreign to you — they are found in lots of computer programs. From left to right, here are the things that may make the AOL screen seem unusual:

Quick Start window

Next and Previous

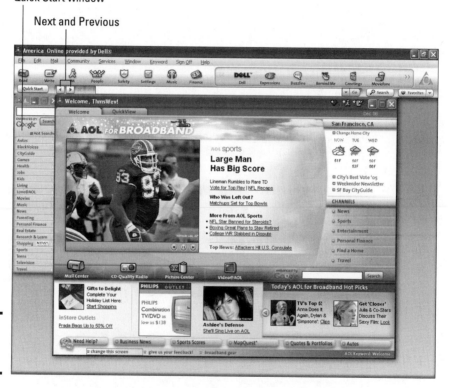

Figure 5-2: The AOL screen.

✦ **Quick Start window:** This window is designed to help you do things quickly. It includes buttons that are found elsewhere in the AOL window. Click its Close button if you don't care to see it. To display the window after you have closed it, click the Quick Start button.

✦ **Next and Previous buttons:** Click these buttons to retreat to or go forward to windows either in AOL or on the Internet that you have visited recently.

✦ **Web Address box:** Enter a Web address here and click the Go button to visit a Web site. You can click the down arrow and select a site from the drop-down list to revisit a site you visited recently.

+ **Search button:** Click the Search button to open a new window and search the Internet.

+ **Favorites:** Click the Favorites button (or its drop-down arrow) to visit a site you bookmarked because you wanted to visit it again.

When you signed up with AOL, you chose a Toolset and Line Up for the Welcome screen that appears when you start AOL. If you would like to rethink those choices, click the Change This Screen link in the lower-left corner of the Welcome screen. You are presented with a series of dialog boxes for constructing a Welcome screen.

Handling Incoming E-Mail

Benjamin Franklin was wrong. He said that nothing is certain except death and taxes. What is just as certain as those inevitabilities is this: Anyone who has an e-mail account will receive ever-increasing amounts of e-mail. Besides reading this mail, the person must devise strategies for sorting and organizing it. These topics are covered in the pages that follow.

Reading incoming mail

When someone sends you e-mail, you hear the words "You've got mail" and a flag rises on the Read button in the upper-left corner of the screen. The number beside this button tells you how many messages are waiting to be read. By moving the pointer over the Read button, you can see a drop-down list with senders' names and message topics. To open your Mailbox and read the mail, click the Read button. You see a Mailbox window similar to the one in Figure 5-3.

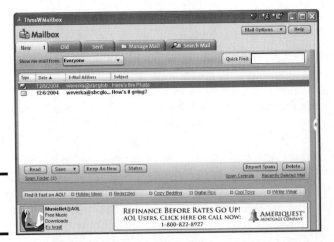

Figure 5-3:
Collecting
the mail.

Here are instructions for reading your mail:

✦ **Reading a message:** Double-click a message or select it and click the
Read button to open it. The message appears in the Message window,
as shown in Figure 5-4. After you open a message, it is moved to the Old
tab. You can read it by opening the Old tab and double-clicking it there.
(Click the Keep As New button to move a message from the Old tab back
to the New tab.)

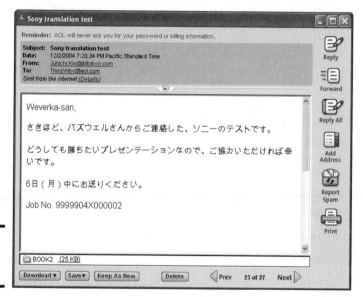

Figure 5-4:
Reading
the mail.

✦ **Deleting a message:** Click the Delete button to remove a message.
Messages you delete are sent to the Recently Deleted folder. To recover
a message, open the Recently Deleted folder, select the message, and
click the Restore button. To open the Recently Deleted folder, open the
Manage Mail tab and select the folder in the My Mail Folder list.

To find a stray message in the Mailbox window, enter a word you remember
from the message's title or text in the Quick Find box (refer to Figure 5-3) and
press Enter.

Receiving a file

You can tell when someone has sent you a file because a little page appears
behind the standard message icon on the left side of the Mailbox window.
The name of the file appears at the bottom of the message window (refer to
Figure 5-4).

✦ To download the file now, double-click its name, click Yes when AOL asks whether you really want to download it, and select a folder for storing the file in the Download Manager dialog box.

✦ To retrieve the file later, click the Download button and choose Download Later. When you want to see the file, choose File⇨Download Manager. You see the Download Manager window. Select the file you want to open and click the Finish Download button. You can find the file in your `C:\My Documents` folder.

Managing your e-mail

If you receive e-mail from many different parties, I strongly suggest creating e-mail folders for storing your mail. That way, when you want to find a message from someone, you will know where to find it. Herewith are instructions for creating folders for e-mail and moving e-mail to different folders.

Creating a folder for storing e-mail

To create new folders for e-mail, start by selecting the Manage Mail tab in the Mailbox window. On the left side of this tab is the My Mail Folders list, which lists the folders where your e-mail is stored. Follow these steps to create a new folder:

1. **Click the Saved on My PC folder.**

All new folders become subfolders of this folder.

2. **Click the Setup Folders button and choose Create Folder.**

You see the Create New Folder dialog box.

3. **Enter a folder name and click the Save button.**

Be sure to choose a descriptive name. The name of your new folder appears under the Saved on My PC folder in the folders list.

Moving e-mail messages to different folders

Follow these steps to move an e-mail message to a different folder:

1. **Select the e-mail message.**

2. **Click the Save button and move the pointer over On My PC on the drop-down list.**

You see a list of folders.

3. **Select the folder you want to move the e-mail to.**

Composing and Sending E-Mail

In order to get invited to parties, you have to issue a few invitations. And in order to get e-mail, you have to send out e-mail. In this section, you find instructions for composing e-mail messages, replying to or forwarding messages, and sending files.

Writing an e-mail

Follow these steps to compose and send an e-mail message:

1. **Click the Write button or press Ctrl+M.**

You see the Write Mail window shown in Figure 5-5.

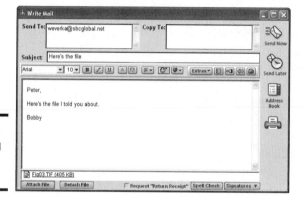

Figure 5-5:
Composing
an e-mail
message.

2. **In the Send To box, enter the address of the person who is to receive the message.**

If the address is on file in your Address Book, just type the first two or three letters to see a list of e-mail addresses that begin with those two or three letters. Choose a name from the list to enter the whole address.

To send the same e-mail to more than one person, press Enter to go to the next line of the Send To box and enter another address there.

Enter an address in the Copy To box to send a copy of the message to someone.

3. **In the Subject line, enter a descriptive subject for the message.**

4. **Enter the body of the message in the text box.**

You can format the message by clicking the Bold or Underline button, for example. However, only people with e-mail software capable of reading HTML formats can see the formatting in your e-mail message.

5. Click the Send Now button to send the message.

Or, to postpone sending it, click the Send Later button. You see the Send Later dialog box. Click the Auto AOL button to schedule a time to send the message. To send the message later on your own, click the Read button to open the Mailbox window. Then click the Manage Mail tab and select the Mail Waiting to Be Sent folder in the My Mail Folders list. Finally, select the message and click the Send button.

Replying to and forwarding messages

Replying to and forwarding messages is a cinch. All you have to do is click the Reply, Forward, or Reply All button in the Message window (refer to Figure 5-4). Immediately, a Write Mail window opens with the sender's e-mail address and subject line already entered. Write a reply or scribble a few words at the top of the forwarded message and click the Send Now or Send Later button.

Sending a file

Follow these steps to send a file to someone:

1. Address and compose the message as you normally would.

2. Click the Attach File button in the Write Mail window.

You can find this button in the lower-left corner of the window. You see the Attached File(s) dialog box.

3. Select the file or files you want to send and click the Open button.

To select more than one file, Ctrl+click the files.

The name of the file or files you want to send appears at the bottom of the Write Mail window. If you change your mind about sending a file, select the file and click the Detach File button.

4. Click the Send Now or Send Later button.

Maintaining an Address Book

You can keep street addresses and phone numbers as well as e-mail addresses in the AOL Address Book. Keeping e-mail addresses is worthwhile because you don't have to type an e-mail address to address an e-mail message if the address is listed in the Address Book. AOL fills in addresses from the book automatically.

Sending e-mails to groups

Create a group in the Address Book if you need to send the same e-mail to several different people at once. For example, if you're the captain of a softball team, you can compose and address a message about upcoming games to all team members. This spares you the trouble of composing a dozen or more e-mail messages.

Here are instructions for handling group addresses:

✔ **Starting a group:** Click the Add Group button in the Address Book window. You see the Manage Group dialog box. Enter a name for your group. In the Contacts List, Ctrl+click to select the names of people you need for the group. Then click the Add button and click the Save button.

✔ **Changing around the group members:** In the Address Book, group names are shown in boldface text. To change around a group, select its name and click the Edit button. You see the Manage Group dialog box. Select names and click the Add or Remove button to change around the group.

✔ **Sending an e-mail to the group's members:** Select the group in the Address Book, click the Send To button, and choose a sending option on the drop-down list. The Write Mail window appears with the addresses of the group members already entered.

✔ **Deleting a group:** Select the group's name and click the Delete button.

Choose Mail⊅Address Book to open the Address Book. Here are instructions for doing this, that, and the other thing with addresses:

✦ **Entering a new address:** Click the Add button. You see the Address Card for New Contact dialog box shown in Figure 5-6. Fill in the pertinent information on the different tabs and click the Save button.

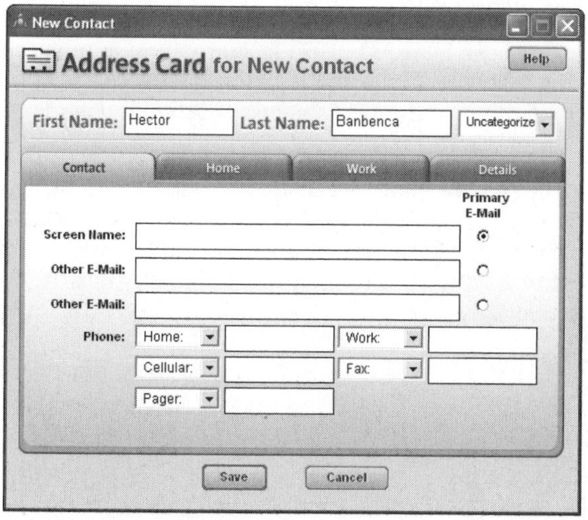

Figure 5-6: Entering an address in the Address Book.

✦ **Changing address information:** Select a name and click the Edit button. You see the Address Card for New Contact dialog box. Change the information there and click the Save button.

✦ **Deleting an entry:** Select a name and click the Delete button.

Exploring the Internet in AOL

As well as conventional ways to search the Internet, AOL offers keywords. Instead of typing an unwieldy Web-site address, you can enter a keyword. As long as that keyword corresponds to one of AOL's channels, you go to an AOL *channel,* a Web site with many links to the subject in question. For example, entering the keyword *autos* takes you to an AOL-maintained Web site with links to many sites that concern cars.

Exploring the Internet by keyword isn't the big deal it used to be. The Internet is much easier to search and navigate than it was when AOL invented its keyword scheme. AOL subscribers can use Internet Explorer or Mozilla to search the Internet. I recommend doing just that. Those browsers are much easier to use than AOL's, in my opinion.

You, of course, are entitled to your opinion, and to that end, here are instructions for exploring the Internet with AOL:

✦ **Entering a keyword:** On the Quick Start toolbar, enter the keyword in the Keyword dialog box or type the keyword directly into the Web-site address box. If the keyword is associated with an AOL channel, you go to the AOL Web site. Choose Keyword➪Explore Keywords to see all the AOL keywords.

✦ **Surfing the Internet:** Enter an address in the Web-site address box and click the Go button.

✦ **Searching:** Click the Search button to go to an AOL-maintained site for searching the Internet. (This site is by no means the best place to start an Internet search. Conducting a search of the Internet is the subject of Book II, Chapter 3.)

✦ **Bookmarking your favorite Web sites:** When you come across a Web site you want to revisit, bookmark it. Click the Favorites button and, in the Favorite Places dialog box, choose Add to Favorites➪Favorite Places. Next time you want to visit the Web site, click the Favorites button and choose the Web site's name in the Favorites window.

Don't forget to click the Previous or Next button to go backward or forward through Web sites you have visited.

Chapter 6: Getting the Plug-Ins You Need

In This Chapter

✔ Finding out what plug-ins are

✔ Choosing which plug-in plays by default

✔ Examining the different plug-ins

*T*his brief chapter describes companion programs called plug-ins that you need to watch videos, hear audio, and read PDF files on the Internet. First you find out precisely what a plug-in is. Then you discover how to decide which plug-in is launched by default, and you take a close look at all the plug-ins.

Introducing Plug-Ins

A *plug-in* is a companion program to a Web browser that handles files that a Web browser can't handle. To make the most of the Internet — to play videos or listen to Internet radio — you need the right plug-ins. For example, the Internet Explorer Web browser can't play videos on its own. When you see a video on a Web page and you click to play it, it doesn't play unless Windows Media Player, QuickTime Player, or another plug-in capable of playing video is installed on your computer.

Table 6-1 lists plug-ins and tells you where to go on the Internet to get information about each one. I describe these plug-ins throughout this chapter. With the exception of the Office programs, you can download the plug-ins in Table 6-1 by going to the Web sites listed in the table or by going to these Web sites: Cnet (www.cnet.com) or TUCOWS (www.tucows.com). All programs in the table except the Office programs are free, although many offer upgraded versions with more features that you can purchase for real green cash.

Table 6-1	Plug-Ins	
Plug-In	*Opens/Plays These Files*	*Web Address*
Audio		
RealPlayer	`.ra, .ram, .rm`	`www.real.com`
Flash Animations		
Flash Player	`.swf`	`www.macromedia.com/` `software/flash`
Microsoft Office Programs		
Excel, Power-Point, Word	`.doc` (Word), `.ppt` (PowerPoint), `.rtf` (Rich Text Format), `.xls` (Excel)	`http://office.` `microsoft.com`
Portable Document Files		
Acrobat Reader	`.pdf`	`www.adobe.com/` `products/acrobat/` `readermain.html`
Video and Audio		
QuickTime Player	`.mov, .mp4`	`www.apple.com/quicktime`
Windows Media Player	`.avi, .MP3,` `.mpeg, .wmv`	`www.microsoft.com/` `windows/windowsmedia`

A Roster of Plug-In Programs

You can't tell who the players are without reading the roster. These pages describe a roster of plug-in programs — Acrobat Reader, Flash Player, Microsoft Office programs, QuickTime Player, RealPlayer, and Windows Media Player. You also find out how to decide which plug-in gets launched automatically when you encounter a certain kind of file on the Internet.

Acrobat Reader

Acrobat Reader is a program for displaying portable document files, better known as PDF files. As shown in Figure 6-1, Acrobat Reader opens inside your Web-browser window when you open a PDF file on the Internet. PDF files are often meant to be printed. Many are Internet versions of brochures and other publications. Search engines read, index, and catalog PDF files as they do Web pages. Google even has a command for searching for PDF files. On the Google Advanced Search page (`www.google.com/advanced_ search`), choose Adobe Acrobat PDF (.pdf) on the File Format drop-down menu. Go to this Web address to read about Acrobat Reader and download the program: `www.adobe.com/products/acrobat/readermain.html`.

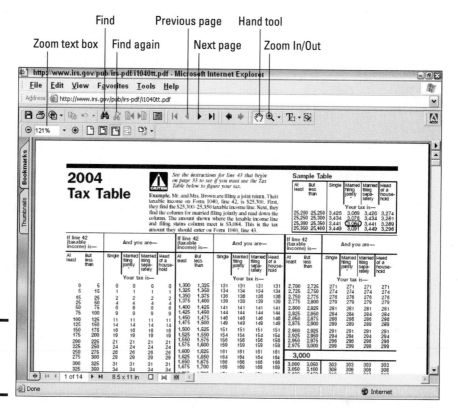

Figure 6-1:
A PDF file
in Acrobat
Reader.

PDF files can be unwieldy and hard to read, but you can take advantage of these Acrobat Reader tools to making reading the files a little easier:

✦ **Going from page to page:** Click the Next Page or Previous Page button, use the scroll bar, or click the Hand Tool button and drag on-screen.

✦ **Zooming in and out:** Click the Zoom Out button, use the Zoom In or Zoom Out tool, or enter a percentage in the Zoom text box to shrink or enlarge the text.

✦ **Finding text:** Click the Find button, enter a word or words in the Acrobat Find dialog box, and click the Find button. Click the Find Again button to search for the next instance of the thing you're looking for.

Copying text from a PDF file can be frustrating. You can click the Text Select tool and drag over the document, but you can only select blocks of text this way. It isn't possible to select one sentence, for example, or a paragraph. Selecting text in a single column is very frustrating because you have to select adjoining text in the other columns as well. If you are in the unenviable position of often having to copy text from PDF files to Word files, check out these programs, which make doing that considerably easier: Solid Converter PDF to Word (www.solidpdf.com) and PDF Converter (www.scan soft.com/pdfconverter).

To convert a Word file to PDF file, try pdf995. You can learn about and download the program at this Web address: http://pdf995.com. OpenOffice, a free alternative to the Microsoft Office programs, can also convert a Word file to a PDF file. Go to this Web address to look into OpenOffice: www.open office.org.

Flash Player

You need Flash Player to play .swf (pronounced "swiff") Flash animations. These animations are lot of fun to watch, which makes Flash Player worth having. You can read about Flash Player and download the program at this Web address: www.macromedia.com/software/flash.

I keep seeing more and more Flash animations on the Internet, although, unfortunately, some of them are advertisements. Check out this Web site for some creative examples of Flash animations: www.albinoblacksheep.com/ flash. This Japanese Flash animation shows how extraordinary Flash animations can be: http://yoga.at.infoseek.co.jp/flash/kikkomaso. swf. You can also find some neat Flash animations at Angry Alien Productions at this Web address: www.angryalien.com. Be sure to check out the 30-second reenactments of popular movies acted out by bunnies.

Some people believe that Flash animations are a security risk to computers because Flash animations are displayed in Internet Explorer using ActiveX controls. ActiveX controls allow programs to interact with the Windows operating system, exposing Windows to security threats. You can disable the Flash Player in Internet Explorer by following these steps:

1. **Choose Tools**⇨**Manage Add-Ons.**

The Manage Add-Ons dialog box appears, as shown in Figure 6-2. It lists add-on programs installed on your computer.

2. **Find Shockwave Flash Object on the list and select it.**

3. **Under Settings, select the Disable option button.**

A message box tells you to exit and restart Internet Explorer.

4. **Click the OK button in the message box and close Internet Explorer.**

You can tell when you need an add-on or plug-in to view a Web page in Internet Explorer because the Manage Add-Ons icon appears on the status bar. You can double-click this icon to open the Manage Add-Ons dialog box.

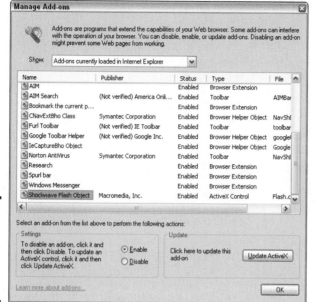

Figure 6-2:
View the
add-on
programs in
Add-Ons
dialog box.

Microsoft Office Programs

Microsoft Excel, PowerPoint, and Word files can be loaded on a Web site
along with standard HTML files. Occasionally you run into one of these files,
and to open it, you need Excel, PowerPoint, or Word. These programs are
part of the Microsoft Office Suite.

By running an advanced search at Google (www.google.com/advanced_
search), you can search for Excel, PowerPoint, and Word files. Open the
File Format drop-down menu and choose Microsoft Excel (.xls), Microsoft
PowerPoint (.ppt), or Microsoft Word (.doc).

QuickTime Player

QuickTime Player was originally invented for Macintosh computers. Apple
came out with a version of QuickTime Player for Windows PCs in 1998.
Nevertheless, QuickTime Player retains its association with Macintoshes. It
is the only media player that can play .mov (movie) files, the video file standard created by Macintosh for its computers. QuickTime Player software has
been folded into iTunes, the program for playing music files (see Book VIII,
Chapter 4). QuickTime Player can play MP4 audio files. You can read about it
as this address: www.apple.com/quicktime. It is shown in Figure 6-3.

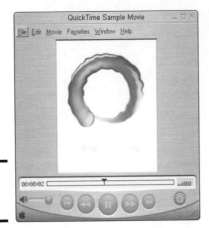

Figure 6-3:
QuickTime
Player.

RealPlayer

RealPlayer, shown in Figure 6-4, has reinvented itself in recent years as multi-purpose media player. You can play MP3 and .wav audio files, as well as .mpeg and .avi video files, with RealPlayer, but I wouldn't bother. The only reason to use this clunky piece of software is to download streaming audio from the Internet. Occasionally you run across a RealAudio (.ra, .ram, or .rm) streaming audio file that can only be played with RealPlayer — and then you have to use the darn thing. You can visit the RealPlayer Web site at this address: www.real.com.

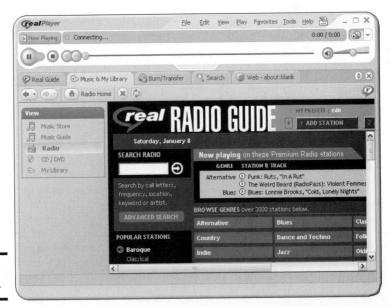

Figure 6-4:
RealPlayer.

Selecting the default plug-in

Suppose you click a video or audio file on a Web page but the wrong plug-in plays or opens the file. Perhaps you want video to play by default in Windows Media Player rather than QuickTime Player or iTunes. You can be the master of your fate. You can decide which plug-in (or program) plays or opens which kind of file by default. You can do that by following these steps:

1. **Choose Start⇨Settings⇨Control Panel.**

2. **If necessary, click the Switch to Classic View link and then double-click the Folder Options icon.**

   You see the Folder Options dialog box.

3. **Click the File Types tab.**

   You see a list of registered file types. Windows recognizes all the files on the list. Windows has preconceived ideas about which plug-in or program to automatically open these files in.

4. **Scroll down the list and select the type of file you want to reassign.**

   In the bottom half of the dialog box, next to the words "Opens With," you can see which plug-in or program automatically opens the file you chose. When you have finished reassigning the file, a new plug-in or program name will appear beside the words "Opens With."

5. **Click the Change button.**

   You see the Open With dialog box. It lists the names of all plug-ins and programs installed on your computer.

6. **Select the name of the plug-in or program with which you want to open files of the type in question.**

7. **Click the OK button in the Open With dialog box.**

8. **Click the OK button in the Folder Options dialog box.**

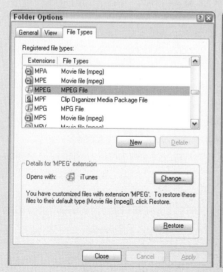

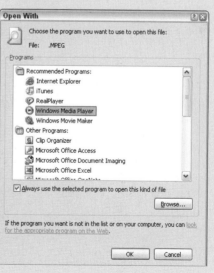

Windows Media Player

Windows Media Player comes with the Windows operating system. If your computer is running Windows, I'll bet that Windows Media Player is on your computer. The program can play movies and audio files as well as tune you into online radio stations and burn CDs (see Book VIII, Chapter 3). To find out more about Windows Media Player, go to this Web address: `www.microsoft.com/windows/windowsmedia`.

Chapter 7: The Internet for Children and Parents

In This Chapter

- ✔ Supervising children's Internet use
- ✔ Comparing the filtering software programs
- ✔ Trying out search engines designed for children
- ✔ Assessing schools on the Internet
- ✔ Answering kids' health questions
- ✔ Looking for colleges and college scholarships

This chapter explains how children and parents can get the most out of the Internet and, in the case of children, do it safely. It looks at supervising children's online time and describes how to safeguard children as they explore the Internet. You look at filtering software programs that weed out objectionable material and some search engines designed especially for children. You find many helpful Web sites in this chapter — for parenting, choosing kids' schools, getting answers to health questions, doing your homework online, and looking at colleges and obtaining college scholarships.

When you find Web sites that you believe are worthwhile for your children, bookmark them. This way, you can return to the Web sites quickly and easily. Book II, Chapter 1 explains bookmarking.

Supervising Kids on the Internet

As you know if you've spent any time on the Internet, it isn't hard to run into objectionable material. Gruesome pictures and Web sites that espouse violence are not hard to come by. You can trip over a pornographic Web site in the course of an innocent Internet search. As a parent, how do you keep your children from finding objectionable material on the Internet?

The only practical way to discourage them from finding this material is to go online with them or, barring that, put your computer in a common room in the house — the living room or family room — where you can keep an eye on who is using your computer. This chapter explains a dozen different ways to steer children away from objectionable material on the Internet. You can enlist software to screen out objectionable material. You can point your children toward Web sites that are kid-friendly. You can employ computer programs that monitor children's online activity. But you must face the fact that most children are more computer-savvy than their parents, and they discover ways to get around your restrictions. This is why I believe in keeping the computer in a common room and why I strongly recommend against letting children have computers in their bedrooms. Besides, letting children have computers in their bedrooms discourages them from playing with their friends and developing the social skills they need for a rewarding life.

Talking to Children about the Internet

Talk to your children about the Internet. Tell them that it was invented for adults but there are many fine things for kids on the Internet, too. Children more than others object to following rules, so I leave it to your creativity to find ways to establish these rules for your children's Internet use without making them sound like rules. You could call them suggestions. You could call them good ideas. Here are some of these ideas:

+ Don't give others your name, age, phone number, or other personal information on the Internet. If a questionnaire on the Internet asks for it, don't fill out the questionnaire.

+ Understand that people who chat with you on the Internet may not be who they say they are. Sometimes adults pose as kids and kids pose as adults.

+ Never meet someone in person whom you met online unless you are with an adult.

+ Don't send your picture to anyone over the Internet unless the person is a family friend or family member.

+ If anyone you don't know asks where you will be or what time you will do something, don't answer, and tell your parents about it.

+ Don't try to buy anything online unless your parents are sitting beside you.

+ If anything upsetting happens on the Internet, tell your parents about it.

After hearing you talk about these rules, if your child asks why adults are so strange and why it's necessary to exercise so much caution when dealing with them over the Internet, just answer, "Someday you'll grow up and you'll understand."

Looking at filtering and monitoring software

Filtering software, also known as *blocking software,* is software that keeps inappropriate material from appearing in a Web-browser window. *Monitoring software* tracks the Web sites that someone has visited on the Internet. Table 7-1 describes well-regarded filtering software. Some of the programs listed in the table are monitors as well. As you use these programs or consider using them, remember that no filtering software can block all objectionable content all the time. The best these programs can do is block most of it.

Table 7-1	Filtering Software Programs		
Program	*Web Address*	*Notes*	*Price*
Content Protect	www.contentwatch.com/products/content protect.php	Offers a variety of different features and controls.	$30
Cyber Patrol	www.cyberpatrol.com	Filters content but does not have monitoring capabilities.	$40
Cybersitter	www.cybersitter.com	Has the most thorough filtering capabilities; you can block content in 32 categories.	$40
iProtectYou	www.softforyou.com	Family members can be assigned "intensity levels" for filtering, with the highest intensity blocking the most Web sites.	$35
Net Nanny	www.netnanny.com	Customizing the list of blocked Web sites for different family members is difficult.	$40
NetFilter Home	www.enologic.com	Rather than lists, uses image and text analysis to determine whether content is objectionable.	$48

Filtering software programs keep lists of Web sites with objectionable material — you can update these lists over the Internet — and they bar children from visiting Web sites on the list. You can configure these programs for different family members so that older siblings have access to more Web sites than younger ones. The programs let you choose whether to block Web sites in different categories — sex, drugs, weapons, violence, extremism, and so on. Some programs can prevent children from visiting newsgroups and chat rooms. You can download trial versions of the programs listed in Table 7-1 by going to Cnet.com (www.cnet.com).

The Internet Filter Review (www.internetfilterreview.com) rates filtering software programs. Go to the Web site to see a detailed chart that shows what each program does and how it compares to the other programs.

By the way, on the subject of monitoring where users of a computer have been on the Internet, you can monitor on your own without the use of monitoring software:

✦ **The cookie trail:** A *cookie* is a text file that Web sites deposit on your computer when you visit them. By studying cookies, you can tell which Web sites someone has been to. In Windows XP, cookies are located in this folder: C:\Documents and Settings*Your Name*\Cookies. In versions of Windows prior to XP, they are found in this folder: C:\Windows\Cookies.

✦ **Temporary Internet files:** When you visit a Web page, you download its component parts — the HTML files, graphic files, and whatnot — to your computer. In Windows XP, these files are kept in the C:\Documents and Settings*Your Name*\Local Settings\Temporary Internet Files folder. In versions of Windows prior to XP, they are kept in the C:\Windows\Temporary Internet Files folder.

Open these folders in Windows Explorer or My Computer to see where you or someone else has been on the Internet.

Discovering search engines designed for children

A *search engine* is a tool for finding information on the Internet (Book II, Chapter 3 explains how search engines work). Search engines designed for children find Web sites that are suitable for children and useful to children. They do that by searching only in prescribed lists of Web sites that have been deemed kid-friendly. Table 7-2 lists search engines for children. Figure 7-1 shows the Yahooligans! Web site, a search engine for children.

Table 7-2	Search Engines for Children	
Search Engine	*Web Address*	*Description*
Ask Jeeves For Kids	www.ajkids.com	Instead of keywords, start your search by putting it in the form of a question.
Cool4Kids	www.cool4kids.com	Search the directory with 18,000 links in 14 categories.
CyberSleuth Kids	http://cybersleuth-kids.com	Search a directory of Web sites suggested by teachers.
Fact Monster	www.factmonster.com	Search the directory or enter keywords to conduct an Internet search.

Search Engine	Web Address	Description
Kids Net	www.kids.net.au	Search the children's portion of the Open Directory Project, the world's leading directory of Web sites, with this search engine.
KidsClick!	www.kidsclick.org	Search a directory of 5,000 Web sites hand-picked by librarians.
Yahooligans!	www.yahooligans.com	Yahoo!'s search engine is meant for children age 7 to 12.

Figure 7-1:
Yahooligans!
is the
Yahoo! Web
site for
children.

With a little tinkering, you can turn a standard search engine into a search engine that is suitable (maybe) for children. To do so, click the Advanced Search link and, on the Advanced Search page, look for a filtering option. For example, Google offers an option called Filter Using SafeSearch (www.google.com/advanced_search). Yahoo! has one called Filter Out Adult Web Search Results (http://search.yahoo.com/search/options). Searching this way, however, is no guarantee that objectionable material won't come up in a search.

Finding Parenting Help on the Internet

Parenting, the cliché goes, is the hardest job in the world. Actually, the hardest job in the world is parenting a teenager. (I'm only kidding. My teenage children have been treating me very kindly except for Friday and Saturday nights, when they insist on staying awake long past my bedtime.) Here are some Web sites for parents:

✦ **Dr. Spock:** For better or for worse, Dr. Benjamin Spock had more influence on raising the Baby Boom generation than anybody else. His *Common Sense Book of Baby and Child Care* was the bible of childrearing in the 1950s and 1960s. This Web site carries forward Dr. Spock's legacy with advice for all stages of childhood: newborns, infants, toddlers, preschoolers, and school-agers. Address: www.drspock.com

✦ **Parent Soup:** As shown in Figure 7-2, this Web site offers a little something for every parent, no matter how old his or her child is. You can get advice about everything from planning a birthday celebration to anger management and nutrition. Address: www.parentsoup.com

Figure 7-2:
Look for parenting advice at Parent Soup.

COOL WEB SITE

I need to fit Behind the Name (www.behindthename.com) somewhere in this book, and it may as well be here, as a parent-to-be may come to this part of the book. Behind the Name is like one of those "what to name the baby" books in that it gives the history and etymology of first names. But what makes this Web site special is the Popularity link. Click this link next to any name and you get a graph generated from census data showing how the name has risen or fallen in popularity over the years. For example, clicking the Popularity link next to my name, Peter, shows that my name was in the top 50 names until 1969, but it has since fallen to ranking 148. Ashley, meanwhile, has risen from ranking 662 in 1969 to become number 8 in 2003. What the hey?

Finding a School for Your Child

Apart from birth, probably no passage in a child's life brings more anxiety for parents than entering elementary school. Finding the right elementary school for a child isn't easy. You can start by searching the Web site of the school district where you reside. The school district is supposed to maintain an accountability report card for each of its schools. These report cards describe the school, list the number of students, and report standardized test results, among other things. Check out these Web sites as well for help with choosing schools:

✦ **Great Schools:** Find profiles and performance ratings for public, private, and charter schools in 50 states. The Web site offers detailed reports about all schools in California, Arizona, Texas, Florida, Colorado, New York, and Washington. Address: `www.greatschools.net`

✦ **Parents for Public Schools:** PPS is a national organization devoted to improving public schools with the help of public-spirited volunteers. From the point of view of a parent looking for a school, the organization can be very helpful in directing you to the right school and advising you in how to get your child admitted. Go to this Web site and see whether your community has a PPS chapter. Address: `www.parents4public schools.com`

By the way, on my authority as the spouse of an elementary school teacher, I know that the best way to judge a school is not by its test scores, but by speaking to the parents of students who attend the school. Every school is a community, and you can find out how vibrant it is from parents, not from statistics.

The motto of Donors Choose (`www.donorschoose.org`) is "Every Teacher a Grant Writer; Every Citizen a Philanthropist." This Web site gives you the opportunity to fund a classroom project large or small somewhere in the United States. Teachers are invited to come to this Web site and describe projects for which they need a donor. Look through the hundreds of projects. If you decide to open your purse or wallet and be a benefactor, you are guaranteed to receive a follow-up report explaining precisely how your money was spent and a raft of thank you notes from students. Here's your chance to really make a difference.

Kids' Health

Besides the numerous Web sites devoted to health in general (WedMD, CBS News HealthWatch, and others), you can also find Web sites devoted to children's health on the Internet. Here are the best ones:

+ **Healthy Kids:** This Web site is brought to you by the editors of *American Baby* magazine. You can find many long, magazine-style articles. Get advice on basic health, development issues, and nutrition. Use the Search text box to search for information and articles. Address: www.healthykids.com

+ **Kids Health:** This Web site is actually three in one. It offers health advice for parents, children, and teenagers. Click the Parents, Kids, or Teens link to read health advice tailored to parents, children, or teenage children. Address: www.kidshealth.org

+ **Teen Advice:** Teenagers can come to this Web site and ask questions about gender issues, family, relationships, and sex, among other topics, and have their questions answered by volunteer advice counselors. Search the Question Archive to see whether your question has already been answered. Address: http://teenadviceonline.org

+ **Teenwire:** Planned Parenthood's award-winning online magazine, Teenwire gives frank and thorough advice to teenagers about contraception and sexual health. Address: www.teenwire.com

Getting Help with Your Homework

Someday computer homework robots will be able to do your homework for you. Until that blesséd day arrives, however, you're stuck with doing it on your own, although you can seek help from these Web sites:

+ **Brain Pop:** If you're the kind of person who learns better from short films than books, check out this Web site. You can see simple cartoons that elucidate topics in science, math, English, social studies, and technology. Address: www.brainpop.com

+ **Hotmath:** Is this too good to be true, or what? Says this Web site, "We show step-by-step explanations for the actual math homework problems in math textbooks (odd-numbered problems only)." If your math textbook is covered at this Web site, you can find out how to solve the odd-numbered problems in today's homework assignment. You'll have to instant-message your friends to find answers to the even-numbered problems. Address: www.hotmath.com

+ **Math.com:** Need a refresher course in classifying angles? How about derivative identities? You can get easy-to-understand math lessons at this Web site. Address: www.math.com

+ **Pink Monkey:** Go to this Web site when you need help writing an essay for an English class. According to its makers, Pink Monkey is "the world's largest library of literature summaries, with 389 booknotes, chapter summaries, and study notes online currently." Address: www.pinkmonkey.com

✦ **Sparknotes:** This Web site offers free online study guides in a number of different academic areas. Click the Math link, for example, to get help with different topics in algebra, geometry, trigonometry, and pre-calculus. Click the Literature link to get plot summaries, character lists, and descriptions of hundreds of different novels. Address: www.sparknotes.com

COOL WEB SITE

Fun Brain, the award-winning Web site shown in Figure 7-3, offers learning games for children. You can find games suitable for kids of different ages in eight different subject areas. Some of these games, by the way, are suitable for adults, too. Fun Brain is located at this Web address: www.funbrain.com.

Figure 7-3:
Fun Brain has a big collection of learning games.

Finding Colleges and College Scholarships

Every college has a Web site. Start your search for the college of your dreams by visiting college Web sites and requesting brochures. While you're at it, check out these Web sites:

✦ **College Board:** This is the all-purpose Web site for high school seniors looking to go to college. Starting here, you can investigate different colleges, sign up to take entrance exams, and take practice SAT tests. Address: www.collegeboard.com

✦ **College Confidential:** Start at this Web site if you are a novice and the whole college admission thing just mystifies you. If what you need to know can't be found on this Web site, post your question on one of the forums and wait for an answer. You won't have to wait long, as this is a crowded Web site. Address: www.collegeconfidential.com

✦ **FastWeb:** After you enter your name and e-mail address, you can describe yourself and enlist the help of FastWeb in finding scholarships for which you are eligible. Be sure to submit a secondary e-mail address. The e-mail address you enter will be barraged by junk mail. Address: `http://fastweb.monster.com`

✦ **FinAid:** This is an all-purpose Web site for people trying to figure out how to pay for their college education. Use the calculators to find out how much money you need. Study your opportunities for loans and scholarships. You can even submit a question to this Web site. Address: `www.finaid.org`

✦ **Thick Envelope:** For a rather hefty fee of $40, this Web site claims to give you a realistic assessment of your chances of being admitted to 80 different colleges. The idea is for you to save money by only applying to colleges that you are qualified for. Address: `www.thickenvelope.com`

✦ **Yahoo! College Search:** To get the bare essentials about a college's tuition costs and enrollment, start at this Web site. Address: `http://education.yahoo.com/college/essentials`

Book II

Exploring the Internet

The 5th Wave   By Rich Tennant

"From now on, let's confine our exploration of ancient Egypt to the computer program."

Contents at a Glance

Chapter 1: Browsing around the Internet

In This Chapter

✔ Finding your way around the Internet

✔ Choosing a home page

✔ Bookmarking Web pages you intend to visit again

✔ Sharing your bookmarks with others

✔ Downloading a file over the Internet

In Internet-speak, *browsing* means to skip merrily along from Web page to Web page. I'm curious why *browsing* was chosen to describe this activity. Before the Internet became available, *to browse* meant to feed on or nibble. Sheep browse on hillsides. Did the makers of Web-browsing software think we're a bunch of sheep?

This chapter describes the basics of getting from place to place on the Internet. It also shows how to bookmark your favorite Web pages, return to the pages you've bookmarked, and manage bookmarks. You also discover social bookmarking, a way to share bookmarked Web pages with other people. Last but not least, you find out how to download and copy files from the Internet.

In case you didn't know, a *Web browser* is the software you use to view Web pages, bookmark Web pages, and get from Web page to Web page. This chapter mentions two browsers — Internet Explorer and Mozilla. Chapter 2 of this minibook describes these and other Web browsers in detail.

Navigation Basics

If you know the least bit about the Internet, you have my permission to skip over this section. It describes the basics of getting around, what hyperlinks are, and how to enter Web addresses in a browser. This information is old hat to most people, but speaking as one who wears old hats from time to time, I understand that not everyone knows the basics, so I describe them here.

Visiting a Web site whose address you know

Every Web page has a *Web address,* also known as a URL, or uniform resource locator. While you're online, you can read the addresses of the Web pages you're visiting by glancing at the Address bar in your browser. (If you don't see the Address bar, choose View⇨Toolbars⇨Address bar in Internet Explorer, or choose View⇨Show/Hide⇨Navigation toolbar in Mozilla.) To go to a Web site whose address you know, carefully type the address in the Address bar and press Enter, as shown in Figure 1-1.

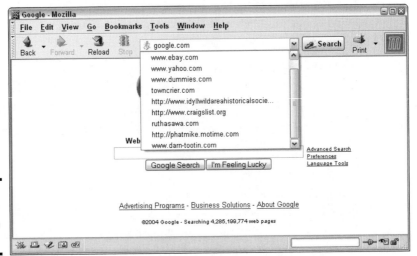

Figure 1-1:
Every Web
page has an
address.

If you've entered the address before, you're in luck. Your browser may recognize the address, in which case the address appears on the drop-down menu and you can select it. If you entered the address recently, you can click the down arrow on the Address bar and, on the drop-down menu, click the address of the Web page you want to visit.

When you enter a Web address, it isn't necessary to enter the *http://* at the beginning of the address. In many instances, you don't have to enter the *www.* either, because your browser assumes that you want to enter those letters and it enters them for you. For example, if you enter **ebay.com,** your browser fills in the rest: `http://www.ebay.com`. Here's another trick you can use in some versions of Internet Explorer: If you click in the Address bar and press Ctrl+Enter, your browser immediately enters `http://www..com/`. All you have to do is fill in the missing parts of the Web address.

Clicking hyperlinks to get from page to page

After you arrive at a Web site, you're sure to find many *hyperlinks*. Hyperlinks come in the form of text and images. Clicking a hyperlink takes you to a different Web page or a different place on the same Web page. You can tell when your pointer is over a hyperlink because the pointer turns into to a hand with the index finger up, and a brief description of where the link will take you appears on-screen as well, as shown in Figure 1-2. By convention, text hyperlinks are shown in blue text and are underlined, although some Web sites break the convention. Image hyperlinks are harder to spot. You can't tell where they are until you move the pointer over them and see your pointer change to a pointing hand.

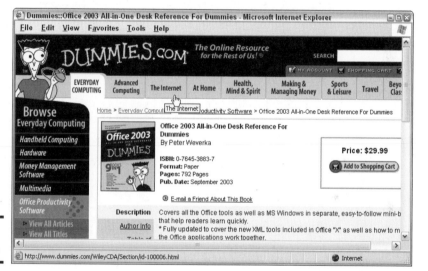

Figure 1-2:
A hyperlink.

Probably the most adventurous way to explore the Internet is to click hyperlinks and see where your journey takes you. You can always backtrack by clicking the Back button, as the next section in this chapter explains.

In the Mozilla browser, you can see a list of all hyperlinks on a Web page by choosing View⇨Page Info (or pressing Ctrl+I) and clicking the Links tab in the Page Info dialog box.

Revisiting Web pages you've been to before

Exploring the Internet is an adventure, but more than a few adventurers travel too far and wish to return to a page that they visited before. Fortunately, backtracking is pretty easy. By clicking the Back button or its drop-down menu, you can revisit the pages you viewed since you opened your Web browser. You can even view a Web page you visited in the past several days.

Clicking the Back and Forward buttons

Following are the different ways to revisit sites:

✦ **Back button:** Click the Back button to see the page you last saw.

✦ **Forward button:** Click the Forward button to move ahead to the page from which you retreated.

✦ **Back and Forward button menus:** Next to the Back and Forward buttons are drop-down menus that you can click to leap backward or forward by several Web pages, as shown in Figure 1-3. Don't be shy about using these drop-down menus. All you have to do to leap forward or backward is to click the down-arrow and click a Web-page name.

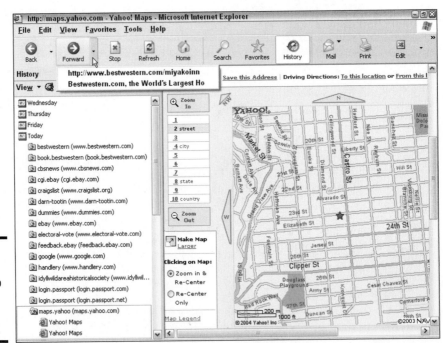

Figure 1-3:
Ways to revisit Web pages you visited before.

Covering your tracks

Your Web browser is watching you! Browsers keep track of the Web sites you've visited, as "Delving into your browsing history" explains later in this chapter. Don't want your boss to know which Web sites you've been visiting? Here are instructions for removing Web addresses from the Address bar drop-down menu and from the History bar or History dialog box:

✔ **Internet Explorer:** Click the History button to see the History bar (refer to Figure 1-3), right-click the address you want to delete, and choose Delete. To remove all the Web addresses on the list, choose Tools⇨ Internet Options and click the Clear History button on the General tab of the Internet

Options dialog box. You can also tell Internet Explorer how many days' worth of Web sites to stockpile by entering a number in the Days to Keep Pages in History text box.

✔ **Mozilla:** Choose Edit⇨Preferences and, in the Preferences dialog box, select the Navigator category and the History sub-category. Then click the Clear History button to remove all Web addresses from the History dialog box, and click the Clear Location Bar button to remove addresses from the Address bar. You can tell Mozilla how many days' worth of addresses to keep on hand by entering a number in the Days text box.

Delving into your browsing history

Your browser is watching you! The program keeps a record of the Web sites and Web pages you visited in the past several days. Follow these instructions to return to one of those Web pages:

✦ **Internet Explorer:** Click the History button and then click a Web address in the History bar. After you click a day of the week button or the Week Of button, you see an alphabetical list of Web addresses (refer to Figure 1-3).

✦ **Mozilla:** Press Ctrl+H or choose Go⇨History. You see the History dialog box. Select a day and double-click a Web address.

Choosing Your Home Page

When you start your Web browser and connect to the Internet, the first place you go is your *home page*. You also go there when you click the Home button in your browser. Unfortunately, software manufacturers and unscrupulous Web sites sometimes commandeer the home page. When you install new software, you sometimes discover that your home page has mysteriously become that of a software manufacturer. And unscrupulous Web sites have been known to load spyware on your computer that changes your home page. Don't let yourself be pushed around this way!

Browsing more than one Web page

You can be in two (or three or four) places at once, at least where browsing Web pages is concerned. While you wait for one Web page to load on your computer, you can examine another one.

To open more than one Web page in Internet Explorer, press Ctrl+N or choose File⇨New⇨Window. Doing so opens a second Internet Explorer window, where you can go to another Web page. You can also open a second window by Shift+clicking a hyperlink. To go back and forth between Web pages that are open, click buttons on the taskbar.

Mozilla is more sophisticated than Internet Explorer when it comes to browsing more than one Web page. In Mozilla, you can open the second (or third or fourth) page in a tab. Use

one of these techniques to open the first tab or another tab:

- Press Ctrl+T or choose File⇨New⇨ Navigator Tab.
- Click the Open a New Tab button.
- Right-click a tab and choose New Tab.

Click tabs to go from Web page to Web page. Use these techniques to close tabs:

- Click the Close button on the right side of the tab bar to close all tabs.
- Right-click and choose Close Tab to close a tab (or press Ctrl+W).
- Right-click and choose Close Other Tabs to close all tabs but the one you're viewing.

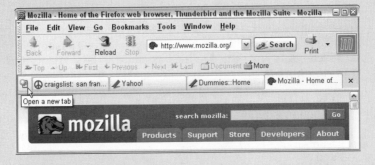

Choose a home page that you are genuinely interested in, one that loads quickly, and one that you visit often. Go to the page you want to make your home and follow these instructions to make it your home page:

- ✦ **Internet Explorer:** Choose Tools⇨Internet Options. You see the General tab of the Internet Options dialog box. Click the Use Current button.

- ✦ **Mozilla:** Choose Edit⇨Preferences. In the Preferences dialog box, select the Navigator category and then click the Use Current button.

Bookmarking Your Favorite Web Pages

In Internet terminology, to *bookmark* means to save a Web address so that you can return to it later. Browsers offer special commands for saving Web addresses. After you have bookmarked a Web page, you need only click its address to visit it. Don't be shy about bookmarking a page — you can always delete the bookmark later. Read on to find out how to go to bookmarked pages, how to bookmark pages, and how to manage your bookmarks.

Going to a page you bookmarked

After you bookmark a Web page, visiting it is simply a matter of clicking once or twice. Everything should be this easy. Following are instructions for going to a bookmarked page in Internet Explorer and Mozilla.

**Book II
Chapter 1**

Browsing around the Internet

Internet Explorer

Internet Explorer offers two ways to visit a favorite Web page that you bookmarked:

+ Click the Favorites button and select the Web page in the Favorites bar, as shown in Figure 1-4. If you put the page in a folder, select the folder's name and then select the bookmark.

+ Open the Favorites menu and choose the bookmark there, as shown in Figure 1-4. If the bookmark is kept in a folder, click a submenu name and then click the bookmark.

Mozilla

To go to a bookmarked page in Mozilla, click the Bookmarks button on the Personal toolbar or open the Bookmarks menu and then choose the bookmark. If the bookmark is in a folder, click the folder name on the submenu and then click the bookmark.

If you are having trouble finding a bookmark, choose Bookmarks⇨Manage Bookmarks (or press Ctrl+B) to open the Bookmark Manager dialog box. Then enter a part of the bookmark name or a keyword you assigned to the bookmark in the Search text box, and press Enter. With luck, your bookmark appears in the dialog box, and you can double-click it there.

People who use Internet Explorer and Mozilla to browse the Web can have their cake and eat it too. Mozilla gives you the chance to visit Web pages you bookmarked with Internet Explorer. To visit one of these pages, choose Bookmarks⇨Imported IE Favorites. The names of pages you bookmarked in Internet Explorer appear on a submenu. Click a bookmark there.

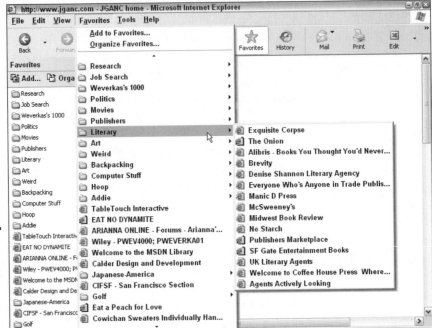

Figure 1-4:
Going to a
bookmarked
page in
Internet
Explorer.

Bookmarking a favorite page

You are hereby encouraged to bookmark a Web page if you feel the least desire to return to it later. Unless you bookmark a page, finding it again can be like finding the proverbial needle in a haystack. As you bookmark pages, give a moment's thought to how you want to organize your bookmarks. If you bookmark more than a handful of pages, finding bookmarks can be difficult, unless you organize your bookmarks into folders. Your Web browser gives you an opportunity to do that, as I explain very shortly.

Internet Explorer

Follow these instruction to bookmark a Web page in Internet Explorer:

1. **Choose Favorites⇨Add to Favorites.**

You see the Add Favorite dialog box, shown on the left side of Figure 1-5.

2. **Select a folder for the Web page (click the New Folder button, if necessary, to create a new folder), and click the OK button.**

Bookmarked Web pages appear on the Favorites menu, as the previous section in this chapter explains. Unless you choose a folder for storing favorite Web pages, the Favorites menu soon fills with Web pages, and you have trouble finding the one you want.

You can quickly bookmark a Web page by pressing Ctrl+D. However, doing so places the Web page on the Favorites menu, and you don't get a chance to put the Web page in a folder for organizational purposes.

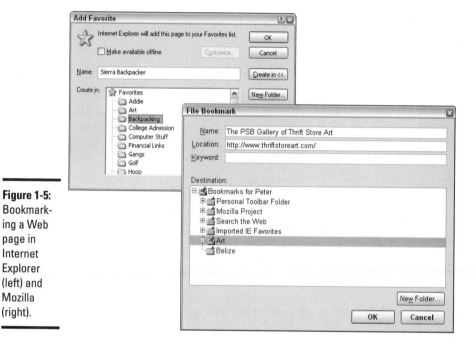

Figure 1-5: Bookmarking a Web page in Internet Explorer (left) and Mozilla (right).

Mozilla

Do one of the following to bookmark a Web page in Mozilla:

✦ Press Ctrl+D (or choose Bookmarks⇨Bookmark This Page) to place the Web page on the Bookmarks menu.

✦ Press Ctrl+Shift+D (or choose Bookmarks⇨File Bookmark) to organize the Web page into a folder in the File Bookmark dialog box, as shown on the right side of Figure 1-5.

Select the folder, enter a name for the bookmark, and enter a keyword as well if you want this page to come up in keyword searches for bookmarks. You can click the New Folder button to create a new folder.

Renaming, deleting, and managing bookmarks

A bookmark collection can be like a crowded garage — it can be a resting place for a lot of old junk as well as useful items. If you collect bookmarks, the time will surely come when you need to rename, delete, or move bookmarks in your collection. These pages explain how to do all that.

Internet Explorer

The easiest way to handle bookmarks in Internet Explorer is to do it by way of the Favorites menu. With this menu open, you can delete a bookmark by right-clicking its name and choosing Delete on the shortcut menu. You can move a bookmark by dragging its name up or down on the menu. You can rename a bookmark by right-clicking its name, choosing Rename, and entering a new name in the Rename dialog box.

Another way to handle bookmarks is to choose Favorites➪Organize Favorites and get to work in the Organize Favorites dialog box, shown on the right side of Figure 1-6. The Create Folder, Rename, and Delete buttons are self-explanatory. What is useful in this dialog box is the Move to Folder button. To move a bookmark into a different folder, select the bookmark's name, click the Move to Folder button, and select a folder in the Browse for Folder dialog box, as shown on the left side of Figure 1-6.

 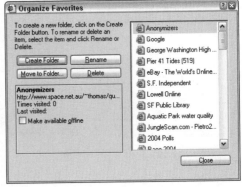

Figure 1-6: Moving a bookmark to a new folder in Internet Explorer.

Yet another way to handle bookmarks is to open My Computer or Windows Explorer and do your moving, renaming, and deleting there. Internet Explorer bookmarks are kept in one of these folders, depending on how your system is set up:

```
C:\Documents and Settings\Your Name\Favorites
C:\Windows\Favorites\Links
```

Open the folder where your bookmarks are located and use standard My Computer or Windows Explorer commands to move, rename, and delete bookmarks. For example, to move a bookmark to a different folder, drag it there.

Mozilla

To manage bookmarks in Mozilla, start by pressing Ctrl+B or choosing Bookmarks⇨Manage Bookmarks. You see the Bookmark Manager dialog box shown in Figure 1-7. Select the bookmark that needs disciplining and follow these instructions to discipline it:

✦ **Moving:** Click the Move button. You see the Choose Folder dialog box shown in Figure 1-7. Select a folder and click the OK button.

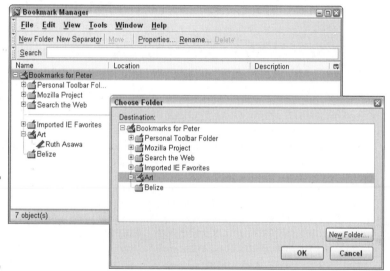

Book II
Chapter 1

Browsing around
the Internet

Figure 1-7:
Moving a
bookmark to
a new folder
in Mozilla.

✦ **Renaming:** Click the Rename button and enter a new name in the Properties For dialog box.

✦ **Deleting:** Click the Delete button, but be careful, because the bookmark is deleted right away. Mozilla isn't a Microsoft-made program. You don't see the Are You Sure You Want to Delete? warning that Microsoft spits out in its programs.

Backing up your bookmarks

Backing up means to make a second copy of computer data and store it on a floppy disk or other medium away from your computer. It would be a sad day if your computer crashed and you lost all your bookmarks. To back up your bookmark collection, open My Computer or Windows Explorer, go to one of these folders, and back up your bookmarks to a floppy disk or other storage medium:

✦ **Internet Explorer:** Bookmarks are located at `C:\Documents and Settings\`*`Your Name`*`\Favorites` or `C:\Windows\Favorites\Links`, depending on your system setup.

✦ **Mozilla:** Bookmarks can be found in a file called `bookmarks.html`. Unfortunately, finding this file can be a chore, as it is buried in a so-called salted (`.slt`) subfolder at `C:\Documents and Settings\`*`Your Name`*`\Application Data\Mozilla\Profiles\`*`Your Profile Name`*`\[random string].slt`. Salted folder, indeed! Sometimes the best way to find this subfolder is to look for it with the Windows Search command.

Social Bookmarking, or Sharing Bookmarks with Others

When you bookmark a Web page, it means you like it well enough to want to return to it someday. Only the best Web pages get bookmarked. If you knew which pages others have bookmarked, you could get a head start in finding useful Web pages. And if you could narrow a search of the Web to bookmarked Web pages, your search would be more rewarding.

On the idea that the only good Web page is a bookmarked Web page, the past couple of years have seen an innovation called *social bookmarking.* Social bookmarking means to share bookmarks with others. Web pages that you bookmark are entered on a master list of bookmarks. Others enter their bookmarked pages on the list as well. The result is a database of bookmarked Web pages that you can search. Most social-bookmarking services also give you the opportunity to store your bookmarks online and organize them in different ways.

Here are the most highly regarded social-bookmarking Web sites:

✦ Backflip (`www.backflip.com`)

✦ del.icio.us (`http://del.icio.us`)

✦ furl (`www.furl.net`)

✦ Spurl.net (`www.spurl.net`)

My favorite is Spurl.net, shown in Figure 1-8. This one is easiest to use and install (although it only works with Internet Explorer). After you register with Spurl.net and load its program on your computer, two buttons — Spurl! and Spurl Bar — appear in your browser window:

✦ Click the Spurl! button (or choose Tools➪Bookmark the Current Page to Spurl.net) to bookmark a Web page and share it with others. A form appears so that you can describe the Web page. The information you enter goes into a database that other Spurl members can search.

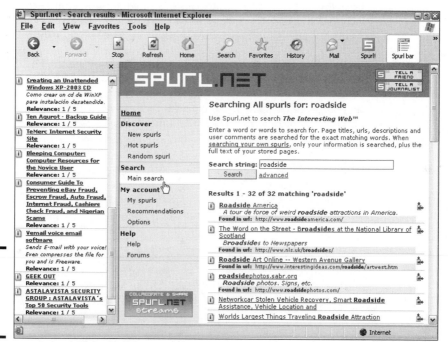

Book II Chapter 1

Browsing around the Internet

Figure 1-8: Social bookmarking with Spurl.

Click the Main Search link at Spurl.net to search among Web pages that others have bookmarked (refer to Figure 1-8). Enter a keyword for the search and click the Search button.

✦ Click the Spurl Bar button to display the Spurl bar on the left side of the browser window (refer to Figure 1-8). In the Spurl bar, you can view a list of pages you bookmarked (click My Spurls), view a list of pages that Spurl recommends for you, given the kind of pages you bookmarked (click Recom), or view a list of pages recently bookmarked by Spurl members (click Hot New). To search pages you bookmarked, enter a keyword in the text box and click the Click to Search button.

Downloading and Copying Files from the Internet

Downloading means to transfer a copy of a file or program from a site on the Internet to your computer. From time to time in your exploration of the Internet, you are given the opportunity to download a file. Book I, Chapter 4 looks into the security implications of downloading files. If you have antivirus software (and you should have it), the software will examine the file after it arrives to make sure that it doesn't carry a virus.

When you click the button to download a file, you see the File Download – Security Warning dialog box shown in Figure 1-9. Click the Save button, choose a folder for the downloaded file in the Save As dialog box, and twiddle your thumbs while the file downloads. To activate the file, go to folder where you stored it, select the file, and double-click it.

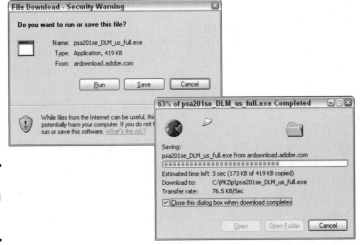

Figure 1-9:
Downloading
a file from
the Internet.

Before you run a file you downloaded, right-click it in Windows Explorer or My Computer and choose Run with AntiVirus to see whether the file contains a virus.

On the subject of grabbing files from the Internet, you can also copy text, pictures, and video files by following these instructions:

◆ **Copying text:** Drag your cursor over the text and press Ctrl+C or choose Edit⇨Copy to copy the text to the Clipboard.

◆ **Copying a picture:** Right-click the picture and choose Save Picture As on the shortcut menu. In the Save As dialog box, select a folder and click the Save button.

◆ **Downloading a video:** Right-click the video image and choose Save Target As on the shortcut menu. In the Save As dialog box, select a folder for storing the video file and click the Save button. You can change the file's name by entering a new name in the File Name text box.

**Book II
Chapter 1**

Browsing around
the Internet

Chapter 2: A Look at Different Browsers

In This Chapter

✔ Looking at the different browsers

✔ Customizing Internet Explorer and Mozilla

This chapter takes a look at different Web browsers, the computer programs you use to explore the Internet. I explain how you can tweak browsers and how to make them work for you. You need a Web browser to cruise the Internet, so you may as well pick the one that works best for you, and after you've picked it, you can then make it run the very best it can.

Comparing the Different Browsers

Table 2-1 offers a thumbnail comparison of the five most commonly used Web browsers. All these browsers are free. The most popular by far is Microsoft's Internet Explorer, shown in Figure 2-1. According to WebSideStory, a company that collects information about how people use the Internet, 94 percent of people who browsed the Internet in July 2004 used Internet Explorer.

Table 2-1	Different Web Browsers	
Browser	*Notes*	*Address*
Internet Explorer	Comes with the Windows operating system. Is compatible with more Web sites than other browsers. Version 6.0 includes pop-up blocking and new security features.	`www.microsoft.com/ windows/ie`
Mozilla	Offers better control of pop-up windows and cookies. Lets you browse more than one Web page with window tabs.	`www.mozilla.org/ releases`

(continued)

Table 2-1 *(continued)*

Browser	Notes	Address
Netscape Navigator	Formerly the most popular browser.	`http://channels.netscape.com/ns/browsers/download.jsp`
Opera	Doesn't offer as many features, but claims to be faster and more secure than other browsers.	`www.opera.com`
Safari	Comes with the Mac operating system (OS).	`www.apple.com/safari`

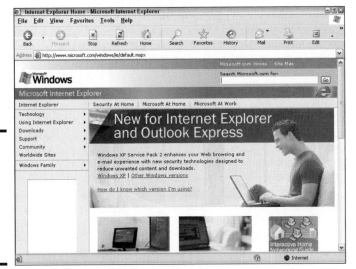

Figure 2-1: Internet Explorer is by far the most popular Web browser.

 Internet Explorer is so popular in part because it comes with Windows. If your computer runs the Windows operating system — and nine of ten computers run Windows — Internet Explorer is installed on your computer automatically. Many Windows users make Internet Explorer their Web browser without giving it any thought. They don't realize that they have a choice of browser software.

Another reason for the popularity of Internet Explorer has to do with Web-site design. Designers know that the vast majority of people who come to their Web sites will use Internet Explorer. Accordingly, they engineer their

Web sites to work best with that browser. The success of Microsoft's browser is self-fulfilling. As more Web sites are designed for Internet Explorer, fewer display properly in other browsers, which causes more people to abandon the browsers they are using in favor of Internet Explorer.

Internet Explorer has been the subject of controversy because of security flaws. In June 2004, the United States government's Computer Emergency Readiness Team (CERT) suggested dropping Internet Explorer. Warned CERT, "There are a number of significant vulnerabilities in technologies relating to the IE domain/zone security model, the DHTML object model, MIME type determination, the graphical user interface (GUI), and ActiveX. It is possible to reduce exposure to these vulnerabilities by using a different Web browser, especially when browsing untrusted sites."

Microsoft responded by introducing Internet Explorer 6.0, an upgrade to its browser, in September 2004. The company also issued a patch for Windows XP called Service Pack 2. Between Service Pack 2 and the upgrade, Internet Explorer was supposed to be safe from attacks.

Is Internet Explorer unsafe? It is no more unsafe than other browsers. In fairness to Microsoft, its browser is more subject to attacks not necessarily because it has more security flaws, but because it presents a bigger and juicier target. Hackers, worm writers, Trojan horsemen, and the other motley malcontents who make attacking browser software their pastime target Internet Explorer because it is found on the majority of computers. If Mozilla or Safari were as ubiquitous as Internet Explorer, they would be attacked just as often.

Throughout this book, I give instructions for using Mozilla because I am very fond of that browser. I think Mozilla is worth checking out. It is easier to customize than Internet Explorer and easier to learn. It handles pop-up windows better. Bookmarks are easier to manage. You can visit more than one Web site at the same time, thanks to Mozilla's window tabs (see the section on browsing multiple Web pages in Chapter 1 of this minibook). And, I must say, it's refreshing to use software that's *not* manufactured by the Microsoft Corporation. Figure 2-2 shows the Mozilla browser.

Besides the Web sites listed in Table 2-1, you can download popular Web browsers at TUCOWS (`www.tucos.com`) and Cnet (`www.cnet.com`). All the browsers are free.

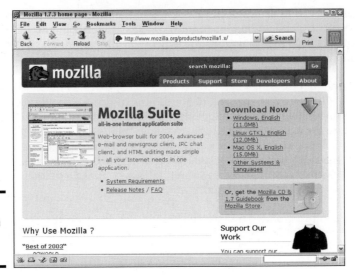

Figure 2-2:
The Mozilla
Web
browser.

Customizing Your Browser

Most people don't realize that they can do a lot inside their browser to make exploring the Internet a more comfortable experience. They don't understand that they can trade their coach seat for first class. Or that they can sit by the window rather than the aisle if they want to. Or that they can forsake the chili mac for the filet mignon.

These pages explain the different ways to customize Internet Explorer and Mozilla. Read on to discover how to make text easier to read, handle toolbars, control pop-up windows, and choose a default search engine for your browser.

As well as this chapter, which discusses customizing your browser, be sure to see Book I, Chapter 4, which explains how to protect your privacy and security as you browse the Internet, and Book I, Chapter 6, which explains plug-in programs such as QuickTime and Acrobat Reader that come into play when you visit certain types of Web pages.

Making the text easier to read

Depending on your computer setup and the Web sites you visit, you may be able to alter the text and background of Web pages by taking advantage of commands in your browser. These commands don't always work, but they are worth a try.

The commands described in this section affect all Web pages you visit, not just the Web page you are looking at when you give the command. If you change the look of text, remember how you changed it in case you change your mind and want to change it back.

Changing text size

Try these commands on your browser's View menu to shrink or enlarge the text on Web pages:

Book II
Chapter 2

✦ **Internet Explorer:** Choose View⇨Text Size, and select a size option on the Text Size menu.

✦ **Mozilla:** Choose View⇨Text Zoom, and then choose a setting on the Text Zoom submenu. You can also press Ctrl+– (Ctrl and the minus sign) or Ctrl++ (Ctrl and the plus sign) to shrink or enlarge the type. Each time you press these key combinations, the text gets smaller or larger.

A Look at Different Browsers

Changing fonts

Check out these commands if you find it necessary to change fonts on a Web page. A *font* is a type style, the complete collection of letters, numbers, and symbols available in a particular typeface. Some fonts are easier to read than others.

✦ **Internet Explorer:** Choose Tools⇨Internet Options, and on the General tab of the Internet Options dialog box, click the Fonts button. You see the Fonts dialog box, shown in Figure 2-3. Choose a font in the Web Page Font list for letters shown in proportional text; choose a font in the Plain Text Font list for letters shown in fixed-width text.

✦ **Mozilla:** Choose Edit⇨Preferences, and then go to the Fonts subcategory under Appearance in the Preferences dialog box, as shown in Figure 2-3. In this category are options for changing proportional fonts, serif fonts, sans-serif fonts, and cursive fonts on Web pages.

Changing text color

Finally, you can change the color of text and the page background color. Resort to these commands, for example, when you come to a Web page that is indecipherable, one of those unreadable pages with a dark background and dark text:

✦ **Internet Explorer:** Choose Tools⇨Internet Options, and on the General tab of the Internet Options dialog box, click the Colors button. You land in the Colors dialog box. Deselect the Use Windows Colors check box. Click the Text button to choose a color for text from the pop-up Color dialog box, and click the Background button to choose a page background from the pop-up Color dialog box.

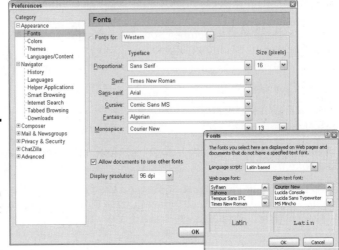

Figure 2-3:
Changing
the look of
text in
Mozilla (left)
and Internet
Explorer
(right).

✦ **Mozilla:** Choose Edit➪Preferences, and then go to the Colors subcategory under Appearance in the Preferences dialog box. Click the Text button and choose a color from the pop-up menu for text; click the Background button and choose a color from the pop-up menu for the page background.

Wrestling with the toolbars and status bar

Sometimes toolbars and other bric-a-brac along the sides of the browser window come between you and the joy of exploring the Internet. To remove all toolbars as well as the status bar along the bottom of the browser window, press F11 (or choose View➪Full Screen). Press F11 again to resuscitate the toolbars.

In all Microsoft programs, Internet Explorer included, you can right-click a toolbar or the menu bar and select the name of a toolbar from the shortcut menu to display or hide a toolbar. Internet Explorer also offers commands on the View➪Toolbars menu for hiding and displaying toolbars.

In Mozilla, you hide or display toolbars by choosing View➪Show/Hide and then selecting or deselecting a toolbar name on the submenu.

The status bar along the bottom of the window tells you when a page has finished downloading (you see the word Done). When you move the pointer over a hyperlink or button, the status bar lists the address of the Web page that will open if you click the hyperlink or button. All of that is well and good, but if you don't care to see the status bar, choose View➪Status bar in Internet Explorer, or choose View➪Hide/Display➪Status bar in Mozilla.

Ways to prevent eyestrain

People who spend many hours working in front of a computer screen owe it to themselves to look after their health. Computers are dangerous to the lower back, the wrists, and the eyes — especially the eyes. Here are some techniques to help prevent eyestrain:

✔ **Keep your monitor in the proper light.** Glare on a monitor screen causes eyestrain. Keep the monitor out of direct light to reduce glare and use an adjustable light to illuminate whatever it is you are working with besides your computer and monitor. If you are using a laptop or flat-screen monitor, you can put the monitor in more direct light because laptops and flat-screens are meant to be sidelit or backlit.

✔ **Play with the knobs on your monitor.** Those goofy knobs on the monitor can be useful indeed. Twist them, turn them, and experiment until you find a look that is comfortable for your eyes.

✔ **Opt for smaller screen resolution.** With a smaller screen resolution, or area, everything looks bigger, although things can get cramped, too. To get a smaller resolution, right-click on the Windows desktop and choose Properties. In the Display Properties dialog box, select the Settings tab. Then drag the Screen Area slider to the left so that the setting reads 640 × 480 pixels, and

click OK. Try this setting on for size. If you don't like it, return to the Settings tab and drag the screen slider to the right. If you can't see the OK button because the screen is too small, just press Enter instead of clicking OK.

✔ **Put large icons on the desktop and in folders.** To make the icons on the Windows desktop and in folders larger, right-click on the desktop and choose Properties. In the Display Properties dialog box, select the Effects tab, select the Use Large Icons check box, and click OK.

✔ **Make the mouse pointer larger.** Another way to make your eyes last longer is to make the mouse pointer larger. Choose Start➪Settings➪Control Panel. Then double-click the Mouse icon (switch to Classic View if necessary), select the Pointers tab in the Mouse Properties dialog box, and choose Windows Standard (extra large) or Windows Standard (large) from the Scheme drop-down menu.

✔ **Gaze at the horizon.** Every so often, leave your desk, step to the window, part the curtains, and stare. Stare at the most faraway point you can see. Stare and dream. Then blink a few times and marvel at how good the world looks when you're not staring at a computer screen.

Preventing and controlling pop-ups

If you have spent any time on the Internet, you know what a *pop-up* is. Pop-ups are new, unwelcome browser windows that leap onto the computer screen when you least expect them. Most pop-ups are advertisements. At best, they are annoying. At worst, several pop-ups appear in succession, and you have to kill them one at a time by closing the browser windows in which they appear. How do you prevent pop-ups? Keep reading.

You can always right-click a link and choose Open in New Window if you want a second window — in other words, if you want a pop-up window — to appear. In Internet Explorer, you can Shift+click a link to open it in a new window.

After you have told your browser how to handle pop-ups, go to Popuptest.com at this address: `www.popuptest.com`. This Web site gives you opportunities to test your pop-up settings.

Handling pop-ups in Internet Explorer

People who are running Version 6 or higher of Internet Explorer can prevent pop-ups from appearing. The pop-up blocking mechanism is turned on automatically. When a pop-up attempts to invade your computer screen, you hear a "blip," and the Information bar appears along the top of the window, as shown in Figure 2-4. `Pop-up blocked`, it tells you. `To see this pop-up or additional options click here.` If you are curious and want to see the pop-up, click the Information bar and choose Temporarily Allow Pop-Ups on the shortcut menu.

Figure 2-4:
In Internet Explorer, the Information bar appears when a pop-up has been blocked.

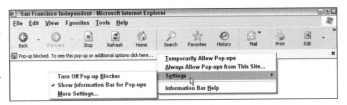

Internet Explorer also offers these options for controlling pop-ups:

✦ **Allow pop-ups to appear:** If pop-ups are your thing and you want to see them, choose Tools⇨Pop-Up Blocker and select Turn Off Pop-Up Blocker on the submenu. You can also reach this command by choosing Settings on the shortcut menu that appears when you click the Information bar (refer to Figure 2-4).

✦ **Allow pop-ups launched from the site you are visiting:** Click the Information bar and choose Always Allow Pop-Ups from This Site on the shortcut menu (refer to Figure 2-4).

To decide for yourself how Internet Explorer handles pop-ups, choose Tools⇨Pop-Up Blocker⇨Pop-Up Blocker Settings. You see the Pop-Up Blocker Settings dialog box. From here, you can keep the Information bar from appearing, decide whether a sound is heard when a pop-up is blocked, and disallow pop-ups in allowed sites by removing the names of allowed sites from the Allowed Sites list.

Handling pop-ups in Mozilla

Follow these steps to stop pop-up windows from appearing in the Mozilla browser:

1. **Choose Edit⇨Preferences.**

   The Preferences dialog box opens.

2. **Open the Privacy & Security category, and click the Popup Windows subcategory.**

3. **Select the Block Unrequested Popup Windows check box.**

4. **Select the Display an Icon in the Navigator Status Bar check box if you want to be informed when a pop-up has been blocked.**

   If you select this option, the pop-up icon appears on the status bar whenever Mozilla blocks a pop-up (you must close and restart Mozilla for the pop-up icon setting to take effect). You can click this icon to permit pop-ups to appear on a Web site.

5. **Click the OK button.**

When Mozilla blocks a pop-up, the pop-up icon appears on the right side of the status bar. Suppose you want to permit pop-ups to appear on the Web site you are visiting? Either click the pop-up icon or choose Tools⇨Popup Manager⇨Allow Popups From This Site. The Allowed Web Sites dialog box appears. Click the Add button.

If you change your mind about permitting pop-ups at a Web site, choose Tools⇨Popup Manager⇨Manage Popups. In the Allowed Web Site dialog box, select the address of the Web site in question and click the Remove button.

Choosing a default search engine

A search engine is a Web site that is devoted to helping you search the Internet. (Chapter 3 of this minibook explains search engines in detail.) When you click the Search button on the Standard toolbar in Internet Explorer, the Search bar opens and you are presented with a mini-search engine, as shown in Figure 2-5. When you click the Search button in Mozilla, you go straight to the home page of the search engine of your choice.

Figure 2-5:
In Internet
Explorer,
the Search
bar offers a
mini-search
engine
for your
convenience.

In both browsers, you get to choose which search engine is the default, the one you use when you click the Search button:

✦ **Internet Explorer:** Click the Search button to open the Search bar, and then click the Customize button (refer to Figure 2-5). You see the Customize Search Settings dialog box. Select the Use Search Service option button, and choose a search engine in the Choose the Search Service list.

✦ **Mozilla:** Choose Edit⇨Preferences to open the Preferences dialog box. In the Navigator category, select the Internet Search subcategory. From the Search Using drop-down menu, choose a search engine.

You can make Google the default search engine in Internet Explorer, but to do so, you have to install the Google Toolbar first. Chapter 4 of this mini-book shows how to make the Google the Internet Explorer default searcher.

Chapter 3: Strategies for Internet Searching

In This Chapter

✔ Understanding how search engines operate

✔ Deciding which search engine to use

✔ Crafting a good search of the Internet

✔ Searching the so-called invisible Web

✔ Determining whether information is valid at a Web site

The Indianapolis 500, the world's most grueling auto race, always begins with this announcement: "Gentlemen, start your engines." In this chapter, I invite you to start your search engine and use it to dig deep into the Internet and find the information you need. This chapter explains how directories, search engines, and meta-search engines work. It describes how to craft a search that brings up the information you need in the search results. You discover how to search the "invisible Web," the part of the Internet that is out of the reach of search engines, and how to tell whether information at a Web site is valuable or just a bunch of hooey.

By the way, Internet researchers often neglect two important ways to get information apart from running a search engine: mailing lists and newsgroups. Mailing lists are discussions conducted by e-mail among people with the same interests and obsessions (Book IV, Chapter 3 explains mailing lists). Newsgroups are online bulletin boards where people debate one another and trade information (Book IV, Chapter 4 looks into newsgroups).

Finding Out about Search Engines

A *search engine* is a tool for finding information on the Internet. To use a search engine, you go to the search engine's Web site and search by category, or you enter *keywords* to describe what you're searching for. The results of your search appear on a results page like the one in Figure 3-1. For each Web page found, you can read a snippet of text with a keyword you used in your search. You can also see the domain names of the Web pages. By studying the text and domain names, you can usually tell whether a Web site is worth visiting. Click a hyperlink on the search results page to visit a Web page.

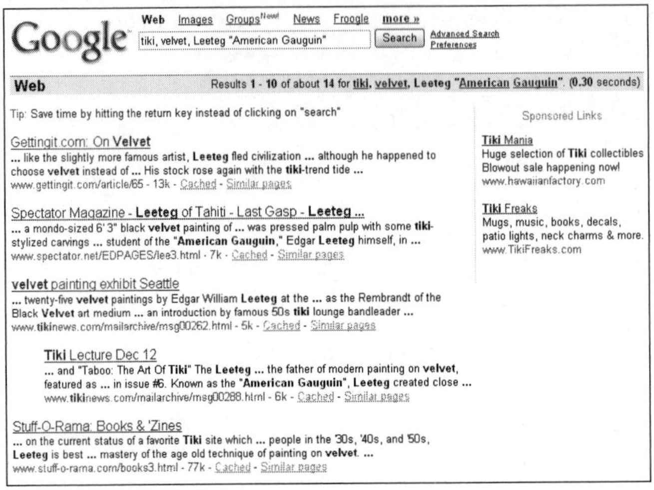

Figure 3-1:
A search results page at Google.

Search engines fall in three categories: directories, standard search engines, and meta-search engines. A *directory* is like a card catalog in a library. You identify a category that describes the information you need and then you get a list of Web sites in the category. With a standard search engine, you enter keywords that describe the information you need, and the search engine provides a list of Web sites with words that match the keywords you entered (refer to Figure 3-1). A meta-search engine employs other search engines to gather information.

How directories work

Directories, you could say, have the human touch. They are operated and maintained by people trained in information science or library science. People, not computers, decide which categories to organize Web sites into and where to place each Web site in the category scheme. Table 3-1 describes directories. Two of them, LookSmart and Yahoo!, are also standard search engines.

Table 3-1	Directories for Searching the Internet		
Directory Name	*Web Address*	*Search Engine Also?*	*Notes*
About	`www.about.com`	No	Not truly a directory, but a network of Web sites maintained by volunteer experts, called *guides*. You can search the About network starting at this Web site: `http://search.about.com/fullsearch.htm`

Directory Name	Web Address	Search Engine Also?	Notes
Librarians to the Internet Index	`http://lii.org`	No	Not truly a directory, but the categories are easy to search in and the Web-site descriptions are excellent.
LookSmart	`www.looksmart.com`	Yes	Presents information in 12 categories (click the Directory tab).
Open Directory Project	`www.dmoz.org`	No	Largest, most comprehensive directory on the Internet. Sends search results to AltaVista, AOL Search, Google, Lycos, and Teoma. (You can also search the Open Directory Project starting at this Google Web page: `http://directory.google.com`).
Yahoo! Search Directory	`http://dir.yahoo.com`	Yes	One of the most comprehensive directories on the Internet.

Figure 3-2 shows the Yahoo! Search Directory. Searching in a directory like Yahoo!'s is a matter of "drilling down" from broad topics to narrower topics. To get to a list of oceanography Web sites starting at the Yahoo! Search Directory, for example, you click the Science category, the Earth Sciences subcategory, and the Oceanography subcategory. You can also enter keywords in the Search text box to search for Web sites that have been cataloged in the directory.

Figure 3-2: Home page of the Yahoo! Search Directory.

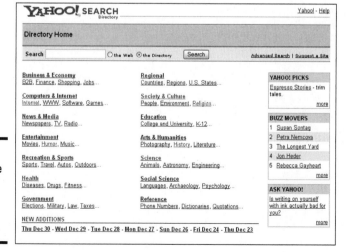

Volunteering for the Open Directory Project

The Open Directory Project aims to be the definitive catalog of the Internet, reaching into and mapping every corner of cyberspace. In the democratic spirit of the Internet, the Directory also aims to remain free of advertisements and other sources of revenue. Rather than pay librarians to catalog Web sites, it relies on volunteers.

If volunteering to catalog the Web strikes you as a good deed, visit this address: `http://dmoz.org/about.html`. It explains what volunteering for the Open Directory Project entails and how to sign up. Each volunteer is assigned a category. Says the Project, "For just a few minutes of your time you can help make the Web a better place, and be recognized as an expert on your chosen topic."

The Open Directory Project isn't the only directory maintained by volunteers. Check out these directories as well when the volunteer spirit moves you:

- **Illumirate:** This directory works in association with the HotBot search engine. Address: `www.illumirate.com`

- **Zeal:** Zeal is the directory behind the LookSmart search engine. Address: `www.zeal.com`

Use a directory to search the Internet when you're researching a broad topic and you know with a fair amount of certainty which category the topic will be in. In other words, use a directory when you have a general question, not a specific one. Web sites that you find in a directory are more likely to be useful than Web sites you find with a standard search engine. After all, someone, somewhere, cataloged the Web site in the directory, which means it has some merit. By contrast, Web sites you find with a search engine may have no merit except for the fact that they include a keyword or two that you used in your search. Search engines have it over directories when it comes to volume. Many more Web sites can be found with a standard search engine than a directory. Search engines illuminate all corners of the Internet, but directories only shine a light on Web sites that catalogers thought worthwhile.

In September 2001, About.com removed a third of the topics from its directory. That left several dozen topic guides — the self-appointed experts who write about topics — stranded. Starting at this Web site, you can investigate topics that were trimmed from the About directory in 2001: `www.formeraboutguides.com`.

How standard search engines work

Standard search engines are sometimes called *spiders* or *crawlers* because they crawl along the Internet, going from link to link, recording what they find and filing it away in a database. When you search the Internet with a standard search engine, you are really rummaging around in the search engine's database. You are finding information brought home to the database by a spider, an automated program for indexing and describing what is on Web pages. Table 3-2 describes the major search engines. (Later in this chapter, "More techniques for narrowing a search" compares the search engines' different features.)

Table 3-2	Major Search Engines	
Name	*Web Address*	*Notes*
All the Web	www.alltheweb.com	Gets search results mostly from Yahoo!. Can search for pictures and video as well as text, as well as search within domains and search by file type.
AltaVista	www.altavista.com	Gets search results from Yahoo!. Can search within domains and by file type. Is the only search engine that permits proximity searches.
AOL Search	http://search.aol.com	Gathers search results from Google. Can search for pictures and video, as well as by file type.
Ask Jeeves	www.ask.com	Groups Web sites in search results by subject. Can search for pictures as well as within domains.
Clusty	http://clusty.com	Arranges search results in "clusters" — subtopics to help you find what you are looking for.
Gigablast	http://gigablast.com	Searches a smaller index of Web sites, but is a good, clean search engine. Can search within domains.
Google	www.google.com	Ranks Web sites in search results largely on the number of times they are linked to other sites. The Cadillac of search engines, it offers just about everything that the others offer, except proximity searching.

(continued)

Table 3-2 *(continued)*

Name	Web Address	Notes
HotBot	www.hotbot.com	Gathers search results from Google, Teoma, and Yahoo!. Can search for images and pictures, within domains, and by region.
LookSmart	www.looksmart.com	Excellent starting point for finding articles by subject or author name (click the Articles tab), but the search engine doesn't offer many features apart from that.
Lycos	www.lycos.com	Gets search results from Yahoo!. Can search within domains.
MSN Search	www.msn.com	Gets search results from Yahoo!. Can search for images and pictures, within domains, and by region.
Teoma	www.teoma.com	Offers a "refine" feature for turning a Web search in a different direction. Ranks Web sites in search results by relevancy based on the context of the Web pages. Can search for images and pictures, and within domains.
WiseNut	http://wisenut.com	Does not offer advanced searching.
Yahoo!	www.yahoo.com	Although Yahoo! is the oldest directory, its search engine was launched in 2004 when it purchased the Overture search engine.

Unlike directories, standard search engines don't employ human beings to decide whether a Web page is relevant to a certain topic. They rely on algorithms to do that. In Internet searching, an *algorithm* is a mathematical formula for scoring a Web page's relevance compared to other Web pages. The Web page that scores highest goes to the top of the list of search results; the Web page that scores lowest goes to the bottom.

Algorithms take into account a Web page's title, headings, meta description tag, and boldface text, among many other things. The success of the Google search engine is usually attributed to Google's ability to accurately rank pages by relevancy in search results. In Google's PageRank algorithm, pages are ranked according to how many times other pages link to them, the idea being that a page to which other pages link is probably more valuable, or relevant, than a page to which no one has bothered to link.

"PageRank," Google explains, "performs an objective measurement of the importance of Web pages by solving an equation of more than 500 million variables and 2 billion terms. Instead of counting direct links, PageRank interprets a link from Page A to Page B as a vote for Page B by Page A. PageRank then assesses a page's importance by the number of votes it receives."

(Go to this Web site for a thorough description of how Google ranks Web pages in search results: `www.google.com/corporate/tech.html`.)

Use a standard search engine to search the Internet for obscure topics or topics that aren't subject to being categorized. Standard search engines reach deeper into the Internet than directories. You can find many more Web sites with a standard search engine than a directory.

Writer and editor Danny Sullivan oversees an excellent online magazine, Search Engine Watch, at this address: `http://searchenginewatch.com`. The magazine rates search engines, describes how they work, offers tips for using them, and even provides an online forum where lovers of search engines trade tips and tricks. You can also get search-engine news and notes at Search Engine Showdown at this address: `http://searchengine showdown.com`.

Google-bombing

Google's PageRank algorithm for judging the relevancy of Web pages has made it susceptible to an armchair sport called *Google-bombing.* Google-bombing means to take advantage of a search engine's method of obtaining search results to artificially raise a Web page's ranking in the search results list. Google judges a Web page's relevancy by how many Web pages are linked to it. By purposefully linking many Web pages to a single page, pranksters can manipulate the Google search results to move a Web page higher in the search results list.

The first Google-bomb was dropped in 1999, when pranksters engineered search results at Google so that a search for "more evil than Satan himself" returned a results list with Microsoft's home page in the first position. Google-bombs have also been launched to link searches for "miserable failure" to online biographies of Michael Moore and President George Bush.

The success of Google-bombers underscores the reason why smart researchers rely on directories as well as search engines. Google is essentially running a popularity contest with its search results. The most popular Web site — the one to which the most other Web pages are linked — wins and takes the top spot on the results list, but as everyone who has attended junior high school knows, the most popular isn't necessarily the best or the smartest. Searching in a directory, you can be sure that the Web sites you turn up are relevant to the topic you are researching.

How meta-search engines work

A *meta-search engine* works much like other search engines, except it doesn't send its own automated spiders onto the Internet to index and describe Web pages. Instead, it rides piggyback on other search engines. A meta-search engine searches using other search engines and gathers the results in one place. The Dogpile meta-search engine, for example, gathers search results from Google, Yahoo!, Ask Jeeves, About, Overture, and FindWhat. Table 3-3 lists meta-search engines.

Table 3-3	Meta-Search Engines
Search Engine	*Web Address*
37.com	www.37.com
800go	http://800go.com/800go.html
Dogpile	www.dogpile.com
Highway61	www.highway61.com
Ixquick	www.ixquick.com
Kanoodle	www.kanoodle.com
Mamma	www.mamma.com
MegaGo	www.megago.com
MetaCrawler	www.metacrawler.com
MetaSpider	www.metaspider.com
Pandia	www.pandia.com/metasearch/index.html
PlanetSearch	www.planetsearch.com
ProFusion	www.profusion.com
Query Server	www.queryserver.com/web.htm
Search.com	www.search.com
Vivisimo	http://vivisimo.com

In theory, a meta-search engine is a useful way to search the Internet because you get the benefit of using more than one search engine. In practice, meta-search engines are a case of "too much all at once." Searches take too long. The search results are too numerous to be useful. Most meta-search engines can't weed out the duplicate Web sites that appear in search results. Duplicates appear because the search engines on which the meta-engine relies often find the same Web site.

Meta-search engines aren't worth a lot unless you know precisely what you are looking for — a digital camera with a product number you can use as a keyword or an out-of-the-way hamlet in Central America whose name is known to very few people. Use a meta-search engine when the topic you are researching is narrow or obscure. This way, you don't have as many search results to look over.

How search engines earn their keep

You may well ask how search engines such as Google and Yahoo! make any income. All search engines do is point you to other Web sites. They don't sell anything. They don't carry advertisements. Right?

Actually, search engines do carry advertisements — subtle ones that point you to different Web sites. On the right side of the Yahoo! Directory, for example, you can find "sponsor results" Web sites. Web sites pay search engines to make their names appear in "sponsor results." When you search for a topic, sponsor-result Web sites related to the topic

you are searching appear under the Sponsor Results heading. A search with the keyword *kimono,* for example, yields Web sites about kimonos, some sponsored and some not. The thinking is that anyone who is searching for information about kimonos will necessarily be interested in Web sites that sell kimonos.

Some search engines place the sponsored Web sites at the top of the list of Web sites on the search results page. When you review search results, make sure that you understand which Web sites are sponsored and which are not.

**Book II
Chapter 3**

**Strategies for
Internet Searching**

Fashion and Beauty > Kimono
Directory > Arts > Design Arts > Fashion and Beauty > **Kimono**

Search | kimono | ○ the Web ◉ just this category | Search | Advanced Search | Suggest a Site

✉ email this category to a friend

CATEGORIES

- Shopping and Services@

SITE LISTINGS

- History of Kimono, A 👓 - online exhibition exploring the types of kimono worn throughout Japanese history.

- Black Moon: Kimono - online exhibition of kimono dating from the late Edo period to the present.
- Homage to Nature: Landscape Kimonos of Itchiku Kubota - gallery of Kubota's designs.
- Kabuki Academy: Kimono Dressing - explains the history and customs of wearing a kimono.
- Kimono - offers a brief history of the kimono.
- Range of Vision: Japanese Kimono - one man's observations on the traditions wearing kimono.
- Weaving & the Japanese Kimono - 1998 feature on kimono and Japanese textiles.

SPONSOR RESULTS

Japanese Kimono for
Gift and Collecting
Chuu offers a large selection
of vintage and contemporary
kimonos, ...
www.chuu.com

Buy Kimonos &
Yukatas at
Asianideas.com
Offering a distinctive product
line, from kimon-ez, chinese
slippers, ...
asianideas.com

Which Search Engine Should I Use?

Which search engine to use is mostly a question of which one you are comfortable with and which one gives you the best results (the next section in this chapter compares and contrasts search commands in the different search engines). Test-drive a few search engines and directories to find the one that gets you to your destination fastest. Meanwhile, here are some basic guidelines for choosing a search technique:

✦ **Specific subject:** If the subject you are researching is specific, well defined, and probably of interest to many people, use a directory such as Yahoo! or the Open Directory Project. Chances are, you can find Web sites cataloged under the subject you are interested in. For example, Web sites devoted to mysticism, ear conditions, and the Holy Roman Empire can likely be found in a directory.

✦ **General subject:** If the subject is likely to have been treated already by others because it is a general subject, see whether you can find it in an online reference. For example, information about California, Aristotle, tsunamis, and supernovae is found in online encyclopedias. (The next chapter in this minibook describes online references.)

✦ **Narrow or unusual subject:** If the subject is quite specific or unusual and is not well known or of interest to many people, use a standard search engine such as Google, Alta Vista, Teoma, or Gigablast. For example, using a search engine is the best way to investigate the pirates of Nosy Boraha, *Ravensara aromatica,* Von Dutch, mustache cups, and the Pentax Optio 750Z.

One thing to consider when choosing a search engine is the incestuous relationships between the search engines. In the previous section of this chapter, I explain that a meta-search engine is a search engine that rides piggyback on other search engines. It searches using other search engines and gathers the results in one place. To some degree, most search engines are meta-search engines in that their search results come in part from other search engines. Google, for example, feeds search results to Ask Jeeves and AOL Search. Teoma also feeds search results to Ask Jeeves. MSN Search and All the Web get some of their search results from Yahoo!. The mother of all search engines, the Open Directory Project, feeds search results to AOL Search, HotBot, and AltaVista, as well as Google itself. (For a graphic representation of how incestuous the search engines really are, take a look at the chart at this address: www.bruceclay.com/searchenginerelationshipchart.htm.)

Because some search engines get their search results secondhand, you may consider using the search engines that feed the others. This way, you get search results straight from the source. These stars light the center of the search engine cosmos, and I suggest getting acquainted with them first if you are new to Internet searching:

✦ **Google:** The Google database of mapped and indexed Web pages is said to be the largest. Address: www.google.com

✦ **Open Directory Project:** This volunteer-staffed directory is highly respected. Address: www.dmoz.org (You can also search the Open Directory Project starting at this Google Web page: http://directory.google.com.)

✦ **Yahoo!:** Yahoo! is the oldest Internet directory. Address: http://dir.yahoo.com

Book II, Chapter 2 explains how to choose the default Internet search engine that gets used when you click the Search button in your Web browser.

Crafting a Thorough but Precise Internet Search

Unless you craft a good Internet search, your search will retrieve far too many Web pages. You'll have to look through many pages to find one that is useful. You'll develop a case of Internet search syndrome, a condition in which the eyes get blurry from staring at too many Web pages for too long. No one wants that.

In the interest of making sure that your Internet searches are short, sweet, and meaningful, these pages explain how to craft a good Internet search. They describe how to conduct a search, use Boolean operators to find useful pages, and narrow your search with advanced search commands and techniques.

**Book II
Chapter 3**

Strategies for Internet Searching

Formulating your search

Not that anyone has counted how many Web pages there are, but Google alone has cataloged over 8 billion. Because there are so many Web pages and search engines are so good at cataloging and indexing them, even a search for an obscure topic can capture hundreds if not thousands of Web pages in the search results. This makes searching the Internet that much harder.

The trick to Internet searching is to decide exactly what you're looking for and then craft a search that pinpoints Web pages that are useful to you. You need to exclude the pages you don't need but, at the same time, reach deep into the Internet for pages that are relevant to the topic you are researching. With respect to the topic you are researching, take these steps to embark on a search of the Internet:

1. **Imagine the ideal Web page, the one with every scrap of information you need.**

2. **Think of the words that are sure to be on your ideal Web page.**

For example, if you are looking for information about John Hicks, the 19th-century chief of the Seminoles, the ideal Web page would contain the word *Hicks* and the word *Seminoles*. To find pages with both words, you use the AND Boolean operator and these keywords (I explain Boolean operators shortly):

```
hicks AND seminoles
```

3. **Think of an exact phrase that is likely to be on your ideal Web page.**

As I explain later, you can search for exact phrases — two or more words that occur one after the other. Rather than search for *hicks* by itself, you could search using this exact phrase (I've put it in quotation marks, the convention for using exact phrases in Internet searches):

```
"john hicks"
```

4. **Think of words to exclude from the search because they may bring up Web pages that aren't useful.**

For example, the Seminole is the mascot of Florida State University. A search for *Seminoles* may bring up Web pages with that school's name, which isn't necessarily a bad thing, because a Florida State University professor may have written a paper about John Hicks. But because Florida State University is football-crazy, a search for *Seminoles* is likely to bring up Web sites about football (there are a ton of those on the Internet!). You could exclude football Web sites from the search by using the NOT Boolean operator, a minus sign (–) placed in front of the word or phrase you want to exclude:

```
-football
```

5. **Run your search.**

As shown in Figure 3-3, the Internet search for information about John Hicks, chief of the Seminoles, looks for Web pages that contain the word *seminoles* and the phrase *john hicks* but don't contain the word *football* (entering uppercase letters in keywords isn't necessary in Internet searches):

```
seminoles AND "john hicks" -football
```

Figure 3-3:
A search using Boolean operators.

6. **Refine your search.**

In a typical Internet search, you have to try, try, try again, and you craft your search as you learn more about the topic you are investigating. You find out which words to exclude. You discover more words to use as keywords in the search. For example, my search for information about John Hicks led me to his Seminole name: *Tuko-see-mathla*. By searching with that name — with that exact phrase — I was able to narrow the number of Web sites in my search results considerably. Later in this chapter, "Using Boolean operators for searching" describes Boolean operators in detail and explains all the different ways of narrowing a search.

In a long Web page, finding the keyword — the word you are searching for — can be a problem. Press Ctrl+F in your browser to search for a keyword in the Find dialog box. In Google search results, you can click the Cached link to see a copy of the Web page with all keywords highlighted.

Avoiding Booleans with advanced search commands

If you read the last couple of pages and you despaired at the idea of using Boolean search operators, you will be glad to find out that you don't necessarily need to know or use Boolean operators to conduct a search. Everything you can do with Boolean operators you can also do by clicking the Advanced Search link at a search engine. Every search engine offers advanced search commands. I suggest always using them. You can run a simple search or a very intricate one from an Advanced Search page.

Figure 3-4 shows the Advanced Search page at Google. In the figure, I am running the same search I ran in Figure 3-3, but without entering Boolean operators (Google enters the operators for me after I tell it how to search). This page offers many ways to narrow a search. I explain all the different ways to narrow a search later in this chapter.

Figure 3-4:
The same
search as
Figure 3-3
using
advanced
commands.

Google	Advanced Search	Advanced Search Tips | About Google

Find results	with **all** of the words	seminoles	10 results	Google Search
	with the **exact phrase**	john hicks		
	with **at least one** of the words			
	without the words	football		
Language	Return pages written in	any language		
File Format	Only return results of the file format	any format		
Date	Return web pages updated in the	anytime		
Numeric Range	Return web pages containing numbers between	and		
Occurrences	Return results where my terms occur	anywhere in the page		
Domain	Only return results from the site or domain	e.g. google.com, .org *More info*		
SafeSearch	⦿ No filtering ◯ Filter using SafeSearch			

Using Boolean operators for searching

Boolean operators are named for their inventor, George Boole, a 19th-century English logician. Use the operators — AND, OR, NOT, and NEAR — in Internet searches to tell search engines how to use keywords in a search. You can enter the operators directly in a search engine's text box or, by going the to Advanced Search page, choose commands and let the search engine enter the Boolean operators for you (see the previous section in this chapter). Enter Boolean operators in all capital letters. Figure 3-5 shows how three Boolean operators work. The following pages explain Boolean operators (sometimes called *search operators*) in detail.

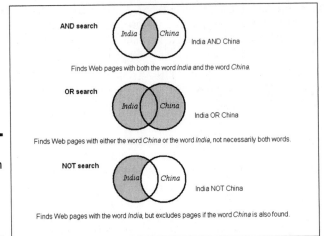

AND search
India AND China
Finds Web pages with both the word *India* and the word *China.*

OR search
India OR China
Finds Web pages with either the word *China* or the word *India,* not necessarily both words.

NOT search
India NOT China
Finds Web pages with the word *India,* but excludes pages if the word *China* is also found.

Figure 3-5:
The Boolean
operators
AND, OR,
and NOT
at work.

Boolean operators are entered in different ways in the different search engines. In Google, for example, you can enter the AND operator with a plus sign (+) instead of the word *AND.* Check the instructions at a search engine's Web site to find out how to enter Boolean operators. In every search engine, enter the operators in all capital letters.

AND operator

The AND operator tells the search engine to return only Web pages with all the keywords you enter. This operator narrows the search and returns fewer search results. Use it to make your search more specific. At some search engines, the operator is entered with a plus sign (+). Some search engines assume when you enter more than one keyword that you want an AND search. Here are examples of the AND operator at work:

```
melungeon AND "charles gibson"
ginkgo +glycosides +flavonoids
```

OR operator

The OR operator tells the search engine to return Web pages if they contain one or more keywords. This operator broadens your search. Use it in searches for esoteric or obscure subjects that are unlikely to turn up many Web pages. Some search engines assume when you enter more than one keyword that you want an OR search. Here are examples of the OR operator at work:

```
ravensara OR "camphor laurel" OR "ravintsara oil"
"monkey's mushroom" OR "hericium erinaceus"
```

NOT operator

The NOT operator tells the search engine to exclude Web pages from a search if they contain the keywords. This operator narrows your search. Use it to disqualify Web pages that would otherwise inflate the search results. In some search engines, this is called the AND NOT operator. In some search engines, you enter the NOT operator with a minus sign (–). Here are examples of the NOT operator at work:

```
portland NOT maine
weverka -robert -karen
```

NEAR operator

The NEAR operator tells the search engine to return Web pages in which the keywords appear within a certain number of words of each other. This operator is like the AND operator, only more so. Use it to find Web pages with keywords not just on the same page, but within a certain distance of one another. As of this writing, only one search engine, Alta Vista, provides proximity searches with the NEAR operator (see "Proximity searching," later in this chapter). Here are examples of the NEAR at work:

```
"david bossie" NEAR whitewater
mexico NEAR immigration
```

Quotation marks

Quotation marks tell the search engine to look for an exact phrase or a string of words. (This one isn't really a Boolean operator, but I'm including it in this list so that you are sure to discover it.) Enclose words in quotation marks to find a name, address, or phrase on a Web page. Here are examples of using quotation marks to find word strings on Web pages:

```
"10086 sunset blvd"
"new york" AND omfug
```

More techniques for narrowing a search

Crafting a good search means cutting to the chase and getting only pages that are useful to you in the search results. By using advanced search commands, you can tailor a search so that it produces a good yield. Table 3-4 lists commands for narrowing a search. It tells you which search engines offer which commands (see Table 3-2, earlier in this chapter, for the Web addresses of these search engines). I describe commands and techniques for narrowing a search in the pages that follow. Combine these techniques, and you will be able to zoom like a laser beam precisely to the Web page you need.

Table 3-4   Search Engines' Advanced Commands for Narrowing a Search

Name	Domain	Date	Language	Page Title	Web Address	File Type	Region	Links	Similar Pages	Proximity
All the Web	✓	✓	✓			✓				
AltaVista	✓	✓			✓	✓				✓
AOL Search	✓	✓	✓	✓	✓	✓				
Ask Jeeves	✓	✓		✓	✓		✓			
Gigablast	✓							✓		
Google	✓	✓	✓	✓	✓	✓		✓	✓	
HotBot	✓	✓	✓			✓	✓			
Lycos	✓	✓	✓	✓	✓					
MSN Search	✓		✓	✓		✓	✓			
Teoma	✓	✓	✓	✓	✓		✓			
Yahoo!	✓	✓	✓	✓	✓	✓	✓			

Here's a handy technique for narrowing the search results when you are running the Google search engine: Click the Search Within Results link at the bottom of the search results page. You go to a Web page for searching only the Web pages that your previous search captured.

Searching inside a domain

Search inside a domain when you want to narrow your search only to Web pages at one Web site. Searching inside a domain is a great way to get information if the Web site you are searching offers information of a specific kind. For example, to get information about computers and computer programs, you can do no better than to search pcworld.com, the domain owned and operated by *PC World* magazine. To get information about traveling to Madagascar, you could search the lonelyplanet.com domain and use *Madagascar* as the keyword for your search.

Don't confuse domain searching with URL searching. Searching a URL means to search the text in Web addresses; searching a domain means to search all the Web pages in one Web site.

Searching by date

Unfortunately, search engines can't accurately tell how up to date Web pages are. Some search engines can tell when a Web page was last modified, or edited. Others record date information merely by noting when they catalog each Web page in their database. By-date searches are not reliable. Still, you can try searching by date when you want recent news about a topic.

Searching by language

Obviously, you are more likely to get information about a French-speaking country by looking on the Internet for Web pages written in French. Language searches turn up Web pages written in a single language to the exclusion of other languages. Search by language if doing so can help you find information and if you either speak the language you are searching for or you can tolerate computerized translations. The next chapter in this minibook describes computerized translation services.

Book II
Chapter 3

Strategies for Internet Searching

Searching in Web page titles

The most descriptive part of a Web page is its title. Making Web page titles part of a search is a good way to narrow a search to Web pages of interest. Google offers two ways to search by title, with the `intitle` (in title) operator and the `allintitle` (all in title) operator. Enter these operators in all lowercase letters:

✦ `intitle` **operator:** Only the first keyword (or exact phrase in quotation marks) entered in the search box must appear in the page title; the other keywords must or can be on the Web page itself. For example, this search finds Web pages with *Barry Bonds* in the title and the word *Balco* or the word *steroid* on the Web page (the `intitle` operator is followed by a colon and no space):

```
intitle:"barry bonds" balco OR steroid
```

✦ `allintitle` **operator:** All keywords entered in the search text box must appear in the Web page title. For example, this search finds Web pages with the words *manga* and *American* in the title (the `allintitle` operator is followed by a colon and no space):

```
allintitle:manga american
```

Searching in Web addresses (URLs)

Searching in Web addresses, also called URLs, is similar to searching in Web-page titles, except you search for text in the Web address of Web pages instead of in Web-page titles. Because people choose Web addresses and folder names that help describe where their Web pages are located, searching by Web address can be a useful way to find information. Google offers two operators, `inurl` (in URL) and `allinurl` (all in URL), for searching the text in Web addresses. Enter these operators in lowercase letters and follow them with a colon and no space.

✦ `inurl` **operator:** Only the first keyword (or exact phrase in quotation marks) entered in the search box must appear in the Web address; the other keywords must or can be on the Web page itself. For example, this search finds Web pages in which the name *Asawa* is in the Web address and the name *Ruth* and the word *Nihonmachi* are on the Web page:

```
inurl:asawa ruth nihonmachi
```

✦ `allinurl` **operator:** All keywords entered in the search text box must appear in the Web address. For example, this search finds Web pages with the words *lions, tigers,* and *bears* in the Web address:

```
allinurl:lions tigers bears
```

Searching by file type

As Book I, Chapter 6 explains, file types apart from HTML files can be published on the Internet. At some search engines, you can search for these file types: Adobe Acrobat (`.pdf`), Adobe Postscript (`.ps`), Microsoft Word (`.doc`), Microsoft Excel (`.xls`), Microsoft PowerPoint (`.pps`), rich-text files (`.rtf`), and others. For example, search by file type when you know that the information you need is posted on the Internet in an Adobe Acrobat file.

Searching by region

At some search engines, you can search by region, usually from a drop-down menu with the names of the different continents. If the information you want is specific to a region or continent, you may as well search by region. Go ahead. Give it a shot.

Searching for links

Searching for links means to find Web pages with hyperlinks that, when you click them, take you to a certain Web page. Searching for links is a great way to find out who or whether anyone has linked his or her Web page to one of yours. Figure 3-6 shows a link search on the Google Advanced search page. This search finds Web pages that have hyperlinks leading to pages at the address shown. You can also conduct a link search at Google with the link operator, like so:

```
link:http://phatmike.motime.com
```

Figure 3-6:
A link search
at Google.

Proximity searching

Proximity searching means to search for keywords that are near to one another. Only one search engine, Alta Vista, offers proximity searches. To construct a proximity search, enter the NEAR operator between the keywords or exact phrases, like so:

```
"peter weverka" NEAR "office 2003"
```

Figure 3-7 shows a proximity search at Alta Vista. The search engine finds Web pages in which the keywords are within ten words of one another. Use proximity searches to research related ideas or to make your AND operator searches more concentrative.

**Book II
Chapter 3**

**Strategies for
Internet Searching**

Figure 3-7:
A proximity
search at
Alta Vista.

Getting "similar pages"

Google offers a special command for finding Web pages that are similar to a page whose address you enter. If you are fond of a particular Web page, Google may be able to find its cousins, uncles, and aunts, which you may find just as useful or enjoy just as much. Look for the Similar text box on the Google Advanced Search page (refer to Figure 3-6).

Searching the "Invisible Web"

The so-called invisible Web is the part of the Internet that search engines can't penetrate. This part of the Internet is private, either because entering requires permission or entering requires a subscription. As I explain earlier in this chapter in "How standard search engines work," search engines troll the Internet, gathering information about Web sites by going from link to link. But in the case of the invisible Web, there are no links to follow. This part of the Internet has been walled off. It consists of private resources — mostly databases such as Lexis-Nexis, UMI Proquest, Infotrac, and JSTOR — that are privately held. The good news about these databases is that, after you've found them, most have excellent searching tools.

Here are some Web sites for searching the invisible Web:

✦ **Complete Planet:** "Discover over 70,000+ searchable databases and specialty search engines," this Web site claims. A search starting here brings up a lot of dreck as well as useful stuff — you've been warned. Address: `http://aip.completeplanet.com`

✦ **GPO (Government Printing Office) Access:** Search databases maintained by the United States government, including annual budgets, bills, and government manuals. (Also try searching Google Uncle Sam at this address: `www.google.com/unclesam`.) Address: `www.gpoaccess.gov/multidb.html`

✦ **InfoMine:** Search databases of use to scholars and academic researchers. Address: `http://infomine.ucr.edu`

✦ **The Invisible Web Directory:** This directory divides the invisible Web into several broad categories for searching — Library Catalogues, Health and Medicine, Public Records, and others. Address: `www.invisible-web.net`

To search the invisible Web, search by category and subcategory. A keyword search for a specific topic is likely to swamp you with far too many search results. See "Discovering Specialty Search Engines," in the next chapter of this minibook, for a list of more search engines that can help you penetrate the invisible Web.

Evaluating Whether Information at a Web Site Is Valid

If "don't believe everything you read in the newspaper" is true, and civilized people think it is, then "don't believe everything you read on the Internet" is the undisputed truth. Most newspaper articles, at least, are fact-checked by editors, but any fool can post anything on the Internet and be certain that somewhere another fool will read and believe it. You owe it to the people who will make use of research you do on the Internet to make certain you get the facts straight. And that begs the question: How do you know whether it's genuine? How do you know whether what you read at Web site is valid?

You can start by examining the Web site itself. I don't mean to be a snob, but a sloppy Web site with grammatical errors and many misspellings is automatically suspect. Next, consider the motive of the people who constructed the Web site. Many sites have a commercial motive. Others are pushing a political agenda. These Web sites have ulterior motives and should be regarded skeptically.

Is the information on the Web site up to date? News about technology and political news, for example, gets stale quickly. Online articles should be marked with the date of publication in plain display. Without the date, it's hard to tell how relevant an online article is. A Web page with a number of dead links — hyperlinks that lead nowhere — is most assuredly out of date and doesn't deserve your attention.

Book II
Chapter 3

Another thing to consider is how close the information is to the original source and whether sources are cited. The Internet can be like Telephone, the children's game in which one person whispers a word or two into the next person's ear, the next person whispers into the next person's ear, and so on, until the original message turns into something completely different. Unless the author or publisher of a Web page can cite a source or preferably give a hyperlink to the source, how do you know what you're getting isn't innuendo or hearsay?

**Strategies for
Internet Searching**

Maybe the best way to judge whether information at a Web site is valid is to use your intuition. What does your gut tell you? When someone stops you on the sidewalk with a long tale about needing a quarter to make a phone call because the car has broken down on account of the rain, et cetera, et cetera, you can usually tell right away whether you're being conned. You just know. The same is true when judging the validity of a Web site.

Chapter 4: Advanced Tools for Scholars and Researchers

In This Chapter

✔ Using a specialty search engine

✔ Taking advantage of the Google Toolbar

✔ Searching the Internet for images, audio, and video files

✔ Getting answers from a Google researcher

✔ Translating text from one language to another

This chapter picks up where the previous one left off and explains commands and techniques for the advanced searcher. In this chapter, you discover a handful of specialty search engines designed for looking into particular parts of the Internet — the sciences, technology, the law, and others. You also find out how convenient the Google Toolbar really is and how to search for images, video files, and audio files on the Internet. Finally, this chapter looks at online translation services and explains how you can search your computer with Google as well as search the Internet.

Discovering Specialty Search Engines

Specialty search engines, sometimes called *vertical search engines,* look into one aspect of the Internet — for example, science, the law, engineering, or the humanities. Most specialty search engines offer advanced commands to make searches more accurate. Table 4-1 describes specialty search engines. If the subject you're interested in happens to be, well, special, you're in luck. Chances are, a specialty search engine can take you precisely where you want to go.

Table 4-1		Specialty Search Engines
Name	*Address*	*Description*
All-Purpose		
DOAJ	http://www.doaj.org	Search the Directory of Open Access Journals for scholarly and scientific articles.
Google Scholar	http://scholar.google.com	Search for scholarly literature — theses, abstracts, peer-reviewed papers, and technical reports.
INFOMINE	http://infomine.ucr.edu	Search "124,710 academically valuable resources" in nine categories.
LookSmart Find Articles	www.findarticles.com	Search for articles by topic, by author name, or in selected publications.
SMEALSearch	http://smealsearch2.psu.edu	Search the Academic Business Literature Library for business documents about a subject or by a specific author.
Computers and Technology		
Google Apple/ Macintosh Search	www.google.com/mac	Search the Internet for information about Macintosh computers.
Google BSD Search	www.google.com/bsd	Search the Internet for information about BSD (Berkeley Software Distribution) open-source operating systems, including Unix.
Google Linux Search	www.google.com/linux	Search the Internet for information about the Linux operating system.
Google Microsoft Search	www.google.com/microsoft	Search the Internet for information about Microsoft software.
Tech Search	www.techweb.com/search/ advancedSearch.jhtml	Search six computer publications.
Economics		
WebEc	www.helsinki.fi/WebEc	Search the Internet for information about economics with the search engine or by browsing in the directory.

Name	Address	Description
Health and Medicine		
Combined Health	`http://chid.nih.gov/ simple/simple.html`	Search a bibliographic database from health-related agencies of the federal government.
Merck Manual	`www.merck.com/mrkshared/ mmanual/home.jsp`	Search by disease name or symptom name in the *Merck Manual,* a physician's desk reference.
MedHunt	`www.hon.ch/MedHunt`	Search for health care information on the Internet.
PubMed	`www.ncbi.nlm.nih.gov/ entrez/query.fcgi`	Search the National Library of Science's 15 million citations for biomedical articles dating to the 1950s.
RxList	`www.rxlist.com`	Search by name or imprint code for information about drugs.
The Humanities		
Artcyclopedia	`www.artcyclopedia.com`	Search museum Web sites by artists' names, artwork names, and museum names.
Art Bridge	`www.art-bridge.com`	Search a directory with categories ranging from Art History to Tribal Art.
Project Gutenberg	`www.gutenberg.org/catalog`	Search the online library for 7,000 different books, most of them classics published prior to 1950.
Social Science Information Gateway	`http://sosig.esrc.bris. ac.uk`	Search for information related to the social sciences, business, and law.
Voice of the Shuttle	`http://vos.ucsb.edu`	Research online Web sites pertaining to the humanities — art, literature, philosophy, and more. Offers a directory and a search engine.
Law		
FindLaw	`http://lawcrawler.find law.com`	Search for information about laws, cases, and codes.

Book II Chapter 4

Advanced Tools for Scholars and Researchers

(continued)

Table 4-1 *(continued)*

Name	Address	Description
Science, Math, and Engineering		
Cite Seer	`http://citeseer.ist.psu.edu`	Search for literature about computer and information science.
Internet Guide to Engineering, Mathematics, and Computing	`www.eevl.ac.uk/index.htm`	Search full-text online scientific journals selected by the editors for relevance and quality.
NASA Image Exchange	`http://nix.nasa.gov`	Search among the 300,000 images in the NASA databases.
NatureServe Explorer	`www.natureserve.org/explorer`	Search a database with information about more than 60,000 plants, animals, and ecosystems of the United States and Canada.
Online Journal Search Engine	`www.ojose.com`	Search scientific publications in in 60 databases.
SciCentral	`www.scicentral.com`	Search for recent news in several scientific disciplines.
Scirus	`www.scirus.com/srsapp`	Search over 167 million science-related Web pages.

By the way, the specialty search engines listed in Table 4-1 are by no means the only ones on the Internet. Book VIII, Chapter 2, for example, describes specialty search engines for finding airline tickets and hotel rooms. Some people believe that Internet searching technology is in its infancy, and as search technology is refined in the coming years, we are soon going to see many more specialized search engines.

Finding Out about the Google Toolbar

If you are a fan of Google, consider using the Google Toolbar, as shown in Figure 4-1. This toolbar makes it possible to do just about anything you can do with the Google search engine without visiting the Google Web site. The toolbar is there at the top of your browser, ready and willing to provide you with a Google service at a moment's notice.

Installing the Google Toolbar

To install the toolbar, go to this Web-site address: `http://toolbar.google.com`. Then click the Download Google Toolbar button. You will be asked

whether you want to disable or enable advanced features. If you enable the
advanced features, you can see a page's rank on the Google Toolbar when
you surf to the page. However, to gather this ranking information, Google
tracks users' surfing habits. What the advanced features question really asks
is whether you consent to sending information about your surfing behavior
to the Google database. Google uses the information to compile data about
people's surfing habits.

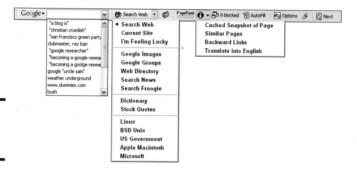

Figure 4-1:
The Google
Toolbar.

**Book II
Chapter 4**

**Advanced Tools for
Scholars and
Researchers**

To turn off the Google Toolbar, right-click any empty place on any toolbar in
your Web browser and deselect the Google option. To remove the Google
Toolbar, do it as though you were removing a computer program. Choose
Start➪Control Panel➪Add or Remove Programs. Select Google Toolbar in the
Add or Remove Programs dialog box, and click the Change/Remove button.

If you've installed the Google Toolbar, you can conduct a search without
manually entering keywords. Either double-click a word on a Web page or
drag across words to highlight them, and then right-click and choose Google
search to run a search.

Using the Google Toolbar

The Google Toolbar is essentially a way to search with Google without visiting the Google Web site. You can find these amenities on the Google Toolbar
(refer to Figure 4-1):

✦ **Google menu:** A drop-down list for going directly to Google.com and its
various pages.

✦ **Search Terms text box:** A text box for entering search terms and
embarking on a new search. Press Enter after you enter a keyword.

✦ **Search Web:** A drop-down list for conducting a specialty search with
Google. Choose Google Images, for example, to search for images.

✦ **News:** Click this button, which is to the right of the Search Web drop-down list, to go to the Google News Web site and see what's happening in the world.

✦ **PageRank:** Displays the page ranking (if you enable the advanced features of the toolbar).

✦ **Blocked:** Click this button to allow or disallow pop-up ads from appearing when you visit this Web site. Allowing pop-ups with this button does not override your browser settings.

✦ **AutoFill:** Click this button to enter your address, name, and credit card information automatically on Web forms. Click the Options button and fill in the AutoFill tab of the Toolbar Options dialog box to provide the Google Toolbar with your name, address, and credit card information.

✦ **Options:** Click this button to open the Toolbar Options dialog box and choose which buttons appear on the Google Toolbar (the Options tab), to describe your search preferences or add more buttons (the More tab), or to enter AutoFill information (the AutoFill tab).

✦ **Highlight:** Click this button to highlight keywords from your search on the Web page you are viewing. This is an excellent way to locate the information you need on a Web page.

✦ **Find Next Occurrence:** Click this button to jump from search term to search term on a Web page. The button is named after a keyword you entered.

By the way, Google isn't the only search engine to offer a toolbar. You can also find the Yahoo! Toolbar (`http://toolbar.yahoo.com`), the Dogpile Search Toolbar (`www.dogpile.com/info.dogpl/tbar`), and the AltaVista Toolbar (`www.altavista.com/toolbar`).

Making Google the Internet Explorer default searcher

When you click the Search button in Internet Explorer, which search engine appears by default in the Search pane, the panel on the left side of the window? You can click the Customize button in the Search pane and choose a search service, but Google is conspicuously absent from the list of services you can choose from. If Google is your favorite search service and you want Google search options to appear when you click the Search button in Internet Explorer, follow these steps:

1. **Click the Options button on the Google Toolbar.**

2. **Select the More tab in the Toolbar Options dialog box.**

3. **Select the Use Google as My Default Search Engine in Internet Explorer check box.**

4. **Click the OK button.**

On the subject of Internet Explorer, you can attach special Google buttons to the Standard Buttons toolbar in Internet Explorer: The Google.com button takes you to the Google home page, and the Google Search button runs a search on a word or group of words you highlighted. To add these buttons to Internet Explorer's Standard Buttons toolbar, go to this Web address: `www.google.com/options/buttons.html`. It explains how to attach the buttons to Internet Explorer.

Googlewhacking

A *Googlewhack* occurs when a search with the Google search engine turns up only one Web page. In *Googlewhacking,* players enter keywords in Google with the aim of producing a single, solitary Web page in the Google search results. At Googlewhack (`www.googlewhack.com`), Googlewhacking's official Web site, you can read a list of keyword combinations — for example, shantytown diddler, serpentine dickybird, and panda nosebags — that have produced Googlewhacks.

Ironically, a Googlewhack ceases being a Googlewhack after it is recorded at the Googlewhack Web site because from that point forward, the keyword combination that produced the Googlewhack appears on more than one Web page. Here are the official rules of Googlewhacking according to the game's Web site:

✔ All keywords you enter must be legitimate words found in the online dictionary at `http://dictionary.reference.com`.

✔ You may not enter exact phrases in quotation marks.

✔ If the keywords appear in a list — an encyclopedia, glossary, or thesaurus, for example — the search doesn't count as a Googlewhack.

Google has inspired a number of oddball games besides Googlewhacking. You can also find Google-bombing (described in the previous chapter of this minibook), Googlelaar (`www.northernlake.com/googlelaar`), GoogleFight (`www.googlefight.com`), and The Random Google Page (`www.bleb.org/random`), but none is as odd as elgooG (`www.alltooflat.com/geeky/elgoog/m/index.cgi`), a backward Google Web page.

Searching for Images, Audio, and Video

As you know if you've spent any time exploring the Internet, Web pages are apt to include images as well as text. And some Web pages offer video and audio as well. Suppose you want to purloin one of these multimedia files for your personal use. You need a photograph of a shiitake mushroom for a PowerPoint presentation. You need a video of a wave crashing to illustrate your ideas about next year's stock market behavior. Maybe you just want to see a video of a late-breaking news event.

Unfortunately, searching the Internet for multimedia files can be a hit-or-miss affair. Be prepared to spend time browsing through Web pages until you find a suitable image or file. Search engines index media files according to their filenames and proximity to words on a Web page. You can't really search by keyword for multimedia files except when the keyword name happens to have the same name as a file. As shown in Figure 4-2, for example, a search for butterfly images with the keyword *butterfly* finds image files with *butterfly* in their names as well as assorted other images, depending on the search engine's criteria for indexing image files.

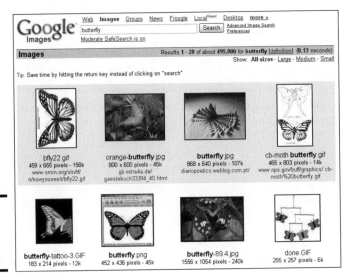

Figure 4-2:
Searching
for images
at Google.

Table 4-2 lists search engines that are capable of searching for multimedia files. In my experience, Google Images is the best choice for searching for images; AltaVista and Singingfish are the best for searching for video. At AltaVista and Singingfish, you can search by file type for `.avi`, `.mpeg`, `.mov`, QuickTime, or `.wma` videos. When searching for audio, best of luck to you. I know of no search engine that does an adequate job of searching for audio files. Find Sounds is fine for what it is, but it only finds short `.wav` files.

Table 4-2   Search Engines Capable of Searching for Multimedia Files

Search Engine	Web Address	Images	Video	Audio	Notes
All the Web	`www.alltheweb.com`	✓	✓	✓	Click the Pictures, Video, or Audio link on the All the Web home page.
AltaVista	`www.altavista.com`	✓	✓	✓	Click the Images, MP3/Audio, or Video link on the Alta Vista home page.
AOL Search	`http://search.aol.com/aolcom/image_home.jsp`	✓			Click the Images link on the AOL Search home page (`http://search.aol.com`).
Ask Jeeves	`http://pictures.ask.com/pictures`	✓			Click the Pictures link on the Ask Jeeves home page (`www.ask.com`).
FindSounds	`www.findsounds.com`			✓	Search the Internet for `.wav` sound effects.
Google	`www.google.com/imghp`	✓			Click the Images link on the Google home page (`www.google.com`).
Ljudo	`www.ljudo.com`			✓	Get sound effects from this Web site.
Lycos	`www.lycos.com`	✓	✓	✓	Click the Advanced Search link on the Lycos home page and then click the Multimedia tab.
Singingfish	`http://search.singingfish.com`		✓	✓	On the left side of the window, choose which kind of files to search for.
Yahoo! Picture Gallery	`http://gallery.yahoo.com`	✓			Search by keyword or by category for pictures and photographs.

By the way, if you come across a multimedia file during your adventures on the Internet and you want to copy it to your computer, follow these instructions:

+ **Image:** Right-click the image and choose Save Picture As. In the Save Picture dialog box, choose a folder for storing the image and then click the Save button.

+ **Video:** Right-click the video image — not the image as it plays, but the still image of the video on the Web page — and choose Save Target As. The Save As dialog box appears. Choose a folder in which to store the video file and click the Save button.

+ **Audio:** Right-click the button or link that starts playing the audio file and choose Save Target As. Then save the file in the Save As dialog box.

This talk of grabbing images, video, and audio from Web sites brings up an important topic: copyrights. Files you take from the Internet were lovingly created by someone, and they belong to their creator. You can use them only under the "fair use" provisions of the copyright laws. These provisions don't allow you to use an image, video, or audio file on a Web site without the creator's permission. One way to find out who owns material is to go to WhoIs.net (`www.whois.net`) and enter the name of the Web address with the copyright material you need. You may be able to find the owner's name that way.

Asking a Google Expert

As fine as the Internet is, sometimes you can't get an answer by searching the Internet, and you have to seek the help of a live, human expert. You can do that by enlisting the services of Google Answers. Google Answers maintains a staff of researchers who are paid to answer questions from registered Google members. It costs 50 cents to post a question. Obtaining an answer costs between $2 and $200, depending on how much you are willing to shell out. Three-quarters of this fee goes to the researcher and one-quarter goes to Google.

To explore the Google Answers Directory, a directory of already-asked questions and already-given answers, you must have a Google account (see Appendix C). To post a question, you must provide Google with your credit card name and number as well.

Either of the following methods takes you to the Google Answers home page:

✦ Go to the Google home page (www.google.com), click the More link and, in the Google Services window, click the Answers link.

✦ Open your Web browser to this address: http://answers.google.com/answers.

Google Answers isn't the only Web site where you can get advice from a living, breathing expert. You can also try out AllExperts at this Web address: www.allexperts.com.

Exploring the Google Answers Directory

At the bottom of the Google Answers home page is a directory with ten categories called the Google Answers Directory. Explore one of the categories or conduct a search to get a sense of the questions being asked and answered. As shown in Figure 4-3, some answers are rated. A five-star answer is considered very satisfactory. Notice the prices and the number of days remaining for questions to be answered. Anyone with a Google Answers account can comment on a question.

Figure 4-3:
Questions
posted to
the Google
Answers
Directory.

Logging in to your Google Answers account

To log in to Google Answers, click the Log In link on the Google Answers home page. The first time you log in, you are asked to create a Google Answers account. Choose a nickname, choose an e-mail notification option, accept the terms of service after you read them, and click the Create My Google Answers Account button.

You go to your Account page. No matter where you travel in Google Answers, you can get to this page by clicking the My Account link. Your Account page offers three tabs for managing your account:

+ **My Questions:** See a list of questions you asked, questions that are awaiting an answer, or questions that were answered.

+ **My Profile:** Change your personal and credit-card information, as well as choose how to be notified by e-mail when a question is answered.

+ **My Invoices:** See what you were charged for submitting questions and getting your questions answered.

Asking a question

To ask a question, enter it in the Google Answers home page and click the Ask Question button. On the following page, enter the subject of your question, choose a category, and name your price. The higher the price, the more likely your question will be answered. The first time you ask a question, Google requests that you provide credit-card information. Your question is posted immediately.

The answer will arrive by e-mail if you opted to be notified by e-mail when a question is answered. Whether you want the answer delivered by e-mail, be sure to revisit your question in the Google Answers Directory to see if it has received any comments.

Online Translation Services

No, translation services on the Internet are not up to the task of doing your French or your Spanish homework for you. Computers are only machines. They have no native concept of language, as Figure 4-4 shows (this translation of Shakespeare's "All's well that ends well" is rendered in Spanish into something like "All's flow that flow to the extremities"). You can, however, cut or copy text from a document or Web site and get an approximate translation of the text at one of these Web sites:

+ **Babel Fish Translation:** Type or paste the words in the Translate a Block of Text box, choose a From and To language combination from the drop-down menu, and click the Translate button. Address: `http://world.altavista.com`

✦ **Google Language Tools:** Type or paste the words in the Translate Text box, choose a From and To language combination, and click the Translate button. (You can also get to this Web page by going to the Google home page at `www.google.com` and clicking the Language Tools link.) Address: `www.google.com/language_tools`

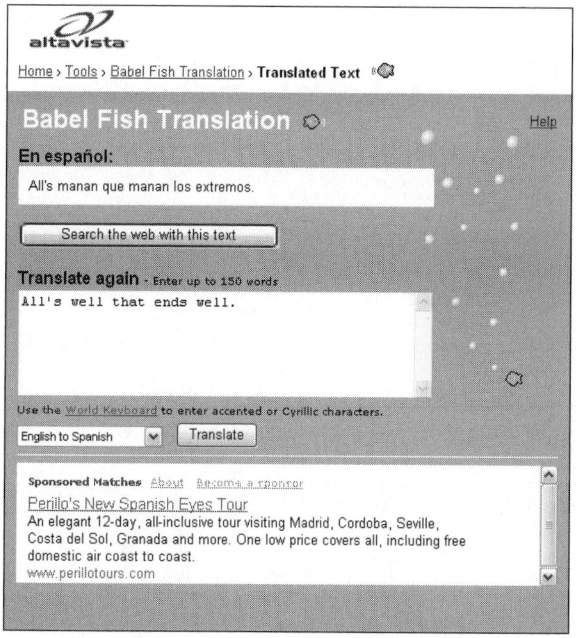

Book II
Chapter 4

Advanced Tools for Scholars and Researchers

Figure 4-4:
Translating from English to Spanish at Babel Fish.

Babel Fish Translation and Google Language Tools both have commands for translating an entire Web page from one language to another. Enter the Web address of the page you want to translate, choose a language combination, and click the Translate button. The Web page appears, but it's rendered in the language you chose, not its original language. In my experiments with Babel Fish Translation and Google Language Tools, Web-page translations were identical, which leads me to think both services run the same translation software.

Google Language Tools does something that Babel Fish can't do: translate Web pages into English as they are found in search results. On the Google Language Tools page, choose a language on the Search Pages Written In drop-down menu, enter keywords for a search, and click the Google Search button. In the search results, click the Translate This Page link to read the Web page in English.

Desktop Search: Searching your computer with Google

The Windows Search command isn't the best. The command is supposed to search your computer for files or text within files, but it doesn't do a very good job. In my experience, at least, it often overlooks files, even when the files are right under its nose.

As of this writing, Google is developing a software program for searching a computer's hard drive using Google search techniques. The program is called Desktop Search and, I'm happy to report, it works great. The program is a big improvement over the Windows Search command. (Microsoft is playing catch-up and is developing a desktop search program of its own called the MSN Toolbar Suite. You can read about it at this address: http://beta. toolbar.msn.com.)

Here are instructions for downloading and using Google's Desktop Search:

- **Downloading the software:** Go to the Web site at this address and click the Agree and Download button: http://desktop. google.com. As soon as the installation is complete, you see a Set Preferences Web page. Choose how you want Google Desktop to work (you can change your mind later), and click the Set Preferences and Continue button. Then click the Start

Searching button so that Google can start indexing the files on your computer — making a map of what is inside it. Indexing may take several hours, but you can work on your computer while Google indexes its contents in the background.

- **Starting Desktop Search:** Click the Google Desktop Search shortcut icon on your Windows desktop or choose Start⇨All Programs⇨Google Desktop Search. Your browser opens to the Google Desktop Search page. It looks and works just like the Google home page.

- **Running a search:** Enter a keyword or keyword combination, and click the Search Desktop button. You can use search operators and conduct an exact search. If files are found, they appear in a search results page. The page tells you where on your computer the files are located. Files are listed by date, with the most recently opened at the top of the list. You can click a filename to open a file.

- **Declaring your search preferences:** Click the Desktop Preferences link on the Google Desktop Search page and choose how you want to search in the Preferences window.

Google™ Desktop Search BETA

Web   Images   Groups   News   Froogle   **Desktop**   more »

Desktop Preferences

antioxidant AND "dimethyl sulfoxide"

[Search Desktop]   [Search the Web]

Search your own computer.

Chapter 5: The Internet as a Reference Library

In This Chapter

✔ Finding general-purpose resources

✔ Finding online encyclopedias, dictionaries, and thesauruses

✔ Searching for people on the Internet

✔ Looking up phone numbers and addresses on the Internet

Many of the cumbersome reference books found on the shelves of the library can be found on the Internet. I'm not suggesting that you forgo a trip to the library the next time you need to consult a reference book, because the walk may do you good and I'm of the opinion that people already spend too much time in front of electronic devices like computers and televisions. Still, if you're in a hurry, you may as well consult one of the online references described in this chapter.

In this chapter, you discover where to find online encyclopedias, dictionaries, and thesauruses, as well as how to find lost friends and look up telephone numbers and addresses anywhere in the world.

Finding General-Purpose Information

First, here are a few general-purpose Web sites where you can get statistics and information about a range of topics:

✦ **FedStats:** Starting at this Web site, you can search United States government databases for statistics about different states or from different federal agencies. Address: www.fedstats.gov

✦ **How Stuff Works:** How Web servers, time, and the Bugatti Veyron's 16-cylinder engine work are among the many subjects you can find at this remarkable Web site, which offers easy-to-understand explanations of many different topics. You can search by topic in the search text box or search by browsing, as shown in Figure 5-1. Address: www.howstuff works.com

✦ **InfoPlease:** This Web site is a sort of old-time country store for information — it offers a little bit of everything, including an almanac, encyclopedia, atlas, and thesaurus. Address: `www.infoplease.com`

✦ **Nation Master:** "Where facts come alive!" this Web site boasts. What makes this place special are the comparison graphs and charts. Compare nations by longevity rates, productivity, and other criteria, and see the results in the form of a chart, not a boring statistical table. Address: `www.nationmaster.com`

✦ **Statistical Abstract of the United States:** This is the U.S. Census Bureau's statistical abstract of the United States divided into 32 categories, from population to industrial outlook. Address: `www.census.gov/prod/www/statistical-abstract-us.html`

Figure 5-1:
How Stuff
Works,
one of my
favorite
Web sites.

Taking Advantage of Online Reference Books

The Internet has relieved the strain of many bookshelves across our land. No longer do as many bookshelves creak and groan from having to support many-volume sets of encyclopedias, hefty dictionaries, and thesauruses. The pages that follow explain how to find the online editions of reference books.

Encyclopedias

You are hereby invited to dip into one of these online encyclopedias when you have a question that's begging to be answered:

✦ **Britannica Online:** *Encyclopædia Britannica* is the old warhorse of encyclopedias; this is the online edition. For $70 per year or $12 per month, you can read full articles in all 32 online volumes. Address: `www.britannica.com`

✦ **Encyclopedia.com:** At last, a free online encyclopedia! Many of this Web site's 57,000 articles come from the *Columbia Encyclopedia, Sixth Edition.* Address: `www.encyclopedia.com`

✦ **MSN Encarta:** With all its resources and wealth, Microsoft ought to be able to offer a better encyclopedia than this one. Besides text articles, Encarta offers pictures and short videos, but you have to be a subscriber to get the good stuff. Subscribing costs $5 per month or $30 per year. Address: `http://encarta.msn.com`

✦ **Wikipedia:** In computer jargon, *wiki* is the term for software that allows collaborative writing at a Web site or blog (the word comes from the Hawaiian for "quickly"). Wikipedia, shown in Figure 5-2, is an online encyclopedia that anyone can read, edit, and help write. It is also a quite interesting ongoing experiment in collaborative writing. Definitions of anything having to do with computers or technology are excellent; avoid the political. (For those who are interested, Wikipedia also offers a thing called a *wiktionary,* a collaboratively written dictionary. You can find it at `http://en.wiktionary.org`). Address: `http://en.wikipedia.org`

Figure 5-2:
Wikipedia,
the ency-
clopedia
and ongoing
collaborative
experiment.

Dictionaries

Next time someone tells you, "I don't know, why don't you look it up?" look it up in one of these online resources:

✦ **Acronym Finder:** Acronyms, like moss and certain kinds of fungi, keep spreading and taking over more of the earth. Go to this Web site when you are stumped for the meaning of an acronym, a word formed from the successive first letters of other words. Address: `www.acronymfinder.com`

✦ **Merriam-Webster Online:** This is the online edition of the old standby dictionary. You can also use the thesaurus starting at this Web site. Address: `www.m-w.com/dictionary.htm`

✦ **OneLook Dictionary Search:** This Web site is a meta-search engine of dictionaries. Enter a word and click the Search button. You get a list of dictionaries on the Internet that offer definitions of your word. Click a dictionary name to go to the online dictionary and read the definition. Address: `www.onelook.com`

✦ **Online Slang Dictionary:** Go to this Web site to decode the speech of your children, nephews, and nieces. You can find a dictionary of American slang. (For English slang, check out A Dictionary of Slang at `www.peevish.co.uk/slang`). **Address:** `www.ocf.berkeley.edu/~wrader/slang`

✦ **Your Dictionary:** This online dictionary doesn't have anything over the other dictionaries listed here. I include it in the list because it can send you a word and its definition each day if you register and are good enough to give it your e-mail address. I'm fond of getting my word of the day in the mail. My vocabulary is increasing. Address: `www.yourdictionary.com`

Here's a quick way to get a word definition: Use the *define* operator in Google (`www.google.com`). Enter **define,** a colon (:), and then, without entering a blank space, the word that needs defining. After you click the Search button, Google gives you a list of Web sites with definitions of the word you entered. For example, enter the following in the Google search text box to find definitions of the word *spyware:*

```
define:spyware
```

Thesauruses

Rooting around in a thesaurus for a good synonym isn't what it used to be now that word-processing programs have built-in thesauruses. In Microsoft Word, for example, you just have to click a word for which you need a synonym and press Shift+F7 to get a list of synonyms for the word. Still, the paltry list of synonyms you get from a word processor can't compare to the synonym lists you can get at these online thesauruses:

✦ **Thesaurus.com:** This is the online edition of *Roget's Thesaurus,* everybody's favorite thesaurus. Address: `http://thesaurus.reference.com`

✦ **The Visual Thesaurus:** This thesaurus could use some improvements. The application that runs it works too slowly for my taste. I include it in this book because it is such an interesting idea. Instead of synonyms appearing in a list, they appear in constellation, with lines showing the words' relationships with one another, as shown in Figure 5-3. You can look up five words in the Visual Thesaurus before you have to pay to download the software. Address: `www.visualthesaurus.com`

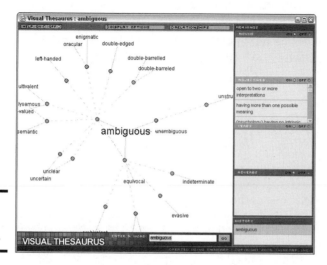

Book II
Chapter 5

The Internet as a Reference Library

Figure 5-3:
The Visual
Thesaurus.

Looking up quotations

A good quote is a great way to enliven a speech. When you're hunting for a good quote, go to these hunting grounds:

✦ **Bartleby Quotations:** You can look up quotations with keywords at this Web site. Address: `www.bartleby.com/quotations`

✦ **The Quotations Page:** Starting here, you can search by keyword or by author name. Address: `http://quotationspage.com`

I'm not sure where to put the next highly unusual Web site in this book, so I may as well put it here. At the Speech Accent Archive (`http://classweb.gmu.edu/accent`), you can hear some 400 examples of different accents, from Afrikaans to Zulu. Says the Web site, "This site examines the accented speech of speakers from many different language backgrounds reading the same sample paragraph. Currently, we have obtained 399 speech samples."

Finding Lost Friends and Lovers

You're supposed to be able to find everything on the Internet. Does that include long-lost friends and lovers? Maybe. You can try your luck with these lookup services. At some of these Web sites, you can pay a fee to run a background check or criminal-history check on someone. You can also trace old telephone numbers and addresses at these sites:

✦ **Docusearch:** This is an online detective agency. Says the Web site, "Docusearch is as intrusive as you need us to be. We investigate the identity, reputation, conduct, affiliations, associations, movements, and whereabouts of just about anyone." Address: www.docusearch.com

✦ **Intelius:** The motto at this Web site is "We know." For some lookups, you can get ages and birthdays. Address: http://find.intelius.com

✦ **Yahoo! People Search:** Search by first and last name. Address: http://people.yahoo.com

Looking Up Phone Numbers and Addresses

The days of the bulky telephone book are coming to an end, thanks to the Internet. Next time you want to look up a telephone number or address, look it up online at one of these Web sites:

✦ **Anywho:** This online directory is owned and operated by AT&T. Address: www.anywho.com

✦ **International White and Yellow Pages:** A directory for looking up addresses and telephone numbers in all continents except Antarctica. Address: www.wayp.com

✦ **Phonenumber:** Offers a reverse telephone and reverse address directory. Enter a phone number or address, and you get a person's name, if it's available. Address: http://www.phonenumber.com

✦ **Reverse Phone Directory:** This one specializes in reverse telephone number and address lookups. Address: www.reversephonedirectory.com

✦ **Smartpages:** This is SBC's online directory. You can also get maps, driving directions, and city guides. For a fee, you can look up someone's criminal history or run a background search on someone. Address: http://smartpages.com

✦ **White Pages:** Offers people searching, as well as reverse address and telephone number lookups. Address: www.whitepages.com

You can look up phone numbers and addresses in Google by using the `phonebook` operator (for looking up residences and businesses), the `rphonebook` operator (for looking up residences), or the `bphonebook` operator (for looking up businesses). At Google (`www.google.com`), enter the operator name, a colon (:), and without entering a blank space, a name followed by the two-letter abbreviation of a state. For example, this search finds people named Dexter Donovan in California:

```
phonebook:dexter donovan ca
```

If you want to opt out of the Google Address book so that your name doesn't come up in searches, go to this Web address: `www.google.com/help/pb removal.html`.

Chapter 6: Read All about It

*L*ong before the Internet, radio, and television, late-breaking news was delivered by newsboys on the street. They shouted, "Extra! Extra! Read all about it!" to peddle the extra editions of their newspapers. An extra edition was a special edition of the newspaper published in the late afternoon, especially to cover a late-breaking news story of importance.

The Internet offers many different ways to "read all about it." This chapter starts by looking at an exciting innovation in Internet news called an aggregator. Aggregators are special programs that collect headlines and story summaries from many news sources so that you can get the latest news without having to travel here, there, and everywhere on the Internet. This chapter also shows how to enlist the help of Google to get the latest news in the form of alerts — e-mail messages sent to you. You also discover search engines designed especially for finding news, news portals, and good sources of foreign news.

Gathering the News with an Aggregator

News fiends who make it their goal to keep up with the latest news get their news from many different Web sites. They get late-breaking news from one place and sports news from another. They get local news from the local daily and financial news from an online financial newspaper. They read their favorite columnists on different Web sites. Some of them even get news from blogs. To catch up on the news, they have to visit many different Web sites.

But instead of going to different Web sites to get the news, what if you could get the news to come to you? Computer programs called *aggregators* and a new Web standard called *RSS,* or Really Simple Syndication, are making this possible. Using an aggregator, you can capture dozens of headlines and story summaries, as shown in Figure 6-1. When you see a headline that interests you, you click it in your aggregator and open a Web page to read the story. Aggregators are convenient. They save time. And they save you the trouble of searching different Web sites for news that matters to you, because you can view part of what is on a Web site — the headlines and story summaries — without actually having to visit the site.

These pages explain how aggregators work, how to subscribe to a Web site with an aggregator, and how to use the Bloglines and Yahoo! aggregators.

How aggregators work

Aggregators are a good thing from the point of view of Web-site developers. The headlines whet readers' appetites and increase the number of Web-site visitors. To make their Web sites available to aggregators, Web-site developers encode headlines and story summaries using the RSS standard. These encoded headlines and story summaries are called *RSS feeds*. To show that their Web sites have been encoded for RSS — that is, to show that their Web sites are capable of feeding headlines and story summaries to aggregators — Web-site developers mark their Web sites with RSS feed icons like the ones shown in Figure 6-2.

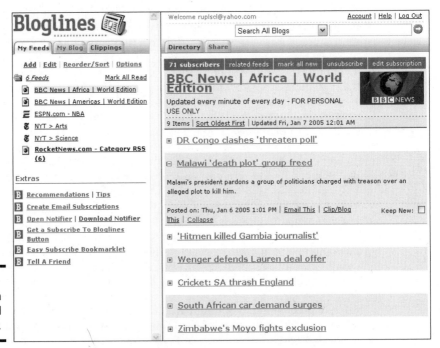

Figure 6-1:
Bloglines, a
Web-based
aggregator.

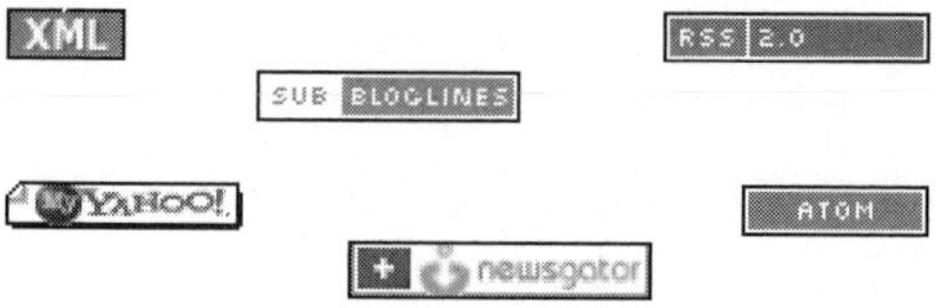

Figure 6-2:
RSS feed
icons.

Book II
Chapter 6

Read All about It

When you see one of these RSS feed icons on a Web site, it means that the Web site can feed headlines and story summaries to an aggregator. Making the connection between your aggregator and a Web site that interests you is called *subscribing*. To subscribe to a Web site so that it can feed your aggregator, you click the RSS feed icon and copy a Web address to your aggregator (I show you how to subscribe in a minute).

The aggregator keeps a list of Web sites to which it subscribes (refer to Figure 6-1). Periodically, or when you ask it to, the aggregator polls each Web site on the list to see whether anything is new, and if something is new, the aggregator downloads the RSS feed from the Web site and displays a new set of headlines and story summaries. In this way, aggregators always present an up-to-date record of what is on each Web site to which they subscribe. In this way, you can keep track of the news at your favorite Web sites.

Aggregators fall in two categories. Some are software programs that you download and install on your computer. Others are Web based; you open them in your Web browser and run them by way of the Internet. Table 6-1 describes the different aggregators, whether they are Web based or are run from a computer, and how much they cost.

Table 6-1	Aggregators			
Aggregator	*Web Site*	*Web Based*	*Software*	*Cost*
Aggie	http://bitworking.org/Aggie.html		Y	Free
Activerefresh	www.activerefresh.com		Y	$30
Awasu	www.awasu.com		Y	Free
Bloglines	www.bloglines.com	Y		Free
BottomFeeder	www.cincomsmalltalk.com/BottomFeeder		Y	Free
FeedReader	www.feedreader.com		Y	Free
InfoSnorkel	www.blueelephantsoftware.com		Y	$40
NewsApp	http://server.com/WebApps/NewsApp	Y		Free

(continued)

Table 6-1 *(continued)*

Aggregator	Web Site	Web Based	Software	Cost
NewsGator	www.newsgator.com	Y		Free
Newz Crawler	www.newzcrawler.com		Y	$25
Rocketinfo	http://reader.rocketinfo.com/desktop	Y		Free
RssReader	www.rssreader.com		Y	Free
SharpReader	www.sharpreader.com		Y	Free
Shortwire	www.shortwire.com	Y		Free
Wildgrape Newsdesk	www.wildgrape.net		Y	Free
WinRSS	www.brindys.com/winrss/iukmenu.html		Y	Free
Yahoo!	http://my.yahoo.com	Y		Free

I prefer Web-based aggregators. The problem with software aggregators is knowing which stories you have read. Aggregators keep track of this for you, but if you have one aggregator on the computer at home and one on your computer at work, the two programs soon get out of sync, and you can't tell which stories you've read. I also like Web-based aggregators because they are more convenient than their software counterparts.

Subscribing to a Web site

In a moment, I describe the particulars of subscribing to a Web site with Bloglines and Yahoo!, but no matter which aggregator you use, the procedure for subscribing is the same:

1. **At a Web site that offers RSS feeds, click an RSS feed icon, as shown in Figure 6-3.**

   Later in this chapter, "Finding RSS feeds with a search engine" explains how to find Web sites with RSS feeds. You can expect to see more RSS feed icons on Web sites in the years to come. Earlier in this chapter, Figure 6-2 shows examples of RSS feed icons. As of this writing, the majority of the icons are marked XML (because RSS feeds are encoded using XML, or eXtensible Markup Language). Some RSS feed icons — Yahoo!, Bloglines, and Newsgator — are named after aggregator programs. Some show the word *Subscribe;* others are labeled *Atom,* which is the name of an RSS encoding format; and others show the letters *RSS.*

   As soon as you click an RSS feed icon, your browser opens a window with RSS XML feed codes, as shown on the right side of Figure 6-3. Yikes! These codes are scary! But don't worry about it. All they do is tell aggregator programs how to fetch RSS feeds.

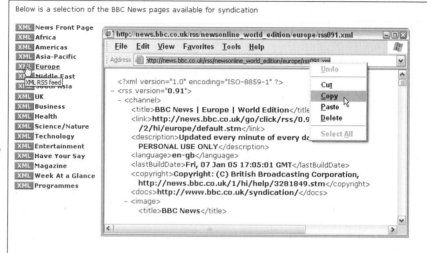

**Book II
Chapter 6**

Read All about It

Figure 6-3:
Copy the
Web
address to
subscribe to
a Web page.

**2. Right-click in your browser's address bar and choose Copy on the
shortcut menu to copy the address to the Windows Clipboard, as
shown in Figure 6-3.**

Make sure that the Web address in the address bar is highlighted when
you choose Copy. The address should be highlighted automatically
when you right-click, but if it isn't, drag over the address before right-
clicking. If the address bar isn't displayed in your browser, right-click the
main menu and choose Address Bar on the shortcut menu.

3. Go to your aggregator and follow the procedure for subscribing.

You are asked to paste the Web address you copied in Step 2 into a text
box. The Web address tells your aggregator where to go on the Internet
to fetch an RSS feed.

Using the Bloglines aggregator

Bloglines (www.bloglines.com) is my favorite aggregator. I like its clean
interface (refer to Figure 6-1). Changing around the headline and story summary displays is easy. Canceling a Web-site subscription is easy as well. You
can also use Bloglines to create a blog and search for Web sites that offer
RSS feeds.

To use Bloglines, click the Register link to register and create an account.
You are interrogated in the usual fashion as you create your account. You are
asked for your e-mail address and a password. To activate the account,
respond to the validation e-mail message.

Subscribing with Bloglines

To subscribe to a Web site, start by signing in and clicking the My Feeds tab. Then open a second browser window and follow the directions in "Subscribing to a Web site," earlier in this chapter, to obtain the Web address of the RSS codes you need to subscribe. Follow these steps to subscribe after you have copied the RSS codes:

1. **Click the Add link.**

   A new panel opens on the right side of the window.

2. **Right-click in the Blog or Feed URL text box in the right side of the window and choose Paste on the shortcut menu.**

   The Web address of the RSS codes appears in the text box.

3. **Click the Subscribe button.**

   The Options window appears so that you can tell Bloglines how to deliver headlines and story summaries to your Bloglines account. You can change these settings at any time by selecting a feed on the My Feeds tab and clicking the Options link.

4. **Click the Subscribe button in the Options window.**

   The name of the Web site you subscribe to appears on the My Feeds tab.

To unsubscribe to a feed, select its name on the My Feeds tab and then click the Unsubscribe link. You can find this link on the right side of the window, above the feed name.

Viewing headlines and story summaries

Feed names on the Feeds tab appear in boldface text if you have not selected them yet. To view headlines and story summaries from a feed, click its name on the Feeds tab. The right side of the window displays headlines and story summaries (refer to Figure 6-1). If a story intrigues you, click its headline to open the story in a Web-browser window.

To see stories from the past that you have already reviewed, click a feed name. On the right side of the window, open the drop-down menu and choose a time period, as shown in Figure 6-4. Then click the Display button.

Using the Yahoo! aggregator

As shown in Figure 6-5, Yahoo! offers an aggregator on the My Yahoo! page. You must be registered and signed in to Yahoo! to take advantage of the Yahoo! aggregator. (Appendix A explains how to register with Yahoo!.) To get to your My Yahoo! page, click the My Yahoo! icon or point your browser to this address: http://my.yahoo.com.

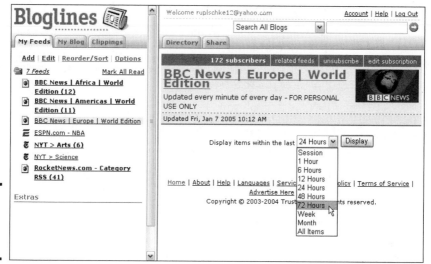

Figure 6-4:
Reviewing
stories from
the past.

Figure 6-5:
The Yahoo!
aggregator
on the My
Yahoo!
page.

Follow these steps to make RSS feeds appear in the My Yahoo! aggregator:

1. **Follow the instructions in "Subscribing to a Web site," earlier in this chapter, to obtain the Web address of the RSS feed codes you need to subscribe.**

2. **On your My Yahoo! page, click the Add Content button.**

You land in the Add Content window.

3. **Click the Add RSS by URL link.**

   You can find this link to the right of the Find button. You go to the Add RSS by URL window.

4. **In the URL text box, right-click and choose Paste to enter the Web address of the RSS feed codes.**

5. **Click the Add button.**

   The Add window appears.

6. **Click the Add button in the Add window.**

   To remove RSS feeds from your My Yahoo! page, click the Remove button (the *X*) next to the headlines. Click the Edit button and choose Edit Content on the shortcut menu to change how headlines are delivered.

Where you see the My Yahoo! RSS feed icon at a Web site, you can click the icon and instantly subscribe to a Web page (as long as you're signed in to Yahoo!, of course).

Finding RSS feeds with a search engine

You can expect to see more RSS feed icons on Web sites in the years ahead. Meanwhile, finding Web sites that offer RSS feeds can be a chore. One way to find them is to enter the name of your favorite news source in Google along with the phrase "RSS feed" (include the quotation marks). I've found many RSS feeds that way. You can also search for RSS feeds with a search engine especially designed for that purpose. Table 6-2 lists RSS-feed search engines.

Table 6-2	RSS-Feed Search Engines
Search Engine	*Address*
BloogZ	www.bloogz.com/rssfinder
Daypop	www.daypop.com
Feedster	www.feedster.com
NewsIsFree	www.newsisfree.com
Syndic8	www.syndic8.com

Getting News Alerts from Google by E-Mail

To help you stay on top of your favorite subject, academic endeavor, or pastime, Google can alert you by e-mail when it discovers something new on the Internet that may be of interest to you. As you know if you read Chapter 3 of this minibook, Google's spiders crawl the Internet looking for updated Web pages and new information, and this information is entered in the Google database. With Google alerts, you can be informed when new information in a particular area has been cataloged by Google. For example, if your area of interest is the hissing cockroach of Madagascar, you can arrange for Google to alert you by e-mail when a Malagasy cockroach hisses anew on the Internet. The e-mail tells you the name of the Web site where the new information is found and invites you to click a link to go straight to the Web site and examine the new information yourself.

Do one of the following to go to the Google Alerts page and tell Google how to alert you:

✦ Go to the Google home page (www.google.com), click the More link, and on the Google Services page, click the Alerts link.

✦ Open your Web browser to this address: www.google.com/alerts.

As shown in Figure 6-6, describe what you want to be alerted about and how you want to be alerted:

✦ **Search Terms:** Enter keywords to describe the news or information you seek. Be very specific, or else you will be inundated with e-mail alerts.

✦ **Type:** Declare whether you want Web pages from news Web sites, from the Internet, or from both places.

✦ **How Often:** Choose from the drop-down menu how often you want Google to send the e-mail alerts.

✦ **Your Email:** Enter your e-mail address.

**Book II
Chapter 6**

Read All about It

Figure 6-6:
Creating a
"Google
alert."

Click the Create Alert button. Google sends you a verification e-mail. Click the link in the e-mail message to start receiving alerts.

News Search Engines

When you want to get the latest news about a topic, search for it with a news search engine. These search engines work just like other search engines. Enter a keyword or a keyword combination in the Search text box to describe the information you are looking for. Table 6-3 describes news search engines (later in this chapter, Table 6-4 describes search engines that focus on international news).

Table 6-3	News Search Engines	
Search Engine	*Web Address*	*Notes*
All the Web News	www.alltheweb.com/?cat=news	Search for news by keyword on the Internet. Click the Advanced Search link to search for news by category. On the All the Web home page (www.alltheweb.com), click the News tab.
AltaVista News	http://news.altavista.com	Search for news by keyword. You can make choices on the Topic, Region, and Time Period drop-down menus to direct your search. At the AltaVista home page (www.altavista.com), click the News tab.
Ananova	www.ananova.com	Browse late-breaking news stories in different categories. Also offers oddball news stories it calls "quirkies."
Columbia Newsblaster	www1.cs.columbia.edu/nlp/newsblaster	This is an experiment of the Columbia Natural Language Processing Group that draws material from 17 Internet news services and "rewrites" the stories onto one page using artificial intelligence techniques.
Daypop	www.daypop.com	Search for news by keyword in traditional news sources as well as blogs, RSS news headlines, and RSS blog posts.
Google News	http://news.google.com	Search for news by keyword in 4,500 news sources or by browsing in different categories. On the Google home page (www.google.com), click the News link.

Search Engine	Web Address	Notes
NewsTrove.com	`www.newstrove.com`	Search for news by keyword or by browsing. Includes many links to online newspapers and newspaper columnists.
Yahoo! News	`http://news.yahoo.com`	Search for news by keyword or by browsing in different categories for stories collected by Yahoo! editors. On the Yahoo! home page (`www.yahoo.com`), click the News link.

Book II
Chapter 6

Read All about It

At Today's Front Pages, you can see what the front page of several dozen daily newspapers look like as of today. Move the pointer over a thumbnail image of a front page to see it on the right side of the screen, as shown in Figure 6-7. Click a thumbnail to see a front page at high resolution in a pop-up window. Today's Front Pages is located at this address: `www.newseum.org/todaysfrontpages`.

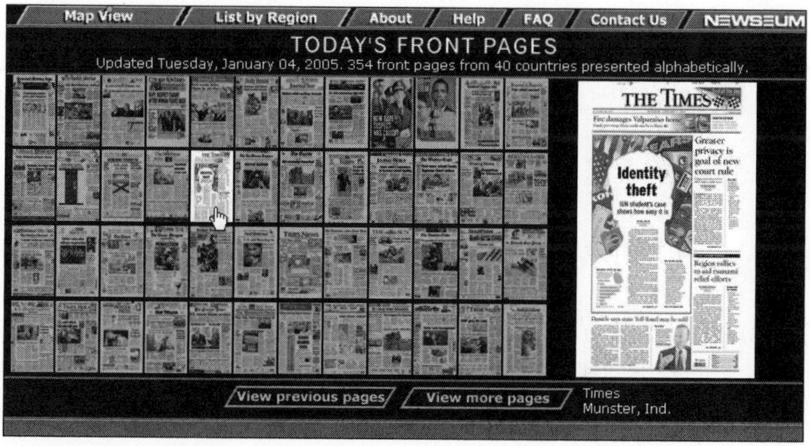

Figure 6-7:
Newspaper front pages, unfolded and ready to read.

Starting from a News Portal

In Internet talk, a *portal*, also called a *Web portal*, is a Web site that delivers many different things — Internet searching, e-mail, shopping, and more. A news portal does the same, only for news. It gives you the news in many different categories. The Web sites listed here represent news organizations. They gather the news on their own without relying on Web sites:

- **BBC:** You can search for world news very easily at this refreshing news portal. Click the name of a continent on the left side of the screen to search for news in one part of the world. Address: `http://news.bbc.co.uk`

- **CNN:** Get news in different categories by clicking links on the left side of the window. Address: `www.cnn.com`

- **MSNBC News:** What do you get when you cross a software monolith with a news behemoth? You get MSNBC News. With so many news categories, finding anything at this Web site is like searching a labyrinth. Address: `www.msnbc.msn.com`

- **Reuters:** Open the drop-down menu and choose an edition — one tailor-made for your part of the world. This Web site gathers news from its 2,000 reporters in the field. Address: `www.reuters.com`

Memigo is a novel Web site that only presents news stories that are of interest to its registered members. Members submit stories and rate stories as they read them. Stories with the highest rating are moved to the top of the Memingo home page. What's more, Memingo keeps track of stories you have rated highly and suggests stories based on your ratings. To check out Memingo or become a registered member of the Web site, go to this address: `www.memigo.com`.

To search for online video news reports, start at Blinkx TV Video Search (`http://blinkx.tv`) and enter a keyword. This search engine looks for video reports in 20 different news sources, including the BBC, CNN, ESPN, and British Television.

Reading Online Newspapers

Chances are, your local newspaper publishes an online edition. Try searching for its name to find out. The following newspapers are on my all-star list because they offer high-quality writing and reporting, and because you can search their archives and use them for historical research:

- **Christian Science Monitor:** This newspaper is known for its even-tempered reporting and the breadth of its coverage of world news. Read articles since 1999 for free; to read articles published before that date, you must pay a fee. Address: `www.csmonitor.com`

- **The New York Times:** That the Gray Lady (as the *Times* is known because the Times building is a shade of gray) is online is almost too good to be true, but you can also search back issues of the *Times* to 1996 for free; you pay a fee to read articles published between 1851 and 1996. You must register to read articles. Address: `www.nytimes.com`

- **Washington Post:** By registering, you can read the *Washington Post* online. For a fee, you can search the newspaper's archives dating to 1877. Address: `www.washingtonpost.com`

Newslink (`http://newslink.org`) offers links to hundreds of small-town newspapers in the United States. You can also find alternative newspapers, online radio stations, and newspapers from other continents. Metagrid (`www.metagrid.com`) is a search engine for locating newspapers' home pages. Enter the name of the town that the newspaper serves and click the Search button. At Crayon.net (`www.crayon.net`), you can create your own newspaper — well, sort of. After registering, you pick a name for your newspaper and tell the Web site from which sources to get the news. Then Crayon.net creates a Web page with links to all your favorite news sources. Over morning coffee, you can go to your "newspaper" at Crayon.net and click a link on the list to quickly check the news.

Getting the News from Abroad

What's going on in the outside world? Table 6-4 shows how you can find out by searching for international news with a search engine. If you aren't using a search engine to get the news of the world, test-drive one of these Web sites:

✦ **All Africa:** This Web site focuses on news from Africa. Search by country from the drop-down menu or investigate a topic by clicking its name on the left side of the window. Address: `http://allafrica.com`

✦ **Kidon Media Link:** Search by country, not just for newspapers but also for magazines, news agencies, and online radio stations. Address: `www.kidon.com/media-link/index.shtml`

✦ **Kiosken:** Find and read online newspapers starting at this Web site by selecting a continent and then a country name. This Web site is brought to you by the Esperanto Federation, an organization bent on teaching the world how to speak Esperanto. Address: `www.esperanto.se/kiosk/engindex.html`

✦ **World Press Review:** This excellent Web site covers compelling world news that doesn't reach our part of the world. Click a region name to read news from one part of the world, or enter a keyword to search the site for news. Address: `www.worldpress.org`

Table 6-4	International News Search Engines	
Search Engine	*Web Address*	*Notes*
NewsTrawler	`www.newstrawler.com`	Search for news by country or by category.
World News Network	`www.wn.com`	Click the Advanced Search link to search with Boolean operators in different languages, or select a region to browse the headlines in different parts of the world.

Book III

E-Mailing

The 5th Wave   By Rich Tennant

"I don't care what your E-Mail friends in Europe say, you're not having a glass of Chianti with your bologna sandwich."

Contents at a Glance

Chapter 1: A Quick Introduction to E-Mailing

In This Chapter

✓ Looking at the difference between Web-based e-mail and e-mail programs

✓ Reading e-mail addresses

✓ Understanding how e-mail is sent and delivered

✓ Compressing files to make them easier to send via e-mail

*I*f you have a modem and an Internet connection, you can send and receive e-mail messages. *E-mail,* or *electronic mail,* is the computer equivalent of letters sent through the post. It goes without saying, but e-mail messages reach their recipients faster than letters and postcards (people who prefer e-mail to conventional mail sometimes call conventional mail services *snail mail*). You can even attach files to e-mail messages, although you can't send e-mail chocolate. Sorry. You can't put a drop of perfume in an e-mail message or enclose a lock of hair either. E-mail may be faster than conventional mail, but it's not nearly as romantic.

This short chapter introduces e-mail basics. It explains the different Web-based e-mail services and e-mail programs. You also find out how to read e-mail addresses and see how e-mail is sent and delivered. Finally, this chapter takes up the practical topic of how to compress files so that you can send them quickly over the Internet.

Web-Based E-Mail and E-Mail Programs

E-mail services come in two distinct varieties — Web-based e-mail and e-mail programs. The two differ with respect to how e-mail is handled and stored. With an e-mail program, all messages are kept on your computer. To compose, send, and receive messages, you give commands in an e-mail program. With a Web-based service, messages are kept on a computer on the Internet, and all e-mailing activity — composing, sending, and receiving messages — is accomplished on the service's computer through a Web browser. Figure 1-1 shows a Web-based e-mail service called ICQmail. In the figure, incoming e-mail messages can be seen in the window of the Mozilla Web browser. It appears that the messages are on a home computer, but they are actually stored on an Internet computer hosted by ICQmail. To read a message, you open it in a browser.

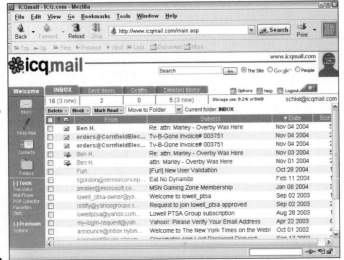

Figure 1-1:
Running
ICQmail, a
Web-based
e-mail
service,
through the
Mozilla Web
browser.

Vagabonds and pilgrims like Web-based e-mail services because they can collect their e-mail wherever they go — well, they can collect it wherever they can find an Internet connection. Collecting Web-based e-mail at an Internet café in Timbuktu or a public library in Cape Town is as easy as collecting it from home or from an office computer. Web-based e-mail services are free, which, of course, is wonderful. And it is easier to set up a Web-based e-mail connection than a conventional connection.

The problem with the services is what happens when you run out of storage space. Web-based e-mail services give you a certain amount of disk space on their computers for storing messages. If someone sends you a large file and you run out of space, so much the worse for you. The Web-based service deletes old messages to make room for new ones when you exceed your storage space.

Table 1-1 lists the most popular e-mail programs. (Chapter 4 of this minibook looks into Web-based e-mail services such as Hotmail and Yahoo! Mail.) I believe that everyone should have at least one Web-based e-mail account as a defensive measure against unsolicited e-mail, also known as spam. As I explain in Chapter 4 of this minibook, you run the risk of being spammed every time you give out your e-mail address. By giving a Web-based account address to people who appear to be suspect, you steer spam and other junk mail to that account instead of the account you use for daily e-mailing — the account that really matters to you.

Table 1-1	Popular E-Mail Programs
Program	*Notes*
Eudora	A user-friendly e-mail program. Named for author Eudora Welty, the muse of Mississippi. Address: `www.eudora.com`
Netscape Mail	Comes with the Netscape Navigator Web browser. Address: `http://netscape.com`
Outlook	Part of the Microsoft Office Suite, this program includes a calendar and task manager. The next chapter of this minibook is devoted to Outlook. Address: `www.microsoft.com/outlook`
Outlook Express	Comes with Windows and Internet Explorer. This program is probably on your computer. Chapter 3 of this minibook explains Outlook Express. Address: `www.microsoft.com/windows/oe`
Pegasus	An easy-to-use e-mailer that is popular outside the United States. Address: `www.pmail.com`

Looking at E-Mail Addresses

An e-mail address comprises a username, a domain name, and a top-level domain. If you were to give the following e-mail address over the telephone, you would say, "Jane at fastmail dot net":

`jane@fastmail.net`

The *username* is the part of the address to the left of the at (@) symbol. It identifies the sender or recipient of the message. When you set up an e-mail account, you are given the opportunity to choose a username for yourself. Sometimes the username includes a first and last name, with the first and last name separated by a period: `jane.smith@fastmail.net`.

The *domain name* identifies the computer where the e-mail messages are sent and stored. When someone sends a message to `jane@fastmail.net`, the message goes to the computer on the Internet — the Web server — that has been assigned the name "fastmail." The message stays there until Jane, collecting her e-mail, gives the command to download the message to her computer so that she can read it. When Jane sends a message, it also goes through the fastmail Web server, to the computer it is addressed to. As I explain in Book I, Chapter 1, each domain name is associated with an Internet protocol (IP) address. When you send e-mail, your computer automatically routes the message to the IP address associated with the domain name in the message address.

The last part of an e-mail address, the two- or three-letter *top-level domain*, identifies a country or address type. You can tell a little something about a person by studying the top-level domain in his or her e-mail address. For example, an address that ends in the letters *edu* probably belongs to someone who works for an educational institution. An address that ends in *au* likely belongs to someone who lives in Australia. Table 1-2 explains what the different three-letter top-level domains mean. The two-letter variety indicates a country. For example, *uk* is the United Kingdom and *jp* is Japan.

Table 1-2	Top-Level Domains
Domain	*Description*
com	A commercial entity
edu	An educational institution
gov	A governmental organization
mil	The United States military
net	A networking organization
org	A nonprofit organization

Discovering How E-Mail Is Sent and Delivered

An e-mail account is similar to a post office box. Mail is delivered to a post office box throughout the day. To collect it, you visit the post office, unlock your box, and grab your mail. Similarly, e-mail messages are delivered to your e-mail address all day long. Until you collect your messages, they reside on an *incoming mail server,* a computer that your Internet service provider (ISP) maintains. This computer receives e-mail that is sent to you. Your ISP also maintains an *outgoing mail server,* a computer responsible for sending your outgoing mail to addresses across the Internet.

For Web-based e-mail services, you don't have to know anything about incoming or outgoing mail servers, but when you set up a conventional e-mail account, you are asked for the names of these servers:

✦ **Incoming mail server:** There are two types of incoming mail servers, POP3 (post office protocol 3) and IMAP (Internet mail access protocol). Before you set up an e-mail account, find out which type of server your ISP uses to receive e-mail, and then get the name of the POP3 or IMAP server.

✦ **Outgoing mail server:** This server is called the SMTP, or simple mail transfer protocol, server. Before you set up an e-mail account, get the name of the SMTP server that your Internet service provider uses to distribute e-mail. Often, the SMTP server's name is the same as that of the POP3 or IMAP server.

Book I, Chapter 3 explains how to connect your computer to your ISP so you can collect and send e-mail.

Compressing Files to Make Sending Them Easier

You can compress files to make them smaller or to roll several files into a single file that's easier to manage and send in an e-mail message. These days, hard drive space isn't difficult to come by, and most people don't compress files to save disk space. However, many people compress files so that they can send files more quickly over the Internet. Depending on what type of file you're dealing with, compressing files can shrink them by 50 to 90 percent. Sending several compressed digital photographs over the Internet takes half to one-tenth the time that it takes to send digital photographs that haven't been compressed. The person to whom you send a compressed file doesn't have to wait as long to get it, nor do you have to wait as long to receive a compressed file. That's the good news. The bad news is that people to whom you send compressed files must have the software and the wherewithal to uncompress them. Without the software, they can't open your compressed file. They can't *extract* it, to use file-compression terminology.

Compressed files are often called *Zip files* because they're usually compressed with WinZip, the most popular utility for compressing and uncompressing files. Everyone with a computer that runs Windows XP can compress and uncompress files because Windows XP offers the Compression utility for doing just that. What's more, the Compression utility can uncompress — or unzip — files that were compressed with WinZip. However, if WinZip or another third-party compression utility is installed on your computer, you can't use the Compression utility to compress files. You have to compress them using the third-party utility. If you try to use the Compression utility, Windows XP runs the third-party utility anyway.

After you compress files into a Zip file, Windows XP attaches a folder icon with a little zipper on it to the file. Zip files in Windows XP take some getting used to. A Zip file is a folder in the sense that the folder holds files, and Windows XP treats it like a folder, but a Zip file is really only a file. Because a Zip file is a hybrid between a folder and a file, I call it a folder-file. At any rate, look for folders with zippers on them when you try to locate Zip files.

Compressing files

Besides shrinking them, compressing files gives you the opportunity to roll a bunch of files into one easy-to-manage file. The 12 digital photographs you want to send to Aunt Enid can be sent in one file attachment rather than 12. The 50 files you want to copy to a CD-R can be stored on the CD as one file rather than 50.

Follow these steps to compress a file or files:

1. **In Windows Explorer or My Computer, select the file or files you want to compress, as shown in Figure 1-2.**

Files of different types can be compressed into the same Zip file.

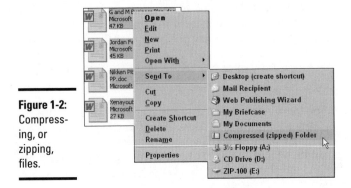

Figure 1-2:
Compress-
ing, or
zipping,
files.

2. **Right-click one of the files and choose Send To⇨Compressed (Zipped) Folder.**

What happens next depends on whether a third-party compression utility is installed on your computer:

- **No third-party utility is installed:** You're done.

- **Third-party utility is installed:** Click the Yes or No button — it doesn't matter which one — when the dialog box asks whether you want to associate compressed files with the Windows XP Compression utility, not the third-party utility.

Windows XP wants to associate each file type with one kind of program. Here, Windows XP is asking you to make its Compression utility the official compression program on your computer, but it doesn't matter what you decide, because you can't compress files with the Compression utility if a third-party compression utility is on your computer.

The third-party utility compresses the files, names the compressed file after the last file you selected, and places the compressed file in the same folder as the files you compressed. In other words, if the last file you selected is called Learning3, the folder-file is called Learning3 as well. To rename a compressed folder-file, right-click it and choose Rename.

Knowing that people like to send compressed files over the Internet, Windows XP offers a convenient command for sending compressed files right after you create them. Right-click the Zip folder-file and choose Send To➪Mail Recipient. Whichever e-mail program you use opens so that you can compose an e-mail message to go along with your compressed file.

Uncompressing files

If someone sends you a Zip, or compressed, file, follow these steps to extract the files from the Zip file:

1. **Right-click the folder-file.**

Which command you choose on the shortcut menu depends on whether a third-party compression utility is installed on your computer:

• **No third-party utility is installed:** Choose Extract All on the shortcut menu.

• **Third-party utility is installed:** Choose Open With➪Compressed (Zipped) Folders. Windows Explorer opens the Zip folder-file in a new window. Now you can see the names of the files that you're about to extract. Click Extract All Files in the Explorer bar.

The Extraction Wizard dialog box appears.

2. **Click the Next button.**

If you want, click the Browse button and choose a folder for the files you're about to extract in the Select a Destination dialog box. If you simply click the Next button, the extracted files land in the folder-file where the Zip file is currently located.

3. **Click the Next button.**

The Extraction Complete dialog box appears.

4. **Click the Finish button.**

You see the extracted files in a new Windows Explorer window. From here, you can open a file or move files elsewhere. Click the Folders button to see where the folder with the extracted files is located on your computer.

The fastest way to uncompress files is to double-click the name of the Zip file. Doing so extracts all the files at once.

**Book III
Chapter 1**

**A Quick
Introduction to
E-Mailing**

Chapter 2: E-Mailing with Outlook

*O*f all the e-mailing software, none is as powerful and all-encompassing as Outlook 2003. The Outlook commands for sending and receiving e-mails and files are easy to pick up. Best of all, the program offers all kinds of ways to handle large loads of e-mail. You can flag it, shunt it automatically into a folder, and even delete it automatically. This long chapter looks into Outlook 2003.

Finding Your Way around Outlook

Outlook is more than an e-mail program, although this chapter focuses on the e-mail side of Outlook. Outlook is also an appointment scheduler, address book, task reminder, and notes receptacle. Outlook is a lot of different things all rolled into one.

Figure 2-1 shows the Outlook Today window with the Folder List on display. The Outlook Today window lists the number of messages in three folders that pertain to e-mail (Inbox, Drafts, and Outbox), calendar appointments, and tasks that need doing. Not that it matters especially, but all Outlook jobs are divided among folders, and these folders are all kept in a master folder called Personal Folders.

Folder list

Figure 2-1:
The Outlook
Today
window.

Here are the ways to get from window to window in Outlook and undertake a new task:

✦ **Navigation pane:** Click a button — Mail, Calendar, Contacts, Tasks, or Notes — on the Navigation pane (refer to Figure 2-1) to change windows and use Outlook a different way.

✦ **Go menu:** Choose an option on the Go menu — Mail, Calendar, Contacts, Tasks, Notes — to go from window to window. You can also change windows by pressing Ctrl and a number (1 through 5).

✦ **Folder List:** Click the Folder List button (it's below the Navigation pane) to see all the folders in the Personal Folder, and then select a folder (refer to Figure 2-1). For example, to read incoming e-mail messages, select the Inbox folder. You can also see the Folder List by pressing Ctrl+6 or choosing Go⇨Folder List.

✦ **Outlook Today button:** No matter where you go in Outlook, you can always click the Outlook Today button to return to the Outlook Today window. You can find this button on the Advanced toolbar.

✦ **Back, Forward, and Up One Level buttons:** Click these buttons to return to a window, revisit a window you retreated from, or climb the hierarchy of personal folders. The three buttons are found on the Advanced toolbar.

When you start Outlook, the program opens to the window you were looking at when you last exited the program. If you were staring at the Inbox when you closed Outlook, for example, you see the Inbox next time you open the program. However, if you prefer to see the Outlook Today window each time you start Outlook, click the Customize Outlook Today button (it's on the right side of the Outlook Today window). Then, in the Outlook Today Options window, select the When Starting, Go Directly to Outlook Today check box and click the Save Changes button.

Addressing and Sending E-Mail Messages

Sorry, you can't send chocolates or locks of hair by e-mail, but you can send pictures and computer files. These pages explain how to do it. You also discover how to send copies and blind copies of e-mail messages, reply to forwarded e-mail, create a distribution list, send e-mail from different accounts, and postpone sending a message. Better keep reading.

The basics: Sending an e-mail message

After you get the hang of it, sending an e-mail message is as easy as falling off a turnip truck. The first half of this chapter addresses everything you need to know about sending e-mail messages. Here are the basics:

1. **In the Mail folder (click the Mail button in the Navigation pane to get there), click the New button or press Ctrl+N.**

A Message window like the one in Figure 2-2 appears.

**Book III
Chapter 2**

**E-Mailing with
Outlook**

Figure 2-2:
Addressing
and
composing
an e-mail
message.

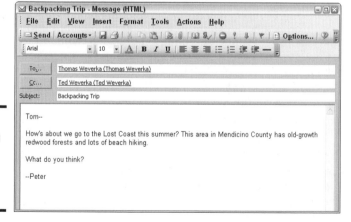

2. Enter the recipient's e-mail address in the To text box.

The next section in this chapter, "Addressing an e-mail message," explains the numerous ways to address an e-mail message. You can address the same message to more than one person by entering more than one address in the To text box. For that matter, you can send copies of the message to others by entering addresses in the Cc text box.

3. In the Subject text box, enter a descriptive title for the message.

When your message arrives on the other end, the recipient sees the subject first. Enter a descriptive subject that helps the recipient decide whether to read the message right away. After you enter the subject, it appears in the title bar of the Message window.

4. Type the message.

Whatever you do, don't forget to enter the message itself! You can spell-check your message by pressing F7 or choosing Tools⇨Spelling.

As long as you compose messages in HTML format and the person receiving your e-mail messages has software capable of reading HTML, you can decorate messages to your heart's content (later in this chapter, "Comparing the Message Formats" explains the HTML issue). Experiment with fonts and font sizes. Boldface and underline text. Throw in a bulleted or numbered list. You can find many formatting commands on the Format menu and Formatting toolbar.

To choose the default font and font size with which messages are written, choose Tools⇨Options, select the Mail Format tab in the Options dialog box, and click the Fonts button. You see the Fonts dialog box. Click a Choose Font button and, in the dialog box that appears, select a font, font style, and font size.

5. Click the Send button.

If you decide in the middle of writing a message to write the rest of it later, choose File⇨Save or press Ctrl+S; then close the Message window. The message will land in the Drafts folder. When you're ready to finish writing the message, open the Drafts folder and double-click your unfinished message to resume writing it.

Copies of e-mail messages you have sent are kept in the Sent Items folder. If you prefer not to keep copies of sent e-mail messages on hand, choose Tools⇨Options and, on the Preferences tab of the Options dialog box, click the E-Mail Options button. You see the E-Mail Options dialog box. Deselect the Save Copies of Messages in Sent Items Folder check box.

Making Outlook your default e-mail program

If you switched to Outlook from Outlook Express or another e-mail program and you like Outlook, you need to tell your computer that Outlook is henceforth the e-mail program you want to use by default. The default e-mail program is the one that opens when you click an e-mail link on a Web page or give the order to send an Office file from inside an Office program. Follow these steps to make Outlook the default e-mail program on your computer:

1. **Click the Start button and choose Control Panel.**

2. **Double-click Internet Options. You see the Internet Properties dialog box.**

3. **On the Programs tab, choose Microsoft Outlook on the E-Mail drop-down menu and click the OK button.**

Addressing an e-mail message

How do you address an e-mail message in the To text box of the Message window (refer to Figure 2-2)? Let me count the ways:

To...

+ **Get the address (or addresses) from the Contacts folder:** Click the To (or Cc) button to send a message to someone whose name is on file in your Contacts folder (later in this chapter, "Maintaining a Happy and Healthy Contacts Folder" explains this folder). You see the Select Names dialog box, shown in Figure 2-3. Click or Ctrl+click to select the names of people to whom you want to send the message. Then click the To (or Cc) button to enter addresses in the To text box (or Cc text box) of the Message window. Click the OK button to return to the Message window. This is best way to address an e-mail message to several different people.

+ **Type a person's name from the Contacts folder:** Simply type a person's name if the name is on file in the Contacts folder. (See the Tip at the end of this list to find out what to do if you aren't sure whether the name is really on file or you aren't sure whether you entered the name correctly.) To send the message to more than one person, enter a comma (,) or semicolon (;) between each name.

+ **Type the address in the To text box:** If you have entered the address recently or the address is on file in your Contacts folder or Address Book, a pop-up message with the complete address appears. Press Enter to enter the address without your having to type all the letters. To send the message to more than one person, enter a comma (,) or semicolon (;) between each address.

Book III
Chapter 2

E-Mailing with Outlook

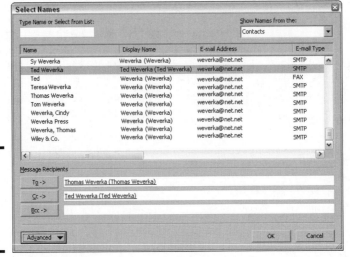

Figure 2-3:
Getting
addresses
from the
Contacts
folder.

✦ **Reply to a message sent to you:** Select the message in the Inbox folder and click the Reply button. The Message window opens with the address of the person to whom you're replying already entered in the To text box. This is the most reliable way (no typos on your part) to enter an e-mail address. You can also click the Reply to All button to reply to the e-mail addresses of all the people to whom the original message was sent.

These days, many people have more than one e-mail address, and when you enter an e-mail address in the To text box of the Message window, it's hard to be sure whether the address you entered is the right one. To make sure that you send an e-mail address to the right person, click the Check Names button or choose Tools⇨Check Names. You see the Check Names dialog box. Select the correct name and address in the dialog box, and click the OK button.

Replying to and forwarding e-mail messages

Replying to and forwarding messages is as easy as pie. For one thing, you don't need to know the recipient's e-mail address to reply to a message. In the Inbox, select the message you want to reply to or forward and do the following:

✦ **Reply to author:** Click the Reply button. The Message window opens with the sender's name already entered in the To box and the original message in the text box below. Write a reply and click the Send button.

✦ **Reply to all parties who received the message:** Click the Reply to All button. The Message window opens with the names of all parties who received the message in the To and Cc boxes and the original message in the text box. Type your reply and click the Send button.

✦ **Forward a message:** Click the Forward button. The Message window opens with the text of the original message. Either enter an e-mail address in the To text box or click the To button to open the Select Names dialog box and select the names of the parties to whom the message is to be forwarded. Add a word or two to the original message if you like; then click the Send button.

Be careful when forwarding a message to a third party without the permission of the original author. How would you like your opinions or ideas scattered hither and yon to strangers you don't know? I could tell you a story about an e-mail message of mine that an unwitting editor forwarded to a cantankerous publisher, but I'm saving that story for the soap opera edition of this book.

To find the e-mail address of someone who sent you an e-mail message, double-click the message to display it in the Message window; then right-click the sender's name in the To box and choose Outlook Properties. The e-mail address appears in the E-Mail Properties dialog box. To add a sender's name to the Contacts folder, right-click the name and choose Add to Outlook Contacts.

Distribution lists for sending messages to groups

Suppose you're the secretary of the PTA at a school and you regularly send the same e-mail messages to 10 or 12 other board members. Entering e-mail addresses for the 10 or 12 people each time you want to send an e-mail message is a drag. Some would also consider it a violation of privacy to list each person by name in a message. To see why, consider Figure 2-4. Anyone who receives the message shown at the top of the figure can learn the e-mail address of anyone on the To list by right-clicking a name and choosing Outlook Properties. Some people don't want their e-mail addresses spread around this way.

To keep from having to enter so many e-mail addresses, and to keep e-mail addresses private as well, you can create a *distribution list,* a list with different e-mail addresses. To address your e-mail message, you simply enter the name of the distribution list. You don't have to enter 10 or 12 different e-mail addresses. People who receive the message see the name of the distribution list on the To line, not the names of 10 or 12 people, as shown in Figure 2-4.

**Book III
Chapter 2**

E-Mailing with
Outlook

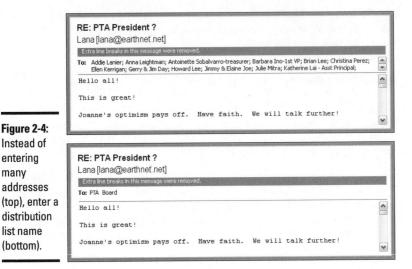

Figure 2-4:
Instead of
entering
many
addresses
(top), enter a
distribution
list name
(bottom).

Creating a distribution list

Follow these steps to bundle e-mail addresses into a distribution list:

1. **Choose File⇨New⇨Distribution List or press Ctrl+Shift+L.**

   You see the Distribution List window, as shown in Figure 2-5.

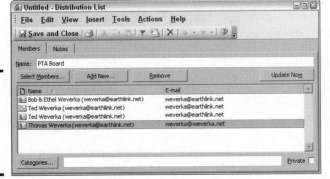

Figure 2-5:
Entering
addresses
for a
distribution
list.

2. **Enter a descriptive name in the Name text box.**

3. **Click the Select Members button to get names and addresses from the Contacts folder.**

   You see the Select Members dialog box.

4. **Hold down Ctrl and select the name of each person you want to be on the list, click the Members button, and click the OK button.**

The names you chose appear in the Distribution List window.

5. **To add the names of people who aren't in your Contacts folder, click the Add New button and, in the Add New Member dialog box, enter a name and e-mail address; then click the OK button.**

6. **Click the Save and Close button in the Distribution List dialog box.**

You did it — you created a distribution list.

Addressing e-mail to a distribution list

To address an e-mail message to a distribution list, click the New button to open the Message window, click the To button to open the Select Names dialog box, and select the distribution list name. Distribution list names appear in boldface and are marked with a Distribution List icon.

Editing a distribution list

 The names of distribution lists appear in the Contacts folder, where they are marked with an icon showing two heads in profile. You can treat the lists like regular contacts. In the Contacts folder, double-click a distribution list name to open the Distribution List window (refer to Figure 2-5). From there, you can add names to the list, remove names from the list, or select new members for the list.

Sending a file along with a message

Sending a file along with an e-mail message is called *attaching* a file in Outlook lingo. Yes, it can be done. You can send a file or several files along with an e-mail message by following these steps:

 1. **With the Message window open, click the Insert File button or choose Insert⇨File.**

You see the Insert File dialog box.

2. **Locate and select the file that you want to send along with your e-mail message.**

Ctrl+click filenames to select more than one file.

3. **Click the Insert button.**

The name of the file (or files) appears in the Attach text box in the Message window. Address the message and type a note to send along with the file. You can right-click a filename in the Attach text box and choose Open on the shortcut menu to open a file you're about to send.

**Book III
Chapter 2**

E-Mailing with
Outlook

TIP

Here's a fast way to attach a file to a message: Find the file in Windows Explorer or My Computer and drag it into the Message window. The file's name appears in the Attach box as though you placed it there with the Insert⇨File command.

Including a picture in an e-mail message

As shown in Figure 2-6, you can include a picture in the body of an e-mail message, but in order to see the picture, the recipient's e-mail software must display messages using HTML (hypertext markup language). As the section "Comparing the Message Formats" explains later in this chapter, not everyone has software that displays e-mail by using HTML. People who don't have HTML e-mail software will get the picture anyhow, but it won't appear in the body of the e-mail message; it will arrive as an attached file (see "Handling Files That Were Sent to You," later in this chapter, to find out about receiving files by e-mail). To view the attached file, the recipient has to open it with a graphics software program such as Paint or Windows Picture and Fax Viewer.

Figure 2-6:
Inserting a picture in an e-mail message.

Follow these steps to adorn an e-mail message with a picture:

1. **In the Message window, click in the body of the e-mail message where you want the picture to go and choose Insert⇨Picture.**

You see the Picture dialog box, shown in Figure 2-6.

2. **Click the Browse button and, in the Picture dialog box, find and select the digital picture you want to send; then click the Open button.**

3. **In the Picture dialog box, click the OK button.**

The picture lands in the Message window. Don't worry about the other settings in the Picture dialog box for now. You can fool with them later.

To change the size of a picture, click to select it and then drag a corner handle. Otherwise, right-click the picture and choose Properties to reopen the Picture dialog box (refer to Figure 2-6) and experiment with these settings:

+ **Alternate Text:** The description you enter here appears while the picture is loading or, if the recipient has turned off images, appears in place of the image.

+ **Alignment:** Experiment with these settings to determine where the picture is in relation to the text of the e-mail message.

+ **Border Thickness:** Determines, in pixels, how thick the border around the picture is. One pixel equals ½ of an inch.

+ **Horizontal and Vertical:** Determines, in pixels, how much empty space appears between the text and the side, top, or bottom of the picture.

Want to remove a picture from an e-mail message? Select the picture and press Delete.

Choosing which account to send messages with

If you have set up more than one e-mail account, you can choose which one to send an e-mail message with. Follow these instructions to choose an account for sending e-mail messages:

+ **Choosing the default account for sending messages:** When you click the Send button in the Message window, the e-mail message is sent by way of the default e-mail account. To tell Outlook which account that is, choose Tools⇨E-Mail Accounts. You see the E-Mail Accounts dialog box. Select the View or Change Existing E-Mail Accounts option button and click the Next button. The next dialog box lists e-mail accounts that have been set up for your computer. Select an account and click the Set As Default button.

Accounts ▾

+ **Sending an individual message:** To bypass the default e-mail account and send a message with a different account, click the Accounts button in the Message window and choose an account name on the drop-down menu. Then click the Send button.

Comparing the Message Formats

Outlook offers three formats for sending e-mail messages: HTML (hypertext markup language), plain text, and rich text. What are the pros and cons of the different formats? Read on to find out.

These days, almost all e-mail is transmitted in HTML format, the same format with which Web pages are made. If HTML is the default format you use for creating messages in Outlook — and it is unless you tinkered with the default settings — the e-mail messages you send are, in effect, little Web pages. HTML gives you the most opportunities for formatting text and graphics. In HTML format, you can place pictures in the body of an e-mail message, use a background theme, and do any number of sophisticated formatting tricks.

However, the HTML format has it share of detractors. First, the messages are larger because they include sophisticated formatting instructions, and being larger, the messages take longer to transmit over the Internet. Some e-mail accounts allocate a fixed amount of disk space for incoming e-mail messages and reject messages when the disk-space allocation is filled. Because they are larger than other e-mail messages, HTML messages fill the disk space quicker. Finally, some e-mail software can't handle HTML messages. In this software, the messages are converted to plain-text format.

In plain-text format, only letters and numbers are transmitted. The format does not permit you to format text or align paragraphs, but you can rest assured that the person who receives the message will be able to read it exactly as you wrote it.

The third e-mail message format, rich text, is proprietary to Microsoft e-mailing software. Only people who use Outlook and Outlook Express can see rich-text formats. I don't recommend choosing the rich-text format. If formatting text in e-mail messages is important to you, choose the HTML format because more people will be able to read your messages.

When someone sends you an e-mail message, you can tell which format it was transmitted in by looking at the title bar, where the terms HTML, Plain Text, or Rich Text appear in parentheses after the subject of the message. Outlook is smart enough to transmit messages in HTML, plain-text, or rich-text format when you reply to a message that was sent to you in that format.

Follow these instructions if you need to change the format in which e-mail messages are transmitted:

✦ **Changing the default format:** Choose Tools➪Options and, in the Options dialog box, select the Mail Format tab. From the Compose in This Message Format drop-down list, choose an option.

✦ **Changing the format for a single e-mail message:** In the Message window, open the Format menu and choose HTML, Plain Text, or Rich Text.

✦ **Always using the plain-text or rich-text format with a contact:** To avoid transmitting in HTML with a contact, start in the Contacts folder, double-click the contact's name, and in the Contact form, double-click the contact's e-mail address. You see the E-Mail Properties dialog box. On the Internet Format drop-down menu, choose Send Plain Text Only or Send Using Outlook Rich Text Format.

Receiving E-Mail Messages

Let's hope that all the e-mail messages you receive carry good news. These pages explain how to collect your e-mail and discuss all the different ways that Outlook notifies you when e-mail has arrived. You can find several tried-and-true techniques for reading e-mail messages in the Inbox window. Outlook offers a bunch of different ways to rearrange the window as well as the messages inside it.

Getting your e-mail

Here are all the different ways to collect e-mail messages that were sent to you:

✦ **Collecting the e-mail:** Click the Send/Receive button, press F9, or choose Tools⇨Send/Receive⇨Send/Receive All.

✦ **Collecting e-mail from a single account (if you have more than one):** Choose Tools⇨Send/Receive and, on the submenu, choose the name of an e-mail account or group (see the sidebar "Groups for handling e-mail from different accounts," later in this chapter, to find out what groups are).

✦ **Collect e-mail automatically every few minutes:** Press Ctrl+Alt+S or choose Tools⇨Send/Receive⇨Send/Receive Settings⇨Define Send/Receive Groups. You see the Send/Receive Groups dialog box, the bottom of which is shown in Figure 2-7. Select a group (groups are explained in the sidebar "Groups for handling e-mail from different accounts"), select a Schedule an Automatic Send/Receive Every check box, and enter a minute setting. To temporarily suspend automatic e-mail collections, choose Tools⇨Send/Receive⇨Send/Receive Settings⇨Disable Scheduled Send/Receive.

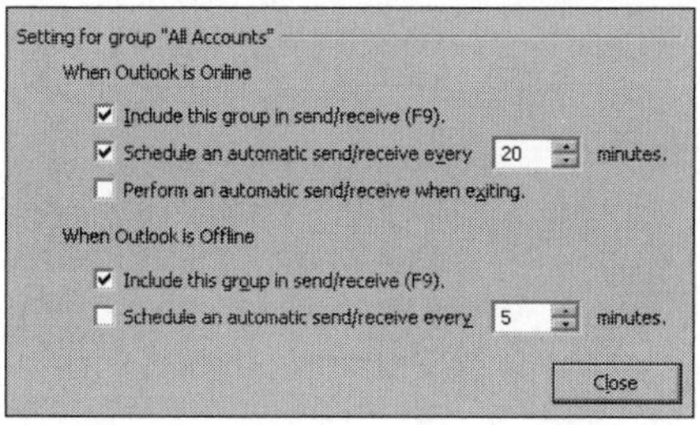

Figure 2-7:
Entering
Group
settings.

> Setting for group "All Accounts"
> When Outlook is Online
> ☑ Include this group in send/receive (F9).
> ☑ Schedule an automatic send/receive every [20] minutes.
> ☐ Perform an automatic send/receive when exiting.
> When Outlook is Offline
> ☑ Include this group in send/receive (F9).
> ☐ Schedule an automatic send/receive every [5] minutes.
>
> [Close]

If you're not on a network or don't have a DSL or cable connection, you shortly see a Connection dialog box. Enter your password, if necessary, and click the Connect button. The Outlook Send/Receive dialog box appears to show you the progress of messages being sent and received.

Being notified that e-mail has arrived

Take the e-mail arrival quiz. Winners get the displeasure of knowing that they understand far more than is healthy about Outlook. You can tell when e-mail has arrived in the Inbox folder because:

A) You hear this sound: *ding.*

B) The mouse cursor briefly changes to a little envelope.

 C) A little envelope appears in the system tray to the left of the Windows clock (and you can double-click the envelope to open the Inbox folder).

D) A pop-up "desktop alert," with the sender's name, the message's subject, and the text of the message, appears briefly on your desktop.

E) All of the above.

Groups for handling e-mail from different accounts

Groups are meant to help people who have more than one e-mail account handle their e-mail. To begin with, all e-mail accounts belong to a group called All Accounts. Unless you change the default settings, all accounts belong to the All Accounts group, and e-mail is sent by and received from all your e-mail accounts when you click the Send/Receive button. If you want to change these default settings, press Ctrl+Alt+S or choose Tools⇨Send/Receive⇨Send/Receive Settings⇨Define Send/Receive Groups. You see the Send/Receive Groups dialog box. Follow these instructions in the dialog box to change how you handle e-mail from different accounts:

✔ **Excluding an account from the All Accounts group:** Exclude an account if you don't want to collect its e-mail when you click the Send/Receive button. Maybe you want to collect mail from this account sporadically. To exclude an account, select the All Accounts group in the Send/Receive Groups dialog box and click the Edit button. You land in the Send/Receive Settings – All Accounts dialog box. In the Accounts list,

select the account you want to exclude and deselect the Include the Selected Account in This Group check box.

✔ **Creating a new group:** Create a new group if you want to establish settings for a single e-mail account or group of accounts. Click the New button in the Send/Receive Groups dialog box, enter a name in the Send/Receive Group Name dialog box, and click the OK button. You see the Send/Receive Settings dialog box. For each account you want to include in your new group, select an account name and then select the Include the Select Account in This Group check box.

✔ **Choosing settings for a group:** In the Send/Receive Groups dialog box, select the group whose settings you want to establish. At the bottom of the dialog box (refer to Figure 2-7), select whether to send and receive e-mail when you click the Send/Receive button or press F9, whether to send and receive automatically every few minutes, and whether to send and receive when you exit Outlook.

The answer is E, "All of the above," but if four arrival notices strikes you as excessive, you can eliminate one or two. Choose Tools⇨Options and, on the Preferences tab of the Options dialog box, click the E-Mail Options button. Then, in the E-Mail Options dialog box, click the Advanced E-Mail Options button. At long last, in the Advanced E-Mail Options dialog box, select or deselect any of the four When New Items Arrive in My Inbox options. To make desktop alerts stay longer on-screen, click the Desktop Alert Settings button and drag the Duration slider in the Desktop Alert Settings dialog box. While you're at it, click the Preview button to see what the alerts look like.

Reading your e-mail in the Inbox window

Messages arrive in the Inbox window, as shown in Figure 2-8. Unread messages are shown in boldface type and have envelope icons next to their names; messages that you've read (or at least opened to view) are shown in Roman type and appear beside open envelope icons. To read a message, select it and look in the Reading pane or, to focus more closely on a message, double-click it to open it in a Message window, as shown in Figure 2-8. In the Folder List, a number beside the Inbox tells you how many unread messages are in the Inbox folder.

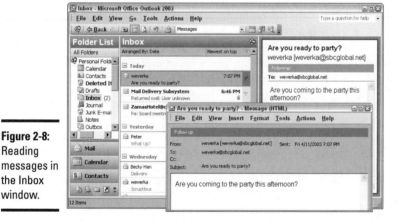

Figure 2-8:
Reading messages in the Inbox window.

Book III
Chapter 2

E-Mailing with
Outlook

Later in this chapter, "Techniques for Organizing E-Mail Messages" explains how to organize messages in the Inbox folder. Meanwhile, here are some simple techniques you can use to unclutter the Inbox folder and make it easier to manage:

✦ **Hiding and displaying the Reading pane:** Click the Reading Pane button to make the Reading pane appear or disappear. With the Reading pane gone, column headings — From, Subject, Received, Size, and Flagged — appear in the Inbox window. You can click a column heading name to sort messages in different ways. For example, click the From column name to arrange messages by sender name.

+ **Hiding and displaying the Navigation pane:** Choose View⇨Navigation Pane or press Alt+F1. By hiding the Navigation pane, you get even more room to display messages.

+ **"Autopreviewing" messages:** Click the AutoPreview button or choose View⇨AutoPreview to read the text of all on-screen messages in small type. The message text appears below the subject heading of each message.

+ **Changing views:** Choose an option on the Current View drop-down menu to reduce the number of messages in the window. For example, you can see only unread messages, or messages that arrived in the past week. The Current View drop-down menu is located on the Advanced toolbar.

Suppose you open an e-mail message but you regret doing so because you want it to look closed. You want the unopened envelope icon to appear beside the message's name so that you know to handle it later on. To make a message in the Inbox window appear as if it has never been opened, right-click the message and choose Mark As Unread.

Handling Files That Were Sent to You

You can tell when someone has sent you files along with an e-mail message because the word *Attachments* appears in the Reading pane along with the filenames, as shown in Figure 2-9. The word *Attachments* and a filename appear as well in the Message window. And if columns are on display in the Inbox window (see the previous section of this chapter), a paper-clip icon appears in the Sort By Attachment column to let you know that the e-mail message includes a file or files, as Figure 2-9 also shows.

Files that are sent to you over the Internet land deep inside your computer in a subfolder of the Temporary Internet Files folder. This is the same obscure folder where Web pages you encounter when surfing the Internet are kept. The best way to handle an incoming file is to open it or save it right away to a folder where you are likely to find it when you need it.

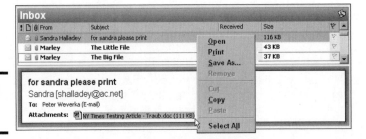

Figure 2-9:
Receiving
a file.

To save a file that was sent to you in a new folder, do one of the following:

✦ Right-click the filename and choose Save As, as shown in Figure 2-9.

✦ Choose File⇨Save Attachments⇨*Filename*.

To open a file that was sent to you, do one of the following:

✦ Double-click the filename in the Reading pane or Message window.

✦ Right-click the filename and choose Open, as shown in Figure 2-9.

✦ Right-click the paper-clip icon in the Inbox window and choose View Attachments⇨*Filename*.

Maintaining a Happy and Healthy Contacts Folder

In pathology, which is the study of diseases and how they are transmitted, a contact is a person who passes on a communicable disease, but in Outlook, a contact is someone about whom you keep information. Information about contacts is kept in the Contacts folder. This folder is a super-powered address book. It has places for storing people's names, addresses, phone numbers, e-mail addresses, Web pages, pager numbers, birthdays, anniversaries, nicknames, and other stuff. When you address an e-mail message, you can get the address straight from the Contacts folder to be sure that the address is entered correctly.

A Contacts folder is only as good and as thorough as the information about contacts that you put into it. These pages explain how to enter information about a contact and update the information if it happens to change.

Entering a new contact in the Contacts folder

To place someone on the Contacts list, open the Contacts folder and start by doing one of the following:

✦ Click the New Contact button.

✦ Press Ctrl+N (in the Contacts Folder window) or Ctrl+Shift+C.

✦ Choose File⇨New⇨Contact.

You see the Contact form, shown in Figure 2-10. On this form are places for entering just about everything there is to know about a person, except his or her love life and secret vices. Enter all the information you care to record, keeping in mind these rules of the road as you go along:

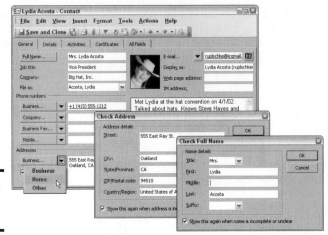

Figure 2-10:
A Contact
form.

+ **Full names, addresses, and so on:** Although you may be tempted to simply enter addresses, phone numbers, names, and so on in the text boxes, don't do it! Click the Full Name button on the General tab, for example, to enter a name (refer to Figure 2-10). Click the Business or Home button to enter an address in the Check Address dialog box (refer to Figure 2-10). By clicking the buttons and entering data in dialog boxes, you permit Outlook to separate the component parts of names, addresses, and phone numbers. As such, Outlook can sort names and addresses more easily, and it can use names and addresses as a source for mass mailings and mass e-mailings with Microsoft Word.

   When entering information about a company, not a person, leave the Full Name field blank and enter the company's name in the Company field.

+ **Information that matters to you:** If the form doesn't appear to have a place for entering a certain kind of information, try clicking a triangle button and choosing a new information category from the pop-up menu. Click the triangle button next to the Business button and choose Home, for example, if you want to enter a home address rather than a business address.

+ **File As:** Open the File As drop-down menu and choose an option for filing the contact in the Contacts folder. Contacts are filed alphabetically by last name, first name, company name, or combinations of the three. Choose the option that best describes how you expect to find the contact in the Contacts folder.

+ **Mailing addresses:** If you keep more than one address for a contact, display the address to which you want to send mail and select the This Is the Mailing Address check box.

+ **E-mail addresses:** You can enter up to three e-mail addresses for each contact (click the triangle button and choose E-mail 2 or E-mail 3 to enter a second or third address). In the Display As text box, Outlook shows you what the To line of e-mail messages will look like when you send e-mail to a contact. By default, the To line shows the contact's name followed by his or her e-mail address in parentheses. However, you can enter whatever you wish in the Display As text box, and if entering something different helps you distinguish between e-mail addresses, enter something different. For example, enter **Lydia – Personal** so that you can tell when you send e-mail to Lydia's personal address as opposed to her business address.

+ **Photos:** To put a digital photo on a Contact form, click the Add Contact Photo button and, in the Add Contact Picture dialog box, select a picture and click the OK button.

Be sure to write a few words on the General tab to describe how and where you met the contact. When the time comes to weed out contacts in the Contacts folder list, reading the descriptions can help you decide who gets weeded and who doesn't.

When you're done entering information, click the Save and Close button. If you're in a hurry to enter contact information, click the Save and New button. Doing so opens an empty form so that you can record information about another contact.

Here's a fast way to enter contact information for someone who has sent you an e-mail message: Open the message, right-click the sender's name on the To line, and choose Add to Outlook Contacts on the shortcut menu. You see the Contact form. Enter more information about the sender if you can and click the Save and Close button.

**Book III
Chapter 2**

**E-Mailing with
Outlook**

Mapping out an address

On the Contact form is an obscure but very useful little button that can be a great help when you need to go somewhere but aren't sure how to get there. This button is called Display Map of Address. As long as your computer is connected to the Internet and an address is on file for a contact, you can click the Display Map of Address button (or choose Actions⇨Display Map of Address) to go online to the Microsoft Expedia Web site and see a map with the address at its center. Double-click a contact name to open the contact in a form. Good luck getting there!

Importing e-mail and addresses from another program

Suppose that you've been using Outlook Express, Eudora, or Lotus Organizer to handle your e-mail and contact addresses, but now you've become a convert to Outlook. What do you do with the e-mail messages and names and addresses in the other program? You can't let them just sit there. You can import them into Outlook and pick up where you left off.

To import e-mail and contact addresses from another program, start by choosing File⇨Import and Export. You see the Import and Export Wizard. What you do next depends on where you now do your e-mailing and address tracking:

- ✦ **Outlook Express:** Select Import Internet Mail and Addresses, and click the Next button. In the Outlook Import Tool dialog box, select Outlook Express, select check boxes to decide what to export (Mail, Addresses, and/or Rules), and click the Next button again. In the next dialog box, choose options to decide what to do about duplicate entries; then click the Finish button.

- ✦ **Eudora:** Select Import Internet Mail and Addresses, and click the Next button. In the Outlook Import Tool dialog box, select Eudora, choose options to decide what to do about duplicate entries, and click the Next button again. In the Browser for Folder dialog box, select the file where the Eudora data is kept and click the OK button.

- ✦ **Lotus Organizer:** Select Import from Another Program or File, click the Next button, select a Lotus Organizer version (4.*x* or 5.*x*), and click the Next button again. Clicking the Next button as you go along, you're asked how to handle duplicate items, to locate the Lotus Organizer data file, and to select an Outlook folder to put the data in.

Some Import and Export filters are not installed automatically by Outlook. Outlook may ask you to insert the Office CD so it can install a filter.

Techniques for Organizing E-Mail Messages

If you are one of those unfortunate souls who receives 20, 30, 40, or more e-mail messages daily, you owe it to yourself and your sanity to figure out a way to organize e-mail messages such that you keep the ones you want, you can find e-mail messages easily, and you can quickly eradicate the e-mail messages that don't matter to you. These pages explain the numerous ways to manage and organize e-mail messages. Pick and choose the techniques that work for you, or else try to convince the Postal Service that you are entitled to your own zip code and that you should be paid to handle all the e-mail you receive.

In a nutshell, here are all the techniques for organizing e-mail messages:

✦ **Change views in the Inbox window:** Open the Current View drop-down menu on the Advanced toolbar and choose Last Seven Days, Unread Messages in This Folder, or another view to shrink the number of e-mail messages in the Inbox window.

✦ **Rearrange, or sort, messages in the Inbox window**: If necessary, click the Reading Pane button to remove the Reading pane and see column heading names in the Inbox window. Then click a column heading name to rearrange, or sort, messages by sender name, subject, receipt date, size, or flagged status. See "Reading your e-mail in the Inbox window," earlier in this chapter, for details.

✦ **Delete the messages that you don't need:** Before they clutter the Inbox, delete messages you're sure you don't need as soon as you get them. To delete a message, select it and click the Delete button, press the Delete key, or choose Edit⇨Delete.

✦ **Move messages to different folders:** Create a folder for each project you're involved with and, when an e-mail message about a project arrives, move it to a folder. See "Looking into the Different E-Mail Folders," later in this chapter.

✦ **Move messages automatically to different folders as they arrive:** See "Earmarking messages as they arrive," later in this chapter.

✦ **Flag messages:** Mark a message with a color-coded flag to let you know to follow up on it. See the next section in this chapter for more information.

✦ **Have Outlook remind you to reply to a message:** Instruct Outlook to make the Reminder message box appear at a date and time in the future so that you know to reply to a message. See "Being reminded to take care of e-mail messages," later in this chapter.

Flagging e-mail messages

One way to call attention to e-mail messages is to flag them. As shown in Figure 2-11, you can make color-coded flags appear in the Inbox window. You can use red flags, for example, to mark urgent messages and green flags to mark the not-so-important ones. Which color you flag a message with is up to you. Outlook offers six colors. As Figure 2-11 shows, you can click the Sort by Flag Status button in the Inbox window to arrange messages in color-coded flag order.

Follow these instructions to flag an e-mail message:

✦ **Starting in the Message window:** Click the Follow Up button. You see the Flag for Follow Up dialog box, as shown in Figure 2-11. If the color you prefer isn't showing, choose a color from the Flag Color drop-down menu. From the Flag To drop-down menu, choose a follow-up notice or type one of your own in the text box. The notice appears across the top of the e-mail message in the Message window.

✦ **Starting in the Inbox folder:** Select the message and choose Actions⇨ Follow Up and a flag color, or right-click and choose Follow Up and a flag color.

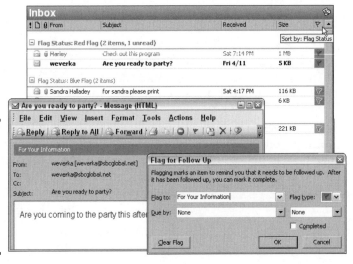

Figure 2-11: Flagging messages so that you can remember to follow up on them.

To "unflag" a message, right-click it and choose Follow Up⇨Clear Flag. You can also right-click and choose Follow Up⇨Flag Complete to put a check mark where the flag used to be and remind yourself that you're done with the message. Later in this chapter, "Earmarking messages as they arrive" explains how you can flag messages automatically as messages arrive.

Being reminded to take care of e-mail messages

If you know your way around the Calendar and Tasks windows, you know that the Reminders message box appears when an appointment or meeting is about to take place or a task deadline is about to fall. What you probably don't know, however, is that you can put the Reminders dialog box to work in regard to e-mail messages.

Follow these steps to remind yourself to reply to an e-mail message or simply to prod yourself into considering an e-mail message in the future:

1. **Select the message and choose Actions➪Follow Up➪Add Reminder.**

You see the Flag for Follow Up dialog box (refer to Figure 2-11). You can also right-click a message and choose Follow Up➪Add Reminder to see the dialog box.

2. **On the Flag To drop-down menu, choose an option that describes why the e-mail message needs your attention later on, or if none of the options suits you, enter a description in the Flag To text box.**

The description you choose or enter appears above the message in the Reading pane and appears as well in the Reminders message box.

3. **Choose the date and time that you want the Reminders message box to appear.**

The Reminders message box will appear 15 minutes before the date and time you enter. If you enter a date but not a time, Outlook assigns the default time, 12:00 a.m.

4. **Click the OK button.**

Items flagged this way appear in red text with a red flag. When the reminder falls due, you see the Reminders message box, where you can click the Open Item button to open the e-mail message.

Earmarking messages as they arrive

To help you organize messages better, Outlook gives you the opportunity to mark messages in various ways and even move messages as they arrive automatically to folders apart from the Inbox folder. Being able to move messages immediately to a folder is a great way to keep e-mail concerning different projects separate. If you belong to a newsgroup that sends many messages a day, being able to move those messages instantly into their own folder is a real blessing, because newsgroup messages have a habit of cluttering the Inbox folder.

To earmark messages for special treatment, Outlook has you create so-called *rules*. To create a rule, start by trying out the Create Rule command, and if that doesn't work, test-drive the more powerful Rules Wizard.

Simple rules with the Create Rule command

Use the Create Rule command to be alerted when e-mail arrives from a certain person or when the Subject line of a message includes a certain word. You can make the incoming message appear in the New Item Alerts window (as shown at the top of Figure 2-12), play a sound when the message arrives, or move the message automatically to a certain folder.

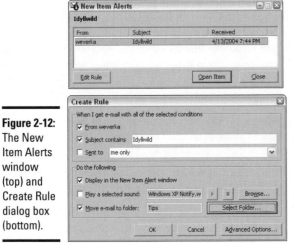

Figure 2-12:
The New
Item Alerts
window
(top) and
Create Rule
dialog box
(bottom).

Follow these steps to create a simple rule:

1. If you want to be alerted when e-mail arrives from a certain person, find an e-mail message from the person, right-click it, and choose Create Rule; otherwise, right-click any message and choose Create Rule.

You see the Create Rule dialog box, shown at the bottom of Figure 2-12.

2. Fill in the dialog box and click the OK button.

These commands are self-explanatory.

Another way to create a simple rule is to choose Tools⇨Organize. The Ways to Organize Inbox panel appears. Starting here, you can move messages from a certain person to a folder or color-code messages as they arrive from a certain person.

Creating complex rules with the Rules Wizard

Use the Rules Wizard to create complex rules that earmark messages with words in the message body or earmark messages sent to distribution lists. You can also create a rule to flag messages automatically or delete a conversation (the original message and all replies).

To run the Rules Wizard, click the Rules and Alerts button or choose Tools⇨ Rules and Alerts. You see the Rules and Alerts dialog box. Click the New Rule button and keep clicking the Next button in the Rules Wizard dialog boxes as you complete the two steps to create a rule:

✦ **Step 1:** Choose the rule you want to create or how you want to be alerted in the New Item Alerts message box (refer to Figure 2-12).

✦ **Step 2:** Click a hyperlink to open a dialog box and describe the rule. For example, click the Specific Words link to open the Search Text dialog box and enter the words that earmark a message. Click the Specified link to open the Rules and Alerts dialog box and choose a folder to move the messages to. You must click each link in the Step 2 box to describe the rule.

To edit a rule, double-click it in the Rules and Alerts dialog box and complete Steps 1 and 2 all over again.

Looking into the Different E-Mail Folders

Where Outlook e-mail is concerned, everything has its place and everything has its folder. E-mail messages land in the Inbox folder when they arrive. Messages you write go to the Outbox folder until you send them. Copies of e-mail messages you send are kept in the Sent folder. And you can create folders of your own for storing e-mail.

If you're one of those unlucky people who receive numerous e-mail messages each day, you owe it to yourself to create folders in which to organize e-mail messages. Create one folder for each project you're working on. That way, you know where to find e-mail messages when you want to reply to or delete them. These pages explain how to move e-mail messages between folders and create folders of your own for storing e-mail.

Moving e-mail messages to different folders

Click to select the message you want to move and use one of these techniques to move an e-mail message to a different folder:

✦ **With the Move to Folder button:** Click the Move to Folder button in the message window and, on the drop-down menu that appears, select a folder. The Move to Folder button is located on the Standard toolbar to the right of the Print button.

✦ **With the Move to Folder command:** Choose Edit⇨Move to Folder, press Ctrl+Shift+V, or right-click and choose Move to Folder. You see the Move Items dialog box. Select a folder a click the OK button.

✦ **By dragging:** Click the Folder List button, if necessary, to see all the folders; then drag the e-mail message into a different folder.

Earlier in this chapter, "Earmarking messages as they arrive" explains how to move e-mail messages automatically to folders as they are sent to you.

Creating a new folder for storing e-mail

Follow these steps to create a new folder:

1. Choose File⇨New⇨Folder.

You see the Create New Folder dialog box, shown in Figure 2-13. You can also open this dialog box by pressing Ctrl+Shift+E or by right-clicking a folder in the Folder List and choosing New Folder.

Figure 2-13:
Creating a
new folder.

2. Select the folder that the new folder is to go inside.

For example, to create a first-level folder, select Personal Folders.

3. Enter a name for the folder.

4. Click the OK button.

To delete a folder you created, select it and click the Delete button. To rename a folder, right-click it, choose Rename, and enter a new name.

Deleting E-Mail Messages (and Contacts, Tasks, and Other Items)

Outlook folders are notorious for filling very quickly. E-mail messages (as well as contacts and tasks) soon clog the folders if you spend any time in Outlook. From time to time, go through the e-mail folders and Contacts window to delete items you no longer need. To delete items, select them and do one of the following:

✦ Click the Delete button (or press the Delete key).

✦ Choose Edit➪Delete (or press Ctrl+D).

✦ Right-click and choose Delete.

Deleted items — e-mail messages, calendar appointments, contacts, or tasks — land in the Deleted Items folder in case you want to recover them. To delete items once and for all, open the Deleted Items folder and start deleting like a madman.

To spare you the trouble of deleting items twice, once in the original folder and again in the Deleted Items folder, Outlook offers these amenities:

✦ **Empty the Deleted Items folder when you close Outlook:** If you're no fan of the Deleted Items folder and you want to remove deleted items without reviewing them, choose Tools➪Options, select the Other tab in the Options dialog box, and select Empty the Deleted Items Folder Upon Exiting.

✦ **Empty the Deleted Items folder yourself:** Choose Tools➪Empty "Deleted Items" Folder to remove all the messages in the Deleted Items folder. You can also right-click the Deleted Items folder in the Folder List and choose Empty "Deleted Items" Folder.

Finding and Backing Up Your Outlook File

All the data you keep in Outlook — e-mail messages, names and addresses, as well as calendar appointments and meetings — is kept in a file called `Outlook.pst`. Locating this file on your computer sometimes requires the services of Sherlock Holmes. The file isn't kept in a standard location. It can be any number of places, depending on the operating system on your computer and whether you upgraded from an earlier version of Office.

The all-important `Outlook.pst` file is hiding deep in your computer, but you need to find it. You need to know where this file is located so that you can back it up to a floppy disk, Zip drive, or other location where you keep backup material. The Outlook Contacts List holds clients' names and the names of relatives and loved ones. It holds the e-mail messages you think are worth keeping. It would be a shame to lose this stuff if your computer failed.

Here's a quick way to find the `Outlook.pst` file on your computer and back it up:

1. Choose File➪Data File Management.

You see the Outlook Data Files dialog box, shown in Figure 2-14.

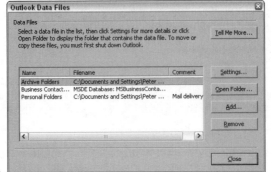

Figure 2-14 :
The Outlook
Data Files
dialog box.

2. **Select Personal Folders and click the Open Folder button.**

   Windows Explorer opens and you see the folder where the Outlook.pst file is kept.

3. **Click the Folders button in Windows Explorer to see the folder hierarchy on your computer.**

   By scrolling in the Folders pane on the left side of the window, you can determine where on your computer the elusive Outlook.pst file really is.

4. **Close Outlook.**

   Sorry, but you can't back up an Outlook.pst file if Outlook is running.

5. **To back up the file, right-click it in Windows Explorer, choose Send To on the shortcut menu, and choose the option on the submenu that represents where you back up files.**

   You can also copy the Outlook.pst file to a Zip drive or CD in Windows Explorer by Ctrl+dragging or copying and pasting.

Chapter 3: E-Mailing with Outlook Express

In This Chapter

✔ Finding your way around Outlook Express

✔ Writing and addressing e-mail messages

✔ Choosing the right format for messages

✔ Getting your e-mail

✔ Organizing your e-mail messages

✔ Keeping an Address Book

*I*ncluded in the Windows operating system is an e-mailing program called Outlook Express. I am a big fan of this program. It has all the virtues of its cousin Outlook without all of Outlook's clumsiness. It is easy to learn. The Address Book that comes with Outlook Express is a great place to keep friends' and coworkers' addresses and phone numbers. As Book IV, Chapter 4 explains, you can even use Outlook Express to subscribe to user groups. Best of all, Outlook Express is free as long as your computer runs Windows. It's there for the taking.

This chapter explains how to handle your e-mail and keep track of addresses with Outlook Express. Along the way, you discover how to send and receive files, organize your e-mail in different folders, and choose message formats.

A Short Geography Lesson

As Figure 3-1 shows, Outlook Express items are kept in folders. Newly arrived messages, for example, land in the Inbox folder. Copies of e-mail messages you send are kept in the Sent Items folder. As I explain "Organizing Your E-Mail Messages," later in this chapter, you can create folders of your own for storing and tracking e-mail messages.

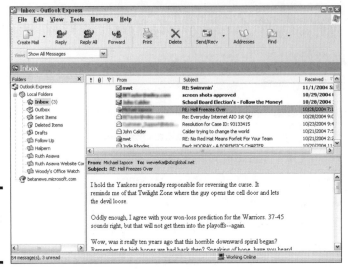

Figure 3-1:
The Outlook
Express
window.

Here are instructions for handling folders:

✦ **Opening a folder:** Choose View➪Go to Folder (or press Ctrl+Y) and
select a folder's name in the Go to Folder dialog box. You may have to
click the plus sign (+) next to a folder to see its subfolders. If the Folder
pane is displayed, click the folder's name in the Folder pane.

✦ **Hiding the Folder pane:** Click the Close button (the *X*) in the upper-right
corner of the Folder pane.

✦ **Displaying the Folder pane:** Click the button named for the folder you
are visiting to briefly display the Folder pane. For example, if you are
in the Inbox folder, click the Inbox button, as shown in Figure 3-2. To
permanently display the Folder pane, click the push-pin button. (If you
don't see a folder button, choose View➪Layout and select the Folder
List check box in the Window Layout Properties dialog box.)

Some people prefer to get right to business and see the Inbox folder as soon
as they start Outlook Express. If you are one of those people, choose Tools➪
Options, select the General tab in the Options dialog box, and select the
When Starting, Go Directly to My 'Inbox' Folder check box.

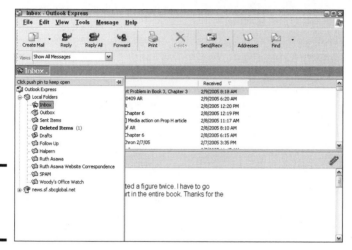

Figure 3-2:
Displaying
the Folder
pane.

Writing and Sending E-Mail Messages

Not so long ago, e-mail messages consisted entirely of text, but now you can
include a picture in an e-mail message and send files along with messages.
These pages explain how to send the whole deal — how to send plain messages, messages with pictures, and messages with files.

**Book III
Chapter 3**

**E-Mailing with
Outlook Express**

Writing an e-mail message

Writing and sending e-mail is quite simple, especially if the address of the
person who is to receive the message is on file in the Address Book (later in
this chapter, "Keeping the Addresses of Friends, Family, and Clients" explains
the Address Book). Follow these steps to write and send an e-mail message:

1. **Click the Create Mail button.**

The New Message window appears, as shown in Figure 3-3.

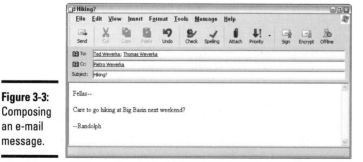

Figure 3-3:
Composing
an e-mail
message.

2. Address the message.

How you address the message depends on whether the recipients' names are on file in your Address Book:

- **Recipients' names are on file:** Click the To button. You see the Select Recipients dialog box with the names of people in the Address Book who have e-mail addresses. Click a name on the list and then click the To button. The name you chose appears in the Message recipients box. You can Ctrl+click to select several names at once. Select names and click the Cc button to send copies of the message. Click the OK button to return to the New Message window.

With a little luck, you don't have to open the Select Recipients dialog box to enter an address. Instead, In the New Message window, type the first few letters of the recipient's name in the To box. If Outlook Express recognizes the name from the Address Book, the name appears.

- **Recipient's names aren't on file:** Type the recipients' e-mail addresses in the To (or Cc) text box. Enter a comma or semicolon between addresses.

3. On the Subject line, briefly describe your message.

When others receive the message, they see what you type on the Subject line first. Notice how the New Message window changes names after you enter a subject.

4. Type your message in the bottom half of the New Message window.

You can use the buttons in the New Message window to format the message in various ways. For example, you can boldface or italicize parts of the message. And don't forget to press F7 or choose Tools⇨Spelling to spell-check your message.

If you get interrupted and want to resume writing the message later, choose File⇨Save (or press Ctrl+S) to place the message in the Drafts folder. You can return to it later by clicking the Drafts folder in the Folders pane and then double-clicking your message to open it.

5. Click the Send button (or choose File⇨Send Later to postpone sending the message).

Messages you postpone sending are kept in the Outbox folder. To edit or perhaps delete a message that you haven't sent yet, click the Outbox folder in the Folders pane on the left side of the screen, select the message, and click the Delete button to delete it or double-click to read and change it.

A copy of every message you send is kept in the Sent Items folder. However, if you prefer not to keep copies of sent messages on hand, choose Tools⇨ Options, select the Send tab in the Options dialog box, and deselect the Save Copy of Sent Messages in 'Sent Items' Folder check box.

Replying to and forwarding e-mail messages

Suppose you receive a message that deserves a reply. Rather than go to the trouble of addressing a reply, you can click the Reply button and simply enter your message. Outlook Express also offers a Reply All button for addressing messages to all parties who received copies of the original message, and a Forward button for forwarding a message to a third party.

After you click one of these buttons, the New Message window appears. Now you can enter your reply or, if you are dealing with a forwarded message, enter a few explanatory words. Address the message as you normally would with the To and Cc buttons, and click the Send button to reply, reply to all, or forward the message.

Sending a file along with a message

Yes, it can be done. You can send files along with e-mail messages by following these steps:

1. **Compose and address the message in the New Message window (refer to Figure 3-3).**

2. **Click the Attach button or choose Insert⇨File Attachment.**

   You see the Insert Attachment dialog box.

3. **Locate and select the file or files you want to send.**

   To select more than one file, hold down Ctrl and click each file that you want to select.

4. **Click the Attach button.**

   A new text box called Attach appears in the New Message window, and you see the names of the file or files you want to send.

5. **Click the Send button to send the e-mail message and its text attachments.**

   Later in this chapter, "Opening and saving files that were sent to you" explains what to do if a friend or enemy sends you a file.

Sending a picture along with a message

In order to view a picture inside an e-mail message, the recipient's e-mail software must be capable of displaying messages in HTML format (see "A Word about Mail-Sending Formats," later in this chapter). Take note of where on your computer the graphic file you want to send is located, and follow these steps to send your graphic inside of a message.

1. **Place the cursor in the New Message window where you want the graphic to go.**

2. **Choose Insert⇨Picture to open the Picture dialog box.**

If the Insert Picture command is grayed out, it isn't available because plain text is your default mail-sending format, and plain text doesn't permit pictures. You can fix this problem by choosing Format⇨Rich Text (HTML) before choosing Insert⇨Picture.

3. **Click the Browse button and, in the Picture dialog box, select the picture you want and click the Open button.**

4. **Choose an Alignment option in the Picture dialog box.**

5. **Click the OK button.**

If you change your mind about how to align a picture or you want to replace the picture with a different one, right-click the picture and choose Properties. You see the Picture dialog box, where you can choose a new picture or change alignments.

A Word about Mail-Sending Formats

Outlook Express offers two formats for sending e-mail messages: HTML and plain text. HTML is the same format that is used to display Web pages. If you intend to include pictures inside your e-mail messages or view pictures that others send you, you must opt for HTML format. HTML-formatted messages take longer to transmit, and some e-mail software doesn't accept them. In plain-text format, only numbers and letters are transmitted.

Follow these steps to choose a default mail-sending format:

1. **Choose Tools⇨Options.**

You see the Options dialog box.

2. **Select the Send tab.**

3. **Under Mail Sending Format, select the HTML or Plain Text option button.**

4. **Click the OK button.**

No matter which format you choose, you can send a particular e-mail message in the HTML or plain-text format. In the New Message window, choose Format⇨Rich Text (HTML) or Format⇨Plain Text.

Receiving and Reading Your E-Mail

As soon as you start Outlook Express, the program, like a loyal dog, fetches your e-mail. And the program fetches your e-mail every 15 minutes, although you can change that, as I explain shortly. No matter how much time has elapsed since you last got your e-mail, you can get it right away by clicking the Send/Recv button (or pressing Ctrl+M).

To merely send or receive your mail, click the down arrow beside the Send/Recv button and choose Receive All or Send All. To receive e-mail from one account if you have more than one, click the down arrow beside the Send/Recv button and choose the name of the account.

To tell Outlook Express how often to fetch your e-mail, choose Tools⇨ Options and, on the General tab of the Options dialog box, enter a number in the Minute(s) text box.

Reading your e-mail messages

If you've received mail, the Inbox folder name appears in boldface, the number of messages you've received appears in parentheses beside the Inbox folder name, and a tiny image of an envelope appears on the right side of the status bar.

Messages arrive in the Inbox folder, where you can read senders' names and the subject of each message, as shown in Figure 3-4. The bottom half of the window shows message text. Click a message to read it. By double-clicking, you can open a message in its own window and read it more easily.

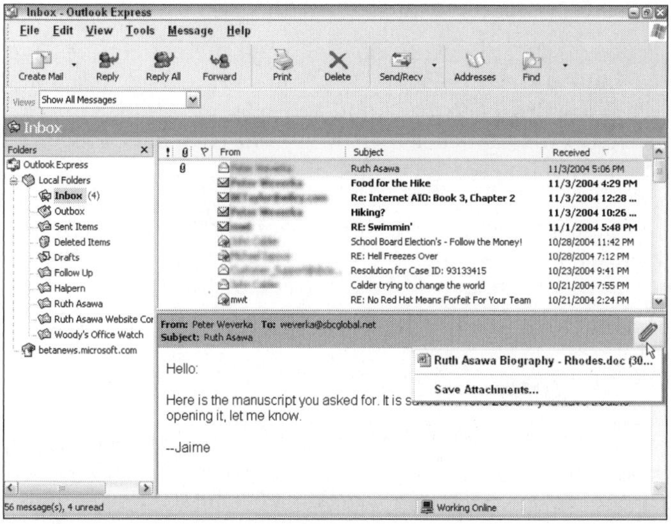

**Book III
Chapter 3**

**E-Mailing with
Outlook Express**

Figure 3-4:
E-mail messages in the Inbox folder. The selected message includes a file.

Observe these conventions of the Inbox folder window:

✦ An open envelope next to a message means that the message hasn't been read. Unread messages also appear in boldface text in the top half of the window. Next to unread messages is a closed envelope.

✦ A paper clip appears next to a message if a file was sent along with the message.

✦ You can click the From button or the Received button (located at the top of the From and Received columns) to arrange messages by name or by date.

To make text easier to read in the Outlook Express window, try this technique: Choose Tools⇨Options and click the Read tab in the Options dialog box. Then click the Fonts button, and in the Fonts dialog box, choose a font you find easy to read. You can also choose a Font Size option to make text larger or smaller.

Opening and saving files that were sent to you

When a file has been sent along with an e-mail message, a paper clip appears next to the message in the Inbox window. If you select the message, a somewhat larger paper clip appears on the stripe between the top and bottom half of the Inbox window. Click the large paper clip, and you can read the names of the files that were sent to you.

Follow these instructions to open or save files that were sent to you:

✦ **Opening a file:** Click the paper clip and then click the name of the file. The file opens on-screen. Choose File⇨Save As to save the file in a folder of your choice (refer to Figure 3-4).

✦ **Saving a file:** Click the paper clip and then select the Save Attachments command (refer to Figure 3-4). You see the Save Attachments dialog box. Click the Browse button, find and select the folder where you want to save the file, and click the OK button. Then click the Save button in the Save Attachments dialog box.

Be careful about opening files from people you don't know because the files may contain viruses. Book I, Chapter 4 explains how to prevent viruses from reaching your computer in e-mail attachments.

Deleting Messages

Unless the Smithsonian Institution wants you to storehouse your e-mail messages for posterity, you may as well delete them. Deleting a message is simply a matter of selecting the message and clicking the Delete button (or pressing

Ctrl+D). You can delete several message at once by Ctrl+clicking them before clicking the Delete button.

Messages you delete don't disappear forever. They land in the Deleted Items folder. Being able to reread a message you deleted is nice, of course, but the Deleted Items folder quickly gets crowded with old messages. To erase all the messages in the Deleted Items folder, right-click the folder and choose Empty 'Deleted Items' Folder on the shortcut menu.

Organizing Your E-Mail Messages

How do you keep track of all the e-mail you get? How do you make sure that every message that deserves a reply gets a reply? To help you stay on top of your e-mailing, Outlook Express offers a bunch of amenities:

✦ **Create a new folder and move messages into it.** Create a folder for storing e-mail that pertains to an important project you are working on and shunt messages into that folder. Or, create a folder for messages that need your urgent attention. The next two sections in this chapter explain how to create a new folder and how to move messages from folder to folder.

✦ **Create message rules so that messages are automatically put in a folder as they arrive.** Message rules save you the trouble of filing messages in the right folder. Messages from The Boss, for example, can all go automatically to the Boss folder. You can even delete messages as they arrive with a message rule. See "Creating message rules," later in this chapter.

✦ **Sort the messages.** By clicking the column heads in a folder window — From, Subject, Received, and so on — you can arrange the messages in different ways and find the one you are looking for.

✦ **Flag messages.** Flagged messages show a flag icon in the Flag column. Choose Message⇨Flag Message to flag a message and be reminded that it needs your attention.

✦ **Watch messages.** A "watched" message is shown in red text. The first time you watch a message, Outlook places the Watch/Ignore column in the folder window, and a pair of spectacles appears in that column next to watched messages. To watch a message, choose Message⇨Watch Conversation. Choose the command a second time to "unwatch" a message. If you decide that you don't want to see the Watch/Ignore column anymore, choose View⇨Columns and deselect the Watch/Ignore check box in the Columns dialog box.

✦ **Ignore messages from someone.** You don't have to bother with messages if they don't arrive, do you? To ignore all incoming messages from a particular address, select a message from the address in question and choose Message⇨Block Sender. To see a list of addresses you have blocked, choose Tools⊏>Message Rules⊏>Blocked Senders List. You see the Blocked Senders tab of the Message Rules dialog box. To remove an address from the list, select it and click the Remove button.

Chapter 5 of this minibook explains how to prevent spam junk mail from arriving in your Inbox.

Creating a new folder

For all I know, the handful of folders that Outlook Express gives you are more than adequate. But you may need a couple of extra folders. You may need one called "Urgent" for messages about a project you are working on. You may need another called "Procrastination" for messages that can be put off to another day. Follow these steps to create a new folder:

***1.* Choose File⊏>New⊏>Folder (or press Ctrl+Shift+E).**

You see the Create Folder dialog box shown in Figure 3-5.

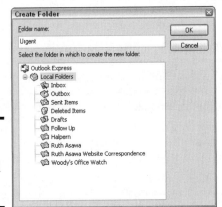

Figure 3-5:
Creating
and naming
a new
folder.

***2.* Enter a name for the folder in the Folder Name text box.**

***3.* In the Select the Folder box, select the folder that your new folder is to go inside of.**

For example, to create a folder on equal footing with Inbox, Outbox, and the other generic folders, choose Local Folders.

***4.* Click the OK button.**

To delete a folder you created, select it in the Folders pane (refer to Figure 3-1) and click the Delete button.

Moving items into different folders

Outlook Express offers two ways to move items into different folders. Select the items you want to move to a different folder and either drag them or move them elsewhere:

+ **Dragging to a different folder:** Drag the items into the Folder pane and drop them into the other folder.

+ **Moving to a different folder:** Choose Edit⇨Move to Folder (or press Ctrl+Shift+V). You see the Move dialog box. Select a folder name and click the OK button.

Creating message rules

A *message rule* tells Outlook Express how to handle a message when it arrives. Message rules can save you a lot of time. For example, the rule being created in Figure 3-6 tells Outlook Express to move incoming messages from a certain person to the Follow Up folder and then forward those messages to two different people. The rule accomplishes in a second what it would take about a minute to do.

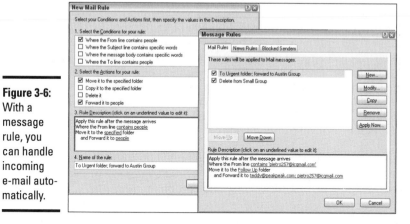

Figure 3-6: With a message rule, you can handle incoming e-mail automatically.

To create a message rule, start by choosing Tools⇨Message Rules⇨Mail. If this is the first time you have attempted to create a rule, you see the New Mail Rule dialog box (refer to Figure 3-6). If you have already created a rule, you see the Message Rules dialog box (refer to Figure 3-6). Click the New button to go to the New Mail Rule dialog box and create a rule.

In the Name of the Rule text box, enter a descriptive name for the rule, and then describe what you want Outlook Express to do to incoming e-mail messages:

+ **Select the Conditions:** Choose the option or options that help Outlook Express identify incoming e-mail.

+ **Select the Actions:** Choose options that describe what you want Outlook Express to do with the e-mail.

+ **Rule Description:** Click the links to open dialog boxes. For example, clicking the Contains People link opens the Select People dialog box so that you can enter an e-mail address. Clicking the Specified link opens the Move dialog box so that you can tell Outlook Express to which folder to move messages.

To refine a rule you already created or to delete a rule, choose Tools⇨Message Rules⇨Mail. In the Message Rules dialog box (refer to Figure 3-6), select a rule and click the Modify button to alter it, or click the Remove button to delete it.

Keeping the Addresses of Friends, Family, and Clients

Rather than enter the e-mail addresses of clients and friends over and over again when you send them e-mail, you can keep addresses in the Address Book. After an address is in the book, all you have to do to address an e-mail message is select a name from a list. Besides e-mail addresses, you can keep street addresses, phone numbers, fax numbers, and other stuff in the Address Book. The Address Book is a good place to store information about clients, coworkers, and friends. Following are instructions for entering a name in the Address Book, looking up a name, and changing the particulars about a person whose name you entered.

To very quickly enter in the Address Book the e-mail address of someone who has sent you e-mail, right-click the sender's message in the Inbox and choose Add Sender to Address Book on the shortcut menu.

Entering names and addresses

To enter a person's name, e-mail address, and other pertinent information in the Address Book, start by clicking the Addresses button or choosing Tools⇨Address Book. You see the Address Book window, as shown on the left side of Figure 3-7. Follow these steps to enter information about someone:

1. **Click the New button and then choose New Contact on the drop-down menu.**

You see the Properties dialog box shown in Figure 3-7.

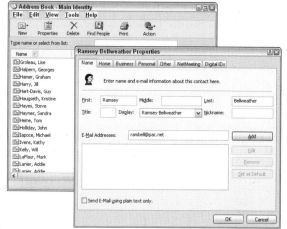

Figure 3-7:
Entering a
person in
the Address
Book.

2. Fill out the different tabs in the Properties dialog box.

On the Name tab, open the Display drop-down menu and choose how you want the name or business to appear in the Address Book. Names appear last name first, unless you choose a different option from the Display drop-down menu.

Also on the Name tab, enter the e-mail address in the E-Mail Addresses text box and click the Add button.

On the Other tab, describe the person and say why you entered him or her in the Address Book. Later, when you remove names from the book, you can go to the Other tab, find out who the person is, and determine whether he or she needs removing.

3. Click the OK button.

Looking up names and addresses

To look up a name and address, start by clicking the Addresses button to open the Address Book. In an Address Book with many names, try these techniques for finding a name if scrolling doesn't do the job:

✦ Enter the first couple of letters in the Type Name or Select from List text box. The list scrolls to the name you entered.

✦ Click the Name button (it's located at the top of the Name column — choose View➪Details if you don't see it). Click once to arrange last names in alphabetical order from Z to A, click again to arrange names by first name, and click again to arrange names by first name from Z to A.

✦ If worst comes to worst, click the Find People button, enter a name, choose Address Book from the Look In drop-down menu, and click the Find Now button in the Find People dialog box.

Losing an Address Book with many important names and addresses would be tragic. To back up the Address Book, go to the `C:\Documents and Settings\`*`Your Name`*`\Application Data\Microsoft\Address Book` folder and copy the Address Book file to a floppy disk. Outlook Express Address Books have the `.wab` extension. You can choose Help⇨About Address Book to open a dialog box that lists the folder where your Address Book is kept.

Chapter 4: Yahoo! and Other Web-Based E-Mail Services

In This Chapter

✔ Looking at the advantages of Web-based e-mail services

✔ Comparing the Web-based e-mail services

✔ Managing your e-mail with Yahoo! Mail

You could do worse than having an e-mail account with Yahoo! Mail. For one thing, the account is free. It doesn't cost you a red cent. And Yahoo! Mail is superior to many conventional e-mail programs when it comes to sending, receiving, and managing e-mail messages.

This chapter looks at the virtues of having a Web-based e-mail account. It compares different accounts, concludes that Yahoo! Mail is the best, and plunges into an exhaustive — and I do mean exhaustive — explanation of all the features of Yahoo! Mail.

Why Have a Free Web-Based E-Mail Account?

As I explain in Chapter 1 of this mini-book, a Web-based e-mail service is one in which e-mail is stored on an Internet computer, not someone's home or office computer. To compose, send, receive, and store e-mail, you use a Web browser, not an e-mail software program. Most Web-based e-mail service accounts are free.

I think everyone should have at least one account with a Web-based e-mail service. Here are the advantages of having one:

✦ **Convenience:** You can retrieve your mail when you are on vacation or a business trip. As long as you can connect to the Internet from your hotel, the local Internet café, or a public library, you can also get your e-mail. You don't need e-mailing software to do it. All you need is a Web browser.

✦ **Permanence:** No matter how many times you change jobs, locales, schools, or Internet service providers, your Web-based e-mail service remains available to you.

✦ **Anonymity:** Corresponding with others under the guise of your superhero or alter-ego persona is easier from a Web-based e-mail account than from a conventional account. After all, bills are sent to your name for having a conventional account. No such bills arrive for Web-based e-mail accounts. Nobody knows who you really are.

✦ **Spam defense:** Whenever you give your e-mail address to a business or merchant on the Internet, you run the risk of getting spam, the unsolicited e-mail advertisements that clog so many mailboxes. Rather than give out the primary e-mail address you use for daily correspondence, give out a secondary address you keep with a Web-based e-mail service. That way, all spam will be directed to an address you don't use often. You can abandon the Web-based e-mail address when it is overwhelmed by spam.

Looking at Some Web-Based E-Mail Services

Table 4-1 briefly describes some Web-based e-mail services. All the services in the table are free (although for a monthly fee, most of them offer extended services, such as more mailbox storage space). In the table, "Mailbox Storage Capacity" refers to how many megabytes' worth of e-mail and files can be kept in an account before the account overflows and the service starts deleting messages and files. "Free POP/IMAP Access" refers to whether the service permits you to download the e-mail you store on a conventional e-mail account into the account you keep with the service.

Table 4-1	Free Web-Based E-Mail Services		
Name	*Address*	*Mailbox Storage (MB) Capacity*	*Free POP/IMAP Access*
Care2 E-mail	www.care2.com	100	
Fastmail	www.fastmail.com	10	✔
GMail	http://gmail.google.com	1,000	
Hotmail	www.hotmail.com	2	
Lycos Mail	http://mail.lycos.com	5	
Mail.com	www.mail.com	10	
My Real Box	www.myrealbox.com	10	✔
My Way Mail	www.myway.com	6	✔
Yahoo! Mail	http://mail.yahoo.com	100	✔

Here are some questions to ponder in your quest for the perfect Web-based e-mail service:

✦ **Mailbox storage capacity:** How many megabytes' worth of files and e-mail messages can pile up in my e-mail account before the service starts deleting them automatically? Mailbox storage capacity is an issue if others frequently send you video files, sound files, and other large files. Table 4-1 lists the mailbox storage capacity of various Web-based e-mail services.

✦ **Attachment capacity:** How large can the files I send or receive be? Most services don't permit you to receive or send files larger than a certain amount of megabytes.

✦ **Unused account policy:** Under what conditions are accounts deactivated automatically? One reason I prefer Yahoo! Mail to Hotmail is that Hotmail deactivates an account if it goes unused for more than a month. Yahoo! Mail deactivates unused accounts after four months. Web-based e-mail services have to be mindful of unused accounts because they occupy valuable disk space on the computers where the services store e-mail and files. Find out how aggressive a service is about kicking out dabblers and dilettantes.

✦ **POP/IMAP access:** Does the Web-based service permit you to collect e-mail from a standard e-mail account? To put it another way, starting from your Web-based account, can you check for mail in your conventional account and bring that mail into your Web-based account? To perform this trick, the Web-based e-mail service must be able to get into the conventional account's POP3 or IMAP incoming mail server. In my experience, many services that claim they have POP/IMAP access don't really have it. Collecting mail from another e-mail account is easier said than done.

✦ **Virus-scanning of e-mail attachments:** Are the files that are sent along with e-mail messages scanned automatically for viruses?

✦ **Spam filters:** Does the service hunt for, detect, and quarantine junk mail automatically?

✦ **Advertisements:** How thick are the advertisements in the e-mail messages? You may well ask yourself, "These services are free, so how do they pay for themselves?" The answer is with advertisements. Some Web-based e-mail services are notorious for their advertising banners and graphics. Sometimes advertisements are attached to the bottom of e-mail messages. The heartfelt e-mail message to the one you love may well conclude with a plea to buy more disk space, and that's not very romantic, is it?

✦ **HTML format:** Does the service allow messages to be composed and received in HTML format? This format is slowly becoming the standard for e-mailing, but some services don't permit HTML messages. The HTML format makes it possible to format text and include pictures in the body of e-mail messages.

Visit the Web pages listed in Table 4-1 to find out the answers to these questions.

Handling Your E-Mail with Yahoo! Mail

Yahoo! Mail is my favorite Web-based e-mail service. The Yahoo! Mail window could stand fewer distracting advertisements, but the drop-down menus make it easy to find and give commands. I like the storage gauge, which shows how much disk space is left in my mailbox. You can send 10MB of file attachments with an e-mail message, which beats most of the other services. And, courtesy of Norton Antivirus, a program I use and respect very much, Yahoo! Mail runs antivirus software over incoming files to make sure they don't contain any viruses.

The remainder of this chapter explains how to handle e-mail at Yahoo! Mail. You discover (take a deep breath) how to check your mail, address and send an e-mail message, read your mail, send and receive files, organize messages into folders, collect mail sent to your conventional account through Yahoo! Mail, and keep an Address Book.

Sorry, but you need a Yahoo! membership before you can set up a Yahoo! Mail account. If you don't have a Yahoo! membership, go to Appendix A and follow the instructions to get one. If you already joined Yahoo! but didn't ask for an e-mail account, don't worry about it. Yahoo! sets up a mail account for you the first time you try to visit your Yahoo! mailbox.

Opening your Yahoo! mailbox

Your Yahoo! e-mail address consists of your Yahoo! ID, the at sign (@), and the domain name (yahoo.com):

YourYahooID@yahoo.com

For example, if your Yahoo! ID is Dave123, your Yahoo! Mail address is Dave123@yahoo.com.

Follow these steps to visit your Yahoo! mailbox and see if anyone sent you an e-mail message:

1. **In your browser, go to** www.yahoo.com.

You land at the Yahoo! home page.

2. **Click the Mail button or the Mail link.**

Both are located in the upper-right corner of the Yahoo! home page.

What happens next depends on whether you have signed into Yahoo!:

✦ **Signed into Yahoo!:** You land in the Yahoo! Mail window shown in Figure 4-1.

✦ **Not signed into Yahoo!:** You are asked to enter your Yahoo! ID and password, after which you see the Yahoo! Mail window shown in Figure 4-1.

Figure 4-1:
The Yahoo!
Mail
window
(pardon
the adver-
tisements).

The Yahoo! Mail window tells you how many unread messages await you.
More importantly, you can click folder names, click buttons, or open the Mail,
Addresses, Calendar, or Notepad menu to give a command. Click the Mail
menu name when you want to return to the Yahoo! Mail window.

You can bypass the Yahoo! home page and go straight to the Yahoo! Mail
window by going to this address: `http://mail.yahoo.com`. If ever an
address was a candidate for a bookmark, this is the one.

Finding your way around the Yahoo! Mail windows

The menus, buttons, and folder names in the Yahoo! windows are meant to
help you get from place to place in a hurry:

✦ **Menus:** Click the down arrow beside a menu name — Mail, Addresses,
   Calendar, or Notepad — to quickly undertake a task or go to a new
   window. You can also click a menu name to go directly to a new window.

✦ **Buttons:** The three buttons — Check Mail, Compose, and Search Mail —
   get you there in a hurry. Click the Check Mail button to go to your mailbox and read mail, the Compose button to write an e-mail message, or
   the Search Mail button to find a message.

✦ **Folder names:** Click a folder name to visit one of the folders where e-mail messages are stored — Inbox, Draft, Sent, and Trash. The Trash folder is where messages you have deleted go to die. Later in this chapter, "Organizing your mail in folders" explains how to create your own folders for storing e-mail.

You can also click the Back and Forward buttons in your browser to revisit various Yahoo! Mail windows.

Reading your e-mail

The Yahoo! Mail window (refer to Figure 4-1) tells you how many unread messages are in your Inbox. Try one of these techniques to go to your Inbox and read messages:

✦ Click the Check Mail button.

✦ Click the Inbox folder name.

✦ Open the Mail menu and choose Check Mail.

Figure 4-2 shows the Inbox window, where you can see who has sent you messages and the subject of the messages. To read a message, click its subject to open a message window like the one in Figure 4-3. In the message window, you can click the Previous or Next link to read the previous or next message you received without having to return to the Inbox window.

To make sure that you follow up messages, you can flag them. A small flag icon appears in the Inbox window on messages that need your attention. To flag a message, select it, click the Mark button, and choose Flag for Follow Up on the drop-down menu.

Figure 4-2:
The Inbox window with incoming messages.

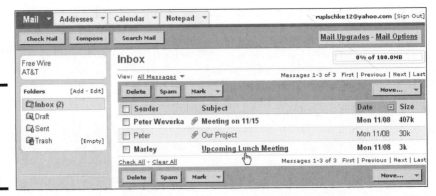

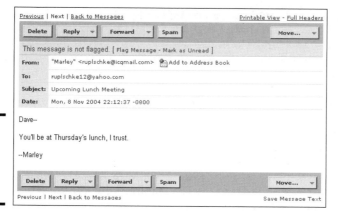

Figure 4-3:
A message
in the
message
window.

Composing (and replying to) e-mail messages

If you want to reply to an e-mail message, you've got it made. All you have to
do is click the Reply button in the e-mail message that was sent to you, and
Yahoo! addresses the e-mail message for you. Composing an original e-mail
message is somewhat different because you have to provide the address.

Follow these steps to compose a new message or to compose a reply to an
e-mail message:

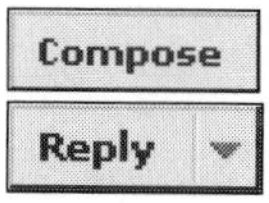

1. The Compose (or Reply) window appears, as shown in Figure 4-4. You
can also get to this window by choosing Mail⇨Compose.

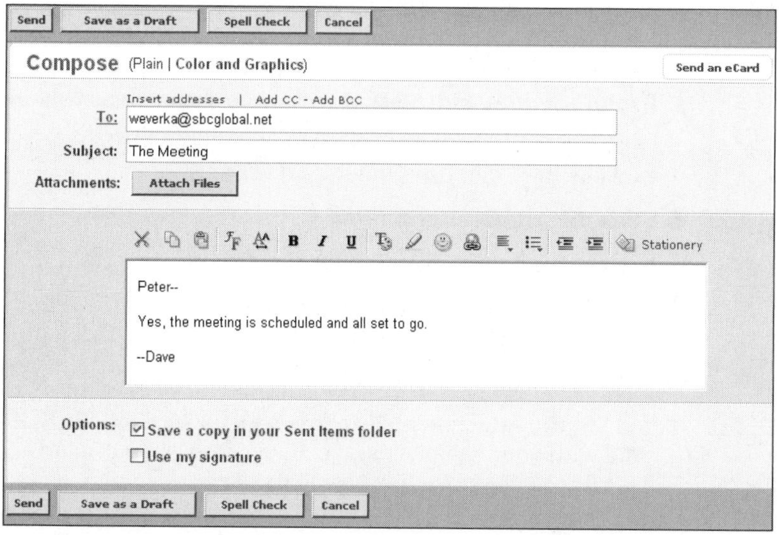

Figure 4-4:
Composing
and
addressing
an e-mail
message.

Book III
Chapter 4

Yahoo! and Other
Web-Based E-Mail
Services

2. **To enter an address (if one isn't entered already), either type the address in the To text box or click the To link and select an address from your Address Book.**

   Later in this chapter, "Keeping an Address Book" explains the Address Book.

   To send copies of your message, click the Add CC link, which places a new text box in the message window called CC for entering the addresses of people who are to receive message copies.

3. **Enter the message in the text box.**

   You can take advantage of the Bold, Align Text, and other buttons to format the text. Be sure to click the Spell Check button to check for misspellings in your message.

4. **Click the Send button to send your message.**

   The only way to postpone sending a message is to click the Save as a Draft button. Doing so places the message in the Drafts folder. When you want to send your message, open the Drafts folder, open your message, finish writing it, and click the Send button.

A copy of every message you send is kept in the Sent Items folder. If you prefer not to keep copies of messages, open the Sent Items folder and click the Turn Save Sent Items Off link.

Sending a file

In e-mail jargon, sending a file to someone is called *attaching* it. Yahoo! Mail permits you to send 10MB worth of file attachments. To attach a file to an e-mail message and send the file along with the message, follow these steps:

1. **Click the Compose button (or the Reply button), and in the Compose (or Reply) window, address and write your message as you normally do.**

   Earlier in this chapter, "Composing (and replying to) e-mail messages" explains the Compose (and Reply) window.

2. **Click the Attach Files button.**

   You see the Attach Files window.

3. **For each file that you want to send, click the Browse button, locate the file in the Choose File dialog box, and click the Open button.**

4. **Click the Attach Files button.**

   You see the Attachments window, which lists each file that you want to send with your e-mail message. If you change your mind about sending a file, click the Remove link beside its name.

Sending a "Sorry, I'm away" response

Suppose you go away on a business trip or vacation and Quentin Tarantino sends you an e-mail message. The world-famous director wants you to be in his next movie. Snubbing the director and missing your big chance at movie fame is, of course, unthinkable. To keep that from happening, you can tell Yahoo! Mail to automatically reply to all who send you e-mail while you're away. Yahoo! calls this kind of response a *vacation response*.

Follow these steps to compose a vacation response and tell Yahoo! Mail how long to keep sending it:

1. **Choose Mail⇨Options or click the Mail Options link to go to the Mail Options window.**

2. **Click the Vacation Response link (you may have to scroll down the window to find it).**

3. **In the Vacation Response window, write the response and declare how long to send it.**

4. **Click the Turn Auto-Response On button.**

If you change your mind about responding, return to the Vacation Response window and click the Turn Auto-Response Off button.

Vacation Response [Back to Mail Options]

Duration

Start Date: November ▾ 09 ▾ 2005 ▾ ▦
End Date: November ▾ 16 ▾ 2005 ▾ ▦

Generic Response

This response will be sent to all incoming mail that you receive during your vacation. You may enter up to 10 lines of text.

    Hello:

    I'm gone away to Madagascar, which means I can't reply
    to the message you sent me.

    But I'll reply as soon as I return from the Red Island.

    --Peter

☑ Send a sample copy of this message to my Inbox

---

5. **Click the Done button.**

You return to the Compose page. It lists the files that you want to send. If you change your mind about sending a file at this point, click the Remove link beside the filename.

Receiving a file that someone sent to you

You can tell when someone sent you a file because the file icon (a paper clip) appears beside the subject of the message in the Inbox. To handle the file, click the file icon or click the subject of the message and scroll to the bottom of the message window. Either way, you see the Attachment options shown in Figure 4-5. Your choices are three:

✦ **Scan and Download Attachment:** Scans the file with Norton AntiVirus software and presents the file in the Scan Results dialog box. Click the Download Attachment link. The File Download dialog box appears. Click the Open button to open the file; click the Save button to save it on your computer.

✦ **Scan and Save to My Yahoo! Briefcase:** Scans the file for viruses and saves it to your Yahoo! Briefcase, an online storage area that Yahoo! maintains. (The Briefcase isn't covered in this book, but you can explore it at `http://briefcase.yahoo.com`.)

✦ **View Attachment:** Opens the file so that you can view it right away. (This option works only with HTML files.)

Figure 4-5:
Handling a
file that was
sent to you.

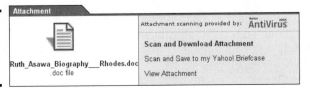

Notice the storage gauge in the upper-right corner of the Inbox. It tells you what percentage of the 10MB you are allotted for files has been used up. Keep an eye on the gauge, and if it climbs above 75 percent, start deleting e-mail messages with file attachments.

Organizing your mail in folders

If you're a poor soul who gets lots of e-mail, you owe it to yourself to create different folders for the e-mail you receive. Create a folder for each project, person, or pest you deal with. This way, you always know where to find e-mail messages. Here are instructions for creating folders and moving messages to other folders:

✦ **Creating a folder:** Choose Mail➪Folders to go to the Folders window. Then enter a name in the Name text box and click the Add Folder button. The Folders window is also the place to go to delete and rename folders.

✦ **Moving messages to a different folder:** Select check boxes to select the messages, and then click the Move button and choose a folder name from the drop-down menu, as shown in Figure 4-6.

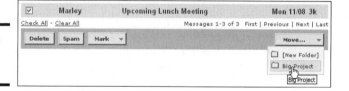

Figure 4-6:
Moving a
message.

You can get Yahoo! Mail's help in moving messages to folders. By *filtering,* you can tell Yahoo! Mail to move messages as they arrive into a certain folder. For example, you can move messages from a certain person or messages with certain words into a folder. This spares you the trouble of moving the messages yourself. Follow these steps to filter this way:

1. Choose Mail⇨Options or click the Mail Options link.

You land in the Mail Options window.

2. Click the Filters link.

You may have to scroll down the window to find this link. You go to the Filters window.

3. Click the Add button.

You see the Add Message Filter window, shown in Figure 4-7.

4. In the Filter Name text box, enter a descriptive name for the action of moving messages to a folder.

You may decide later on to click the Edit button in the Filters window to change the way this filter works. By writing a descriptive name, you know which filter you are dealing with.

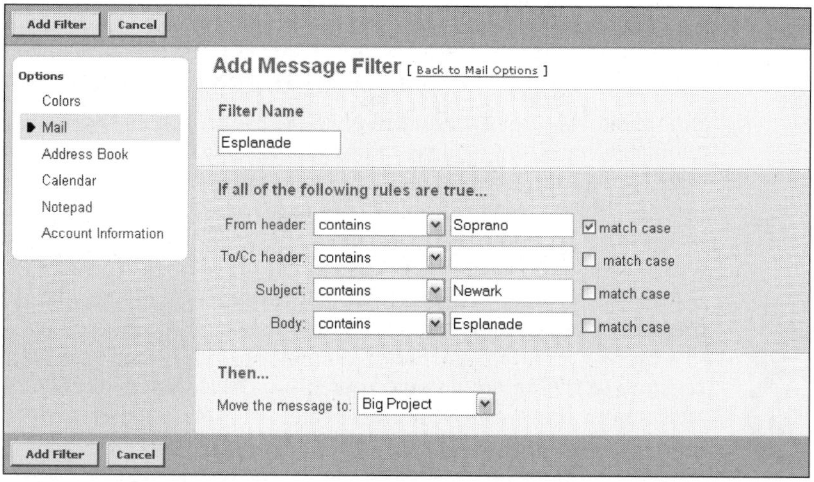

Figure 4-7:
Telling
Yahoo! Mail
to move a
message
automat-
ically into
a folder.

Add Filter	Cancel

Options

  Colors

▶ Mail

  Address Book

  Calendar

  Notepad

  Account Information

Add Message Filter [Back to Mail Options]

Filter Name

`Esplanade`

If all of the following rules are true...

From header:	contains ▾	Soprano	☑ match case
To/Cc header:	contains ▾		☐ match case
Subject:	contains ▾	Newark	☐ match case
Body:	contains ▾	Esplanade	☐ match case

Then...

Move the message to: `Big Project` ▾

Add Filter	Cancel

Bulking and blocking

Yahoo! Mail offers two ways to prevent unwanted e-mail from infesting your Inbox folder — blocking and bulking. *Blocking* means to delete messages from certain addresses automatically as they arrive. *Bulking* is when Yahoo! routes what it thinks is spam to a special folder called the Bulk folder. For the most part, Yahoo! is good about impounding the right messages in the Bulk folder, but Yahoo! is only human, and sometimes it makes mistakes. Messages remain in the Bulk folder for one month in case you want to examine them, and then they are deleted automatically. Follow these tips to get the most from bulking and blocking:

✔ **Bulking:** Periodically open the Bulk folder to see whether the messages stored there really qualify as spam. A real message may have slipped in unawares. To decide how long messages remain in the Bulk folder before they are deleted, click the Mail Options link and then the Spam Protection link in the Mail Options window. In the Spam Protection windows (you'll find three), tell Yahoo! Mail how long to impound spam and whether to block all messages from addresses that have sent you spam.

✔ **Blocking:** To block all mail from a certain Web address, click the Mail Options link and then the Block Addresses link in the Mail Options window. In the Block Addresses window, enter the address to block and click the Add Block button.

5. **Use the Rule drop-down menus and text boxes to describe the messages you want to move.**

6. **Choose a folder from the Move the Message To drop-down menu.**

7. **Click the Add Filter button.**

   You return to the Filters window. If a rule isn't doing its job right, revisit this window, select the rule, click the Edit button, and change the rule till it works right.

Collecting your mail from a conventional mail service

Yahoo! Mail is one of a handful of Web-based e-mail services that permit you to collect mail from a conventional e-mail account. Yahoo! Mail goes into your conventional service's POP incoming mail server, scoops up the mail, and brings it to your Yahoo! Mail Inbox. To perform this bit of wizardry, however, you must know the name of your conventional service's incoming mail server (you can't collect your e-mail if your service runs an IMAP or POP3, not a POP, server). You must also know the password for getting into your conventional e-mail account.

To find out the name of your conventional e-mail service's POP incoming mail server, open your standard e-mail program and get it there:

✦ **Outlook Express:** Choose Tools⇨Accounts, select the account name on the Mail tab of the Internet Accounts dialog box, click the Properties button, and read the server name on the Servers tab of the Properties dialog box.

✦ **Outlook 2003:** Choose Tools⇨E-Mail Accounts, select the View or Change Existing E-Mail Accounts option button in the dialog box that appears, and click the Next button. Then select the name of your account and click the Change button. The next dialog box lists service information, including the name of your incoming POP mail server. Be sure to click the Cancel button to get out of this dialog box.

Follow these steps to set up Yahoo! Mail to collect mail from your conventional e-mail account:

1. **Choose Mail⇨Options or click the Mail Options link.**

You go to the Mail Options window.

2. **Click the Mail Accounts link.**

You land in the Mail Accounts window. This window lists each account that is connected to your Yahoo! Mail account.

3. **Click the Add button.**

The first of several Add Account windows appears.

4. **Enter an account name and click the Continue button.**

The name you enter will appear in the Mail Accounts window when you are finished adding this account.

5. **Enter your POP mail server name, your username, and your password.**

The username is the part of your e-mail address that appears to the left of the at sign (@). Notice the Indicator options buttons. If you so choose, you can color-code incoming mail sent to you through this account by selecting a color.

6. **Click the Setup Mail Server button.**

If all goes well, the account is added to the list of accounts you can manage in Yahoo! Mail.

To see whether mail has arrived at your conventional account, click the Check Other Mail link in the Inbox window.

Keeping an Address Book

The Yahoo! Mail Address Book is a pretty good place to keep the addresses of friends, family members, and coworkers. And keeping addresses on hand in Yahoo! Mail makes it easier to address e-mail messages. Instead of entering an address by hand, you can click the To link in the Compose window, select a name in the Address Book, and click the Insert Checked Contacts button.

To open the Address Book:

1. **Click the Addresses menu name.**

2. **Choose Addresses⇨View Contacts.**

As shown in Figure 4-8, you can enter an addressee's name and other information either by filling out the Quick Add Contact form at the bottom of the window or by clicking the Add Contact button at the top of the window and entering detailed information in the Add Contact window.

To quickly enter the address of someone who sent you an e-mail message in the Address Book, click the Add to Address Book link in the message window. The Add to Address Book window opens so you can describe the sender in detail.

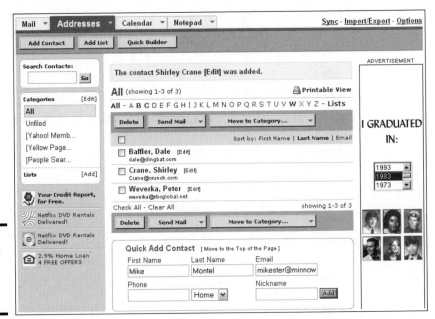

Figure 4-8:
The Yahoo!
Mail
Address
Book.

Chapter 5: Only You Can Prevent Spam

In This Chapter

✔ **Seeing the spammers' side**

✔ **Understanding how spammers get your e-mail address**

✔ **Taking preventative measures against spam**

✔ **Using spam-filtering software**

Smokey the Bear's "Only You Can Prevent Forest Fires" campaign was a great success. In fact, it succeeded too well, and the Forest Service had to retire the bear. It turns out a wildfire now and then is actually good for the ecology. I would like to propose a campaign against spam modeled after Smokey the Bear's campaign: Only you can prevent spam. *Spam* is unsolicited advertising junk e-mail. If you've been on the Internet for any length of time trading e-mail messages, you have very likely received unwanted spam in your mail box. By some estimates, 80 percent of e-mail sent on the Internet is spam. Software manufacturers have come to the rescue of people whose mailboxes are clogged with spam, and some of their programs work some of the time, but realistically, the only way to prevent spam from landing in your mailbox is to observe some simple preventative rules and remain vigilant. You have to rely on yourself to prevent spam. Only you can prevent it.

This chapter explains who the spammers are and how they obtain e-mail addresses. It lays out strategies for preventing spam. And it describes some software programs for dealing with e-mail accounts that are clotted with spam.

SPAM ("spicy ham"), of course, is a luncheon meat. Supposedly, junk e-mail was given the name "spam" (in lowercase letters) thanks to Monty Python's Flying Circus, the English comedy troupe, which used to perform a sketch with men dressed as Vikings singing a song called *The Spam Song* in a crowed café. The song's lyrics consist of only three words: *spam, lovely,* and *wonderful,* with *spam* being repeated many times over during the song. Spam is e-mail that gets delivered many times over to great annoyance — much like the word *spam* in the song. To hear *The Spam Song,* go to this Web page and click the Spam Song link at the bottom of the page:

www.mailmsg.com/SPAM_python.htm

Looking at It from the Spammer's Point of View

Look at it from the spammer's point of view: Spamming is good for business. For the cost of a computer, an Internet connection, an address list, and some software, you can send 100,000 e-mail advertisements like the ones shown in Figure 5-1. Sending the e-mail doesn't cost anything. Even if your modem is slow, it takes only an hour or two to send the messages. And if only 10 people (0.01 percent) reply and purchase whatever it is you're selling, you have recouped your costs, because the cost of sending the 100,000 messages is so low.

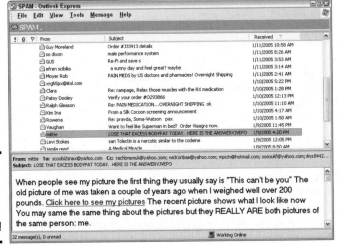

Figure 5-1:
Spam
messages,
every last
one of them!

On January 1, 2004, the CAN-SPAM (Controlling the Assault of Non-Solicited Pornography and Marketing Act) act went into effect in the United States. This act requires unsolicited e-mail messages to be labeled, include the sender's physical (not e-mail) address, and include opt-out instructions so the person who received the e-mail can request not to be sent any more e-mail. The act also prohibits anyone from misleading others by putting a false return address on an e-mail message. However, the CAN-SPAM act hasn't decreased the amount of spam. Spammers have simply picked up shop and moved outside the United States or routed their messages so they can't be traced. The majority of spam is now sent from China. The messages are routed through several computers before they reach the United States.

As long as people reply to spam messages and purchase items they learned about from spam messages, spam will remain with us. Spam is too easy to send and too easy to profit from.

Spamware

You've heard of software, of course. If you read Book I, Chapter 4, you know about *spyware* (software designed to track your doings on the Internet) and *adware* (software designed to make advertisements appear in your Web browser). Here's another "-ware" for you: *spamware*. Spammers use spamware programs to send spam e-mail messages. Spamware services and programs can do these tasks:

✔ Send e-mail messages in bulk, and send them in such a way that spam-filtering programs don't recognize them as spam.

✔ Locate and collect e-mail addresses from Web sites, message boards, and newsgroups. There is even a name for this variety of spamware — *harvestware*.

✔ Provide a false sender name and address in e-mail messages to make the messages look legitimate. This is called *e-mail spoofing*.

✔ Disguise the sender's Internet service provider in spam messages so that the sender doesn't get in trouble for sending spam.

✔ Provide relay stations called *zombie PCs* that forward spam messages through many different computers before they are delivered. These zombie PCs make it harder to trace where spam messages originate.

Sending e-mail messages in bulk isn't necessarily spamming. A company that sends the same e-mail message to its customers, clients, or subscribers is not spamming, but bulk e-mailing. In a bulk e-mailing, the senders make no attempt to hide their names or addresses, and all the recipients voluntarily submitted their addresses to the sender. In a spam mailing, senders usually hide their identities, and the addresses were obtained secondhand either by purchasing them or by collecting them on the Internet from the unwitting.

You can find companies that sell spamware and spamware services on the Internet. But don't look with the keyword "spamware." Search for "bulk e-mail service resources" or "bulk e-mail marketing." Bulk e-mailing companies all claim that they send only non-spam. Some of these companies are telling the truth; some are not.

How Spammers Obtain E-Mail Addresses

Spammers can't send spam unless they have e-mail addresses and lots of them. They obtain addresses in different ways. Knowing how spammers get e-mail addresses can help you keep your address from falling into their clutches. Here are the ways that spammers acquire addresses:

✦ **Purchasing e-mail address lists:** These lists are for sale on the Internet. Try searching for "bulk e-mail list" to see what I mean. The people who sell the lists claim that the addresses are "opt-in," meaning that addressees opted, or chose, to make their e-mail addresses available to others. If you ever signed up for something on the Internet and checked the box that said, "I agree to receive offers and opportunities via e-mail from our advertisers," your address is on at least one spam address list.

✦ **Running spamware:** *Spamware* is software designed to assist spammers. Some kinds of spamware can gather addresses from Web sites, news-groups, and message boards. This software looks for the at symbol (@) on Web pages, copies the words on either side of the at symbol, and in so doing collects e-mail addresses.

✦ **Collecting addresses on the Internet:** Some Web sites are actually traps meant to collect e-mail addresses. If you voted for something online, entered a contest or sweepstakes, or took a quiz that required entering your e-mail address, you made your address available to spammers.

Some spammers get addresses by using a dictionary attack rather than an e-mail address list. A *dictionary attack* is a technique for detecting "live" e-mail addresses. In a dictionary attack, names and randomly generated numbers are combined with `msn.com`, `compuserve.com`, or another e-mail domain name to form e-mail addresses, and the addresses are sent a test message. For example, suppose the e-mail domain target of the attack is named `funnyfreemail.com`. Using names and random numbers, a test message is sent to these and hundreds of thousands of other addresses:

```
pat@funnyfreemail.com
pat1@funnyfreemail.com
pat21@funnyfreemail.com
paul@funnyfreemail.com
paul1@funnyfreemail.com
paul21@funnyfreemail.com
peter@funnyfreemail.com
peter1@funnyfreemail.com
peter21@funnyfreemail.com
```

If the test message is returned as undeliverable — if it *bounces,* to use e-mail terminology — the address is discarded. But if the test message is delivered, the address is known to be "live." Spam messages are then sent to all live addresses at the e-mail domain.

Preventative Medicine for Spam

As the saying goes, an ounce of prevention is worth a pound of cure. I'm sorry to say it, but the only way to realistically prevent spam from coming to your mailbox is to take preventative measures. Later in this chapter, "Looking at Spam-Filtering Software" describes software programs for blocking and filtering spam, but you don't need those programs if you take preventative measures in the first place to keep the spammers from finding you. These pages explain rules you can follow to keep spammers at bay. You also find out an e-mail strategy for making sure the e-mail address you care about is clean of spam.

Rules for preventing spam from reaching your mailbox

By following the simple rules I describe here, you can keep spammers from discovering your e-mail address and prevent spam from arriving in your mailbox. These rules are easy to follow. All you have to do is remember them and stick to them.

Don't reply to spam

Don't reply to spam messages under any circumstances. By replying, all you do is alert the spammer to the fact that your e-mail address is legitimate, and that makes you a target of even more spam. And don't write a reply complaining about being sent spam. Spam messages are sent by computers. Nobody will read your complaint.

Don't "unsubscribe" to spam messages

Some spam messages contain an Unsubscribe link that you can click to prevent more messages from coming. In a survey conducted in 2003 by Yahoo!, 48 percent of e-mail users believed you can stop spam by clicking Unsubscribe links. But the links are a rouse. All you do by clicking them is make spammers aware that your e-mail address is live and therefore worth targeting with more spam.

Don't buy anything advertised by spam

Even if the spam message is selling what looks to be a terrific bargain, resist the temptation. By buying, you expose yourself to all the risks of replying to spam. Your address is known to be live. As such, it becomes a target for spammers. What's more, most of the items offered by spammers are illegal or fraudulent. And if the products don't work or aren't what they say they are, what recourse do you have? You can't complain or call the police. And here's another thing: If you pay for the item with a credit card, how good do you feel about giving your credit card number to a Web site associated with spammers? Me, I'd feel kind of queasy. Some spam operations are run by organized crime cartels.

Don't be fooled by sneaky spam

Spammers are very good about disguising spam. They have to be because spam-filtering software is good at recognizing it. When certain words — *sale, free, bargain,* and others — appear in the subject line of messages or in the messages themselves, the messages are flagged automatically as spam. To get around this obstacle, spammers sometimes write business-like message headings to trick you into opening messages: "This Needs Your Attention," "Urgent and Confidential," "Meeting Agenda." Some message headings play on the fact that many people order items online: "Your Order #31334," "Confirmation of Purchase."

To get around the problem of words marking an e-mail message as spam, spammers put spaces or underscores between the letters in suspect words. For example, *Viagra* is spelled V_I_A_G_R_A in spam messages. Sometimes the spammer inserts a punctuation symbol in the middle of a word to beat the spam-filtering software: V*IAGRA. Underscores, blank spaces, and misplaced punctuation marks are a sure sign of spam.

Spoofing a return address isn't hard to do. Just because the return address lists the name of a well-known institution, don't assume the e-mail was sent from there.

Be careful where (and how) you post your e-mail address

Spammers gather e-mail addresses from the Internet. They get the addresses from Web pages, newsgroups, chat rooms, and message boards. Harvestware, a variety of spamware, can scour the Internet for the tell-tale at symbol (@) found in e-mail addresses and copy those addresses back to a spammer's computer.

Sometimes you have to post your e-mail address on the Internet. To get around the problem of posting your address without it being discovered by spammers, try one of these techniques:

+ Create a graphic with your address and post the graphic. Spamware can't read letters and numbers in a graphic, but people can.

+ Put blank spaces between the letters. Others will be able to read and understand your e-mail address, but spamware won't be able to make heads or tails of it. For example, the e-mail address johndoe@earthlink.net would look like this (some might even find the address easier to read this way):

    `j o h n d o e @ e a r t h l i n k . n e t`

+ Spell out your address. Again, others will be able to read it, but computers won't understand it.

    `johndoe at earthlink dot net`

+ Include the words "no spam" in your address. Others will know to remove these words when they enter your e-mail address, but computers won't have a clue what's going on.

    `johndoeNOSPAM@earthlink.net`

Don't choose an address that's subject to dictionary attacks

A *dictionary attack* is a technique spammers use to generate e-mail addresses. To generate them, common names are randomly assigned number combinations and then joined to a domain name. To keep your e-mail address from being subjected to dictionary attacks, choose an uncommon name for your address. Use your last name, for example, if it isn't common. If your is a common last name, consider using a different name in your e-mail address.

Don't display images in e-mail messages

HTML-formatted e-mail messages can contain images. Sometimes, to keep a message from being too large, images are not sent inside an e-mail message. Instead, the e-mail message includes instructions to get the images from a Web server on the Internet. This is precisely what happens when you view a Web page in a Web browser. Instructions on the Web page tell your Web browser to get image files from a Web server and display the images. In an e-mail message, likewise, instructions inside the message get the images from a Web server and display the images in the message window.

The problem with retrieving images this way, however, is that the retrieval notice signals the Web server that you have opened the message. Spammers can use this signal — it's called a *Web beacon* — to detect a live e-mail address. By including Web-beacon images in e-mail messages, spammers receive signals indicating that e-mail addresses are legitimate and good targets for spam.

To prevent your e-mail address from being discovered this way, turn off images in your e-mail program, as shown on the left side of Figure 5-2. When someone you trust sends a message with an image, you can temporarily enable images again, as shown on the right side of Figure 5-2. Follow these instructions in Outlook and Outlook Express to turn off images in e-mail messages:

Outlook:

1. **Choose Tools⇨Options.**

2. **On the Security tab of the Options dialog box, click the Change Automatic Download Settings button.**

You see the Automatic Pictures Download Settings dialog box.

3. **Deselect the Don't Download Pictures or Other Content Automatically in HTML E-Mail check box.**

To view images in a message whose sender you trust, open the message and choose Format⇨Send Pictures from the Internet.

Outlook Express:

1. **Choose Tools⇨Options.**

2. **On the Security tab of the Options dialog box, select the Block Images and Other External Content in HTML E-Mail check box.**

To view images in a message whose sender you trust, open the message and choose View➪Blocked Images (see Figure 5-2).

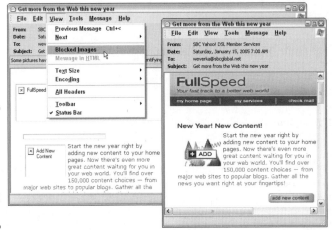

Figure 5-2:
Turning off images in e-mail messages protects you from spam.

The secondary e-mail address strategy for preventing spam

The surest way to prevent spam is to reconsider how you use e-mail. Most people keep one e-mail account. Or at best they keep two, one at home and one at work. To prevent spam, your first and foremost task is to create a secondary e-mail account with an e-mail address that you can give to people and companies who are suspect.

When you subscribe to some Web sites and services on the Internet, you are asked to provide an e-mail address. Online stores ask you for an e-mail address when shop with them. Message boards and newsgroups require an e-mail address when you sign up with them. The more often you give out an e-mail address, the more likely the address is to receive spam. But if you give the address of a secondary e-mail account you don't care very much about, it doesn't matter whether the account is flooded with spam, because the account doesn't matter much to you anyway.

Create a secondary e-mail account and give its e-mail address to businesses and merchants on the Internet who might sell your address to spammers or might themselves be spammers. The Internet offers many places to create free Web-based e-mail accounts. (See Chapter 4 of this mini-book for a list of such places.) Create one, two, or three extra e-mail accounts. When a Web site asks you to register with your e-mail address, give the address of a secondary account. Eventually, your secondary account will become the target of many dozen spammers. It will fill with spam, like the e-mail account shown in Figure 5-3. When that happens, abandon your account and don't look back. Eventually, the Web-based e-mail service where you keep the account will cancel the account after you cease using it.

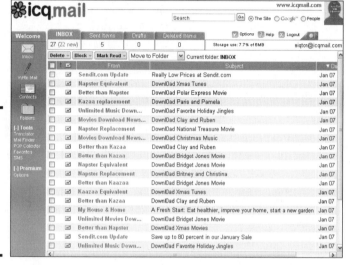

Figure 5-3:
A spam-choked e-mail account. This one is almost due to be abandoned.

Use your primary e-mail accounts for correspondence from friends, family, and business associates. Give these accounts' e-mail addresses only to people you know and want to hear from. As part of your strategy for preventing spam, primary e-mail account addresses are sacrosanct! Do not give them to any business or merchant because they, in turn, might give them to a spammer.

The Cheat Sheet on the inside front cover of this book has places for entering e-mail addresses and passwords. If writing down the addresses and passwords of secondary e-mail accounts will help you remember their addresses and passwords, write them on the Cheat Sheet. It really doesn't matter if anyone besides you accesses these accounts. They are there only as repositories for spam.

Looking at Spam-Filtering Software

Most e-mailing programs have commands for filtering (or blocking) spam as it arrives. You can block all e-mail messages from particular addresses. You can filter out all e-mail messages with certain words. The problem with these commands is that spammers have figured out how to thwart them. No self-respecting spammer sends e-mail messages twice from the same e-mail address. The commands in your e-mail program for blocking spam from a

**Book III
Chapter 5**

**Only You Can
Prevent Spam**

particular address are meaningless. No self-respecting spammer includes words in his or her e-mail messages that are likely to be flagged and filtered out. Spammers simply put blank spaces or punctuation marks in the middle of words to keep their spam messages from being flagged. Consider the spam message shown in Figure 5-4. I can read what it says, but the spam-blocking mechanism in my e-mail program can't read it the same way that I can, so the spam blocker let the message through.

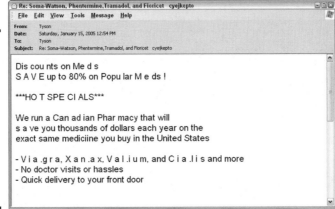

Figure 5-4: Spammers sprinkle blank spaces and punctuation marks in messages to evade filtering software.

Content-filtering spam software has become obsolete. Merely recognizing and blocking e-mail messages from different addresses isn't enough. Filtering out messages that contain certain words doesn't do the job either. In light of these failures, two kinds of spam-filtering software have emerged to battle spam: Bayesian filtering software and challenge-response software. Table 5-1 describes leading Bayesian and challenge-response spam-filtering programs. You can download these programs at Cnet (`www.cnet.com`). The pages that follow explain how this software works.

Table 5-1	**Spam-Filtering Software**	
Program	*Notes*	*Cost*
Bayesian Filtering Software		
602LAN Suite		
`www.software602.com`	Also an antivirus program and firewall.	Free
Outclass		
`www.vargonsoft.com`	An Outlook plug-in that makes POPFile available to Outlook users.	Free

Program	Notes	Cost
PocoMail		
`www.pocosystems.com`	An e-mail program as well as a filtering software.	$40
POPFile		
`http://popfile.sourceforge.net`	Very configurable program.	Free
SpamBayes		
`http://spambayes.sourceforge.net`	From the makers of POPFile; designed for Outlook.	Free
Challenge-Response Filtering Software		
ChoiceMail Free		
`www.digiportal.com`	Includes content-filtering.	Free
UseBestMail		
`www.usebestmail.com`	Works with Eudora, Netscape, Outlook, Outlook Express, and Pegasus.	$30

Bayesian filtering software

Bayesian filtering software uses statistical analysis methods to identify spam messages. The software is supposed to customize itself for each person who uses it. After you install the software, you subject it to a hundred or more e-mail messages and tell it which messages are spam. On the basis of these test messages, the software builds a statistical model for what spam arriving in your mailbox is. Then it filters out spam using this model as a guide.

The problem with Bayesian filtering software is that you have to continuously tinker with the statistical model to keep it up to date. And Bayesian software shares a problem with content-filtering software: A legitimate message could be mistaken for spam and be sent to the Spam folder. Bayesian and content-filtering spam software programs give you the opportunity to examine the Spam folder to make sure a real e-mail message didn't get put there by accident. But the purpose of spam-filtering software is to save yourself the trouble of examining e-mail for spam. In my judgment, Bayesian filtering software isn't worth the trouble. Tinkering with the statistical model and examining spam messages takes too much time and effort. After all, how long does it take to just delete spam messages when you see them in your mailbox? If it takes less time to do that than fiddle with Bayesian software, what's the point of running Bayesian software?

Challenge-response software

Challenge-response spam-filtering software is the way to go if you receive hundreds or thousands of spam messages daily and you can't abandon your e-mail address. This software blocks all spam. The software works like this:

**Book III
Chapter 5**

**Only You Can
Prevent Spam**

Have you considered ditching your e-mail address?

Rather than use spam-filtering software, why not abandon your e-mail address, get a new one, and start all over? Any Internet service provider worthy of the name will give you a new address. If your current e-mail address is the lifeblood of your business, abandoning it might be out of the question, but if you can get by with a new address, I suggest abandoning the current one.

I've abandoned a couple primary e-mail addresses in my day, and I discovered an unsuspecting benefit of abandoning e-mail addresses: It's a good opportunity to reconnect with people. Before you abandon your address, you send a message to everyone in your Address Book

explaining that you have a new e-mail address. Some of these messages go out to people who haven't heard from you in years. Think of it as a chance to revive old friendships and renew business contacts.

E-mail programs make it easy to send the same message to everyone in your Address Book, Contact List, or whatever your e-mail program calls its list of addresses. And that brings up an ethical question: If you send the same message to all your contacts to inform them of your new e-mail address, are you, in effect, spamming them? Are you sending spam to stay a step ahead of the spammers? I leave these ethical questions to people more erudite than I.

When someone sends you an e-mail message, the software immediately sends a reply message (the challenge) asking the sender to please send the message again but with a code word this time. If the message along with the code word is sent a second time (the response), the software accepts the e-mail message and places the sender's name on a list of addresses from which e-mail is accepted. The sender can now send messages without receiving a challenge. The premise of challenge-response spam-filtering is that spammers never meet the challenge. They never respond to challenge messages, much less include the right code word in their responses.

Ironically, challenge messages sent by challenge-response spam-filtering software have been confused for spam. In November 2004, spam filters at AOL and Earthlink blocked challenge messages sent by Mailblocks, a Web-based e-mail service. The messages were mistakenly quarantined in Spam folders. I doubt that this kind of thing happens very often, but it's something to think about.

If you use challenge-response filtering, make sure that the challenge e-mail message you send explains why you use the software. Be sure to tell your friends and co-workers that they have to reply to the challenge message only once. No doubt they receive spam, too. They will probably be delighted to help you in the heroic twilight struggle against spam.

Book IV

Quick Communicating

The 5th Wave
By Rich Tennant

"TELL THE BOSS HE'S GOT MORE FLAME MAIL FROM YOU-KNOW-WHO."

Contents at a Glance

Chapter 1: Instant Messaging

In This Chapter

✓ **Getting acquainted with instant messaging**

✓ **Maintaining your privacy**

✓ **Messaging with AOL Instant Messenger**

✓ **Exchanging messages with MSN Messenger**

✓ **Trading messages with Yahoo! Messenger**

✓ **Seeking others with ICQ**

*I*f you have teenage children, you probably already know what instant messaging is. *Instant messaging* (IM) is something between chatting online and exchanging e-mail messages. What makes instant messaging so popular with teenagers and others is being able to know which of your friends are online at the same time as you and being able to communicate with all of them at once. Instant messaging gives you the opportunity to have an instant online party — or in a business setting, an instant online meeting.

Instant-messaging programs all have a version of the contact list, which is a list that shows the names of your friends who are online. As soon as the name of someone with whom you want to gossip appears on the list, well, the dirt gets dished and the party starts flowing. This chapter looks at the four most popular instant-messaging programs: AOL Instant Messenger, MSN Messenger, Yahoo! Messenger, and ICQ.

Introducing Instant Messaging

Besides an Internet connection, you need an account with an instant-messaging service to trade instant messages. To help you choose an instant-messaging service, Table 1-1 compares them, although there isn't very much to compare. The instant messengers are quite similar. If anyone ever needed proof that the Internet is crowded with copycats, instant messaging is it. All the services are free. Each has a variation of the contact list, a list of people with whom you care to stay in touch. When a friend from your list comes online, the instant-messaging service alerts you, and you can start trading instant messages with your friend. All the messengers give you the opportunity to engage in multiparty messaging, that is, communicating with more than one person at a time. All messengers want you to submit a personal profile in which you describe your interests and give your address, phone number, gender, and other private information (I don't recommend doing it). For the sake of privacy, you can ignore people of your choice or fly under the radar so that your friends don't know you're online.

Table 1-1	Instant Messengers	
Messenger	*Description*	*Web Address*
AOL Instant Messenger	The most popular messenger, with several million members, most in English-speaking countries.	www.aim.com
ICQ	The original instant messenger that's still very popular outside the United States. ICQ is loaded down with all kinds of features that make it unwieldy and hard to use.	www.icq.com
MSN Messenger	Microsoft's offering, not to be confused with Windows Messenger, the Windows XP component.	http://messenger.msn.com
Trillian	An all-in-one service for people who use more than one instant messenger. With this software, you can trade messages simultaneously with people who run AOL Instant Messenger, MSN Messenger, and Yahoo! Messenger.	www.cerulean studios.com
Yahoo! Messenger	Well integrated with Yahoo!'s other services. You can use your Yahoo! Mail ID and password to log on to this instant messenger.	http://messenger.yahoo.com

You'll be glad to know that instant messengers are so popular in part because they are very easy to learn and use. They differ only insofar as the number of extras they offer. For example, devotees of ICQ, MSN Messenger, and Yahoo! Messenger can exchange SMS (short messaging services) messages on their cell phones. Some of the services offer audio and video chatting. Some permit you to trade files as well as instant messages.

The BigBlueBall (so named because that's what the earth looks like from afar) offers tips, forums, and old-fashioned advice for using the different instant-messaging services. You can also download the software for running the services at this Web site. Its address is www.bigblueball.com.

Knowing How to Preserve Your Privacy

No matter which instant messenger you choose, you need to know how to preserve your privacy while you instant-message. Instant messengers pose something of a problem because they alert others when you are online and they invite all kinds of people into your computer. But sometimes, like the film star Greta Garbo, you *vant* to be alone. You want to get the benefits of instant messaging without every Tom, Dick, and Harry knowing that you are online and sitting at your computer. Here are some tasks worth knowing if you are to preserve your privacy as you instant-message (I explain shortly how to complete these tasks in the different messengers):

✦ **Make yourself invisible:** When you run an instant-messaging program, all who have your name on their contact list know that you are at your computer. They know that unless you make yourself invisible. All the messengers have commands for being invisible so that others don't know you're online.

✦ **Ignore somebody:** Is somebody pestering you? All the messengers have commands for ignoring pests so that their attempts to bother you come to nothing.

✦ **Control whether the program starts when you start your computer:** Most messengers want to run every moment that your computer is running. When you start your computer, they start running, too. But starting a program automatically this way puts a burden on your computer and makes it slower to start. Be sure to take the bull by the horns and decide when the instant messenger starts and stops.

✦ **Change your profile:** Your profile is the personal information that you make available to others who use the instant messenger. All the messengers would like you to submit your name, address, gender, and phone number, but submitting that information is unwise. Your privacy is at stake. Identity thieves, stalkers, and spammers scour instant-messenger profiles for unwitting victims. Make sure that your profile reveals only what you want it to reveal.

By the way, Greta Garbo claims *not* to have said, "I want to be alone." She explained, "I only said, 'I want to be left alone.' There is a whole world of difference."

Using AOL Instant Messenger

You don't have to be a member of America Online to use the AOL Instant Messenger, sometimes called AIM by its loyal users. The program is free and anyone can download it. AOL pioneered instant messaging in the United States. For that reason, its instant messenger is by far the most popular in North America. Figure 1-1 shows the Buddy List window and a Chat Room window in the AOL Instant Messenger.

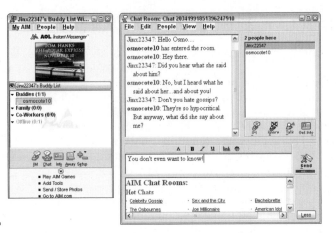

Figure 1-1:
The AOL Instant Messenger Buddy List window (left) and Chat Room window (right).

Go to this Web address to download the AOL Instant Messenger software: www.aim.com. You are asked to submit a screen name, password, and e-mail address where AOL Instant Messenger can send a membership verification.

Here are the basics of using AOL Instant Messenger:

✦ **Adding friends to your Buddy List:** Click the Setup button and choose Buddy List on the pop-up menu. Then click the Add a Buddy button and enter your buddy's screen name. To add the name of someone you meet in a chat window, right-click the name and choose Add to Buddy List.

✦ **Engaging someone in a chat or message exchange:** Right-click a name on your Buddy List and choose Send Chat Invitation or Send Instant Message. If someone invites you to chat or instant-message, you see the Invitation From window or Instant Message window. Take it from there.

Here are some useful techniques for protecting your privacy:

✦ **Make yourself invisible:** Choose My AIM⇨Manage Linked Screen Names to open the Manage Linked Screen Names window. Select the Invisible At Sign On check box next to each screen name under which you want to be invisible.

✦ **Ignore somebody:** Right-click the name of a buddy and choose Block Buddy on the shortcut menu. You can also click the Block button when someone sends you an invitation to chat or exchange instant messages. And you can click the Setup button, choose Preferences on the pop-up menu, and enter the names of people to be blocked in the Privacy category of the Preferences dialog box.

+ **Control whether the program starts when you start your computer:** Click the Setup button and choose Preferences on the pop-up menu. In the Sign On/Off category of the Preferences dialog box, deselect the Start AIM When Windows Starts check box.

+ **Change your profile:** Choose My AIM⇨Edit Profile and describe yourself anew in the Create a Profile dialog box.

Using MSN Messenger

You have to love the mighty Microsoft Corporation. The company does what the Japanese are always being accused of doing — it doesn't invent anything, but it comes in after the fact to refine and perfect others' inventions. MSN Messenger is a case in point. It isn't the first instant messenger, but it may be the best. It has less clutter than the others and is very easy to use. Figure 1-2 shows the MSN Messenger window and a conversation window.

Cleaning up the notification area

Instant messengers have a bad habit of dropping icons in the notification area. This area is located in the lower-right corner of the desktop next to the clock. The idea is for the icons to be there at the ready in case you want to start an instant-messaging program, but all those icons can make the notification area awfully crowded.

Follow these steps to clean up the notification area:

1. Right-click a blank space in the notification area, being careful not to click the clock or an icon.

2. Choose Customize Notifications on the pop-up menu. If you don't see this menu, you're not right-clicking in the correct place.

3. In the Customize Notifications dialog box, open the drop-down menu for each icon

and choose Always Hide, Always Show, or Hide When Inactive.

4. Click the OK button.

Figure 1-2:
The MSN
Messenger
window
(left) and
conversa-
tion window
(right).

To trade instant messages with MSN Messenger, you need a .NET passport. Appendix B of this book explains what .NET passports are and how to get one. To download the MSN Messenger software, go to this address: `http://messenger.msn.com/download`. Then click the Go button under Registered MSN User (click this Go button regardless of whether you are registered with the Microsoft Network). To sign on to MSN Messenger, use your .NET passport ID and password.

The basics of using MSN Messenger are as follows:

+ **Adding friends to your Contact list:** Click the Add a Contact link (in the I Want To section at the bottom of the window). In the wizard dialog boxes that appear, either select a name from your MSN Messenger dialog box or enter an e-mail address.

+ **Engaging someone in a message exchange:** Double-click a name on your Contact list. The Conversation window shown on the right side of Figure 1-2 opens. Enter a message and click the Send button.

Do the following to maintain your privacy while you are traveling aboard the flagship MSN Messenger:

+ **Make yourself invisible:** Choose File⇨My Status⇨Appear Offline.

+ **Ignore somebody:** Right-click a name on your Contact list and choose Block. To see a list of the people you have blocked, choose Tools⇨ Options and select the Privacy tab in the Options dialog box.

+ **Control whether the program starts when you start your computer:** Choose Tools⇨Options and select the General tab in the Options dialog box. Then deselect the Automatically Run Messenger When I Log on to Windows check box if you do not want Messenger to start when you boot your computer.

+ **Change your profile:** Choose Tools⇨Options and select the Personal tab in the Options dialog box. Then click the Edit Profile button.

Using Yahoo! Messenger

Yahoo! Messenger is the Yahoo! entry in the instant-messenger sweepstakes. To use Yahoo! Messenger, you must have a Yahoo! account. Appendix A of this book explains how to get one of those. If you have a Yahoo! Mail account, you have it made, because your Yahoo! ID and password get you straight into Yahoo! Messenger without having to argue with the doorman. Figure 1-3 shows the Yahoo! Messenger window and the conversation window.

Figure 1-3:
The Yahoo! Messenger window (left) and conversation window (right).

The basics of using Yahoo! Messenger are as follows:

✦ **Adding friends to your Contact list:** Choose Contacts⇨Add a Contact and then enter your friend's Yahoo! ID or e-mail address in the dialog box.

✦ **Engaging someone in a message exchange:** Double-click a name on your Friends list to open the conversation window (refer to Figure 1-3). Then enter a greeting and click the Send button.

Here is the straight dope on how to maintain your privacy while you are trading messages with Yahoo! Messenger:

✦ **Make yourself invisible:** Choose Messenger⇨Change My Status⇨Invisible to Everyone.

✦ **Ignore somebody:** Choose Messenger⇨Preferences to open the Yahoo! Messenger Preferences dialog box. In the Ignore List category, click the Add button and enter the name of the contact you want to ignore.

✦ **Control whether the program starts when you start your computer:** Choose Messenger⇨Preferences and, in the Yahoo! Messenger Preferences dialog box, select the General category. Deselect the Automatically Start Yahoo! Messenger check box.

✦ **Change your profile:** Choose Contacts⇨Profile and describe yourself anew.

Using ICQ

ICQ ("I Seek You"), an Israeli invention and the oldest instant messenger, was purchased by America Online in 2000. Over 100 million people have registered with ICQ, according to the service, and that may well be true, but most of them tried ICQ on a lark and then abandoned it. Compared to the other instant messengers, ICQ is difficult to use. It tries to be too many things at once — an Internet portal, an e-mail service, a search engine, and a lonely hearts club, among other things. Doing something that should be as simple as making yourself invisible to other ICQers requires leaping through hoops and balancing flaming torches. Figure 1-4 shows the ICQ window.

Figure 1-4: The ICQ window.

To test-drive ICQ, go to this Web site and download the software: www.icq.com. Here are the basics of using ICQ:

✦ **Adding friends to your Contact list:** Click the Add/Invite Users button. In the Find/Add Users to Your List dialog box, enter the e-mail address, nickname, or ICQ number of the person you want to add to your list.

✦ **Engaging someone in a message exchange:** Double-click a name on your Contact list, enter a greeting in the Message Session dialog box, and click the Send button.

To run ICQ and maintain a modicum of privacy, follow these instructions:

✦ **Make yourself invisible:** Click the ICQ button and choose Security & Privacy on the pop-up menu. On the General tab of the Security For dialog box, deselect the Allow Others to View My Online/Offline Status on the Web check box.

✦ **Ignore somebody:** Click the name of the person on your Contact list that you want to ignore and then select Alert/Accept Modes. In the User Preferences For dialog box, select the General category and then the Status tab. Select the Invisible to User check box.

✦ **Control whether the program starts when you start your computer:** Click the ICQ button and choose Preferences. In the Owner Preferences For dialog box, select the Connections category, and then select the General tab. Deselect the Start ICQ on Startup check box.

✦ **Change your profile:** Click the My ICQ button and choose View/Change My Details on the pop-up menu. Then fill in the View/Change My Details dialog boxes.

Chapter 2: Blogs and Online Journals

In This Chapter

- ✔ Looking at the differences between blogs and online journals

- ✔ Understanding what makes a good blog or online journal

- ✔ Using search engines for searching in blogs and online journals

- ✔ Finding places on the Internet to create blogs and online journals for free

- ✔ Creating a blog at Mótime

According to Technorati, an Internet market research company, 12,000 new blogs are created every day. What's all the fuss about? And what is a blog, anyway? This chapter explains what blogs and online journals are and how to create one of your own for free. You also find out what constitutes a good blog or online journal and how you can search the Internet for blogs and online journals. The second half of this chapter gives hands-on instructions for creating a free blog at Mótime, a free Web service for creating and managing blogs.

What Are Blogs and Online Journals?

The word *blog* is shorthand for *Web log*. A typical blog is a hodgepodge of commentary and links — to online news sources and often to other blogs — where topics of concern to the blogger are discussed. A good blog gathers news stories and commentary from sources that you would not find on your own. Like journals, blogs are updated frequently. They mean to keep you abreast of the latest news. You get a picture of whatever the blogger is interested in — the day's politics, advances in technology, or the state of the Internet, for example. One person runs the show, but the links and the quotes from other writers make each blog a collaborative effort. Even visitors to a blog can get into the act by writing comments for all to read.

Figure 2-1 shows Radio Free Blogistan (`http://radiofreeblogistan. com`), a blog devoted to blogging and online community building written by Internet philosopher Christian Crumlish and others. This is a classic example of a blog. On the left side of the page is commentary written by Crumlish, but even there, he quotes liberally from other authors and includes links in his commentary so that you can click a link and read source material. On the right side of the page is an archive of past entries and links to other blogs. By clicking a Commentary link, you can enter a comment, and your comment is recorded on the blog for others to read.

A handful of blogs have become famous — or notorious, as the case may be. The Daily Kos (`www.dailykos.com`), Calico Cat (`www.calicocat.com`), and Wonkette (`www.wonkette.com`) cover politics. Gizmodo (`www.gizmodo.com`) stays on top of the latest electronic gadgets. Slashdot (`http://slashdot.org`) and Techdirt (`http://techdirt.com`) look into the newest technologies. BoingBoing (`www.boingboing.net`) covers the strange and unusual. These blogs attract many readers. A handful of blog authors have been able to quit their day jobs and make a living from advertisements on their blogs.

Sometimes what passes for a blog is really an online journal. Online journals precede blogs on the Internet by a half-dozen years (blogs began appearing in 2000 but online journals go back to 1994). An *online journal* is a diary, usually written anonymously, that records someone's daily life and thoughts. Sometimes online journalers (as the people who write the journals call themselves) link their journals to other online journals, but for the most part, each online journal is personal and distinctive. It's not a collaboration, but the private record of someone's life.

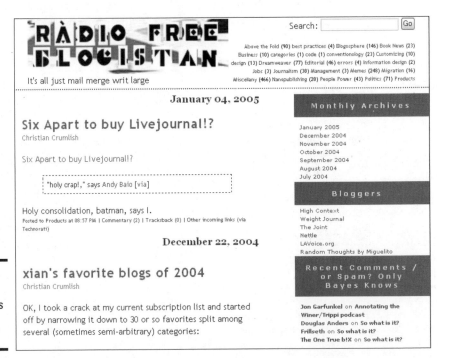

Figure 2-1: Radio Free Blogistan is a classic blog.

Speaking for myself (and why not speak for myself; it's my book isn't it?), I find online journals much more interesting than blogs. You can get a voyeuristic kick, of course, from reading an online journal, but more than that, if it's well written, an online journal can be fascinating. Reading a good one can be like reading a good novel in that you peer very deeply into someone else's life and view the world through different eyes.

Rob Rummel-Hudson, for example, the author of an online journal he calls Darn-Tootin (www.darn-tootin.com), writes movingly and sometimes humorously about his family, the ups and downs of his career, Texas, and a host of other topics, including dwarf hamsters, of all things. I realized a few years ago how addicted I was to his online journal when I found myself worrying about Rob being out of work, and this in spite of the fact that I had never met Rob, and he knew absolutely nothing about me (I have since interviewed him for this book and, in case you're curious, he has a job now). Figure 2-2 shows Rob's Darn-Tootin online journal. His journal is more sophisticated than most because it offers photographs and short videos as well as journal entries. And Rob's journal dates to January 1996, a long run by the standards of most bloggers and online journalists.

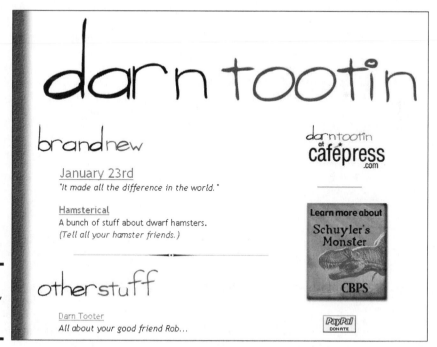

Figure 2-2:
Darn-Tootin,
an online
journal.

Another favorite journal of mine is More Laowai Chronicles (www.20six.co.uk/laowaimono), which is written by a self-styled "redneck in China," an American expatriate from Georgia living deep in the Chinese hinterland. The author has no shortage of exotic material to write about, and he writes about it with gusto and humor. I'm also a fan of Eat a Peach for Love (http://phatmike.motime.com) because the author is a friend, the writing style is unique, and I sometimes make an appearance in this online journal. I enjoy seeing myself, too. I'm always surprised by what a heroic, dashing figure I cut.

By the way, one of the most famous diaries in English letters is now online and being presented like a blog. You can read day-to-day entries in the diary of Samuel Pepys (1633–1703) at this Web address: www.pepysdiary.com.

What Makes for a Good Blog or Online Journal?

What makes a good blog or online journal is first of all the writing. Not everyone can be a good writer, but even middling writers can write better if they write about a subject that they love or are passionate about. That subject may be yourself, and that's quite all right, because an online journal is by definition about its author. Try to write in your own voice; it makes keeping your blog or journal up to date easier and makes your writing more credible. Nearly 95 percent of all blogs are abandoned. Writing in your own voice about something you love can encourage you to keep going.

Unless you update your blog or online journal frequently, it won't attract a readership. Make it a point to update frequently. Here are other practical suggestions for making your blog or online journal a success:

✦ Link to other blogs and online journals. By doing so, you join the network of blogs and journals and encourage more people to visit your blog.

✦ Give readers a chance to comment on your entries. You benefit from the praise and criticism, and readers feel like they're a part of your blog or journal.

✦ Include some kind of calendar mechanism so that readers can get to past entries. This way, readers can look into your past and learn more about you. Include a short biography as well.

You'll be glad to know that the blogging services I describe later in this chapter make it easy to link to other blogs or journals and include a calendar mechanism and biography (see "Free Web Sites for Creating Blogs and Online Journals," later in this chapter). What's more, all the services permit visitors to comment on the blogs and journals they visit.

Blog Search Engines and Directories

The best way to find out whether you're interested in blogs and online journals is to read a few and see what all the fuss is about. Starting from the Web sites that follow, you can search by keyword in blogs and online journals to find out what bloggers are saying about a topic of interest to you. Try entering the name of your hometown. Or, enter the name of your school or a school you used to attend. You can also rummage through blog directories at some of these Web sites:

✦ **Bloogz World Wide Blog:** Search blogs the world over from this Web site. You can choose a language from the drop-down menu to search for blogs written in French, Spanish, German, or English. Address: www.bloogz.com

✦ **Globe of Blogs:** This is a directory. Search for blogs by category and subcategory. Address: www.globeofblogs.com

✦ **Technorati:** You can use Boolean operators in searches at this search engine. Address: www.technorati.com

At Threeway Action (www.threewayaction.com), people who write online journals trade ideas about writing online as well as a number of other topics. You can find many links to online journals at Threeway Action. Online journalers also congregate at The Usual Suspects (http://theusuals.net), which offers message boards and links to online journals and blogs. Would you like to meet online journalers in the flesh? You can do that at Journalcon, their annual conference. Go to this Web address for information: www.journalcon.com.

Free Web Sites for Creating Blogs and Online Journals

By the strictest definition, blogs and online journals are just Web sites where people describe what they are up to and give their opinions on this, that, and the other thing. You don't need special software to create an online blog or journal. Technically savvy people write the HTML codes and lay out their blogs and online journals on their own. Still, because blogging is such a popular activity, all kinds of Web sites and Web services have sprung up to assist bloggers.

Table 2-1 lists Web services with which you can create a blog or online journal. I chose these services because they are free and easy to operate. They all work the same way. You register, choose a name for your blog, select a template design, and start writing. The blogs all have a place where others can comment on your writing, a place for links to other blogs or Web sites, and a way to store past entries so that others can find and read them. People with similar ideas and obsessions tend to assemble at the same blogging services. Live Journal and Diaryland, for example, are popular with teenagers. Before you choose a blogging service, read a few of its blogs to find out whether the service is the right one for you. I like Mótime, partly because (how do I put this diplomatically?) most of the Mótime bloggers are grownups. The rest of this chapter explains how to operate a blog at Mótime.

Table 2-1	Free Blog- and Online Journal–Creation Services		
Service	*Web Address*	*Notes*	*Example Blog*
Blogger	`www.blogger.com`	Google owns Blogger (before the Internet, this sentence would make no sense whatsoever!).	`http://riverbendblog.blogspot.com`
Diaryland	`www.diaryland.com`	Create a blog from simple templates.	`http://kelsncarrie.diaryland.com`
Live Journal	`www.livejournal.com`	Known for its tight-knit community; popular with teenagers.	`www.livejournal.com/users/jenny`
Mótime	`www.motime.com`	More adults than teenage bloggers here.	`http://phatmike.motime.com`

Running a Blog or Online Journal at Mótime

In my humble opinion, Mótime is the best place on the Internet to create a blog or online journal for free. The commands for creating, formatting, and editing entries are easy to use. Mótime blogs don't carry garish advertisements. Mótime even archives past entries for you. Past entries are archived under month names. Anyone who wants to read an entry you wrote in the past can click the name of a month and year to open a Web page with entries from that month and year.

The sections that follow explain how to sign up for a Mótime blog, create the blog, and write and edit entries. You also find out how to put links and photographs on your blog page, update your profile, and send e-mail messages to people who contact you through Mótime. (I'm going to refer to them as blogs for the rest of this chapter to keep readers from getting tongue-tied.) However, you can create a blog or online journal at Mótime. Earlier in this chapter, "What Are Blogs and Online Journals?" distinguishes between these two kinds of online writing.)

Signing up with Mótime

Before you can create a blog with Mótime, you need to sign up. Go to the Mótime home page (www.motime.com) and click the Create Your Blog button. You land in the Create a New Account page. You know the drill, I'm sure — enter all the information you are asked for on this page and click the Create New Account button. Be sure to choose a User Name carefully. The name sticks with you throughout your adventures with Mótime.

As you are instructed to do, go to the e-mail account whose address you gave to Mótime and open the validation e-mail message. It's called "Welcome to Mótime." Click the confirmation link in the message to go to the User Registration page at Mótime.

Now you're getting somewhere. Enter your username, enter your password, and click the Log-In button.

You land in the Control Center (what is this, a science fiction movie?). The Control Center is the starting point for doing everything you want to do in Mótime — write a blog entry and edit past entries, for example. Click the Add New Blog button to go to the Create a New Blog page.

Creating a new blog

On the Create a New Blog page, enter this information and click the Create button:

✦ **Title:** The title tells readers right away what your blog is all about, so choose a descriptive, clever (but not too clever) name. The title appears across the top of your blog for all to see.

✦ **URL:** Enter a word to form the Web address of your blog. Most people enter their username or the name of their blog. For example, if you enter **Johnny**, the Web address of your blog is:

```
http://johnny.motime.com
```

✦ **Description:** Write what amounts to a subtitle for your blog. The words appear along the top of your blog.

✦ **Show Blog on Newly Update Menu:** Mótime keeps a page called Read Latest Posts, where you can go to read recently updated blogs. Select the Yes, Show the Blog option button if you want your blog to appear on the list after you update it.

After you click the Create button, you come to the Template page, where you choose a layout and design for your blog. You can click an Enlarge link to get a good look at a template. Unfortunately, you can't edit these layouts unless you know something about HTML encoding, although you can choose a different template later.

Book IV
Chapter 2

Blogs and Online
Journals

You see the Edit Blog tab of the Blogs user window, as shown in Figure 2-3. This is where you write blog entries. Go to the section "Writing and editing blog entries," later in this chapter, if you want to write your first entry now.

To change the title and subtitle of your blog, go to the Edit Blog tab of the Blogs user window (see Figure 2-3) and click the Basic link. Then enter a new title and subtitle. To choose a different template for your blog, go to the Edit Blog tab of the Blogs user window and select the Template tab. Then click the New link and choose a different template.

Starting from the Control Center

When your blog needs care and attention, go to Mótime (www.motime.com) and sign in with your username and password. You come to the Control Center window shown in Figure 2-4. From here, you choose what you want to do next:

- ✦ **Blogs:** Click the name of your blog to open the Edit Blog tab of the Blogs user window (see Figure 2-3) and write or edit a blog entry.

- ✦ **Messages:** People who visit your blog can click the Contact Me link to send you an e-mail message at Mótime. Click the Messages link to read these e-mails. You can reply to messages as well as read them.

- ✦ **Community:** Subscribe to blogs and chat with other Mótime subscribers. After you subscribe to a blog, you can click its name to open it in your Web browser.

- ✦ **Account:** You can change your username or password, as well as describe yourself in a profile. People who click the My Profile link on your blog can read your profile.

- ✦ **Mótime News**: Read the latest news from Mótime.

Writing and editing blog entries

To write a blog entry, start from the Edit Blog tab of the Blogs user window (see Figure 2-3). Type your entry in the text box. I trust you recognize most of the buttons and commands for formatting text. These are the same buttons and commands found in word processors. For example, choose a font and font size from the Font and Size drop-down menus to change the look of text. Indent text with the Increase Indent and Decrease Indent buttons. Click the Post and Publish button when you are finished writing.

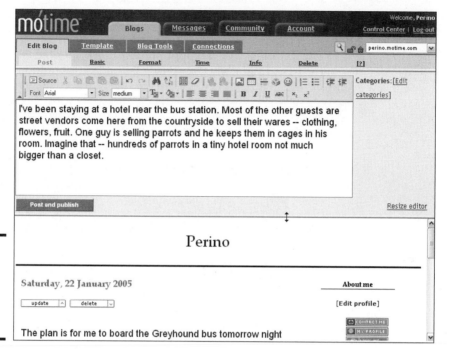

Figure 2-3:
The Edit Blog tab of the Blogs user window.

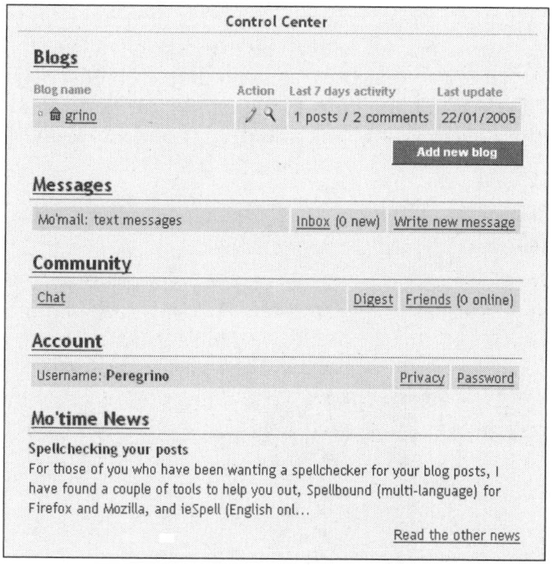

Figure 2-4:
The Control Center.

Here are a handful of tasks worth knowing about:

✦ **Making a hyperlink:** To link to another Web site or blog in an entry, drag to select the text that is to form the link. Then click the Insert/Edit Link button. The Link – Web Page Dialog box appears. Enter the Web address of the page to which you want to link. By copying the address from your Web browser's Address text box, you can paste it into the Link – Web Page Dialog box by right-clicking and choosing Paste.

✦ **Removing a hyperlink:** Click the link and then click the Remove link button.

✦ **Inserting a photograph:** To insert a photograph, it must be located on the Internet. You can't upload a photo from your computer to Mótime because Mótime doesn't offer server space to its subscribers (if it did, the service would not be free anymore). Take note of the Web address of the photo and click the Insert/Edit Image button. In the Image Properties – Web Page Dialog box, as shown in Figure 2-5, enter the Web address of the photograph, as well as the dimensions you want for it (in pixels), and indicate whether you want a border and how you want it aligned. (The easiest way to get the Web address of a photo is to right-click it, choose Properties, and copy the address from the Properties dialog box.)

✦ **Editing or removing a photograph:** Click to select the photograph and then press Delete to delete it, or click the Insert/Edit Image button to edit it in the Image Properties – Web Page Dialog box (refer to Figure 2-5).

To edit an entry you wrote before, display your blog page on the Edit Blog tab of the Blogs user window (refer to Figure 2-3), click the Update button, and edit your entry in the text box. You can delete an entry by clicking the Delete button. If you can't see your blog page in the bottom half of the window, click the Resize Editor link and drag the window divider upward.

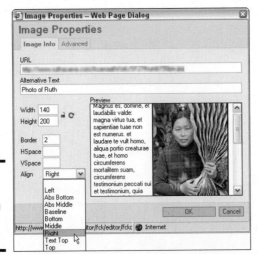

Figure 2-5: Inserting a photograph in a blog entry.

Rather than write an entry on the Edit Blog tab, you can write it in Microsoft Word or another word processor and paste it into the text box. This way, you can spell-check your writing. Click the Paste button to paste text into the Edit Blog tab. You can also create hyperlinks in a word processor and paste them into the Edit Blog tab.

As you write your blog, you can see what it will look like to people who visit it by clicking the Preview button. You can find this button in the upper-right corner of the window (refer to Figure 2-3). Clicking it opens your blog in a second Web-browser window.

Putting links on your blog page

Under the heading "Link," your blog page has a place for listing links to other blogs and Web sites. To enter a link, start from the Blogs user window (refer to Figure 2-3), select the Blog Tools tab, and then click the Links tab. You see a form for naming the link and entering its address. Fill out the form and click the Add button.

Be sure to periodically click these links to make sure that they are still active and go to the right Web site or blog.

Chapter 3: Mailing Lists and Message Boards

In This Chapter

✔ Discussing ideas on a mailing list

✔ Subscribing to a mailing list

✔ Giving your opinion on a message board

This chapter looks at two ways to exercise your ideas and obsessions on the Internet — mailing lists and message boards. A mailing list is a sort of continuous discussion conducted by e-mail among likeminded people. A message board is a place where you can deposit your opinion on the Internet and, with a little luck, find someone to engage you in a thought-provoking debate or discussion.

Most of this chapter is devoted to mailing lists. Mailing lists are one of the most underused resources for Internet researchers. A good mailing list — one where the members are helpful and erudite — is like having a team of researchers working alongside you.

Trading Ideas on a Mailing List

A *mailing list,* also known as an *e-mail discussion list* or *e-mail newsletter,* is an online club in which members who share the same interests, problems, or passions exchange ideas by e-mail. A mailing list works like this: Any message sent to the list is immediately forwarded to all the subscribers. When you have a question that you think another subscriber can answer, you send it to the list and hope for a reply. When you receive a question from the list and you have the answer, you send it to the list for the benefit of the subscriber who asked the question and all others who care to read or comment on your answer.

Subscribing to a mailing list is like subscribing to a special-interest newsletter, with the advantage that you can comment on the newsletter and pose questions to its editors and readers. For a researcher, mailing lists can be invaluable if the topic under investigation is well defined — the Dead Sea Scrolls, Joaquin Murieta, or the Welsh language, for example. Civic organizations, scholars, and clubs can use mailing lists to trade information and ideas. Some years ago, I coauthored a book about botanicals from Madagascar. By luck and careful searching, I found a mailing list in England where botanists and chemists discussed the properties of different plants, some of them grown in Madagascar. The subscribers to the list were very helpful to me. They answered my questions, pointed me to useful reference books, and steered me to useful Web sites.

No one knows how many mailing lists are out there. People who try to count them quickly run out of fingers and toes. Suffice it to say, there are as many mailing lists as there are pigeons in Paris. Later in this chapter, "Finding a mailing list" explains how to search for mailing lists.

The difference between a mailing list and a newsgroup is that information posted to a newsgroup is open to everyone with a Web browser, whereas mailing-list information is delivered by e-mail and is shared only by the people on the mailing list (Book IV, Chapter 4 explains newsgroups). A Yahoo! group is a hybrid between a mailing list and a newsgroup. In a Yahoo! group, subscribers can view submissions to the group on the Internet as well as have submissions forwarded to them by e-mail (Book IV, Chapter 5 looks into Yahoo! groups).

Categories of mailing lists

Mailing lists fall in three categories. Which category a mailing list falls in matters when it is time to subscribe to a list or send it an e-mail message. The following list describes the types of mailing lists:

✦ **Manually administered:** In this kind of list, a moderator reads each message as it is submitted and either passes it along to subscribers or deems it unworthy of being passed along. You don't need special software to administer a manual list. All you need is an e-mail program like Outlook or Outlook Express to receive and send e-mail messages.

✦ **Computer-administered:** As e-mail arrives, a *list server program* passes it along immediately to subscribers. Most mailing lists fall in the computer-administered category. With this kind of mailing list, you need to know special commands for subscribing and unsubscribing to the list, and you need to know which list server program you are dealing with. Later in this chapter, Table 3-1 describes list-server commands.

✦ **Web-based, computer-administered:** As e-mail arrives, a Web-based mailing list service distributes it to subscribers. Topica and Coollist are examples of Web-based mailing list services. These services are ad supported, meaning that all e-mail messages are accompanied by advertisements.

Finding a mailing list

Most people join mailing lists by invitation. They hear about them from friends or coworkers. Researchers wandering lonely in the darkness of the Internet can find mailing lists by starting at one of these Web sites:

✦ **Catalist:** Search in the L-Soft Catalog, a catalog of mailing lists maintained by the makers of LISTSERV, the most popular list server program. Some 60,000 mailing lists are in the catalog. Address: `www.lsoft.com/lists/listref.html`

✦ **Coollist:** Search for mailing lists hosted by Coollist, a Web-based mailing list service. Address: `www.coollist.com`

✦ **JISCMail:** Search this database of mailing lists run by scholars in England. You can find some very interesting lists here. Address: `www.jiscmail.ac.uk`

✦ **Tile.net:** Search for mailing lists by name, description, or domain name. Address: `www.tile.net/lists`

✦ **Topica:** Search for mailing lists hosted by Topica, a Web-based mailing-list service. Address: `http://lists.topica.com`

Another way to find mailing lists is to query Catalist by e-mail. Address an e-mail message to this address: `listserv@listserv.net`. In the text of the message (not the subject line), type **list global *keyword***, where *keyword* describes the mailing list you are searching for. For example, a query for mailing lists with warts as the subject would read **list global warts**. Catalist then sends you an e-mail with mailing lists that fit your description, or if no lists can be found, it sends you an e-mail telling you as much.

Distinguishing between the list address and administrative address

Every mailing list has two addresses, the *administrative address* for messages that have to do with housekeeping matters, and the *list address* for messages that are to be forwarded to subscribers:

✦ **Administrative address:** Send subscription requests and requests pertaining to how and when you want messages delivered to the administrative address. Table 3-1 describes commands you can send to the administrative address of a computer-administered mailing list. These commands go in the body of the e-mail message, not the subject line. A typical administrative address consists of the name of the list server program with which the list is administered (LISTSERV, ListProc, Mailbase, Mailserv, or Majordomo), followed by the at sign (@), and a domain name:

`listserv@lists.maryland.edu`

✦ **List address:** After you subscribe to a mailing list, you are sent its list address, and you can contribute to the list by sending comments and queries to the list address. The messages you send are read by all list subscribers.

Table 3-1   Sending Messages to Computer-Administered Mailing Lists

List Server Program	Enter This in the E-Mail Message Body	Example
Subscribing to a Mailing List		
Listproc	SUBSCRIBE *listname* Firstname Lastname	SUBSCRIBE warts Bob Smith
LISTSERV	SUBSCRIBE *listname* Firstname Lastname	SUBSCRIBE warts Bob Smith
Mailbase	JOIN *listname* Firstname Lastname	JOIN warts Bob Smith
Mailserv	SUBSCRIBE *listname* Firstname Lastname	SUBSCRIBE warts Bob Smith
Majordomo	SUBSCRIBE *listname*	SUBSCRIBE warts
Unsubscribing from a Mailing List		
Listproc	UNSUBSCRIBE *listname*	UNSUBSCRIBE warts
LISTSERV	UNSUBSCRIBE *listname*	UNSUBSCRIBE warts
Mailbase	LEAVE *listname*	LEAVE warts
Mailserv	UNSUBSCRIBE *listname*	UNSUBSCRIBE warts
Majordomo	UNSUBSCRIBE *listname*	UNSUBSCRIBE warts
Getting a Mailing List in Digest Form		
Listproc	SET *listname* MAIL DIGEST	SET warts MAIL DIGEST
LISTSERV	SET *listname* DIGEST	SET warts DIGEST
Mailbase	Not available	
Mailserv	Not available	
Majordomo	SUBSCRIBE *listname*-DIGEST	SUBSCRIBE warts-DIGEST
Ceasing to Get a Mailing List in Digest Form		
Listproc	SET *listname* MAIL ACK	SET warts MAIL ACK
LISTSERV	SET *listname* MAIL	SET warts MAIL
Mailbase	Not available	
Mailserv	Not available	
Majordomo	UNSUBSCRIBE *listname*-DIGEST	UNSUBSCRIBE warts-DIGEST
Ceasing to Receive Copies of Messages You Send to a Mailing List		
Listproc	SET *listname* MAIL NOACK	SET warts MAIL NOACK
LISTSERV	SET *listname* NOREPRO	SET warts NOREPRO
Mailbase	Not available	
Mailserv	Not available	
Majordomo	Not available	

List Server Program	Enter This in the E-Mail Message Body	Example
Suspending Mail Delivery without Unsubscribing from a Mailing List		
Listproc	SET *listname* MAIL POSTPONE	SET warts MAIL POSTPONE
LISTSERV	SET *listname* NOMAIL	SET warts NOMAIL
Mailbase	SUSPEND MAIL *listname*	SUSPEND MAIL warts
Mailserv	Not available	
Majordomo	Not available	
Receiving Mail Again after You Have Suspended Mail Delivery		
Listproc	SET *listname* MAIL ACK	SET warts MAIL ACK
LISTSERV	SET *listname* MAIL	SET warts MAIL
Mailbase	RESUME MAIL *listname*	RESUME MAIL warts
Mailserv	Not available	
Majordomo	Not available	
Getting a List of People Who Subscribe to a Mailing List		
Listproc	RECIPIENTS *listname*	RECIPIENTS warts
LISTSERV	REVIEW *listname* F=MAIL	REVIEW warts F=MAIL
Mailbase	REVIEW *listname*	REVIEW warts
Mailserv	SEND/LIST *listname*	SEND/LIST warts
Majordomo	WHO *listname*	WHO warts
Concealing Your Name from Other List Subscribers		
Listproc	SET *listname* CONCEAL YES	SET warts CONCEAL YES
LISTSERV	SET *listname* CONCEAL	SET warts CONCEAL
Mailbase	Not available	
Mailserv	Not available	
Majordomo	Not available	

The difference between the administrative and list address is like the difference between a newspaper's business offices and its editorial offices. You wouldn't subscribe to a newspaper or complain about late deliveries by sending a letter to the editorial offices, nor would you send a letter to the editor to the person in charge of delivering newspapers. When you send a message to a mailing list, make sure that you send it to the right address.

Subscribing to a Mailing List

To receive e-mail from a mailing list, you have to subscribe to it. Usually you get instructions for subscribing when you find a mailing list in an Internet search. The instructions tell you the administrative address where you can send your subscription request and what to enter in the body of the e-mail message. If your list is manually administered, you just send the list manager an e-mail explaining why you want to join. Be sure to include your name and address in the e-mail.

Subscribing to a computer-administered list is more problematic because how you subscribe depends on which list-server program is used to administer the list. The five list-server programs are LISTSERV, ListProc, Mailbase, Mailserv, and Majordomo. Earlier in this chapter, Table 3-1 explains how to submit a subscription request. Subscribing is easier than it looks. Just be sure to carefully follow the instructions for subscribing, and put the SUBSCRIBE command in the body of the e-mail message, not the subject line. Also, be sure to send the request from the e-mail address to which you want messages mailed.

After you subscribe, you get a welcome message announcing what a lucky person you are to have found such a wonderful mailing list. Save the message. It has directions for sending e-mail to the list. It also has instructions for unsubscribing. You may need those directions if you decide that the mailing list isn't for you. With luck, the welcome message tells you which list-server program — LISTSERV, ListProc, Mailbase, Mailserv, or Majordomo — administers the list. You will be asked to reply to the welcome message to confirm that you really want to subscribe. We can't have some prankster submitting your e-mail address to a kooky mailing list, can we?

Sending messages to a mailing list

To send a message to a mailing list and all its subscribers, send it to the list address. Make sure that the subject line thoroughly describes what your message is all about. Remember: Subscribers have to sort through messages from the list. A descriptive subject line helps them quickly decide whether your message is worth reading.

By the way, you are wise to read e-mail messages from the mailing list for a week or more before you start contributing. Find out what the mailing list is all about. Take its temperature. See who the personalities are, how you can fit in, and how you can make a genuine contribution to the list before you start showering it with e-mail messages.

Digesting and organizing the mail

You're in for a flood of e-mail if the mailing list to which you subscribe is a busy one. How do you keep the deluge of e-mail messages from overwhelming the other messages that need your attention? You have a choice. You can

WARNING!

Signatures and HTML formatting

E-mail that you send to a mailing list's administrative address goes nowhere if it contains a signature or is formatted for HTML or rich text. A signature is a saying, slogan, or advertisement found at the bottom of e-mail messages. Many free, Web-based e-mail services attach signatures to messages automatically, but computer-administered lists are programmed to read terse commands (refer to Table 3-1), and they don't know what to do with the extra words in a signature, so they reject the message. Likewise, computer-administered lists can't handle HTML-formatted messages or rich-text messages. They don't know what to do with the all those formatting commands, and they reject messages with HTML or rich-text formatting. They prefer plain-text messages.

Before you send an e-mail message to an administrative address, make sure that the e-mail doesn't contain a signature or fancy formats. Follow these instructions to keep signatures from appearing in an e-mail message you send with Outlook, Outlook Express, and Yahoo! Mail:

✔ **Outlook and Outlook Express:** In the message window, select the signature and press Delete.

✔ **Yahoo! Mail:** In the Compose window, deselect the Use My Signature check box.

Follow these instructions to send your messages in plain text, not HTML or rich text:

✔ **Outlook and Outlook Express:** In the message window, choose Format➪Plain Text.

✔ **Yahoo! Mail:** In the Compose window, click the Plain link (you can find it at the top of the message window next to the word *Compose*).

Compose (Plain | Color and Graphics)   Send an eCard

Insert addresses | Add CC - Add BCC
To: listserv@lists.maryland.edu
Subject:
Attachments: Attach Files

SUBSCRIBE warts Bob Smith

Options: ☑ Save a copy in your Sent Items folder
☐ Use my signature

receive the messages in digest form or create rules in your e-mail program that move incoming messages into special folders.

In digest form, messages from a single day or two are bundled into one message with a table of contents. Rather than negotiate dozens of messages, you look through a single message, albeit a long one. Earlier in this chapter, Table 3-1 describes commands for receiving messages in digest form (the table also describes how to cease getting messages that way).

Shunting e-mail into different folders as it arrives is a great way to organize mail so that you can find it when you need it. Messages from a mailing list all come from the same address. On the basis of the address from which the messages come, you can create rules that put mailing-list messages into a specific folder. You can find instructions in this book for creating rules in Outlook, Outlook Express, and Yahoo! Mail:

✦ **Outlook:** See Book III, Chapter 2.

✦ **Outlook Express:** See Book III, Chapter 3.

✦ **Yahoo! Mail:** See Book III, Chapter 4.

Unsubscribing and other tasks

Earlier in this chapter, Table 3-1 describes a handful of other tasks that are worth knowing as you wrestle with your mailing list of choice. Refer to Table 3-1 for the commands you need to complete these tasks:

✦ **Unsubscribing from a mailing list:** By all means, unsubscribe if the list isn't working for you. Who needs all those e-mail messages? And you can resubscribe if you want to.

✦ **Ceasing to receive copies of messages you send to a mailing list:** Some mailing lists send copies of messages to senders on the idea that senders want to be sure that their e-mail arrived on the list. But all those copies can fill a mailbox quickly.

✦ **Suspending mail delivery without unsubscribing:** While you're on vacation in glorious Acapulco, you can tell the mailing list to stop sending messages. That way, you have fewer messages to read when you return with your suntan and your newfound sunny disposition.

✦ **Getting a list of people who subscribe to the mailing list:** If you want a comprehensive list with names and e-mail addresses of people who subscribe to the list, you can get it.

✦ **Concealing your name from other list subscribers:** For privacy's sake, you can prevent your name and e-mail address from appearing on subscriber lists.

Spouting Your Opinion on a Message Board

A *message board* is a place on the Internet where you can vent, philosophize, or opine alongside others. Figure 3-1 shows the Current Events message board at Arianna Online (www.ariannaonline.com), a Web site run by the newspaper columnist Arianna Huffington. Message boards are sometimes called *discussion boards, online forums,* and *Web forums.*

It used to be that running a message board on a Web site was a major undertaking, but advances in software have made it much easier to run a message board, and the number of message boards has risen accordingly. Some message boards are open to everyone; most require you to register by giving a name and e-mail address. Because people operate under pseudonyms when they post their opinions on message boards, opinions tend toward the outlandish and the extreme. If you stick around a message board long enough, you are sure to make new friends and enemies.

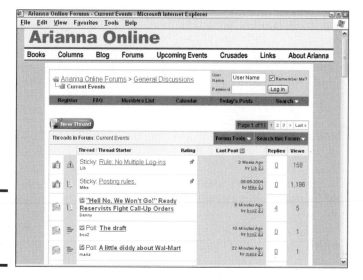

Figure 3-1:
A typical message board.

To see what message boards are all about and to find one that suits your tastes, start at one of these Web sites:

✦ **Delphi Forums:** Search message boards hosted by Delphi forums. Address: `www.delphiforums.com`

✦ **EZBoard:** Search by keyword at the self-proclaimed "world's largest message board network." Address: `www.ezboard.com`

Chapter 4: Newsgroups and the Usenet

In This Chapter

✓ Understanding newsgroups

✓ Reading newsgroup names

✓ Comparing Google Groups to newsreaders

✓ Searching the Usenet with Google

✓ Subscribing to newsgroups with Outlook Express

✓ Downloading music and video files from newsgroups

*W*elcome to the Usenet, the shadowy, untamed corner of the Internet where people post messages and files in newsgroups. There are some 35,000 to 40,000 newsgroups altogether. A *newsgroup* is an online bulletin board where people debate, rant, philosophize, deliberate, and argue. About 800 million messages dating to 1981 can be found on the Usenet. People also post image files, music files, and videos on the Usenet for others to download. If you look carefully, you can find a newsgroup devoted to almost any topic, but I can't promise you that the people who post to a newsgroup stick to its topic. Newsgroups are not moderated. No one oversees a newsgroup to make sure that people stay on topic. No one removes objectionable material such as advertisements or pornography.

This chapter looks at how newsgroups work and describes the cryptic manner in which they are named. It explains how to search for newsgroup postings, subscribe to newsgroups, and post messages in newsgroups on the Web in Google Groups or from your computer with Outlook Express. The end of this chapter describes how to download pictures, music files, and video files from newsgroups with Outlook Express and a quirky little computer program called Binary Boy.

A lot of objectionable material is found in newsgroups. Cranks and crackpots like nothing better than exercising their obsessions in newsgroups. If you are easily offended or have a low opinion of others' ability to argue intelligently, be careful which newsgroups you visit.

Introducing Newsgroups

The term *newsgroup* is something of a misnomer. Visitors to newsgroups don't usually discuss the latest news. The "news" portion of the name is a throwback to the early days of the Usenet, when scholars and researchers used it to discuss the latest technology. The Usenet, a decentralized network of computers that holds the newsgroup postings, actually predates the Internet. You can find newsgroup postings on the Usenet from as early as 1981. Figure 4-1 shows a posting to the net.bugs newsgroup from January 18, 1985. In this post, the author introduces the idea that computers will fail in 2000 because they will mistakenly think the year is 1900, not 2000. It was 15 years before the famous Y2K bug, and computer hobbyists were already discussing it on the Usenet! Newsgroups are sometimes called *user groups* and *discussion groups,* two terms that more accurately describe what newsgroups really are.

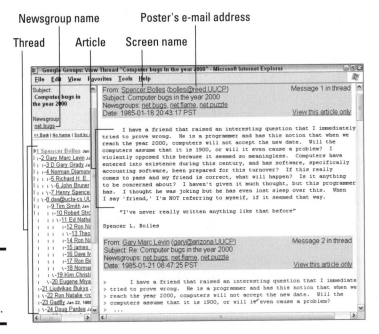

Figure 4-1:
An article on a newsgroup.

For many years, you needed a newsreader to explore the Usenet, subscribe to newsgroups, read messages, and post messages. A *newsreader* is a software program for negotiating the Usenet. Outlook Express is a newsreader as well as a program for handling e-mail. Starting in 1995, an outfit called DejaNews started archiving messages posted to newsgroups. You could open DejaNews in your Web browser and explore the Usenet without needing a newsreader. In 2001, Google purchased DejaNews. Now you can explore the Usenet in a Web browser starting from Google.com as well as explore it with a newsreader. Both ways are covered in this chapter.

Newsgroups have their own terminology. As shown in Figure 4-1, a contribution to a newsgroup is called an *article*. The initial article and its follow-up posts are collectively called a *thread*. The person who writes an article does so under his or her *screen name*. Bookmarking a newsgroup so that you can visit again it is called *subscribing*.

In theory, each newsgroup concerns one topic, but newsgroups are not regulated. No rules pertain. Any fool can drop a message about any topic in a newsgroup, and nobody can stop him or her. To enjoy or make use of newsgroups, you have to be able to tolerate a fair amount of junk — advertisements, loony opinions, weird obsessions, and pornography.

So what are newsgroups good for? In my experience, they are good for looking into very narrow, well-defined topics. For example, if you have a question about a software program, look up its name on the Usenet. You can likely find a newsgroup that's devoted to the software program where friendly people can answer your question and advise you. The Usenet is also a wonderful place for getting others' opinions about consumer products, especially electronics. Finally — and I'm surprised so few people know about this — the Usenet is an excellent source of music files and other digital files such as movies and pictures. You can download files from a newsgroup. I think being able to download music and video files is the best thing going in newsgroups.

Figuring Out Newsgroup Names

A newsgroup name comprises a hierarchy, followed by a period (.), followed by at least one descriptive word. A *hierarchy* is a newsgroup classification. Table 4-1 describes common newsgroup hierarchies. By glancing at the hierarchy and the descriptive word or words after the period, you can tell what a newsgroup is all about. Here are some examples of newsgroup names:

```
alt.horror.video.collectable
comp.hackers
rec.outdoors.fishing
talk.philosophy.humanism
```

Table 4-1	Common Newsgroup Hierarchies
Hierarchy	*Description*
alt	Alternative — for the weird and strange and unconventional.
biz	Business — for business topics.
comp	Computers — for hardware and software issues and high-tech stuff.
humanities	Humanities — for history, philosophy, and the arts.
misc	Miscellaneous — for newsgroups that don't fit elsewhere.

(continued)

Table 4-1 *(continued)*

Hierarchy	Description
news	News — for discussions about the Usenet (not the daily news).
rec	Recreation — for hobbies, sports, and leisure activities.
sci	Science — for science topics.
soc	Social groups — for socializing.
talk	Talk — for politics and general-purpose yakking.

Another word to look for in newsgroup names is *binaries*. When you see this word in a name, it means that you can download files from and post files to the newsgroup. Binaries is the newsgroup term for binary files. A *binary file* is a nontext file whose contents must be interpreted by a program, in this case a program that displays pictures or plays sounds or video. Look in the alt hierarchy for newsgroups that offer binary files. Here are some examples of newsgroups that offer binaries:

```
alt.binaries.multimedia.3-stooges
alt.binaries.pictures.motorcycles
alt.binaries.sounds.1970s.mp3
alt.binaries.sounds.radio.oldtime
```

Tile.net keeps an index of newsgroups. You can search the index by name, subject, or newsgroup hierarchy. To search the index, go to this address: http://tile.net/news. For a quick tutorial in newsgroups, you could do no worse than visiting Slyck's Guide at this address: www.slyck.com/ng.php. Want to search for binary files available in newsgroups? Try this site: http://alt.binaries.nl.

Google versus the Newsreaders

As I mention earlier in this chapter in "Introducing Newsgroups," you can explore the Usenet inside your Web browser starting at Google.com, or you can use a newsreader, a software program designed for handling newsgroups. Using Google gives you the advantage of being able to search for specific topics — for example, muscle cars, Madagascar, or manatees. You can also search by screen name to see who posted what or search by date to see what the newsgroup chatter was 10 or 20 years ago. Searching the Usenet with a Web browser is easier than searching it with a newsreader. You don't have to go to the technical trouble of hooking up your computer to a news server (more about that later) or understand all the commands for downloading messages and subscribing.

Using a newsreader is the way to go if you find a newsgroup you like and want to visit regularly. You can download messages to the newsgroup right into your computer and read them at your leisure. The biggest advantage of newsreaders over a Web browser is being able to download music files and videos from newsgroups. You can't do that by starting at Google.com and wandering the Internet in your Web browser.

Exploring Newsgroups with Google

For the sake of convenience, it's hard to beat Google for exploring the Usenet and reading messages posted in newsgroups. To post a message, you have to acquire a Google account. Other than that, searching for newsgroups, searching for messages in newsgroups, and subscribing to newsgroups couldn't be easier. If only Google would come up with a way to download multimedia files from newsgroups. You can't do that in Google — yet.

Searching for newsgroup postings

As you probably already know, Google is a very powerful tool for searching the Internet. Google can also reach deep into the Usenet to find messages posted in newsgroups. In fact, Google can reach all the way back to messages posted in 1981. Here's some good news if you are a past master at searching with Google: You can use the same techniques to search the Usenet with Google as you can to search the Internet (Book II, Chapter 3 explains searching the Internet with Google).

To search the Usenet with Google, open your browser to `http://groups.google.com` or go to the Google home page and click the Groups link. You land in the Google Groups page, the starting point for searching the Usenet. These tips can help you search the Usenet with Google:

✦ **Browsing the newsgroup directory:** Chose a category name and, on the Web page that appears, either open a newsgroup or continue searching deeper into the categories and subcategories. Figure 4-2 shows the page for searching Science and Technology groups.

✦ **Searching by keyword:** Enter search terms in the text box and click the Search Groups button. In the search results page, click a post that piques your interest. As shown in Figure 4-3, the post appears in its own window along with the thread to which it belongs. The search terms you entered are highlighted. You can scroll down the window to read the entire thread. Click the newsgroup name to make the newsgroup appear in your browser.

✦ **Conducting an advanced search:** Click the Advanced Groups Search link on the Google Groups page to conduct a thorough search. You go to the Advanced Groups Search page, where you get the opportunity to search by exact phrase, date, and other nifty criteria.

Figure 4-2:
Searching
inside the
Science and
Technology
hierarchy.

Figure 4-3:
Reading a
message
found in a
keyword
search.
Notice the
highlighted
search
terms.

Subscribing to a newsgroup

To subscribe to a newsgroup and be able to visit it regularly, bookmark it:

✦ **Internet Explorer:** Choose Favorites⇨Add to Favorites and, in the Add
   Favorite dialog box, select a folder, enter a bookmark name, and click
   the OK button.

✦ **Mozilla:** Choose Bookmarks⇨File Bookmark and, in the File Bookmark dialog box, select a folder, enter a name for the bookmark, and click the OK button.

Book II, Chapter 1 explains everything a mortal needs to know about bookmarking.

Posting messages to a newsgroup

To post a message to a newsgroup or reply to a message someone else posted, you need a Google account. Appendix C explains how to get one of those. After you have your account and post for the first time, Google asks you to choose a screen name, the name that identifies you as the author of the messages you deposit in newsgroups. Choose a name carefully. You can't change it. If you want to change names, your only resort is to create a new Google account.

Follow these instructions to post a message, reply to a message, or reply directly to the author of a message in a newsgroup:

✦ **Posting a new message for the whole newsgroup:** Click the Start a New Topic link. In the form that appears, enter the subject of your message and the message itself in the Message window. Then click the Post Message button (or click the Preview Message button to proofread your message before you post it).

✦ **Posting a reply to a message someone else wrote:** Click the Reply link. You can find this link at the bottom of messages. Enter your reply and click the Post button (or the Preview button if you want to proofread your reply first).

✦ **Replying personally to the author of a message:** Click the Reply to author link (you may have to click the Show Options link first to see the author's e-mail address). Then enter your reply and click the Send Message button. Be aware that most people don't leave their correct e-mail address in newsgroup messages to prevent their mailboxes from being flooded with spam. Chances are, your e-mail message won't reach its destination.

TIP

To keep messages you write on the Usenet from being put in the Google archive of newsgroup messages, type **X-No-Archive: yes** (with a single space between the colon and *yes*) in the first line of the message.

Exploring Newsgroups with Outlook Express

Every computer that runs the Windows operating system has Outlook Express. Most people know this program as an e-mailer, but Outlook Express has a dark little secret — the program doubles as a newsreader. To visit a newsgroup with Outlook Express, you connect to a news server that tracks the names of newsgroups. Then you visit a newsgroup that interests you and read a few messages. If the newsgroup is one that piques your interest, you can subscribe to it. Subscribing makes it easy to revisit a newsgroup later. Of course, you can also add your two cents' worth and post a message of your own in a newsgroup. Better read on.

Book III, Chapter 3 explains the e-mailing side of Outlook Express and how to handle the Folder pane.

Connecting to a news server

A *news server* is a networked computer that stores messages in its own newsgroups. The server also communicates with other news servers to retrieve the messages that other news servers store. News servers have large storage capacities — really big storage capacities. They hold text messages as well as files that have been encoded into text. As you explore the Usenet, you download messages from news servers.

Before you can explore the Usenet with Outlook Express, you need to tell Outlook Express which news server to connect to. To be specific, you need to tell Outlook Express the name of the Internet News (NNTP) server that your ISP uses. To get this name, call your Internet service provider. Sorry — you can't get around it. You have to make the phone call even if it means climbing tree-sloth-like up a phone tree for many minutes. Ask your ISP, "What is the name of the Internet News (NNTP) server — the news server — that I need to look at newsgroups on the Usenet?" Besides the news server name, ask your ISP whether you need to provide an account name and password to access the news server. Usually, your e-mail address and password for e-mail get you into the news server, but if this isn't the case, get an account name and a password.

You've finished doing that? Congratulations. Follow these steps to tell Outlook Express how to connect to the news server:

1. **In Outlook Express, choose Tools⇨Accounts.**

You see the Internet Accounts dialog box.

2. **Select the News tab.**

3. **Click the Add button and choose News on the pop-up menu.**

You see the first of four Internet Connection dialog boxes.

4. **Enter your name; then click the Next button.**

The name you enter is your screen name, the name that appears next to your e-mail address at the top of articles you post.

5. **Enter an e-mail address so that people can reply directly to you; then click the Next button.**

Entering an e-mail address is mandatory. The address appears with your posts. Anyone can click the address and send you an e-mail straight-away. However, to keep spammers from getting your e-mail address, include the words NOSPAM in the address. This way, anyone who wants to e-mail you can remove those letters, but the computers that crawl the Internet for e-mail addresses on behalf of spammers will not be able to collect your correct address. (Book III, Chapter 5 explains how to pre-vent spam from flooding your mailbox.)

6. **Enter the name of the Internet News (NNTP) server that your ISP pro-vided you; then click the Next button.**

As shown in Figure 4-4, the news server name you enter appears in the Folder pane of Outlook Express. To explore the Usenet, you click the news server's name in the Folder pane.

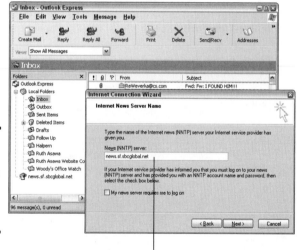

Figure 4-4:
The news server name appears in the Folder pane.

News server name

7. **If your ISP requires you to provide a password to read newsgroups, select the My News Server Requires Me to Log On check box and, in the following dialog box, enter your account name and password.**

You probably enter your e-mail address and the password you use to collect your e-mail.

8. **Click the Finish button.**

You return to the Internet Accounts dialog box.

9. **Click the Close button.**

10. **Click the Yes button in the dialog box that asks "Would you like to download newsgroups from the news account you just added?"**

The next section in this chapter explains what downloading newsgroups is all about. Notice the new folder in the Outlook Express Folder pane. Just like I said, it is named after the Internet News (NNTP) server address you entered.

If you have a problem connecting to the Usenet, return to the Internet Accounts dialog box, select the name of the account you just created, and click the Properties button. You get the chance to change connection settings in the Properties dialog box.

Downloading newsgroups to Outlook Express

The first time you connect to a news server or click the server's name in the Outlook Express Folder pane, a dialog box asks whether you would like to view a list of available newsgroups. Click the Yes button. Downloading the names takes a while if you have a slow connection to the Internet, but when the names have downloaded, you see the Newsgroup Subscriptions dialog box shown in Figure 4-5.

Periodically right-click the news server's name in the Folder pane and choose Reset List on the shortcut menu. Doing so updates the list of newsgroups on the Usenet.

How's your news server?

Some ISPs don't offer their customers a news server for connecting to the Usenet. MSN (the Microsoft Network) is one such ISP. And the news servers that some ISPs offer are too slow, don't give you access to binary newsgroups, or don't offer binary files in their entirety. If you are hankering to explore the Usenet but your news server isn't working for you, you can resort to a private company. Here are some private companies that offer subscription news servers. Prices for subscribing vary from $10 to $50 per month, depending on how many files you download.

✔ Astraweb: `http://news.astraweb.com`

✔ EasyNews: `www.easynews.com`

✔ Giganews: `www.giganews.com`

✔ NewsHosting: `www.newshosting.com`

✔ Usenet Monster: `www.usenetmonster.com`

✔ UseNetServer: `www.usenetserver.com`

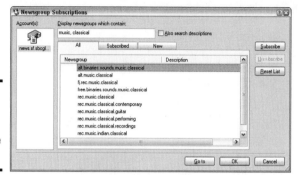

Figure 4-5:
Finding a
newsgroup
to subscribe
to.

Exploring the different newsgroups

Starting in the Newsgroup window (click the news server name in the
Outlook Express Folder pane to get there), follow these steps to explore different newsgroups:

1. **Click the Newsgroups button.**

You see the Newsgroup Subscriptions dialog box (refer to Figure 4-5).

2. **In the Display Newsgroups Which Contain text box, enter keywords
that describe the newsgroup you are looking for.**

To enter more than one keyword, separate the words with commas. The
dialog box shows the names of newsgroups with the keywords you
entered.

3. **Select a newsgroup that looks interesting and click the Go To button
to visit it.**

You see a message window similar to the one in Figure 4-6. Read a few
messages and see what you think of this newsgroup. (Later in this chapter, "Reading and posting messages in newsgroups" explains in more
detail how to read messages.) The next section in this chapter explains
how to subscribe if you decide to do that.

4. **Click the name of your news server to return to the Newsgroup
window.**

The news server name and its icon work just like the other icons in the
Outlook Express Folder pane. No matter how far you travel, you can
click the news server icon to return to the Newsgroup window.

Whether or not you subscribe to a newsgroup you've visited, Outlook
Express keeps its name in the Folder pane. To remove a newsgroup name
from the Folder pane, click the name to select it and press Delete.

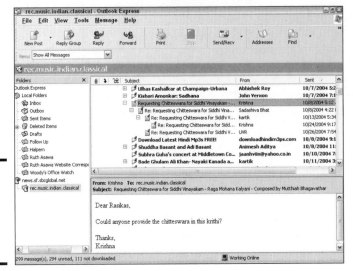

Figure 4-6:
Reading
messages
in the
message
window.

Subscribing and unsubscribing

Subscribe to a newsgroup if there is even the slightest chance that you want to visit it again. Newsgroups are so numerous, and their names are so cryptic, that finding one you've been to before is nearly impossible unless you subscribe. Besides, unsubscribing is easy. Follow these instructions to subscribe to a newsgroup after you have found it:

✦ **In the Newsgroup Subscriptions dialog box:** Select a newsgroup name and then click the Subscribe button (refer to Figure 4-5).

✦ **In the Newsgroup window:** Right-click the newsgroup's name in the Folder pane and choose Subscribe on the shortcut menu.

To unsubscribe, right-click the newsgroup's name in the Folder pane and choose Unsubscribe from the shortcut menu. You can also select a name on the Subscribed tab of the Newsgroup Subscriptions dialog box and click the Unsubscribe button.

Getting the latest messages from a newsgroup

A busy newsgroup receives hundreds or thousands of postings a day. After you subscribe to a newsgroup, you can download these new messages to your computer. Then you can read the messages at your leisure in Outlook Express. Downloading the latest messages this way is called *synchronizing*.

To start synchronizing, select the news server icon in the Folder pane to open the Synchronization window shown in Figure 4-7. This window lists the name of each newsgroup to which you subscribe. Click the Synchronize Account button to download messages.

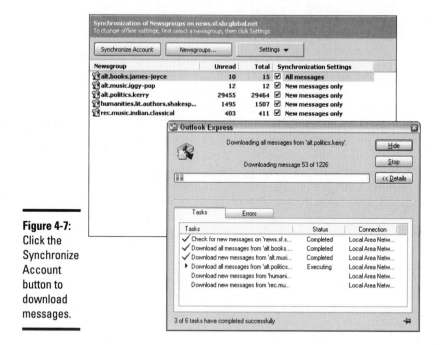

Figure 4-7:
Click the
Synchronize
Account
button to
download
messages.

By selecting Synchronization Settings check boxes and choosing options from the Settings button, you can decide how many messages to download. Deselect a check box if you prefer not to download messages from a newsgroup. Select a newsgroup and click the Settings button to open a menu with these downloading options:

✦ **All Messages:** Downloads all messages posted to the newsgroup.

✦ **New Messages Only:** Downloads only messages that have been downloaded since the last time you synchronized.

✦ **Headers Only:** Downloads only the headers — the subject of messages — not the message text. You can click a header to download the message.

Reading and posting messages in newsgroups

To read messages posted to a newsgroup, double-click the newsgroup's name in the Folder pane or the Synchronization window. Soon, messages appear in the top of the message window (refer to Figure 4-6). To read a message, click it and read the text at the bottom of the window, or, to open the message in its own window and read it more comfortably, double-click the message. A plus sign (+) appears beside messages to which others have responded. To read the responses, click the plus sign next to a message and view the responses.

Outlook Express offers three ways to register your opinion in a newsgroup and either post a message or send a message directly to another author. Click the message that deserves a reply and follow these instructions:

+ **Posting a new message for the whole newsgroup:** Click the New Post button. You see the New Message window with the newsgroup's address where the To box usually is. Enter a subject for your post, type the message, and click the Send button.

+ **Posting a reply to a message someone else wrote:** Click the message you want to reply to and then click the Reply Group button. The New Message window opens with the text of the message to which you are replying. A subject is already entered in the Subject box. Type your reply and click the Send button. Be sure to erase the text in the message to which you are replying before you write your reply.

+ **Replying personally to the author of a message:** Click the Reply button. The New Message window opens with the author's e-mail address, usually disguised, in the To box and the text of the original message. Correct the e-mail address, enter your reply, and click the Send button. Your message goes straight to the person named in the To box — it is not posted on the newsgroup.

Choose Tools⇨Get Next 300 Headers to view more message headers in the message window and get the chance to read more messages.

Downloading Multimedia Files with a Binary Newsreader

A *binary newsreader* is one that specializes in getting binary files — multimedia files such as music files and video files — from newsgroups. Binary files are difficult to manage for two reasons. First, news servers, the computers that handle messages on the Usenet, are only capable of handling text messages. When an MP3 music file, for example, is deposited on a news server, it is encoded into text, as shown in Figure 4-8. When the music file is retrieved, the encoded text has to be decoded into a binary file. Second, news servers can't handle messages longer than 10,000 lines of text. An MP3 music file that is 3MB in size would require about 65,000 lines of text — many more lines than can fit in a single text message. Therefore, the music file has to be divided into several text messages when it is deposited in a newsgroup. A binary newsreader has to be capable of, first, assembling a file from several different text messages, and second, decoding the message text into a binary music or video file.

Another issue with downloading binary files is that many news servers don't make the files available in their entirety. To piece together a binary file, you download text message 1 of 20, 2 of 20, 3 of 20, and so on, and then you decode the messages and run the files together to create a multimedia file. But if one text message is missing — say, message 9 of 20 — you end up with a gap in the file. Part of the song or part of the movie is missing and the file can't be played. News servers that are run by the major ISPs purposely leave at least one text message out of the sequence to protect themselves against copyright violations. This is their way of defending themselves against music publishers and movie companies. Most subscription news servers, however, don't deliberately leave out text messages in the file sequence. Earlier in this chapter, the sidebar "How's your news server?" lists some of these subscription news servers. A good binary newsreader can detect when part of a binary file is missing and tell you as much in case you prefer not to download an incomplete file.

Figure 4-8:
An MP3 file encoded into numbers and letters.

Table 4-2 describes several binary newsreaders. I prefer the Binary Boy newsreader. Because this book isn't as much a book as it is a long game of follow the leader, I discuss Binary Boy in this chapter. I also explain how to download binary files with Outlook Express in case you're a fan of that program. Outlook Express is nowhere near the best program for downloading binary files from a newsgroup, but if you are dealing with images or with a few text messages and all are clearly labeled in a newsgroup, Outlook Express is just fine for downloading the messages and assembling them into a file.

Table 4-2   **Binary Newsreaders**

Name	*Web Address*	*Cost*
Binary Boy	www.binaryboy.com	$24.95/30-day trial
BNR (Binary News Reaper)	www.bnr2.org	Free
GrabIt	www.shemes.com	Free
NewsBin Pro	www.newsbin.com	$35 with time trial
NewsShark	www.wmhsoft.com/NewsShark	$49.95
Power-Grab	www.cosmicwolf.com	Free

In many binary file newsgroups, you can request a song or movie. The convention is to put the letters REQ, a colon, and the name of the thing you are requesting in the message header of your request. With a little luck, you can come back to the newsgroup a day or two later and find the song or movie you requested.

Downloading binary files with Outlook Express

The biggest obstacle to downloading binary files with Outlook Express is telling which text messages in a newsgroup are parts of binary files and which are plain-old text messages. In most newsgroups, the message header reveals whether the text message is part of a binary file. Scroll to the right to see whether the message reads 1 of 2, 2 of 2, and so on. You can also glance in the lower half of the message window after you select a message. If you see a bunch of gibberish (refer to Figure 4-8), you've selected part of a binary file.

Follow these steps to download a binary file from a newsgroup using Outlook Express:

1. **Select all the text messages that, taken together, form the binary file.**

   The fastest way to do that is to select the first message and Shift+click the last. You can also hold down Ctrl and click each message. The selected messages are highlighted, as shown in Figure 4-9.

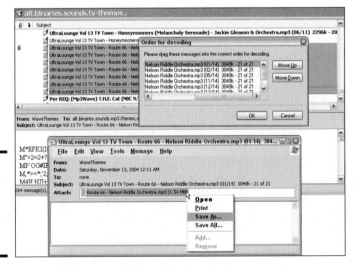

Figure 4-9: You can download files in Outlook Express.

2. **Choose Message⇨Combine and Decode.**

   You see the Order for Decoding dialog box (refer to Figure 4-9).

3. **Make sure that the messages are in the correct order.**

   Select messages and click the Move Up or Move Down button, as necessary.

4. **Click the OK button in the Order for Decoding dialog box.**

   The Combine and Decode message box appears as the messages are decoded and joined into a file. As shown in Figure 4-9, a message window appears, with the binary file in the Attach line.

5. **Right-click the binary file and choose Open to play the file, or choose Save As to save it in a folder.**

   I hope the song you downloaded is sweet, and if you downloaded a movie, I hope it has a happy ending.

Downloading binary files with Binary Boy

The biggest advantage of Binary Boy (`www.binaryboy.com`) over Outlook Express is that Binary Boy can separate text messages from binary file messages right away. And Binary Boy makes downloading the binary file messages easier too, because you just click a button to download several files at once. The program costs $30, but you can use the trial version for free for 30 days. Following is a quick tutorial in the Binary Boy newsreader.

Doing the setup work

Download Binary Boy by going to this address: `www.binaryboy.com`. As part of installing the program, you are asked where you want to store it in your menu structure. Choose carefully. The first time I downloaded Binary Boy, I forgot where I put the program on my menus. I had to dig into the `C:\Program Files\Binary Boy` folder and double-click the `Binboy.exe` file to start Binary Boy.

The installation procedure asks about your newsreader and what kind of connection your computer has to the Internet. Don't worry about answering those questions right away. Just click the Cancel button to go to the next dialog box. When the program is finished downloading, choose Edit⇨Settings (or press Alt+T) to open the Binary Boy Settings dialog box and tell Binary Boy about your Internet connection and newsreader:

✦ **Internet connection:** On the Dialer tab, choose I'm Using a Permanent Internet Connection if you connect through a DSL service or network. If yours is a dialup connection, choose Dial Using a Phone Book Entry, choose your ISP, and enter your username and password.

✦ **Newsreader:** On the Server tab, enter the address (the name) of the news server your ISP provides. See "Connecting to a news server," earlier in this chapter, for an explanation of news servers. Also enter your e-mail address and password.

Next, click the Newsgroups button or choose Connection⇨Refresh Newsgroup List to download the list of newsgroups into Binary Boy.

Creating group lists

In Binary Boy parlance, a *group list* is a collection of newsgroups from which you want to download binary files. When the time comes to see what is on different newsgroups, you open a group list and look in the newsgroups one at a time, downloading binary files as you go along. In Figure 4-10, for example, .jpg files are being downloaded from the alt.binaries.pictures.tall-ships newsgroup. This newsgroup is part of a group list called Historic Pictures.

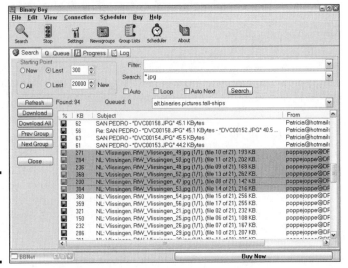

Figure 4-10: Downloading files with Binary Boy.

Group lists make it possible to search many newsgroups very quickly for multimedia files. Follow these steps to create a group list of newsgroups you are interested in:

1. **Click the Group Lists button or choose Edit⇨Edit Group List.**

2. **Click the Yes button in the dialog box that asks "Would you like to create a new group list?"**

You see the Newsgroups dialog box. The Master Newsgroup List in the bottom half of the dialog box shows newsgroup names.

3. **Enter a search term in the Search text box to describe the kind of newsgroup you are searching for.**

   For example, enter **binaries** to see the names of groups with the word *binaries* in their name.

4. **Select each newsgroup you want to add to your list and click the Add button.**

   After you click the Add button, the name of the newsgroup you selected appears in the Subscribed Groups list at top of the dialog box.

5. **Click the OK button when you have finished adding newsgroups to your groups list.**

   The Save As dialog box appears. Notice that Binary Boy has created some lists already — audiobooks, e-books, jobs, and others. Their names appear in the dialog box.

6. **Enter a name for your list in the File Name text box.**

7. **Click the Save button.**

   You did it — you created a group list.

To change a group list around or delete a group list, click the Search button or choose Collection⇨Search for Attachments. You see the Search dialog box. Choose the name of a list on the Group List to Search drop-down menu. To delete the list, click the Delete List button. To change a list, click the Edit List button. You see the Newsgroups dialog box, the same dialog box you used to created the group list. Add more newsgroups or delete newsgroups as you please.

Downloading multimedia files

After you create a group list, you can get down to the business of downloading binary files from newsgroups. Follow these steps to download binary files from newsgroups whose names you put in a group list:

1. **Click the Search button or choose Collection⇨Search for Attachments.**

   The Search dialog box appears.

2. **On the Group List to Search drop-down menu, choose the name of the group list whose newsgroups you want to search, and click the OK button.**

   You see the Search window (refer to Figure 4-10).

3. **Select the name of a newsgroup from the drop-down menu.**

4. **In the Search text box, enter a wildcard to describe the kind of binary files you want to download.**

   For example, to download jpeg image files, enter ***.jpeg** or ***.jpg**. To find music files, enter ***.mp3**. To find movie files, enter ***.wmv**. If you've entered these wildcards before, you can choose them from the drop-down menu instead of entering them. And if you want to see all messages on the newsgroup, enter ***.***.

   Notice the disk icons next to messages. When you see a green half-disk icon, the text message in question is part of a larger binary file with at least one part missing. A red half-disk icon means that the file is missing part 1 and can't be decoded. A whole green disk icon (which you can see in Figure 4-10) means that the entire file is available to your newsreader.

5. **Select the file or files you want to download.**

   To do so, click filenames. You can select several files at once by Ctrl+clicking or Shift+clicking them. To download an entire binary file, you need only select one part (a message with a green half-disk icon by its name).

6. **Click the Download button to download files you selected, or click the Download All button to download all files that are part of a large binary file, one part of which you selected in the previous step.**

   If you don't see the Download buttons, choose View⇨Resize Subject List (or press Alt+R) as many times as necessary to make the buttons appear. After the files download, you can choose another newsgroup name from the drop-down list and download files from another newsgroup.

Files downloaded to your computer land in the `C:\Documents and Settings\`*Your Name*`\My Documents\My Attachments` folder. You can quickly open this folder by pressing Alt+A or by choosing File⇨Open Attachments Folder. The folder opens in Windows Explorer.

What to do about incomplete files

If you download a music or video file, it may be incomplete. Parts are missing. What can you do about that? One thing you can do is try to stitch the file together with the help of Dr. Binary. This strangely named utility fills in gaps in files and tries its best to assemble them. Follow these steps to try to make an incomplete file whole again:

1. **Choose File⇨Send All Parts to Dr. Binary.**

2. **Click the Yes button in the dialog box that asks whether you want to send the** `Parts` **folder to Dr. Binary.**

   The `Parts` folder is located at `C:\Documents and Settings\`*Your Name*`\My Documents\Parts`. (To open this folder from Binary Boy, choose File⇨Open Parts Folder.) Text files that have yet to be decoded because they are incomplete are kept in the `Parts` folder.

3. Choose File⇨Dr. Binary or press Alt+D.

You see the Select One Part from Set dialog box. A set is the text messages that make up a binary file.

4. Select the first file and click the Open button.

You see the Dr. Binary dialog box shown in Figure 4-11.

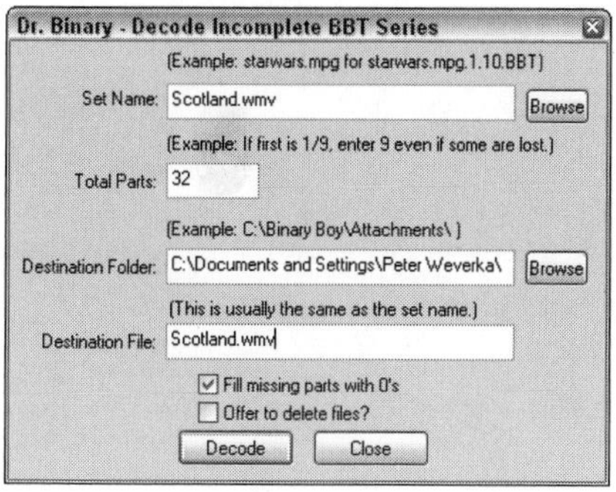

Figure 4-11:
Decoding an
incomplete
file.

5. Click the Decode button.

With any luck, the good doctor is able to decode the files and create the semblance of a music file or video. You can find the file in the `C:\Documents and Settings\`*`Your Name`*`\My Documents\My Attachments` folder (press Alt+A to get there).

Chapter 5: Joining, Starting, and Managing a Yahoo! Group

In This Chapter

✔ Discovering Yahoo! groups

✔ Searching for and joining a group

✔ Canceling your membership

✔ Posting messages, files, and photos to groups

✔ Starting your own Yahoo! group

This chapter takes on the subject of Yahoo! groups, how to join them, and how to create them. You are hereby invited to join a Yahoo! group to find and commune with kindred spirits, and if no such group exists, you can start one of your own.

When you think about it, a Yahoo! group is really a canned, preformatted Web site where people can post messages, download files, and view photographs. The groups are like conventional mailing lists, only they're much easier to manage (mailing lists are the subject of Book IV, Chapter 3). The only disadvantage of Yahoo! groups is having to create an account with Yahoo! and sign in to Yahoo! to make use of them. Some people find that inconvenient.

To join or create a Yahoo! group, you need a Yahoo! account. Appendix A explains how to get one of those. You also need to sign in to Yahoo! before you can join or create a group.

Introducing Yahoo! Groups

A Yahoo! group is more of a club than a group. In fact, Yahoo! groups used to be called clubs. Join a group to discuss your favorite topic with people who share your interest in bowling, Madagascar, UFOs, or whatever your favorite topic is. Some groups are not as much for discussing as they are for making announcements. A civic club or softball team, for example, can post meeting days or game schedules in its Yahoo! group. My son's Spanish teacher keeps a Yahoo! group for his students. He invited parents to join, too. I can find out when my son's homework assignments are due and when tests are forthcoming. Now when I ask the boy, "Shouldn't you be studying for a Spanish test?" I know the answer beforehand.

Each Yahoo! group gets a page like the one shown in Figure 5-1. You can read messages posted to the group starting from this page. You can also search for messages posted in months or years past. This page is also the place to download files or look at photographs, if the group offers files and photographs to its members. It's possible to join a group and never visit its Yahoo! page. You can have messages to the group delivered to your Yahoo! e-mail account without ever going to the Yahoo! page that the group calls home.

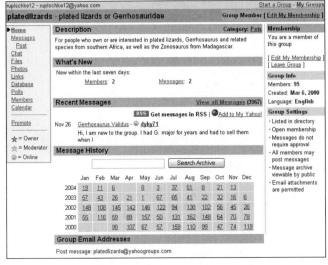

Figure 5-1:
The Yahoo!
group page
belonging
to the
platedlizards
group.

To find a group worth joining or visit a group you've already joined, start by going to the Yahoo! Groups page (after you've signed in to Yahoo!, of course). Figure 5-2 shows this page. One of these methods can get you there:

✦ Go to the Yahoo! home page (www.yahoo.com) and click the Groups link.

✦ Go straight to the Yahoo! Groups page at this address: http://groups.yahoo.com.

Figure 5-2:
The Yahoo!
Groups
page.

Finding and Joining a Yahoo! Group

Yahoo! groups come and go, so getting an accurate count of how many groups are out there is difficult. But there must be at least 10,000 Yahoo! groups. Usually, you can find one devoted to a topic you're interested in. These pages explain how to find a Yahoo! group that suits your taste and temperament, and how to join a group. You also discover how to visit a group you've joined, read its messages, download its files, and view its photographs.

Finding a group

Starting from the Yahoo! Groups page at `http://groups.yahoo.com` (refer to Figure 5-2), you can look for groups worth joining with one of these methods:

✦ **By search terms:** Enter search terms in the Join a Group text box and click the Search button. For example, to search for groups devoted to the actor Marlon Brando, enter **"marlon brando"** (include the quotation marks) and click the Search button.

✦ **By category:** Click categories and subcategories until you come to a group that tickles your fancy. To find groups devoted to Marlon Brando, for example, click the Entertainment & Arts category; the Actors and Actresses subcategory; the letter B subcategory; the Brando, Marlon subcategory; and finally, the Brando, Marlon Groups subcategory. Notice as you search that a number in parentheses next to subcategory names tells you how many groups are in each subcategory.

No matter where a search takes you or how far you stray in the Yahoo! groups pages, you can always return to the Yahoo! Groups page (refer to Figure 5-2) by clicking the Groups or the Groups Home link. You can find this link in the upper-right corner of pages.

Joining a Yahoo! group

Before you join a group, look around and see whether it's worth joining. The calendar on the group page tells you how many new messages have been posted to the group this month. Take note of how many members are in the group. Is this a lively party or a dud with everyone standing around the potato chips hardly saying anything? If the group is public (more about that in a minute), you can read messages posted to the group. Read a few and see whether the discussion is interesting. Unfortunately, public groups are susceptible to junk mail. Have many spam messages been posted to the group? If so, the group may not be worth joining.

Look under Group Info on the right side of the page to see which kind of group you are dealing with. Yahoo! groups fall in two categories:

✦ **Public group:** Anyone can join this group without getting the permission of the owner. Look for the words *Open membership* under Group Info.

✦ **Private group:** You must get the owner's permission to join this group. Look for *Membership requires approval* under Group Info.

If you decide to join a group, click the Join This Group button. You come to the Join This Group page, where you negotiate these all-important questions:

✦ **Yahoo! Profile:** If you have more than one Yahoo! profile and you want to join under a profile different from the one you are currently operating under, choose a profile from the drop-down menu.

✦ **E-Mail Address:** If you have more than one Yahoo! e-mail address, choose the one you want to use to post messages to this group.

✦ **E-Mail Display:** If the group permits you to hide your e-mail address from the moderators, you see this check box. To hide your address, select the check box.

✦ **Comment to Owner:** In the case of a private group, write a note to the owner explaining why you want to join.

✦ **Message Delivery:** Choose how you want to read messages posted to the group:

  • **Individual Emails:** Messages posted to the group (and approved by the owner in the case of private groups) are sent to your e-mail address right away.

- **Daily Digest:** Instead of getting individual messages, you receive one message each day with a day's worth of e-mail. This option keeps you from being flooded with e-mail from the group.

- **Special Notices:** Only notices from the owner or a group moderator are sent to you, and they are sent by e-mail.

- **No Email:** No messages posted to the group are sent to you by e-mail. You want to go to the group page to read and post messages.

✦ **Message Format:** Choose HTML or plain text. HTML-formatted e-mail messages can include color, boldface text, pictures, and other froufrou stuff. Some e-mail programs can't handle HTML-formatted messages.

✦ **Word Verification:** Enter the combination of letters and numbers in the text box. The word-verification mechanism is meant to keep evil robots from joining groups and hosing them down with junk mail.

Don't fret or ponder very long over these questions. You can always change your mind about how your e-mail address is displayed and how messages from the group are delivered by e-mail, as the next section in this chapter explains.

After you click the Join button, you are admitted to the group, or, in the case of private groups, a Membership Pending page tells you that you will receive confirmation by e-mail if the group's owner decides to let you in.

Visiting a group to which you belong

A list of the groups you joined can be found on these pages. Click the name of a group to open its page and visit it.

✦ **Yahoo! Groups page:** To get to this page, go to the Yahoo! home page and click the Groups link or go straight to the page by steering your browser to this address: `http://groups.yahoo.com`. You can find the list of groups to which you belong on the left side of the page in the My Groups section (refer to Figure 5-2).

✦ **My Groups page:** Click the My Groups link on any Yahoo! page having to do with groups. The My Groups page lists each group you belong to, as well as the profile, e-mail address, and message-delivery mode you chose for each group.

Reading messages and downloading files and photos

A Yahoo! group page is really a mini-Web site in that you can view photos and download files as well as post messages. As shown in Figure 5-3, the left side of the group window offers links you can click to open the Messages window, download files, or view photos.

To read a message, click the Messages link and then click a message's subject in the Messages window. Doing so opens a message window, where you can read the message comfortably. Here are some tips for preventing claustrophobia as you read messages:

✦ Click the Previous or Next link in a message window to read the previous or following message posted to the group.

✦ Click the Up Thread link to read the original message if you are reading a reply (a message with the term *Re:* in its subject line).

✦ Click the Expand Messages link to be able to scroll down the screen and read messages, as shown in Figure 5-3. In an expanded window, subject lines as well as messages appear. Click the Collapse Messages link to go back to seeing a list of message subjects.

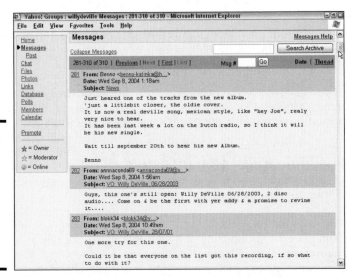

Figure 5-3:
Click the Expand Messages link to be able to scroll through messages.

Not every group offers photos or files for downloading, but if a group to which you belong does, follow these instructions to view photos and download files:

✦ **Viewing photos:** Click the Photos link on the group page. You come to the Photos page, where you see either photo thumbnails or folders where photos are stored. To open a folder, click it. Click a thumbnail to view the larger version of a photo. You can click the Slideshow link to make the photos appear one at a time.

✦ **Downloading a file:** Click the Files link on the group page. You land in the Files page, where you see either a list of files or folders where files are kept. Click a folder to open it. To open a file, click it. If the file is one that can carry a virus, the File Download dialog box appears. Book II, Chapter 1 explains all the vagaries of downloading and copying files from the Internet.

To save a photo to your computer, right-click it, choose Save Picture As, choose a folder in the Save Picture dialog box, and click the Save button. You can enter a name of your own for the photograph in the File Name text box before clicking the Save button.

Changing how messages from a group are delivered

Sometimes you join a group and get flooded with e-mail messages. Or, you register the wrong e-mail address in a group. Or, you wish you had joined a group under a different profile. In times like those, you can visit the Edit My Groups window, shown in Figure 5-4, and change how messages are delivered, your e-mail address, or your profile.

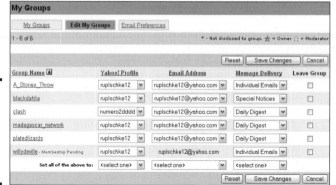

Figure 5-4: The Edit My Groups window, for changing your mind.

Follow these dance steps to get to the Edit My Groups window:

1. **Go to the Yahoo! Groups page (**`http://groups.yahoo.com`**).**

2. **Click the My Groups link.**

You can find this link in the upper-right corner of the page. You land in the My Groups window. It lists each group to which you belong.

3. **Click the Edit My Groups link.**

Not a moment too soon, you come to the Edit My Groups window (refer to Figure 5-4).

4. **Using the drop-down menus, choose a new profile, e-mail address, and message-delivery mode for each group to which you belong.**

5. **Click the Save Changes button.**

 You return to the My Groups window. It correctly lists each setting you chose in the Edit My Groups window.

Leaving a Yahoo! Group

Groucho Marx said, "I don't want to belong to any club that will accept me as a member." If you were accepted as a member of a Yahoo! group and, like Groucho Marx, you think it reflects badly on your character, you can resign from the group two different ways:

✦ Go to the group's page and click the Leave Group link. You can find this link in the upper-right corner of the page.

✦ Go to the Edit My Groups window (refer to Figure 5-4), select the Leave Group check box for the group you want to leave, and click the Save Changes button. The previous section in this chapter explains how to get to the Edit My Groups window.

Posting a Message to a Group

So you want to drop your two cents' worth in a group you've joined? You can do that in three ways:

✦ **Posting on the group's page:** Click the Post link. You can find this link on the left side of the page, as shown in Figure 5-5. Then fill out the Post Message form and click the Send button.

✦ **Replying to a post:** Click the Reply link in the Messages window. The Post Message form displays the message you are replying to. Notice the letters *Re:* in the subject line. These letters indicate that you are posting a reply. Enter your reply and click the Send button.

✦ **Posting by e-mail program:** Address your message to the group's post-message address: *groupname*@yahoogroups.com. You can find this address at the bottom of the group's page. Then write the message and send it. And be sure to send it from the address you listed when you joined the group. If you send it from a different address, your post will be rejected.

Figure 5-5:
Posting a
message to
a group.

To send a message to someone who posted a message in a group, not to the group itself, click the person's e-mail address. You can find this address at the top of the message window near the person's name. After you click it, a form page opens so that you can write an e-mail message.

Sending Files and Photos to a Group

Not every group allows its members to post files and photos. If you try to post a file or photo but can't do it, don't take it personally. It could be that the group moderator doesn't allow files or photos to be posted. It could be that only certain members can post. Yahoo! only allots 20MB of file space for each group to post files and photos. Twenty megabytes isn't very much file space, so moderators have to be careful how they use it.

Follow these steps to post a file or photo to a group:

1. **Click the Files link or the Photos link in the group page.**

You land in the Files window or the Photos window. If files or photos are stored in folders, the window displays several folder names. Click the folder where you want to post the file or photo.

2. **Click the Add File link or the Add Photo link.**

As shown in Figure 5-6, you see the Add File window if you are posting a file. The Add Photos window looks and works much like this window.

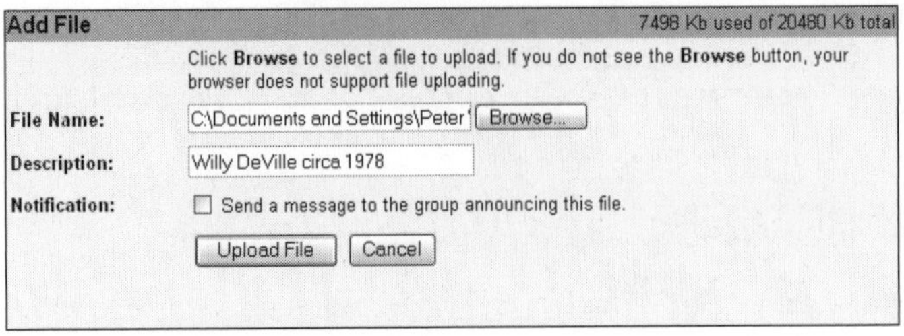

Figure 5-6:
Posting a
file to a
group.

3. **Click the Browse button, and in the Choose File dialog box, locate your file or photo, select it, and click the Open button.**

4. **Enter a few descriptive words in the Description text box.**

The words you enter appear under the file's name in the Files window, or under the photo's filename in the Photos window.

If you are in the Photos window, you can upload more than one photo at a time by entering more filenames.

5. **Click the Upload File button or the Upload button.**

Your file or photos aren't posted right away. It takes a moment for the Yahoo! computers to swallow and digest them.

Conducting a poll

Polls can be a lot of fun. Poll a group for practical reasons — to find out the best day to hold a meeting or the best place to eat lunch. Or poll a group to find out which song it likes best or what its favorite movie is. To conduct a poll, click the Polls link on the group page. Then, in the Polls window, click the Create a Poll link. In the Create Poll window, enter the question, enter the answer choices, and choose when the poll concludes.

To see the results of your poll, click the Polls link and, in the Polls window, click the name of your poll.

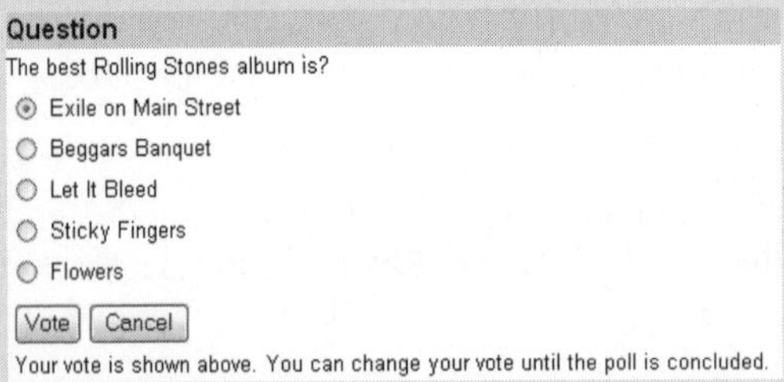

If you posted a file or photo to the wrong folder, don't despair. Click the Cut link next to the file or photo to move it to the Clipboard. Then open the folder where you want the file or photo to be and click the Paste link.

Starting and Managing a Yahoo! Group

So you scoured the Yahoo! groups but couldn't find one devoted to the topic that warms your heart or excites your intellect. You have but one recourse — create a group of your own. The rest of this chapter explains how to do that. You discover how to create a group, control who can join, and review or delete messages as they are posted. You also find out how to remove members and confer moderator status on a member. I hope your Yahoo! group attracts many, many groupies.

Before you begin . . .

Before you create a Yahoo! group, find a good hammock to lie in and ponder these matters:

✦ **Is there already a Yahoo! group for the topic you want to cover?** As I write this, 70 Yahoo! groups are devoted to the actor Tom Cruise. Do we need another group for the diminutive superstar? Search the groups thoroughly to find out whether someone beat you to it (see "Finding a group," earlier in this chapter).

✦ **Which category does the group belong in?** When you create your group, you are asked to select a category to place it in. Rummage around the Yahoo! categories until you find the ideal category for your group. Find the category that people who are searching for a group like yours will look in first.

✦ **What is the name of your group?** Choose a descriptive name. You want people to know what your group is about as soon as they read its name.

After you create your group, you get the opportunity to decide whether it is public or private, whether posts made to the group need your approval, and other such-like stuff. I explain it all later in this chapter.

Starting a Yahoo! group

Yahoo! seems to want everyone to start a group. Right there at the top of the Yahoo! Groups page (refer to Figure 5-2) is the Start a New Group link. Click that link to get going.

Starting a group is a three-step process. Sign in to Yahoo! under the profile and e-mail address that you want to use to manage your Yahoo! group after you create it. Then click the Start a New Group link and take Step 1, Step 2, and Step 3.

Step 1 of 3: Select a Yahoo! Groups category

Select the category that you want your group to be in. To select the category, use the same techniques for searching that you use to look for a group starting from the Yahoo! Groups page (see "Finding a group" and Figure 5-2, earlier in this chapter). Either enter search terms in the text box or search by selecting categories and subcategories.

When you arrive at the category you want from your group, click the Place My Group in *Category Name* link. You can find this link to the right of the category name.

Step 2 of 3: Describe your group

On the next page, describe your group:

✦ **Group Name:** Enter a name for your group. As shown in Figure 5-7, the name you choose appears at the top of the group page.

✦ **Enter Your Group Email Address:** Choose an e-mail address for your group. Members can send e-mail to all members of your group by sending a message to the address you enter. The address appears at the bottom of your group page.

✦ **Describe Your Group:** Enter a concise description of your group. The words you enter appear on your group page, as shown in Figure 5-7. Tell what your group is about and why it is worth joining. Remember: This is your best chance to attract the kind of members who will contribute to the group and make it a lively community.

✦ Write and spell-check the description in a word-processing program. Then copy and paste your description into the Describe Your Group text box (on the Yahoo! page, right-click and choose Paste). This way, you can comfortably write and proofread your description.

Click the Continue button to move on to Step 3.

Figure 5-7:
The group page for the Rosenda Monteros group.

The owner of the group

The person who creates and manages a Yahoo! group is called the *owner*. Only the owner can customize the group, decide who can join, delete e-mail messages, and designate someone else to be a moderator, a person who can take over some of the owner's responsibilities.

If you are the owner of a group, a blue star appears beside the group's name in the My Groups section on the Yahoo! Groups page. On the group page itself, meanwhile, the owner sees three extra links on the left side that members don't see:

🖊 **Promote:** Click this link to get and copy HTML code that you can use to place invitations to join the group on a Web page.

🖊 **Invite:** Click this link to send e-mail invitations to friends, family, and coworkers, inviting them to join the group.

🖊 **Management:** Click this link to customize and manage your group. See "Customizing and managing a group."

On the group page, the Messages, Files, Photos, and Members links along the left side work a bit differently if you are the owner. When you click one of these links, you see messages, files, photos, or a membership list, but you also see tools for removing messages, files, photos, and members. You're the owner! You're the boss!

My Groups
★RosendaMonteros
A_Stones_Throw
blackdahlia
clash
platedlizards
willydeville
Order these groups

Step 3 of 3: Select your Yahoo! profile and e-mail address

Finally, a wee bit of housekeeping:

✦ **Email Address:** Choose the e-mail address where you want to receive messages that are sent to you from members of the group. For example, requests to join your group are sent to this address.

✦ **Yahoo! Profile:** If you have more than one Yahoo! profile, choose the one for which you want to be known to members of the group.

✦ **Word Verification:** You know the drill. Enter the combination of letters and numbers in the text box.

Click the Continue button to go to the Congratulations window, where you see your group's name, the address of its home page, and its e-mail address. Yahoo! removes spaces from names, so if your group's name comprises two or more words, the words are run together (refer to Figure 5-7). Don't worry about it. On your group page, the name isn't run together. The run-together name is just the official name.

Try right-clicking the Group Home Page address and choosing Open in New Window on the pop-up menu. Doing so opens your Yahoo! group page in your Web browser. How do you like your group page? If you want to customize it, read on.

Customizing and managing a group

To start with, each group is a public group that's open to anybody. Replies to messages are posted to the group without being reviewed first. But you can change these and other settings by customizing the group.

Yahoo! gives you the chance to customize a group right after you create it. By clicking the Customize Group button in the Congratulations window, you can open a so-called Customize Wizard and answer a bunch of survey questions about your group. Go ahead and take the wizard survey if you want. Whatever you do with the wizard, however, you can always customize and refine your group by going to the Management window shown in Figure 5-8.

Figure 5-8: Start at the Management window to customize and manage a group.

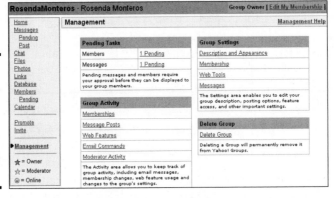

The Management window is your starting point for customizing and managing a group. Click a link in this window to handle members, messages, and the appearance of the group page. Follow these initial steps to customize or manage your group:

1. **Sign in to Yahoo! under the name and profile you use to manage your Yahoo! group.**

2. **Go to the Yahoo! Groups page at** `http://groups.yahoo.com`.

3. **In the My Groups section, click the name of the group you own.**

   A blue star appears beside its name. After you click the name, you go to the group page.

4. Click the Management link on the left side of the page (refer to Figure 5-8).

You're there! You've arrived at the Management window and you're ready to go.

Deciding how members may join the group

In the Management window, click the Membership link (the link in the Group Settings section, not the Memberships link in the Group Activity section) to decide how people can join your group. You see the Group Settings window. Click Edit link in this window to change the membership rules and the e-mail message that is sent to members when they join.

Be careful, because the Membership Type and Email Display settings cannot be changed after you make the initial selection:

✦ **Membership Type:** Choose Open to permit anyone to join or Restricted to require members to get your approval. Choose the Closed option if you want only people you invite to be able to join the group.

✦ **Email Address Display:** With this option, you permit members to hide their e-mail addresses from other group members. Members can't bypass the group and send e-mail to one another.

Changing the group settings and page appearance

Click the Description and Appearance link in the Management window (refer to Figure 5-8) to change the group settings and appearance of your page. You land in the Group Settings window. By clicking an Edit link in this window, you can change the group's Web address, its description, its category, and the description that you wrote when you created the Yahoo! group.

You can also change the colors of the page and place a photograph on the page. To decorate your page with a photo, click the Edit link next to the word *Photo* in the lower-right corner of the window and, in the Change Picture For window, either click the Browse button and choose a photo file or enter a link to a photo on the Internet.

Giving members access to Web tools

"Web tools" refers to the ability to post photos and files to your group, as well as view profiles and chat. Click the Web Tools link in the Management window (refer to Figure 5-8) to decide which tools members get.

Admitting new members

If you opted to make prospective members get your approval before they can join your group, you are alerted when someone wants to join in three different ways:

+ **On your group page:** The top of your group page reads "Pending members require your attention. Activity pending for 14 days will be automatically rejected." Click the Members link in this notice to go to the Pending tab of the Pending Members page. You can also click the Members link in the Pending Activity section on the right side of the page, or the Pending link in the Members section on the left side.

+ **In the Management window:** In the Pending Tasks section (refer to Figure 5-8), click the Pending link next to the word *Members* to go to the Pending tab of the Pending Members page.

+ **In your Yahoo! mail account:** An APPROVE message appears in the Inbox. To allow the person to join, simply reply to the message. To decline, forward the message as you are instructed to do in the body of the e-mail.

Figure 5-9 shows part of the Pending tab of the Pending Members page. To admit a new member or reject someone's application for membership, open the Action drop-down menu, choose Approve or Deny, and click the Save Changes button.

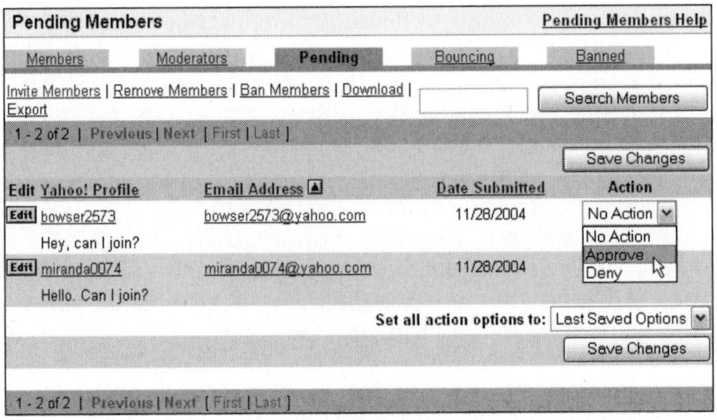

Figure 5-9: Approving or denying a membership.

Accepting and rejecting messages

If your group is moderated, you must approve each message before it gets posted. Yahoo! lets you know when messages need your review in three ways:

✦ **On your group page:** The top of your group page reads "Pending messages require your attention." Click the Messages link to go to the Pending page. You can also click the Pending link in the Messages section on the left side of the page or the Messages link in the Pending Activity section on the right side to go to the Pending page.

✦ **In the Management window:** In the Pending Tasks section (refer to Figure 5-8), click the Pending link next to the word *Messages* to go to Pending window.

✦ **In your Yahoo! mail account:** A MODERATE message appears in your Inbox. To allow the person to join, simply reply to the message. To decline, forward the message as you are so instructed in the e-mail.

To accept or reject a message in the Pending window, open the drop-down menu next to the message and choose Approve or Delete. Then click the Save Changes button. You can also click the Edit button to edit the message before you approve it. You might — ahem! — use this opportunity to repair the poster's grammatical or spelling errors.

Dealing with trusted or troublesome group members

To save yourself the trouble of accepting or rejecting messages from a trusted or troublesome member of your group, you can accept or reject the poster's messages automatically regardless of whether your group is moderated or unmoderated. In a moderated group, you can accept the poster's messages without having to review them. In an unmoderated group, you can review messages from a troublesome poster so that they aren't posted without your approval. Follow these steps to override the message-moderation settings for a member of your group:

1. **Click the Members link on the group page.**

   You see the Members window. It lists each member of your group.

2. **Click the Edit button beside the member's name.**

The Edit Member window appears.

3. **Scroll to Posting Messages and click the Edit link.**

   You come to the Edit Message Posting Privileges window.

4. **In the Override Your Group Posting Setting section, select the option that describes how you want messages from this poster to be treated automatically.**

   Select the Messages Posted by This Member Are Not Moderated option button to accept messages automatically or select the Messages Posted by This Member Are Moderated option button to review messages before they are posted.

5. **Click the Save Changes button.**

To switch from having a moderated group to having an unmoderated group or vice versa, go to the Management window (refer to Figure 5-8) and click the Messages link in the Group Settings section. In the Group Settings window, scroll to Posting and Archives, and click the Edit link. In the Moderation section in the following window, select the Unmoderated or Moderated option button. Then click the Save Changes button.

Removing messages, files, and photos

Suppose someone posts an unpleasant or off-topic message, a file that has no business being offered by your group, or an offensive photo? Here's what you can do about it:

✦ **Removing a message:** On the group page (not in the Management window), click the Messages link (you can find it on the left side of the page right below the Home link). You see a list of messages posted to your group. Find the message that needs deleting, select its check box, and click the Delete button.

✦ **Removing a file:** On the group page (not in the Management window), click the Files link to go to the Files window. Click the Delete link next to the name of the file you want to delete.

✦ **Removing a photo:** Click the Photos link on the group page. You land in the Photos window. Select the photo that you want to remove and click the Delete button.

Each Yahoo! group is allotted about 20MB for files and photos. The upper-right corner of the Files window tells you how much space remains in your allotment: "250 Kb used of 20480 Kb total." As you approach the 20480KB allotment, you may have to delete some files and photos.

To prevent a member from uploading files, click the Members link on the group page and, in the Members window, click the Edit button beside the member's name. You go to the Edit Member window. Select the Disallow This Member from Uploading Files check box and then click the Save Changes button.

Handling the membership

Occasionally it is necessary to make a member stand in the corner, or, quite the opposite, award a member with moderator status. Moderators have almost all the rights and responsibilities of owners. Make a trusted member of your group a moderator, and the work of managing your group gets a little easier.

To remove a member, ban someone from your group, or make a member into a moderator, start in the group page and click the Members link. You can find this link on the left side of the page. You come to the Members window shown in Figure 5-10. Get to work:

✦ **Removing a member:** Find the member, select his or her Remove check box, and click the Save Changes button.

✦ **Banning a member:** Get the e-mail address of the person you want to ban. Then click the Ban Members link and, in the Ban Members window, enter the e-mail address and click the Ban Members button.

✦ **Making a member into a moderator:** Click the Edit button to go the Edit Member window. Then click the Change to Moderator link. In the Make Moderator window, select Moderator Privileges check boxes to confer rights and responsibilities on the moderator, and click the Make a Moderator button.

Figure 5-10:
The
Members
window
lists each
member of
the group.

A yellow star appears beside the names of moderators in the Members window. To turn a moderator back into a mere member, go to the Members window (refer to Figure 5-10), click the Edit button next to the moderator's name, and in the Edit Moderator window, click the Change to Member link.

Chapter 6: Chatting Online

Chatting is to the Internet what Elvis is to rock-and-roll. Before Web sites, online auctions, MP3 files, instant messaging, blogs, and social networking, there was online chatting. Chatting made the Internet famous. Along about 1995, it was the thing to do. You could converse with people on the other side of the world, make exotic new friends, confess your darkest sins to sympathetic strangers, or pretend to be something you weren't with people who didn't mind at all because they, too, were pretending. In the 1990s, America Online became the biggest Internet service provider because its "anything goes" chat-room policy attracted millions of customers.

Chatting is not the popular activity it used to be, but thousands of people still engage in chats. Interestingly, chat rooms have become a preferred hangout for people who live in countries where free speech is banned or suppressed. Because you can be anonymous in a chat room (indeed, you *should* be anonymous for privacy's sake), people can discuss politics without fear of reprisal.

This short chapter looks at everything you need to know to chat on the Internet. It describes online chats, takes you into a chat room, and explains how to safeguard your privacy as you chat. It also shows how to use mIRC, which is special software for chatting.

Introducing Online Chats

Chatting takes place in a *chat room,* a locale in cyberspace where people meet and greet each other anonymously in real time. Each chat room is supposed to be devoted to one topic. Figure 6-1 shows a typical chat room, this one devoted to Cultures and Community at Yahoo! Chat (`http://chat.yahoo.com`). Chatters' nicknames — the pseudonyms under which they talk to one another — are listed on the right side of the chat window. By double-clicking a nickname on the list, you can open a smaller chat window and engage in a *private chat,* a conversation of two, as shown at the bottom of Figure 6-1.

Most chat services and programs allow private chatting. Unfortunately, they also permit chatters to use different fonts and emoticons — smiley faces and so on — not to mention foul language. The result isn't as much a conversation as a chaotic mish-mash of words. In my experience, meaningful chats take place privately between people who have met each other in the main chat window.

Chat services fall in two categories — IRC and private, Web-based chat services. IRC stands for *Internet Relay Chat.* IRC is an Internet chat network by which people who have joined different channels — the IRC word for "chat rooms" — can type messages to one another. Think of IRC as an Internet for chatters. Some Web-based chat services, namely MSN and America Online, allow their members to chat on IRC channels.

Advances in software have made it much easier to maintain a chat room. Consequently, every Tom, Dick, and Harry can put one on a Web site. Even a modest Web site without many amenities may have a chat room these days.

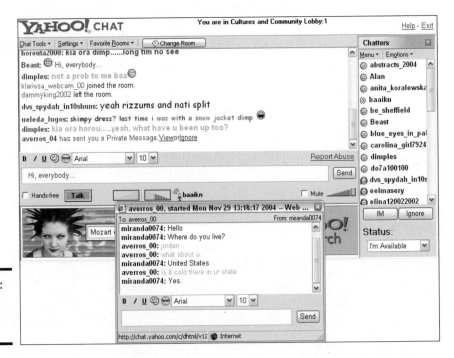

Figure 6-1:
A typical
chat
window.

Finding Out the Rules of the Road

To protect your privacy and safeguard your identity as you chat, here are the rules of the road where chatting is concerned:

✦ Don't give out personal information in a chat room. Your name, phone number, the school you attend, your place of work — guard them carefully. I don't mean to be a paranoid, but stalkers have tracked people down with information they got in chat rooms.

✦ Be civil. This rule is abused quite often in chat rooms, but try your best.

✦ Warn your children if they visit chat rooms that many chatters are not who they claim to be. Somebody who they think is a kid like they are could well be an adult.

Private, Web-Based Chat Services

As I explained earlier, private Web-based chat rooms are so numerous it would be impossible to catalog them. Table 6-1 lists the addresses of major online services that offer chatting. To use these services, you have to have an account. To chat on MSN, you can use your .NET passport (Appendix B explains what that is).

Table 6-1	Chatting at the Major Online Services
Service	*Address*
America Online	(Click the People link on AOL home page.)
MSN Chat	`http://groups.msn.com/people`
Yahoo! Chat	`http://chat.yahoo.com`

Raidersoft offers a special search engine for searching for chat rooms. Run the search engine starting at this address: `http://chat.raidersoft.com/index.pl`. While you're there, check out the top-25 list of the most popular Web sites with chat rooms. Raidersoft ranks these Web sites each week according to how many hits they've received.

**Book IV
Chapter 6**

Chatting Online

Chatting on IRC

Figure 6-2 shows a rather odd-looking program called mIRC for engaging in IRC chats. You can download this program for free from Cnet (`www.cnet.com`), TUCOWS (`www.tucows.com`), or the office home page of mIRC (www.mirc.com). Mac users can use Ircle, the Mac equivalent of mIRC. mIRC? Ircle? Why the strange names? Did these programs originate on Mars?

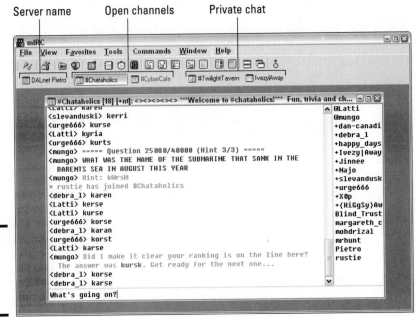

Figure 6-2:
Chatting in mIRC, the IRC chat program.

When you start mIRC, you see the mIRC Options dialog box. Click the Connect to Server button to find a server that can connect you to IRC. You see the mIRC Favorites dialog box with a list of channels you can go to. If you know the name of a channel you want to visit, enter its name and click the Join button. Just close the dialog box if you don't have a channel to visit. I show you how to visit a channel shortly.

Finding and bookmarking channels

You can open as many chat windows as your sanity allows. Here are instructions for finding, opening, and bookmarking channels with mIRC:

✦ **Connecting to a server:** If your server connection fails or your initial attempt to connect to a server doesn't work out, choose File⇨Select Server (or press Alt+E) to open the Servers category of the mIRC Options dialog box. Then select a server from the IRC Server drop-down menu and click the Connect to Server button.

✦ **Finding and entering a new channel (a chat room):** Choose Tools⇨Channels List and click the Get List button in the mIRC Channels List dialog box. You see the Channels dialog box. Scroll through the *very* long list of channels until you find one that interests you. Then right-click the name and choose Join Channel on the shortcut menu.

✦ **Going from channel to channel:** An icon along the top of the window appears for each channel that is open (refer to Figure 6-2). To go from open channel to open channel, click these icons.

✦ **Bookmarking a channel:** To bookmark a channel so that you can visit it again, choose Favorites⇨Add to Favorites and click the OK button in the Add Channel dialog box. Bookmark a channel if there is even a remote possibility you will visit it again.

✦ **Visiting a channel you bookmarked:** Open the Favorites menu and click the name of a channel you bookmarked. (Click the More option at the bottom of the menu and double-click the channel in the mIRC Favorites dialog box if the channel isn't on the list.)

✦ **Revisiting a channel:** Choose Favorites⇨Recent Channels and select a channel name on the submenu to revisit a channel you recently visited.

✦ **Leaving a channel:** Click the channel's Close button.

Starting your own channel

Believe it or not, you can start your own channel. The channel will last until the moment you shut it down. After you start your channel, you can invite others to come and join you there.

To start a channel, type the following in the text box of a channel you are currently visiting and press Enter:

```
/JOIN #yourchannelname
```

Make sure *yourchannelname* is an original name that no one else is using for his or her channel. Be sure to begin your name with a number sign (#) and put a space between the word JOIN and the name. The name cannot include blank spaces.

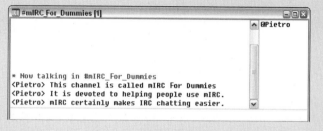

Engaging in a chat

Here are the rules of engagement for chatting:

✦ **Chatting:** Enter your words in the text box and press Enter (refer to Figure 6-2).

✦ **Starting a private chat:** On the right side of the window, double-click the name of the person you want to chat with privately. A new window opens so that you can start chatting. Meanwhile, a private window icon appears to let you know that a private chat window is open (refer to Figure 6-2).

✦ **Being invited to a private chat:** Along the top of the window, you see the private chat icon blinking on and off, as well as the name of the person who wants to chat with you. Click the icon to open a private chat window.

✦ **Changing your nickname:** Choose Commands⇨Change Nick and enter a name in the Input Request dialog box.

✦ **Ignoring a chatter:** Choose Commands⇨Ignore User and enter the chatter's nickname in the Input Request dialog box.

For a complete list of IRC commands, go to this address: www.mirc.com/ cmds.html. You can get help with IRC at the IRChelp.org Internet Relay Chat (IRC) Help Archive at this address: www.irchelp.org.

Chapter 7: Free Web Sites at Yahoo! GeoCities

In This Chapter

- ✔ Comparing free Web-hosting services
- ✔ Tips for designing Web pages and Web sites
- ✔ Creating a Web site
- ✔ Building your site in the Web Site Accounts window
- ✔ Using PageBuilder to construct a Web site
- ✔ Managing the files on your Web site
- ✔ Submitting a Web site to search engines

*T*his chapter is devoted to the idea that everyone should have a Web site and that you can put a Web site on the Internet without paying a nickel.

Why does everyone need a Web site? For the sake of convenience, if nothing else. Posting notices and announcements on a Web page and directing people to the Web page is easier than sending notices by e-mail and definitely easier than sending them by snail mail. I keep my résumé on a Web page at Yahoo! GeoCities, a free Web-hosting service. When someone asks to see my résumé, I direct them to my Yahoo! GeoCities Web page. All I have to do is put the address of the Web page in an e-mail message. All the recipient of the e-mail has to do is click the address, a hyperlink, to go straight to my Web page and read my résumé. I don't have to squeeze my résumé into the body of an e-mail message or, if I send it as a file attachment, hope that the recipient can open it and read it. Having my résumé on a Web page is convenient for everybody.

This chapter compares the different free Web-hosting services. It gives you guidelines for designing a Web site and tells you how to build a Web site at Yahoo! GeoCities with PageWizards, the PageBuilder, and other Web-site-building tools. Finally, you get advice for submitting your Web site to search engines to increase its chances of being found on Internet searches.

To create a Web site at Yahoo! GeoCities and host it for free, you need a Yahoo! account. Appendix A explains how to get one and how to sign in to Yahoo!

Deciding on a Free Web-Hosting Service

Web hosting is not what a spider does to a fly. *Web hosting* means to make disk space for a Web site available on a Web server, a computer connected to the Internet where Web pages are stored. To view a Web page in your browser, you download it from a Web server to your computer. A Web-hosting service is a company that rents disk space on its Web servers to people so that they can present their Web pages on the Internet.

It used to be that you always had to pay for Web-hosting services. Most people still pay. The cost of renting space on a Web server runs from $12 to many hundreds of dollars per month, depending on how big your Web site is and how much server space it requires. You can, however, get free Web-hosting services if you are willing to put up with advertisements on your Web site.

Figure 7-1 shows a Web page hosted by Yahoo! GeoCities, a free Web-hosting service. Notice the advertisement. Free Web-hosting services earn their keep with ads like this, pop-up ads, and pop-up windows. By the way, if you look closely, you can see that the ad is for Abebooks.com. The ad software detected the word *Abe* on the Web page and immediately inserted an ad for Abebooks.com, thinking that Abe is a bookseller and not an American president. Don't let anyone tell you computers are smart.

Figure 7-1:
Nothing is free or adless — an advertisement on a GeoCities Web page.

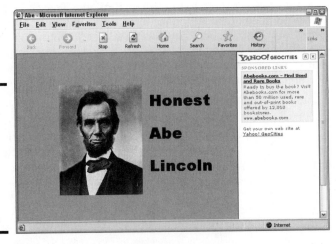

In Yahoo! GeoCities, advertisements like the one in Figure 7-1 appear on every Web page, and they can be very annoying. Some people shy away from Web pages hosted by the free services because they can't bear the advertisements. Before you can read the Web page shown in Figure 7-1, you have to click the Close button on the advertisement to make it go away. Having to close advertisements like this is tiresome. If the purpose of your Web site is to report on matters of consequence, promote a business, or engage in a serious scholarly endeavor, or if you want splashy stuff like animations that the free services can't accommodate, you are better off paying a Web-hosting service to handle your Web site. But if all you want to do is post an announcement or simply tell the world about yourself in a fun kind of way, you may as well do it for free.

Table 7-1 describes the most popular free Web-hosting services. I chose these services from among the 300 that offer free Web hosting because they are known to be reliable and they provide tools for building Web sites. As you choose a free Web-hosting service, take these matters into consideration:

✦ **Reliability:** Because they rely on income from advertisers, free Web-hosting services come and go. Make sure that the service you choose has been in business for a few years and is reliable.

✦ **Web-site-building tools:** If you are not adept with FrontPage, Dreamweaver, or another software program for constructing Web pages and Web sites, choose a service that offers Web-site-building tools. Some services offer special tools for constructing blogs, online forums, and other fancy stuff. These tools are usually designed for novices and are easy to use.

✦ **Disk space**: How much space on the Web server are you allotted? If you plan to create many Web pages or offer files for downloading, you need more space than you need if you just want to post a Web page or two.

✦ **Bandwidth:** This term refers to how fast data is transmitted on a given path or medium, in this case, how fast data is sent from the Web server. Bandwidth is expressed in bits per second (bps). No one likes a slow server. If you can, find out what a service's bandwidth is. A fast rate is 75 Mbps (megabits per second) or higher.

✦ **Data transfer rate:** For measuring Web-server use, the data transfer rate describes how much data, in gigabytes, a Web server transfers in a month. Some Web-hosting services place a limit on how much data can be transferred monthly; others charge fees or charge more if the rate climbs above a certain amount. The data transfer rate is a function of the bandwidth, because a narrow, or slow, bandwidth can't transfer data as quickly. A good data transfer rate is 3GB or higher per month.

✦ **File size limit:** Some services place a limit on the size of files you can place on their server. File size is an issue if you plan to offer music files or video files for downloading on your Web site.

Table 7-1	Popular Free Web-Hosting Services	
Service	*Description*	*Web Address*
Angelfire	Free server space as well as tools for building Web sites. Offers a "blog builder" especially for creating blogs.	`http://angelfire.lycos.com`
AOL	For America Online subscribers, free home pages and online journals. Offers many templates as well as tools for creating blogs.	`http://hometown.aol.com`
Bravenet	Free service space and many Web-site-building tools. Offers tools for building chat rooms and hit counters.	`www.bravenet.com`
FortuneCity	Free server space, domain names, and e-mail services.	`www.fortunecity.com`
Freeservers	Free server space, e-mail services, Web-site-building tools, and FTP access.	`www.freeservers.com`
FreeWebs	Free server space and tools for building Web sites.	`http://members.freewebs.com`
Netfirms	Free server space and Web-site templates.	`http://www.netfirms.com`
Tripod	Free server space and Web-site-building tools, including one for making blogs.	`www.tripod.lycos.com`
Yahoo! GeoCities	Free server space and tools for building Web sites.	`http://geocities.yahoo.com`

Free Web Hosting, a Web site, keeps an index of 800 or more free Web-hosting services. You can search for services based on how much free space they offer, whether they offer site-building tools, and other criteria. Free Web Hosting is located at this address: `www.free-webhosts.com`.

I prefer Yahoo! GeoCities for free Web hosting. As the oldest free service, it is certainly reliable. The service is ten years old (ancient by Internet standards). It has been owned and operated — not to mention refined — by Yahoo! since 1999, when Yahoo! bought it for a mere $4.7 billion. What especially appeals to me about Yahoo! GeoCities is the Web-site-building tools that the service offers. These impressive tools are the subject of most of this chapter.

Yahoo! GeoCities and other free Web-hosting services present a serious drawback in regard to spider-style search engines such as Google. These search engines continuously troll the Internet, mapping and indexing Web sites (Book II, Chapter 3 describes what spider-style search engines are). The information that these search engines collect is put in a database. When you search the Internet starting at Google, for example, you are really searching a database with detailed information about many different Web pages. However, Google and other spider-style search engines don't troll Web sites that are hosted at GeoCities and other free hosting sites. Your GeoCities Web site won't turn up in Google searches unless you submit your Web site to Google and other spider-style search engines on your own. Later in this chapter, "Submitting Your Web Site to Search Engines" explains how to do that.

A Few Design Considerations

The following pages are devoted to what Web pages should look like. It explains how to make Web pages that others will admire. By heeding this advice, you can create Web pages that are useful, pleasant to look at, and easy to read.

Ask yourself, "Who's my audience?"

The cardinal rule for developing Web sites is to always remember who your audience is. Obviously, a Web site whose purpose is to publicize an amusement park needs to be livelier than a Web site whose purpose is more solemn, say, to post students' final examination scores. Likewise, a Web site that posts pictures of a newborn baby should be brighter and more colorful than one that promotes a funeral parlor.

More so than "Who's my audience?" a better question to ask may be, "Why exactly am I developing this Web site?" You are doing the hard work of creating a Web site for a good reason. Ask yourself what that reason is and then think of compelling ways to present the topic so that others become as passionate about it as you are.

Be consistent from page to page

If you opened a magazine at a newsstand and discovered that the text on each page had a different font, each page was laid out differently, and each page was a different size, you wouldn't buy the magazine. The same goes for Web sites. A Web site that isn't consistent from page to page gives a bad impression. Visitors will conclude that little thought was put into the site, and they won't stick around.

To be consistent, lay out your Web pages in a similar manner. Make sure that headings are the same size. Pages don't have to have the same background, but backgrounds should be similar. For example, you can use the same pattern but a different hue. Or, you can use different shades of the same color. The point is to give visitors the impression that a lot of thought was put into your Web site and that you care very much about its presentation.

Use the home page as an introductory page to your site

The home page is the first page, or introductory page, of a Web site. Usually the home page offers hyperlinks that you can click to go to other pages on the Web site. Because visitors go to the home page first, be sure that the home page makes a fine introduction to your Web site. The home page should include lots of hyperlinks to the other pages on the site. It should be enticing. It should be alluring. It should make people want to stay and explore your Web site in its entirety. However, to make the home page serve as an introduction, you have to do a little planning. You can sketch a diagram showing how the introductory stuff that you write on the home page is linked to the other pages on the Web site.

Divide your Web site into distinct topics

An unwritten rule of Web-site developers is to never create a Web page that is so long that you have to scroll far to reach the bottom. Topics on Web pages should be presented in small, bite-sized chunks. Rather than dwell on a topic at length, divide the topic across several pages.

What's more, a Web site isn't like a book or article. No one reads Web sites from start to finish. A Web site is like a garden of forking paths in that visitors can click hyperlinks and take different routes through a Web site. (Visitors don't hesitate to try different routes because they know they can always click the Back button to return to where they came from.)

When you build your Web pages, consider using hyperlinks to take visitors to other pages on the site, to other places on the same Web page, and to other sites on the Internet. Use hyperlinks to give your visitors the option of going many different places. Instead of presenting long pages that visitors have to scroll to read, let visitors choose what to read next.

Hyperlink your site to other sites on the Internet

Most Web sites include a page called "My Favorite Links" or "Other Sites of Interest" or just "Links." Go to that page, and you find hyperlinks that you can click to go other places on the Internet. Everybody knows how hard finding interesting sites is. A "My Favorite Links" page is always appreciated because visitors can be sure that the sites on the page are worth visiting.

Including hyperlinks on your site gives you another advantage: It helps make your site part of the Internet community. Link your site to someone else's and often the other person reciprocates. Pretty soon your site starts popping up on "My Favorite Links" lists. The traffic on your site increases. You site becomes a known quantity on the Internet.

Choose page backgrounds carefully

One of the hardest design decisions you have to make concerns page backgrounds. Choose a dark background and visitors to your site have trouble reading the text. A busy background also distracts visitors. You can, of course, opt for white text and a dark background, but too much white text has been known to strain the eyes. Choose the background before you make any other design decision. That way, as you construct your Web pages, you will be sure to decorate them with items that work well on the background.

Write the text and assemble the graphics beforehand

Before you start constructing your Web site, write the text. Rewriting and editing text after it has been placed on a Web page isn't easy. Open your word processor, start typing, say exactly what you want to say on your Web pages, correct all misspellings and grammatical errors, and save the file. Later, you can import the text from the word-processed file to the Web page.

If you intend to use graphics or pictures, set them apart in a folder where you can find them easily. While you're at it, take a good look at them. Which graphics you use can influence the design decisions you make as you construct your Web page. Make sure that you know the graphics you intend to use intimately so that you can use them wisely and well.

Avoid using too many gizmos

More than a few Web-site developers have ruined their efforts by loading their sites with too many exotic gizmos. Yes, those toys are fun to play with, and yes, they make for a nice Web site. Problem is, visitors to a site have to wait for all those gizmos to load before they can appreciate them. Not only that, all those gizmos can be very distracting.

Creating the Web Site

When you are done creating your Web site, Yahoo! assigns a Web address to the home page of the site; the address consists of the domain name `geocities.com` followed by a forward slash (/) and your Yahoo! account ID. For example, if your Yahoo! ID is Barney123, the address of your Web site is

`http://www.geocities.com/Barney123`

To create a Web site at Yahoo! GeoCities, you must have a Yahoo! account (see Appendix A). Sign in to Yahoo! and follow these baby steps to begin creating a Yahoo! GeoCities Web site:

1. Go to the Yahoo! home page at `www.yahoo.com` **and click the Groups link.**

You land in the Yahoo! GeoCities page. You can also get there by going straight to this address: `http://geocities.yahoo.com/home`.

2. In the GeoCities Free Web Hosting section, click the Sign Up button.

3. Choose an option to describe what kind of ads should appear beside your Web site; then click the Continue button.

Strange to say it, but choose carefully because the advertisement category you select tells visitors to your Web site a lot about who you are.

You come to the Welcome to Yahoo! GeoCities window. It lists your ID, your Yahoo! e-mail address, and the Web address of your Yahoo! GeoCities Web site.

4. Click the Build Your Web Site Now! link.

In case you didn't notice, the people at Yahoo! are very fond of exclamation points. Now you're getting somewhere. You come to the Web Site Accounts window shown in Figure 7-2, where you can start constructing your Web site.

Figure 7-2: The Web Site accounts window, the starting point for creating and managing a Web site.

Google AdSense

How would you like — well, maybe — to make some pocket change by putting Google ads on your Web site? You can do that by hosting advertisements by way of Google. The program is called Google AdSense. According to Google, the ads that appear on your Web site are related to what your users are looking for on your site. Says Google, "You'll finally have a way to both monetize and enhance your content pages." Monetize? Does that mean to turn lead into gold? For information about Google AdSense, go to this Web address: `www.google.com/adsense`.

Building Your Site from the Web Site Accounts Window

The Web Site Accounts window (refer to Figure 7-2) is the starting point for building and managing your Web site. Go here to create new Web pages or to work on pages you've already created. The window offers these amenities for constructing a Web site:

✦ **Yahoo! PageWizards:** Templates you can use to create new Web pages. See "Creating a page with a PageWizard," later in this chapter.

✦ **Yahoo! PageBuilder:** A computer program for creating and refining Web sites. The first time you attempt to use this program, it is installed on your computer. See "Creating a page with PageBuilder," later in this chapter.

✦ **File Manager:** A utility for copying, renaming, and deleting the files from which your Web site is made. See "Managing the Files," later in this chapter.

No matter where you are in Yahoo!, you can get to the Web Site Accounts window with either of these techniques:

✦ Click the GeoCities link on the Yahoo! home page (`www.yahoo.com`).

✦ Go to this address: `http://geocities.yahoo.com/home`.

As part of creating a page, Yahoo! GeoCities asks you to name it. Names are given to Web addresses like so:

`http://www.geocities.com/`*Your_Web_Site_Name*`/`*Page_Name*`.html`

For example, a page named `About_Me` made for a Web site at `http://www.geocities.com/Barney123` gets this name:

`http://www.geocities.com/Barney123/About_Me.html`

Creating a page with a PageWizard

Creating a page with a PageWizard involves choosing a basic design and then completing three to five steps, depending on which design you choose. In my experience, pages created with the PageWizard are a mixed blessing. You are spared the trouble of doing most of the layout work, but you still have to tweak the page to make it your own. You have to move graphics, text boxes, and other page elements around. And you have to do that without upsetting the page design. Sometimes using a PageWizard proves more trouble than it's worth.

Designating your home page

The home page is the first page you come to in a Web site. By default, a GeoCities home page is called `index.html`. Web browsers look for the `index.html` file when they arrive at a Web site so that they can open the home page first. When you create a Web site, Yahoo! GeoCities creates a placeholder home page for you called `index.html`. Until you create an `index.html` file of your own, you see the ugly placeholder home page whenever you go to your Web site from the Web Site Accounts window or view it in a browser.

Creating a home page is one of the first tasks to complete as you create a Web site. If you already created a home page but forgot to name

it `index.html`, follow these steps to give a page you created the name `index.html`:

1. Open the File Manager. To do so, click the File Manager link in the Advanced Toolbox section of the Web Site Accounts window.

2. In the File Manager window, click the Open File Manager link.

3. Select the check box beside the name of the page you want to be your home page.

4. Click the Rename button.

5. Enter **Index.html** in the New Name text box and click the Rename Files button.

To get going, click the Yahoo! PageWizards link in the Web Site Accounts window (refer to Figure 7-2). Then choose a basic design and click the Begin button.

As you construct your page, keep your eyes on the sample page in the Build Your Quick Start Page dialog box, shown in Figure 7-3. The sample page plainly shows what the choices you make mean in real terms. The numbers on the page show which part of the page you are altering as you complete each numbered step. You can always click the Preview button to open the page in a browser window and get a good look at it. If you don't like what you see, click the Back button and start all over. You are asked to do these things:

✦ Enter a page title and a description of the page.

✦ Choose a picture or photograph for the page.

✦ Enter some hyperlinks.

✦ Provide your name and e-mail address.

✦ Name your page. Don't enter the .html file extension — the PageWizard does it for you.

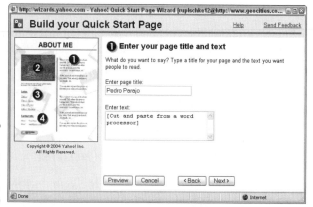

Figure 7-3:
Fashioning a
page with a
PageWizard.

**Book IV
Chapter 7**

**Free Web Sites at
Yahoo! GeoCities**

Creating a page with PageBuilder

PageBuilder is a computer program in its own right. To get technical about it, PageBuilder is a *Java applet,* a small software program written in the Java language that is designed to run on a Web browser. Each time you start PageBuilder, it installs itself on your computer. Figure 7-4 shows PageBuilder in action. To start this program, click the Yahoo! PageBuilder link in the Web Site Accounts window (refer to Figure 7-2). Then, on the Yahoo! PageBuilder page, click the Launch PageBuilder link.

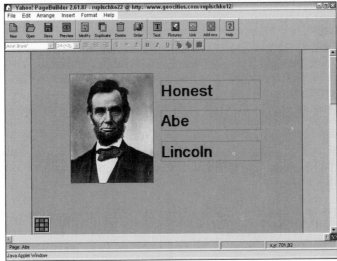

Figure 7-4:
PageBuilder
is a Java
applet for
constructing
Web pages.

PageBuilder offers two different ways to create a new Web page:

+ **Blank page:** Click the New button or choose File➪New.

+ **Page from a template:** Choose File➪New Page from Template. You see the Open Page dialog box. Select the name of a template and click the Open button.

Don't forget to save and name your page. Click the Save button, enter a name in the Save Page dialog box, and click the Save button.

Constructing a Web Page with PageBuilder

You can't rely on Yahoo! PageWizards to do all the layout work. At some point, you have to open PageBuilder, get your hands dirty, and do the layout work yourself. The remainder of this chapter explains how to do that. You find out how to choose a background color for pages, enter and format the text, handle hyperlinks, and include pictures on Web pages.

As the previous section in this chapter explains, you start PageBuilder in the Web Site Accounts window (refer to Figure 7-2) by clicking the Yahoo! PageBuilder link.

As you lay out Web pages, occasionally click the Preview button or choose File➪Page Preview to open your Web page in a browser window and see how it will look to people who stumble upon it on the Internet.

Choosing a background color or picture

Web pages should be pleasing to the eye and easy to read. To that end, your first task in dealing with a Web page is to choose the background. Choosing the right background for a Web page is like choosing the right clothes for a job interview. The background sets the tone. Viewers see the background first. It tells them what kind of Web page they are viewing — a sober Web page with a white background, for example, or a playful Web page with a colorful background.

To choose a background color or picture for a Web page, start by choosing Format⇨Background. You see the Background Properties dialog box. Take it from there:

- ✦ **Choosing a color:** Click the Set Background Color button, and in the Choose Background Color dialog box, select a color.

- ✦ **Using a picture for a background:** Click the Upload button to open the Upload Files window. Then click the Browse button and choose a picture file from your computer in the Choose File dialog box.

Be careful about choosing blue and violet backgrounds because text hyperlinks on the page are blue and text hyperlinks that have been clicked are violet. If you are fond of blue and violet backgrounds, you can still use them without obscuring hyperlinks. To do so, choose new colors for hyperlinks (see "Putting hyperlinks on your Web pages," later in this chapter).

Entering text and headings on a Web page

To enter text on a Web page, start by entering a text boxes like the ones shown in Figure 7-5. A text box is a holding tank for text. You can move text boxes around the page and change their size as necessary. Providing you followed my advice, you can paste text that you wrote earlier with a word processor into a text box. Here are the basics of entering and laying out text on a Web page:

- ✦ **Entering a text box:** Click the Text button or choose Insert⇨Basic⇨Text. A text box appears on the Web page.

- ✦ **Typing the text:** Start typing. The text box changes size to accommodate text as you enter it.

- ✦ **Copying text from a word processor:** You can't simply copy the text in a word processor and choose Edit⇨Paste to put it in a text box, but you can paste text by taking an extra step or two. Copy the text in your word processor and, in PageBuilder, click the Clipboard button. This button is the rightmost on the Formatting toolbar. You see the Text Clipboard dialog box. Right-click in this dialog box and choose Paste to paste the text into the dialog box. Then click the Paste button to enter the text in the text box.

✦ **Using text effects:** Select the text and click the Boldface, Italic, or Underline button to boldface, italicize, or underline the words.

✦ **Choosing a font for text:** Select the text and choose a font on the Font drop-down menu.

✦ **Changing the size of text:** Select the text and choose a measurement on the Font Size drop-down menu.

✦ **Choosing a color for text:** Select the text, click the Text Color button, and select a color in the Choose Text Color dialog box.

✦ **Filling in a text box with color:** Click the text box to select it, and then click the Fill button. In the Choose Background Color dialog box, select a color.

✦ **Aligning the text:** Click the Left Align, Center, or Right Align button to align the text horizontally in the text box; click the Top, Middle, or Bottom button to align text vertically. These buttons are found on the Formatting toolbar.

✦ **Changing the shape of a text box:** Move the pointer over a corner or a side of the text box, and when you see the double-arrow, start dragging.

✦ **Moving a text box:** Move the pointer over the text box, and when you see the four-headed arrow, start dragging.

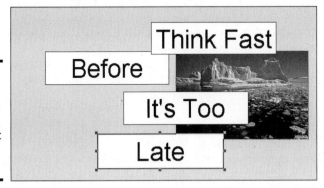

Figure 7-5: Four text boxes and a graphic, with the last text box selected.

Putting hyperlinks on your Web pages

A hyperlink is a secret passage from one place on the Internet to another. Click a hyperlink and something new appears on-screen — a different Web page or different Web site. You can also click a hyperlink to activate an e-mail program or start downloading a file. Hyperlinks give Web-site visitors the opportunity to choose what they read or view next. Hyperlinks connect a Web site to other sites and to the Internet community. They make a Web site livelier and more inviting.

To create a hyperlink, start by selecting the thing — a word, phrase, or picture — that will form the hyperlink. Then either click the Link button or choose Format⇨Create Link. You see the Hot Link dialog box shown in Figure 7-6. On the Link to a Location drop-down menu, choose the target for your link, the thing that will appear or happen when the link is clicked:

✦ **Another Web site:** Choose Web URL and enter the Web address of the page you want to link to. The easiest way to do this is to copy the address from the Address bar of your browser, right-click in the dialog box, and choose Paste.

✦ **A different page on your Web site:** Choose My Page and click the Choose button. In the Pick File dialog box, select the name of a Web page on your site.

✦ **An e-mail message window:** Choose E-Mail and enter an e-mail address. When someone clicks the link, his or her default e-mail program opens. The message is already addressed to the e-mail address you entered.

✦ **A file to download:** Choose My File and click the Choose button. In the Choose File dialog box, select the name of a file you uploaded to your Web site. To upload a file, choose File⇨Upload Files and Images. Then choose a file on your computer in the Upload Files dialog box.

Figure 7-6:
Creating a hyperlink.

Book IV
Chapter 7

Free Web Sites at
Yahoo! GeoCities

By default, text hyperlinks are blue and links that have been clicked are violet. To change these default colors, choose Format⇨Page Properties. In the Page Properties dialog box, click the Links or Visited Links button and select a color in the Choose Default Hot Link Color dialog box.

Putting a picture or photograph on a Web page

Pictures stored on your computer, pictures on Web pages on the Internet, and PageBuilder's library of clip art files can all be put to use on your Web site. What's a Web page without a picture or two? It's like an emperor without any clothes. To insert a picture on a Web page, either click the Pictures button or choose Insert⇨Basics⇨Pictures. You see the Select Picture dialog box. Insert your picture:

✦ **Clip art:** In the Picture List box, double-click [Clip Art]. A list of categories appears in the box. Double-click a category name that intrigues you. You see a list of pictures. Select a picture to see it in the Picture Preview box.

✦ **A picture file from your computer:** Click the Upload button. You go to the Upload Files window. Click the Browse button, select the picture file, and click the Upload button.

✦ **A picture on another Web site:** Make sure that Web URL is chosen on the Link to a Location drop-down menu. Then enter the Web address of the picture on another Web site that you want to appear on your Web site. To get this address, right-click the picture and choose Properties. Then, in the Properties dialog box, look for the address. To select the address, drag over the address in the Properties dialog box, right-click, and choose Copy. Next, right-click and choose Paste in the Select Picture dialog box to enter the address.

In the Screen Tip text box, enter a word or two to describe the picture. When a visitor to your Web site moves the mouse over the picture, a pop-up box with the words you entered will appear. Finally, click the OK button to enter the picture.

To move a picture on a Web page, move the pointer over the picture's perimeter, and when you see the four-headed arrow, click and start dragging. To change a picture's size, move the pointer over a corner or side, and when you see the double-headed arrow, start dragging. Drag a corner to maintain the picture's proportions; drag a side to stretch or squeeze the picture.

Managing the Files

Use the File Manager to handle the files from which your Web site is made. Starting from the File Manager, you can view, rename, delete, and copy Web pages on your site, as well as edit HTML codes. To start the File Manager, click the File Manager link in the Advanced Toolbox section of the Web Site Accounts window and then click the Open File Manager link. Figure 7-7 shows the File Manager window.

The File Manager window lists every file on your Web site and all files that you uploaded. To work with a file, select its check box. Then click the Copy, Rename, or Delete button. Click the Edit button to edit the HTML codes from which a page is constructed, if you feel competent enough to do that.

Yahoo! GeoCities

		Name		Last Modified (GMT)		Size (KB)
☐	🔳	Abe.html	View	Dec 01 09:18am	Stats	2
☐	🔳	Pano.html	View	Dec 01 09:24am	Stats	1
☐		Pano_Arte.jpg	View	Dec 01 09:22am		22
☐	✏	index.htm	View	Dec 01 01:39am	Stats	3
☐		lydia.jpg	View	Dec 01 06:00am		23
☐		sunnyosuna.jpg	View	Dec 01 05:59am		12
☐	✏	temporarypreviewfile.html	View	Dec 01 06:56am	Stats	1

New Edit Copy Rename Delete checked files Upload Files

Check All - Clear All   🗀 = Subdirectory 🔳 = PageBuilder 🔳 = PageWizard

New Edit Copy Rename Delete checked files Upload Files

🗀 **Subdirectories**
New (Create Subdirectories to organize your files)

Disk Space Usage	View Files - File list too long? Select just the file types you want to see.	Quick Links
Used: 0.1 MB	⦿ List files with extensions ☑ html ☑ gif ☑ jpg ☑ other	Add-Ons
Available: 14.9 MB	- that begin with ANY ▾ character.	Site Statistics Home Page Settings
Total Allocated: 15.0 MB	○ Or, manually type in filenames.	File Manager Help
	Refresh File Manager	

Figure 7-7:
The File
Manager
window.

The bottom of the File Manager tells you how much of the 15MB of disk
space you were allotted has been used and how much remains. Keep an eye
on these numbers. If your are close to the 15MB allotment, you'd better start
deleting files from your Web site.

Submitting Your Web Site to Search Engines

Earlier in this chapter, in "Deciding on a Free Web-Hosting Service," I
explained that spider search engines don't search GeoCities Web sites. If
yours is a GeoCities Web site, the only way for you to get your site listed at
different search engines is to submit it yourself. Table 7-2 provides Web
addresses and e-mail addresses where you can submit your Web site to a
search engine and in so doing increase the chances of your Web site being
found in Internet searches.

Table 7-2	Submitting a Web Site to Search Engines
Search Engine	*Web or E-Mail Address for Submission*
All the Web	www.alltheweb.com/help/webmaster/ submit_site
Alta Vista	www.altavista.com/addurl/default
AOL Search	http://search.aol.com/aolcom/add.jsp
Ask Jeeves	http://ask.ineedhits.com; sitesubmit@ askjeeves.com
Ask Jeeves for Kids	http://web.ask.com/ContactUsKids
Education World	www.education-world.com/navigation/add_ url_form.shtml

(continued)

Table 7-2 *(continued)*

Search Engine	Web or E-Mail Address for Submission
Excite	`https://secure.ah-ha.com/guaranteed_inclusion/step1a.aspx`
Google	`www.google.com/addurl.html`
Librarians' Index to the Internet	`suggestions@lii.org`
Open Directory Project	`www.dmoz.org/add.html`
Snap	`www.snap.com/about/site.php`
Teoma	`www.seoposition.com/teoma-search-engine.html`
Wisenut	`http://wisenut.com/submit.html`
Yahoo!	`http://search.yahoo.com/info/submit.html`
Yahooligans!	`http://add.yahoo.com/fast/add?+Kids`

Each search engine has different rules and procedures for submitting a Web site. Sometimes you have to register. Sometimes you have to write a descriptive paragraph about your Web site. Follow the submission rules carefully. In your description, be sure to explain why your Web site is useful, entertaining, meaningful, or whatever our Web site happens to be. When you submit your Web site to a directory-style search engine, the people who review your submission will be interested in knowing how to catalog your Web site, so be sure to suggest a category and subcategory where your Web site should be placed (Book II, Chapter 3 explains what directory-style search engines are).

As I explain in Book II, Chapter 3, most search engines rely on other search engines to do some of their searching. Because the majority of search engines rely on these three to obtain their search results, you are wise to submit your Web site to these three search engines first:

+ **Google (`www.google.com`):** Submit your Web site to this address: `www.google.com/addurl.html`

+ **Open Directory Project (`www.dmoz.org`):** Submit your Web site to this address: `www.dmoz.org/add.html`

+ **Yahoo! (`www.yahoo.com`):** Submit your Web site to this address: `http://search.yahoo.com/info/submit.html`

Chapter 8: Making Friends and Connections Online

In This Chapter

✔ Looking at the online social-networking services

✔ Finding new friends on the Internet

✔ Dating online in the Yahoo! Personals

✔ Finding long-lost friends on the Internet

The pioneers of the Internet thought that the Internet would bring people closer together. They thought it would connect people in the far-flung corners of the earth. They saw cyberspace as a meeting ground in which people could join forces to work for the common good or, on a more prosaic note, join forces to converge on the same Chinese restaurant.

The last couple of years have seen a resurgence of Internet activity in the area of connecting people. Social-networking services such as Friendster have transformed online dating and friend making. Web sites such as Meetup.com have helped hundreds of thousands of people find others who have common bonds and interests. This chapter looks at a handful of Web sites and services with which you can connect with others and make new friends.

Social Networking

In case you didn't know it yet, social networking is The Next Big Thing where the Internet is concerned. A better name for social networking would be "cyber-schmoozing." *Social networking* means to make new friends or meet new business associates at an online social-networking service. It doesn't cost anything join these services, although some charge for extras such as e-mailing and instant messaging with other members.

Friendster (`www.friendster.com`), shown in Figure 8-1, was the original and is still the most popular service. When membership in Friendster surpassed 2 million in 2003, copycats from across the software industry started salivating, meowing, and sharpening their claws. Now there are at least a dozen social-networking services. Table 8-1 describes the most prominent ones.

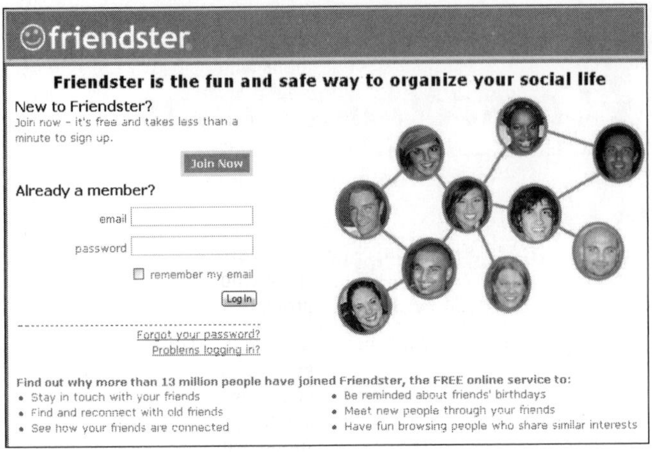

Figure 8-1:
Friendster,
the original
social-
networking
service.

Table 8-1	Social-Networking Services	
Service	*Description*	*Web Address*
Everyone's Connected	Members keep Web logs and contribute to online newspapers that friends and potential friends can read. "You can matchmake your friends," the site says, "or use Secret Match to anonymously express an interest in someone." For the younger crowd. Membership is free.	`www.everyonesconnected.com`
Friendster	Members keep detailed profile pages and can write testimonials about their friends for others to read. Friendster is the original social-networking Web site, with 3.9 million members. "The fun and safe way to organize your social life," the site says. Most members are in their 20s and 30s.	`www.friendster.com`
hi5	For young people to make new friends. Members keep journals and testimonials that others may read. "Let your friends share their experiences and tell everyone what they think of you. It's a great way to learn about new people from people you trust." This is a matchmaking site for people in their 20s.	`www.sona.com`

Service	Description	Web Address
Knowmentum	Members make connections with other business professionals. "Knowing these connections can help you obtain your next job, find that key client, start a business relationship, and more," the site says. Membership is free, although $3 to $4 per month gets you extra services, such as finding out who has been viewing your profile.	www.itsnotwhatyouknow.com
LinkedIn	Business professionals connect with one another. "LinkedIn helps you discover inside connections to recommended job candidates," the site claims. As of October 2004, it had 1 million members. Memberships are free, although you are charged if you receive more than a thousand referrals each day.	www.linkedin.com
Myspace	Young people make friends and declare their interests at this site. Profiles often include sexually explicit information. You can browse profiles without being a member.	www.myspace.com
Orkut	Members create profiles and join communities of like-minded people. Orkut is owned and operated by Google.	www.orkut.com
Ryze	For businesspeople, the networks are organized around different industries and geographical locations. It's called Ryze, the site says, because "it's about people helping each other 'rise up' through quality networking." Includes classified ads.	www.ryze.com
Tickle	At this unusual matchmaking and networking site, members connect with others on the basis of their score on various quizzes. For example, you can take the "Who's your hip-hop heartthrob" quiz and the "What kind of kisser are you?" quiz. The site connects you to members who score similarly to you.	www.emode.com

**Book IV
Chapter 8**

**Making Friends and
Connections Online**

(continued)

Table 8-1 *(continued)*

Service	Description	Web Address
Tribe.net	Members join tribes to find like-minded people — and the typical member, it appears, joins many dozen tribes. The site includes discussion boards, job listings, and personal ads. Membership is free, and you can browse profiles and the entire site without being a member. For the alternative set.	`www.tribe.net`
Yafro	Members post photos of themselves about which other members are free to comment. Members earn points according to how well their photographs are regarded. Includes sexually explicit descriptions.	`www.yafro.com`

All the services are modeled after Friendster. Whichever service you join, you can expect the same. First, you create a profile, a Web page that describes your interests, wants, desires, obsessions, hobbies, and line of work. Then you post photographs of yourself on your profile page. (Credit the digital camera with the popularity of social-networking services as much as anything else. Digital photos make it possible to see as well as read about potential friends and business associates.)

So far, it sounds like an online dating service, but what makes Friendster and the other social-networking services different is the way that connections are made. Each member's profile page lists his or her circle of friends, called a *network,* as shown in Figure 8-2. Before you can talk to another member, you have to get an introduction from somebody who is in the same network as the person you want to talk to. For example, before Dick can talk to Jane, he has to get an introduction from someone in his network who is also in Jane's network. Perhaps that person is Nan. On Nan's profile page, Dick sees that Jane is in Nan's network, he studies Jane's profile, and he wants to meet Jane. He asks Nan for an introduction. If she agrees to vouch for Dick and introduce him to Jane, the connection is made, and if Dick and Jane become friends, she may join his network and he hers. In this way, each member's network of friends is always expanding — well, it expands if a member is someone worth knowing.

Craigslist

A chapter about finding friends and making connections online would be incomplete without a mention of Craigslist. Craigslist was invented in San Francisco in 1995 by a computer programmer named Craig Newmark. Originally, the list's only purpose was to announce upcoming events in the Bay Area, but because the software that Newmark developed for posting items to his list was so easy to use, his site soon became a place for listing jobs, selling items, and listing apartment rentals. Eventually, Craigslist turned into an all-purpose Web page for bartering, selling, debating, sharing rides, swapping houses, and doing any number of things. Today, Craigslists are

found in 57 cities in the United States and 14 cities abroad. To see whether your city has a Craigslist, go to this Web address: www.craigslist.org/about/cities.html.

Amazingly, Craigslist to this day does not accept advertisements. The list has maintained its down-to-earth idealism and commitment to helping people help themselves. Craigslist only charges for job listings. If you want to buy tickets to sporting events at the last minute, help your local school (click the Teacher's Wishlists link), hold an online garage sale, seek donations for a worthy cause, buy cheap second-hand electronics, post a personal ad, or find a job, stop by Craigslist.

craigslist	indianapolis			albany / raleigh
				albuquerque / reno
				anchorage / sacramento
				atlanta / salt lake
post to classifieds	**community** (222)	**housing** (115)	**jobs** (142)	austin / san antonio
help subscriptions	activity partners	apts / housing	accounting / finance	baltimore / san diego
	artists lost+found	rooms / shared	admin / office	boise / santa barbara
	childcare musicians	sublets / temporary	art / media / design	boston / seattle
search craigslist	general politics	housing wanted	biotech / science	buffalo / spokane
	groups rideshare	housing swap	business / mgmt	charlotte / st louis
[ ]	pets volunteers	vacation rentals	customer service	chicago / SF bay
community ▼ [▷]	events classes	parking / storage	education / teaching	cincinnati / tampa bay
		office / commercial	engineering / arch	cleveland / tucson
	personals (615)	real estate for sale	human resources	columbus / tulsa
	strictly platonic		internet engineering	dallas / wash, DC
event calendar (5)	women seek women		legal / government	denver
S M T W T F S	women seeking men	**for sale** (395)	marketing / pr / adv	detroit
28 29 30 1 2 3 4	men seeking women	barter baby+kids	medical / healthcare	eugene / **canada:**
5 6 7 8 9 10 11	men seeking men	bikes cars+trucks	nonprofit sector	fresno / montreal
12 13 14 15 16 17 18	misc romance	books clothes+acc	retail / food / hosp	hartford / ottawa
19 20 21 22 23 24 25	casual encounters	free collectibles	sales / biz dev	honolulu / toronto
	missed connections	furniture computer	skilled trade / craft	houston / vancouver
best-of-craigslist	rants and raves	general electronics	software / qa / dba	indianapolis
::: craig blog :::		sporting garage sales		inland empire / **americas:**
				kansas city / são paulo
				las vegas
				los angeles / **uk & ie:**
				memphis / dublin
				miami

This built-in screening mechanism in which members introduce one another makes online connections safer and more rewarding. It's based on an age-old idea — that your friend's friend is a candidate to become your friend, too, because the two of you probably have interests in common. Friendster was designed to be an online dating service, but its success inspired software developers to carry the social-networking idea into the business realm. Services such as Knowmentum and Ryze link people with common business interests. Other services are designed to help you find new friends, not necessarily romance.

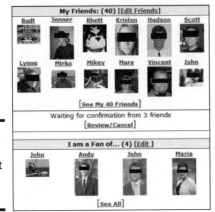

Figure 8-2:
A network
of friends at
Friendster.
com.

If the social-networking adventure appeals to you, check out the services listed in Table 8-1. Take a tour of the services and see what's what. Each service caters to a different crowd. The same precautions about safeguarding your privacy that apply to all online activity apply to social-networking as well. Never give out personal information such as phone numbers and addresses. Never take it for granted that the people you encounter online are who they say they are, or are even real people. Recently, Webmasters at Friendster removed 8,000 "Pretendsters" — people pretending to be someone else — from their service.

Finding New Friends in Your Town or City

Somewhere in the town or city in which you live are people who would like to know you and share the same interests as you. How can you find them? You can paint a sign listing your interests and walk the streets until someone sees the sign and shouts, "Eureka!" Or, you can go online and take advantage of Meetup.com or Upcoming.org to find kindred souls. Read on.

Meeting new people at Meetup.com

Meetup.com gained national attention during the 2004 presidential election when the Howard Dean campaign made use of the service to organize neighborhood meetings on behalf of its candidate. Meetup.com has a million and a half members. They gather at monthly "meetups" to discuss . . . you name it. Chihuahuas. Belly dancing. Literary theory. Meetup.com is a great way to meet people whose interests are the same as yours. Visit the Meetup.com Web site at this address: www.meetup.com.

After you join and log in, you see the home page shown in Figure 8-3. Starting here, you can look for meetup groups to join or start your own meetup group:

✦ **Searching for a meetup group:** On the home page, click the Find a Meetup Group button. Then search using the Topic text box or click Topic links until you come to a Meetup Group page. Read messages on its message board and get a sense of what the group is all about. Do you want to join?

✦ **Joining a meetup group:** To join a meetup group and attend its meetings, click the Sign In Now button on the Meetup Group page. On the Your Profile page, write a note to the group and click the Submit button. The meetup's organizer will send you an e-mail explaining when and where meetups occur. Don't be shy about replying to the organizer to ask a question about the group.

✦ **Changing your profile or memberships:** To update your member profile or leave a group you joined, click the Your Account link and get to work on the Your Account page.

✦ **Starting a group:** Click the Start a Meetup Group button on the home page. You are asked to pick a topic, name your group, and describe your group. As the group organizer, you are responsible for scheduling the meeting, choosing its location, welcoming members, and communicating with members by e-mail.

Figure 8-3:
The home page at Meetup.org.

Planning nighttime adventures at Upcoming.org

Upcoming.org is for city folk who enjoy the nightlife and want to find companions who enjoy the nightlife as much as they do. Using the service, you can find out what's going on in the way of nightlife in the metropolitan area in which you live, see which events other members are attending, and call members' attention to events you want to attend in case anyone wants to go with you. To visit Upcoming.org and perhaps join, go to this Web address: `www.upcoming.org`.

Figure 8-4 shows the home page at Upcoming.org. This is the page you see after you log in. It lists the events you plan to attend and events your friends plan to attend. Starting on this page, you can do all things necessary to make your nightlife more adventurous:

✦ **Choosing metro areas:** Declare the metro area in which you live so that you can find out what's going on there and discover who from Upcoming.org is attending. You can choose more than one metro area. To choose a metro area, click the Metros link on the home page and select a country, state, and finally, a city or area. Then click the Join Metro button. The names of the metro areas you chose appear on the home page (refer to Figure 8-4).

✦ **Checking out events in your area:** Click the name of a metro area on the home page to see a list of events that other members in the metro area added to the site. You come to the All Events page, which lists each event, its venue, and how many Upcoming.org members are attending. Click an event to find out when and where it occurs, and who is attending. You can click a member name to see a member's profile.

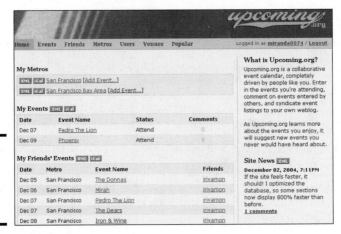

Figure 8-4: The home page at Upcoming.org.

✦ **Adding an event to the list:** To add an event to the list of events in your metro area so that other members are alerted to its occurrence, click the Add Event link on the home page. Then, on the Add Event page, categorize the even, tell when it will occur, give it a name, and enter its venue.

✦ **Seeing what your friends are doing:** Wherever you see a member name in Upcoming.org, you can click the name to see the member's profile. And if you click the Add to My Friends link on the Profile page, the person is added to your Friends list. To see which events a friend is attending, click the Friends link and then click your friend's name on the My Friends page.

Looking for Love in the Yahoo! Personals

"I feel pretty strange about using the personals, because I've never done it before, but here goes . . ." Many Yahoo! profiles begin this way, but why feel strange about it? You're not the only one looking for love on the Internet. Anybody can browse the profiles at Yahoo! Personals, but if you want to get in touch with someone or make yourself available, you have to submit a profile of your own. The following pages explain how to do all that.

To search for love in the Yahoo! Personals, you must have a Yahoo! account and you must sign in to Yahoo!. Appendix A explains how to do both.

Searching for Mr. or Ms. Right

To search for Mr. or Ms. Right in the Yahoo! Personals, sign in to Yahoo! and go to the Personals home page. To get there, either go to Yahoo! (www.yahoo.com) and click the Personals link or go straight to the Personals home page at this address: http://personals.yahoo.com.

On the Personals home page, conduct your search using one of these methods:

✦ **Quick search:** Fill in the fields and click the Find My Match button.

✦ **Refined search:** On the Search Results page, click a link on the left side of the page to enter more search criteria and refine your search. For example, click the Love Style link and select a Love Style from the pop-up menu, as shown in Figure 8-5. Click the Update Results button to run the search again.

✦ **Keyword search:** Click the Keyword Search link on the Personals home page, and in the form that appears, enter a search term and click the Find My Match button.

Book IV
Chapter 8

Making Friends and
Connections Online

Figure 8-5:
Refining the
search.

If a search yields any results, you see a list of profiles — descriptions and, in some cases, photos that you can read or view and ponder. Click an ad headline or the More link, and you come to the Profile Details page with detailed information about the person. From here, you can:

✦ **Save a profile:** Click the Save Profile link to save a profile and be able to view it later. To see profiles you've saved, click the My Saved Profiles link on the Personals home page.

✦ **Get in touch with the person:** Click the Break the Ice link and send the person a brief message. You must have created a profile of yourself to "break the ice" (see the next section in this chapter). Unless you are a paying subscriber to Yahoo! Personals, you can only send one icebreaker message to a person (and receive one reply). You can, however, include your e-mail address in the icebreaker message in order to communicate, but by doing that, you leave the confines of Yahoo! Personals. All communications after that are done by conventional e-mail outside of Yahoo!.

Submitting a profile to Yahoo! Personals

Rather than search for love, you can try to get love to come knocking at your door by submitting your profile to Yahoo! Personals. A *profile* is a self-portrait by which others can find and learn something about you.

Starting on the Personals home page, click the Create a Free Profile link. You come to the Create a Profile questionnaire. Fill in the required fields plus whatever personal information you want to share. You are asked to describe yourself, describe your perfect love match, write a headline and a self-description for your ad, enter a personals name, and state whether you want people rummaging through the personal ads to be able to find you. Be sure to submit flattering photos to increase the chances of someone responding to your ad.

If someone responds to your profile

You can tell whether someone has sent to an icebreaker message because the My Personals module on the Personals home page tells you how many messages have been sent. Click the Mailbox link to go to the Mailbox page and read the message.

As I mentioned earlier, you can only reply once unless you are a paid subscriber, in which case you can communicate by e-mail and instant message. You can, however, include an e-mail address in your reply and communicate outside the confines of Yahoo! Personals.

To be notified by e-mail when someone has responded to your profile, click the Set Up Matches by E-mail link on the Personals home page. On the Matches by Mail page, choose your e-mail address (if you have more than one). From the drop-down menu, choose how often you want the messages sent to you.

Reuniting with Old Friends

Who hasn't searched the Internet late at night for lost loves, friends from days gone by, and boon travel companions from long ago? The Internet is supposed to reach into every corner of the earth to drudge up information, so shouldn't it be able to find long-lost friends, too?

Frank Zappa said, "High school isn't a time or place — it's a state of mind." If you care to revisit that particular state of mind, you can do it at Classmates. com (www.classmates.com). Registering is free, and after you register, you can look up classmates by year at the high school you attended, as shown in Figure 8-6. You can also search the message boards, but to post messages, send classmates e-mail, post photographs, or put up a profile, you need a Gold account, which costs $35 per year — kind of steep in my opinion.

I hope that somebody starts a Friends Reunited Web site for the United States. The one in England (www.friendsreunited.com) has been a phenomenal success, with 11 million members. Old school chums, army pals, and even ex-convicts have used the site to find one another. According to the Web site, half the adult school population of Britain has visited Friends Reunited, and graduates from every school in the nation use the service. Why has it been so successful? For one thing, it's free. And even members who don't opt for full membership can receive e-mails at the site. That makes it very easy for old friends to get back in touch.

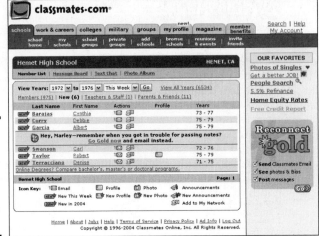

Figure 8-6:
Rummaging
through
the past
darkly at
Classmates.
com.

Book II, Chapter 5 explains how to search for people by name on the Internet. You can always search for long-lost friends that way.

Chapter 9: Using Your PC as a Telephone

In This Chapter

✔ Using VoIP services for telephone calling

✔ Talking to others on your computer with Skype

*A*s fast as e-mail and instant messaging are, the fastest way to communicate with someone who is not in the same room as you is by telephone. The computer has yet to catch up with the instrument invented by Antonio Meucci in 1889. Or has it?

This chapter looks at how to make telephone calls with the assistance of your computer and the Internet. You can save money calling with your computer, especially if you often make long-distance calls. The Internet offers two ways to make these calls. You can use a VoIP service or Skype, a peer-to-peer data-transmission software. Both techniques are covered in this chapter.

Unless you have a fast broadband connection, don't even consider talking on the telephone by computer. People with DSL service and cable modems can talk on the telephone by computer, but if you have a dialup connection, you're out of luck. Book I, Chapter 2 explains the difference between broadband and dialup connections.

Calling with a VoIP Service

Some years ago, telephone companies developed the VoIP (voice over Internet protocol) to transmit telephone calls faster over the telephone lines. The protocol converts analog sounds to digital data. It uses the Internet's packet-switching capabilities to squeeze more data into the telephone lines (Book I, Chapter 1 explains packet switching). Now a half-dozen telephone companies offer VoIP service plans directly to homes and offices. Under these plans, you can call anywhere in the United States and Canada for a flat rate of $30 to $40 per month (the Lingo plan offers a flat rate as well for landline calls to Western Europe). Check out VoIP telephone services if you spend more than $30 to $40 per month calling long-distance to the United States and Canada. You could save money by switching to a VoIP service.

Table 9-1 describes the VoIP telephone service plans. Comparing the plans can be difficult because they offer different options and vary in price. Fortunately, all offer a trial period, so if you don't like a plan, you can cancel it after two weeks or a month.

Table 9-1	VoIP Telephone Service Plans*		
Plan Name/ Company	Web Site	Cost per Month	Activation/ Termination Fee
CallVantage/AT&T	www.att.com/ callvantage	$30	$30/None
Freedom Unlimited/ Packet8	www.packet8.net	$20	$30/$60
Lingo/Primus Telecommunications	www.lingo.com	$20	$30/$40
Optimum Voice/ Cablevision	www.optimumvoice. com	$35	None/None
Premium Unlimited/ Vonage	www.vonage.com	$25	$29/$39
VoiceWing/Verizon	www.verizon.com/ voicewing	$35	$40/$20

*Prices current as of February 2004

When you sign up to use a VoIP telephone service plan, you are given a *telephone adaptor*. This hardware device — it's about the size of a wallet and is more accurately called an *analog telephone adaptor* — is the intermediary between the telephone and the computer. It turns the analog signal from the telephone into digital data that can be sent over the Internet. As shown in Figure 9-1, the telephone adaptor is plugged into the modem. The wire that normally goes from the computer to the modem is instead plugged into the telephone adaptor, and the telephone is plugged into the telephone adaptor as well. As you speak on the telephone, the telephone adaptor renders your voice into digital data that can be sent over the Internet.

As a marriage between the Internet and the telephone, VoIP services have the benefits and the drawbacks of both parents. Telephone calls can be treated like e-mail messages. You can save them, copy them, and forward them. You can listen to your voice mail in a Web browser and open your browser to an online list of the calls you've made showing how much each call cost. You can be alerted by e-mail when someone has called you on the telephone.

Unfortunately, most services charge for calling 411 (directory assistance). And you never really know what will turn up on your bill when you call overseas. Charges vary greatly depending on the country you call. VoIP service plans charge higher for calling cell phones than landline phones. Sometimes voices lag in the telephone conversation. Don't give up your conventional phone service just yet if you opt for VoIP calling. See whether you like it before you abandon the telephone as we know it today.

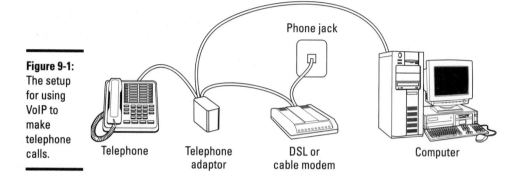

Figure 9-1:
The setup for using VoIP to make telephone calls.

Phone jack

Telephone   Telephone   DSL or   Computer
             adaptor   cable modem

Free Telephone Calling with Skype

Skype, a computer program for talking over the Internet, isn't as much an online telephone as it is an instant-messaging program that transmits sound instead of text. To talk with Skype, both parties must be logged on to the Skype network, just as both parties must be logged on to AOL to trade instant messages with AOL Instant Messenger. Rather than talk on the telephone, parties speak into microphones on their computers. They hear the other party through their computer speakers. Transmitting sound this way over the Internet is nothing new. What makes Skype extraordinary is its peer-to-peer technology, which makes digitized sound travel quickly over the Internet. You can talk to someone on Skype without echoes or lag time. Well, you can usually do that. Talking with Skype is not very different from talking on the telephone. And talking on Skype is free, whether you're talking to someone next door or someone in Timbuktu. Skype is a wonderful program for talking to friends and relatives in distant places.

With *peer-to-peer* (or P2P) technology, data isn't routed through a central management point. Instead, every computer connected to the network transmits as well as receives data. Data traveling from computer A to computer B can take many different routes through the network and reach its destination that much faster. Kazaa, the notorious file-sharing program, uses peer-to-peer technology. The technology makes it possible to transmit and download music files quickly. The same principle applies to Skype, except you're transmitting voices, not music files.

**Book IV
Chapter 9**

Using Your PC as a Telephone

Downloading and configuring the software

As I mention in the previous section, both parties have to download the Skype software and register with Skype before they can start talking. Both parties also need a working microphone, speakers, and a sound card on their computers. Here's how to get Skype software, register with Skype, and sign in:

✦ **Downloading Skype:** Go to this Web address and click the Download Now link: www.skype.com.

✦ **Registering with Skype:** The first time you run Skype, you are asked for a username and password. Remember your name well. Others will know you and call you by the name you enter. The program also asks you to describe yourself in a profile. Other people can find you on the network using the information you enter. Your name is what matters most. To change the information in your profile later, choose File➪Your Personal Profile.

✦ **Logging in to Skype:** After you start Skype, click the Click Here to Log In link on the Start tab and then enter your username and password.

Figure 9-2 shows two of the five tabs in the Skype window. Does the Skype window look familiar? If you read Chapter 1 of this minibook about instant messaging, you probably have a case of déjà vu right now. Skype is an instant-messaging program. It has a Contacts list, commands for safeguarding your privacy online, and even commands for sending instant messages.

Figure 9-2:
The Skype Start tab (left) and the tab for making a phone call (right).

Choose File⇨Log Off to close Skype. If you simply close the Skype window, the program runs in the background and continues to receive incoming phone calls.

Assembling a Contacts list

You can only call people whose names appear on your Contacts list. Your first task, before you call anybody, is to enter the names of friends and family on the Contacts list. You can do that in two ways:

✦ **If you know the person's name:** Choose Tools⇨Add a Contact or click the Add a Contact button. In the Add a Contact dialog box, enter the name under which your friend or coworker is registered in Skype, and click the Next button. If the name is found, it is entered automatically on your Contacts list.

✦ **If you aren't sure of the person's name:** Choose Tools⇨Search for Skype Users and click the Advanced button in the Search for Skype Users dialog box. Enter what you know about the person and click the Search button. If you succeed in locating the person, right-click his or her name and choose Add to Contacts.

To remove a name from your Contacts list, click the Contacts tab, right-click the name, and choose Remove from Contacts.

If someone wants to put your on his Contacts list, you see the Authorize This User message box. Choose an option that describes how and whether you want the other person to see you when you're online, and click the OK button.

Talking on the Skype phone

How you handle the Skype phone depends on whether the call originates with you or the other party:

✦ **Calling:** To make a phone call, select the Contacts tab. Then either double-click the person's name or select it and click the Call button.

✦ **Receiving:** To receive a phone call, select the tab with the name of the person who is calling you. Then click the Call button. You'll know when you're getting a call because you'll hear a ringing noise. (If you don't hear the ring and you want to or if you don't care to hear it, choose File⇨Options and, on the Call Alerts tab of the Options dialog box, select or deselect the Play Ringtone check box.)

During a call, the Skype icon blinks on and off in the Notification area by the clock on your computer screen. To end a phone call, click the End Call button or choose Call⇨Hangup⇨*Caller's Name*.

Guarding your privacy

Here are instructions for guarding your privacy while you are running Skype:

+ **Make yourself invisible:** Choose File⇨Change Status⇨Invisible. You can tell which status you are operating under by glancing at the icon in the Notification area.

+ **Control whether the program starts when you start your computer:** Choose File⇨Options and, on the General tab of the Options dialog box, select or deselect the Start Skype when I Start Windows check box.

+ **Change your profile:** Choose File⇨Your Personal Profile and fill in the User Profile dialog box.

Book V

Your Personal Finances

The 5th Wave   By Rich Tennant

"You know, it dawned on me last night why we aren't getting any hits on our Web site."

Contents at a Glance

Chapter 1: Searching for Financial Information

In This Chapter

- ✔ Discovering the basics of how to invest
- ✔ Developing your investment strategy
- ✔ Investigating a company you want to invest in
- ✔ Getting the latest financial news
- ✔ Investigating a mutual fund, stock, or bond
- ✔ Choosing a broker

*P*revious to the Internet, only the wizards of Wall Street had enough information at their fingertips to evaluate stocks, mutual funds, and other investments. A tickertape told them the value of each stock. Expensive newspapers, magazines, and newsletters told them about trends, investments worth buying, and investments worth shunning.

Nowadays, anyone with a PC can plug into the Internet and find all kinds of information about investing. All across the Internet are Web sites that offer investment advice and information. If you are careful and know where to look, you can get your hands on the same information that experts use to play the markets. You can read company prospectuses, financial newsletters, and magazines. You can visit a Web site tailor-made to provide a certain kind of information to investors. The only trouble is wading through all the Web sites until you find the one that works well for you.

This chapter looks into how the Internet can help you start investing and become a better investor. It demonstrates how to research a company, points the way to financial news services on the Internet, and spells out how to research stocks, bonds, and mutual funds.

Getting Lessons in How to Invest

Looking before you leap is always the best policy, so before you take the leap and start investing, go on the Internet and discover what investing is all about. Many brokers and banks are eager for you to start investing. For that reason, the Internet is filled with tutorials, online classes, and courses that you can take to learn the ropes.

Can't decide how much of your savings to devote to investments? Don't know what a market index is? Check out these Web sites, which offer online tutorials in investing:

- ✦ **American Association of Individual Investors:** Read articles about choosing and evaluating investments. Most of the articles are free. Address: www.aaii.com/invbas/index.shtml

- ✦ **The Investment FAQ:** Search for investor information by category, or conduct a keyword search. This site also offers tours for beginning investors (click the For Beginners link). Address: http://invest-faq.com

- ✦ **Money 101:** Starting here, you can get 21 lessons in investing, with advice about everything from investing in stocks to planning for your retirement. Address: http://money.cnn.com/pf/101

- ✦ **Vanguard Group:** Click the Personal Investors link to attend classes at "Vanguard University" and discover the basics of investing and retirement planning. Address: www.vanguard.com

No terminology is harder to understand than investment terminology. Do you know what a price/earnings (P/E) ratio is? A short sell? A put? A shot-put? When you get stumped by an investment term, go to the Yahoo! Finance Glossary at http://biz.yahoo.com/f/g.

Devising an Investment Strategy

To make your money work for you, you need an investment strategy. Experts differ about the fine points of investment strategies, but they agree on these basic principles:

- ✦ **Determine how much income you can devote to investing:** How much you can devote is a matter of how much you can save. Before you make investments, you need to understand your spending habits and how much is left after you pay for groceries, rent, and other necessities.

- ✦ **Decide on your financial goals:** Do you want to retire early? Do you want to live luxuriously or modestly when you retire? How much income from your investments will you need when you stop working? Your financial goals determine how much you invest and how risky your investments are.

✦ **Allocate your investments wisely:** On the theory that you shouldn't put all your eggs in one basket, many investment counselors advocate diversifying investments across many different investment types — blue-chip stocks, high-risk stocks, bonds, and mutual funds, for example. You minimize your risks this way, because if one class of investments falters, the others theoretically pick up the slack.

✦ **Set aside rainy-day money:** Put away as much money as you need to live on for four months in a savings account. This way, if you lose your job, have a medical emergency, or face another setback, you have enough to live on without tapping into your investments.

✦ **Find the right broker:** Some brokers charge a commission and some an annual fee. Some badger you with investment opportunities every week, and others are as silent as the lambs. Later in this chapter, "Finding a Broker" explains how to choose a broker.

✦ **Decide how to monitor your investments:** You can't tell how well or poorly your investments are doing unless you monitor them. The next chapter looks into monitoring investments. You can track your investments online or use a software program such as Money or Quicken.

Here are some Web sites that can help you devise a financial plan:

✦ **Fidelity Investments:** Click the Retirement Planning link at this Web site to go to the Retirement Resource Center, where you can find advice and worksheets for planning your retirement. Address: `www.fidelity.com`

✦ **Money 101:** You can't find a better simple investment tutorial than this one offered by Money 101. Address: `http://money.cnn.com/pf/101/lessons/4`

✦ **Yahoo! Financial:** The Planning Basics page at the Finances portion of Yahoo! offers excellent tutorials for planning your retirement and devising an investment strategy. Address: `http://planning.yahoo.com/pb.html`

You are not ready to become an investor if you are not paying your credit card bills in full every month. Carrying a credit card balance from month to month is the surest sign that you are not saving correctly to be an investor. Look at it this way: Even if your investments earn 10 percent a year, the 10-percent profit is more than offset by the 16 to 21 percent in interest you pay annually to service your credit card debt.

Discovering Basic Researching Techniques

Later in this chapter, "Researching Mutual Funds, Stocks, and Bonds on the Internet" explains how to do specific research online. These pages explain general-purpose researching. Follow me to find out where the big, gaudy financial portals are, how to research a company online, and why mailing lists and newsgroups can be valuable for getting investment advice.

The big, gaudy financial portals

The Web sites described here provide information about stocks, mutual funds, companies, markets, and nearly everything under the sun. They are usually called *portals* because they offer so much information, but I call these Web sites "big" and "gaudy" because you can get lost in them so easily. They are useful to investors, but it takes time to know your way around these Web sites:

✦ **CBS MarketWatch:** This site offer reports from global markets, investor tools, articles, and mutual fund advice — it has everything but the proverbial kitchen sink. Address: `http://cbs.marketwatch.com`

✦ **Motley Fool:** "The Fool," as it is known to its admirers, offers stock screeners, advice for buying stocks and mutual funds, articles, and a host of other stuff, as shown in Figure 1-1. "The Motley Fool exists to educate, amuse, and enrich the individual investor" is the Fool's motto. Address. `www.fool.com`

✦ **Money Central:** This is another mazelike financial portal for the investor to get lost and occasionally find useful stuff in. Address: `http://moneycentral.msn.com`

Figure 1-1:
Motley Fool,
a financial
portal.

Researching a company online

Before you invest in a company, you owe it to yourself to research it. Has the company undergone a financial setback? Has management experienced a shakeup? What were the company's profits or losses in the last quarter?

To research a company, start by finding the company's Web site on the Internet. You can often make an educated guess as to the company's Web-site address by typing **www.*companyname*.com** (where *companyname* is the name of the company) in the Address text box of your browser, pressing Enter, and hoping for the best. If that strategy doesn't work, try searching for the company's Web site by using a search engine such as Google (see Book II, Chapter 3 for more about searching the Web).

Next, visit one of these Web sites to track down a company's profile:

✦ **Company News On-Call:** Search by company name in the PR Newswire database for articles published in the past year. Beware, however, because only news about large companies is available here. Address: `www.prnewswire.com/cnoc.html`

✦ **Hoover's Online:** This site provides profiles, revenue reports, balance sheets, and charts on some 8,500 companies. Address: `www.hoovers.com`

✦ **OneSource CorpTech:** The focus here is high-tech companies. The site offers company profiles, links to news articles about companies, and stock charts. CorpTech is very good at listing the names of company executives. Give one a call and see what happens. Address: `www.corptech.com`

✦ **Public Register's Annual Report Service:** This site presents free annual reports from over 3,600 companies. Mind you, the companies themselves provide these reports, so give them a shrewd reading. Address: `www.prars.com`

✦ **Silicon Valley.com:** This is the place to research high-tech companies operating out of the Silicon Valley. Address: `www.sv.com`

✦ **U.S. Securities and Exchange Commission:** Publicly traded companies are required to file financial data with the Securities and Exchange Commission (SEC). From the SEC Web site, shown in Figure 1-2, you can download details about a company's operations, including financial statements, executive pay, and other information. (Click the EDGAR Filers link.) Address: `www.sec.gov`

Besides visiting the Web sites listed here, try running a conventional Internet search for information about a company (see Book II, Chapter 3). You might find news articles and opinions about the company that way.

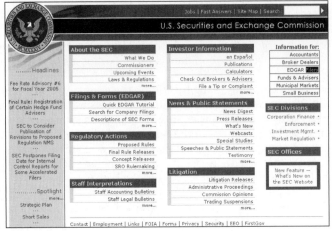

Figure 1-2:
Go to the
Securities
and
Exchange
Commission
to research
companies.

Researching in mailing lists and newsgroups

Don't underestimate mailing lists and newsgroups when it comes to researching investments, companies, and markets. A mailing list is an ongoing discussion conducted by e-mail among people in the know (Book IV, Chapter 3 explains mailing lists and how to find them on the Internet). A newsgroup is an online bulletin board where people discuss different topics. (Book IV, Chapter 4 explains newsgroups and how to find one on the Usenet.) When heavily guarded financial information escapes from a company, more often than not its point of exit is a newsgroup or mailing list.

Getting the Latest Financial News

Savvy investors stay on top of late-breaking financial news. And keeping abreast of changes in the economy and the political climate isn't a bad idea either. A smart investor gets there first, before the fools rush in.

The Internet offers a daunting number of newspapers, magazines, newsletters, and news organizations that are devoted to financial news and opinions. Visit a few Web sites. Soon you will find a favorite site that focuses on news that matters to the kind of investing you want to do.

Major news services

First, here are a few mammoth corporate Web sites. Most of these sites — such as CNN and MSNBC — are sponsored by news services that predate the Internet. You don't find eccentric opinions here, but the news stories are trustworthy and the financial advice is as solid (if as plain) as granite:

✦ **Bloomberg Personal Finance:** Advice for money management, news about financial markets, and columnists can be found here. Address: www.bloomberg.com

✦ **CBS MarketWatch:** This all-purpose site does more than offer financial news. You can get market data, stock quotes, company portfolios, advice for managing your personal finances, and performance charts. Address: http://cbs.marketwatch.com

✦ **CNN Money:** This is the financial section of CNN's news Web site. You can find up-to-the-minute financial news here, as well as commentary and tools for investigating stocks and mutual funds. Address: http://money.cnn.com

✦ **MSNBC:** Click the Business link to go to a Web page with business news, stock market news, and news about e-commerce. Address: www.msnbc.com

✦ **TheStreet.com:** This site offers financial news but, better yet, it includes a nice selection of columnists. This is the place to go when you want to sample others' financial opinions. Address: www.thestreet.com

Financial newspapers and magazines

Perhaps financial newspapers and magazines are more to your taste. The online editions of these popular newspapers and magazines are not as comprehensive as the ones you can buy at the newsstand. However, they can still be very valuable:

✦ **Business Week Online:** This site offers news from the financial world, as well as technology and small-business news. Address: www.businessweek.com

✦ **The Economist:** *The Economist,* an English financial magazine, is simply the best magazine of its kind in the world. Its cosmopolitan outlook puts to shame some of the narrow-minded, homegrown magazines on the news rack. Read the current issue of this magazine for its world view of economics and business. Figure 1-3 shows the online Economist. Address: www.economist.com

✦ **FT.com:** The online version of the *Financial Times* offers market data, news, and analysis. Address: www.ft.com

✦ **Kiplinger Online:** More than a magazine, the online edition of *Kiplinger's Personal Finance Magazine* offers shopping services, advice for buying insurance, and other valuable stuff. Of course, you also get business and market news. Address: www.kiplinger.com

+ **Money:** The online edition of *Money* magazine provides many news articles and expert opinions. You can also get stock quotes and company profiles here. Address: `www.money.cnn.com`

+ **Wall Street Journal:** The online edition of this well-regarded newspaper also presents news summaries and insider information about American businesses. You can also get company reports and stock quotes. You must register to read the articles. Address: `www.wallstreetjournal.com`

Figure 1-3:
Reading
*The
Economist*
online.

Online newsletters

The Internet has made it possible for every Tom, Dick, and Harry to post a Web page and call it an investor newsletter. Far be it from me to decide which newsletters are worthy. Instead, you be the judge. Go to the Newsletter Access Web site (`www.newsletteraccess.com`) and search for a newsletter that whets your appetite. To conduct the search, enter a keyword or browse the different categories.

Researching Mutual Funds, Stocks, and Bonds on the Internet

Mutual funds and stocks are the two most popular kinds of investments. Not coincidentally, numerous Web sites devoted to stocks and mutual funds can be found on the Internet. From these sites, you can check the latest price of a stock or mutual fund. You can also dig deeper to investigate or screen funds and stocks. In the following pages, I unscrew the inscrutable and show you where to go on the Internet to research mutual funds, stocks, and bonds.

To find out anything about a security on the Internet, you usually have to know its ticker symbol. A *ticker symbol* is a one- to five-letter abbreviation that is used for tracking the performance of stocks, mutual funds, and bonds. You can usually find these symbols on the statements that you receive from brokers. If you don't know a security's ticker symbol, go to Yahoo Finance! (`http://finance.yahoo.com`) and use the search engine there to find it (click the Symbol Lookup link).

Researching a mutual fund on the Internet

Mutual funds are the favorite of investors who want to reap the benefits of investing without doing the legwork. A *mutual fund* is a company that buys stocks, bonds, precious metals, and other securities. Investors buy shares in the fund. If the fund managers know their stuff, the securities that the mutual fund owns increase in value — and shares in the fund increase in value as well. Owning shares in a mutual fund is like owning shares of stock in a company. The difference is that a share of a mutual fund represents ownership in many different companies, as well as bonds and other securities.

Many people don't have the time, the expertise, or the inclination to research investment opportunities. For those people, mutual funds are ideal. You can rely on the fund managers' investing know-how. You can buy shares in a mutual fund without speaking to a broker. By definition, a mutual fund is diversified because it owns shares of many different securities, so you don't have to worry as much about diversification when you invest in a mutual fund.

Before you start dabbling in mutual funds, you need to know how fees are levied, about the different kinds of funds, and about the risks. After you know that, you can start looking for a fund that meets your needs. Here are some Web sites where you can acquire the basics of mutual-fund investing:

✦ **Brill's Mutual Funds Interactive:** This is the all-purpose Web site for mutual fund investing. Here, you can read about mutual fund investing or search for funds by name and read about them. Address: `www.fundsinteractive.com`

✦ **Mutual Fund Investor's Center:** This excellent Web site, shown in Figure 1-4, offers articles about mutual-fund investing and ranks mutual funds in various ways. You can also search for mutual funds using different criteria. Address: `www.mfea.com`

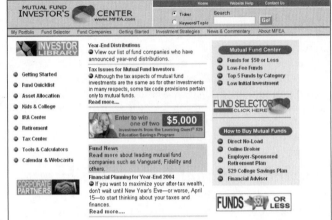

Figure 1-4:
Checking
out mutual
funds at the
Mutual Fund
Investor's
Center.

At last count, investors could choose from among 10,000 mutual funds. After you know what you want in a mutual fund, check out these Web sites, where you can search for a mutual fund that fits your investment strategy:

✦ **Fund Alarm:** "Know when to hold 'em, know when to fold 'em," advises this unusual Web site. Instead of advising you what to buy, it tells you when to sell your mutual funds. Address: www.fundalarm.com

✦ **Morningstar.com:** The granddaddy of mutual fund analysis, this site offers reports on 7,000 mutual funds. You can get fund profiles, performance reports, financial statements, and news articles. (Click the Funds link.) Address: www.morningstar.com

✦ **SmartMoney.com:** This site offers a sophisticated search engine for pinpointing mutual funds. (Click the Funds link and then click the Fund Finder link.) Address: www.smartmoney.com

Researching stocks on the Internet

The stock market, it has been said, is 85 percent psychology and 15 percent economics. And that's only half the problem. The other half has to do with its hard-to-understand terminology and the numerous confusing ways to buy and sell stock.

If you decide to jump into the stock market on your own, more power to you. This book cannot possibly delve into everything you need to know to invest in the stock market, but I can point the way to a few Web sites that can help you on the road to riches.

Socially conscious investing

Investing is a bit like casting a vote. When you invest in a company, you endorse its products, its business practices, and its labor practices. For better or worse, your investment helps shape the world in which we live.

On the idea that most people object to child labor, unsafe working conditions, pollution, and unhealthy products, a number of mutual fund managers have taken the lead and established socially conscious mutual funds. These funds do not buy into companies that practice what the managers think is bad business or social behavior.

To find out more about socially conscious investing and perhaps buy shares of a socially conscious mutual fund, check out the Co-op America Web site (www.coopamerica.org) and the Social Investment Forum (www.socialinvest.org). By the way, studies show that socially conscious mutual funds perform on average as well as other mutual funds.

To get general-purpose information about stocks and stock markets, read stock tips, and discover stock-picking strategies, try these sites, which are good starting places:

✦ **DailyStocks:** This site provides links to market indexes, news sources, earnings figures, and newsletters. Address: www.dailystocks.com

✦ **InternetNews:** This site offers links to many financial resources, including brokers' sites and government data. Address: http://stocks.internetnews.com

When you want to hunker down and examine specific stocks, go to one of these sites (and be sure to read "Researching a company online," earlier in this chapter, as well):

✦ **Free Realtime:** Get financial news, the latest stock quotes, and company profiles at this Web site. Address: http://quotes.freerealtime.com

✦ **MoneyCentral Investor:** Look in the Stocks section and click a link to find a stock quote, a chart, and analyst ratings. You can also screen stocks from this Web site. Address: http://investor.msn.com

✦ **PCQuote:** You can enter a ticker symbol and get stock quotes and charts. This site also presents market news, a "stock pick of the week," and news articles about the markets. Address: www.pcquote.com

✦ **Yahoo! Finance:** Enter a ticker symbol and you can get a price chart, news articles about a stock, charts that track its performance, and links to the company's SEC filings. As Figure 1-5 shows, you can also compare the performance of two different stocks. Address: http://finance.yahoo.com

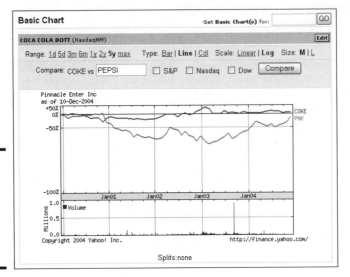

Figure 1-5:
Comparing
one stock
against
another at
Yahoo!
Finance.

Suppose that you want to target a stock but you don't know what it is yet. In other words, you believe that the future is bright for a certain industry and you want to buy shares in companies in that industry. Or, you want to buy a certain kind of stock — stock in a foreign corporation, a small-cap stock, or a blue-chip stock. Searching for stocks this way is called *screening*. The Reuters' Investor Web site offers stock-screening databases that you can search using different variables. (Look for the Reuters PowerScreener.) Its address is www.investor.reuters.com.

Researching bonds on the Internet

A bond is really a loan that you make to a government agency or private corporation. During the life of the loan, the government agency or corporation pays you interest, known as the *coupon rate*. Interest payments are usually made twice yearly. Bonds are considered safer, less-volatile investments than stocks and mutual funds because the amount of the bond is paid back at the end of the loan term, known as the *maturity date*. Instead of owning part of the company, which is the case with stocks, bond holders own a debt that the company or government agency that issued the bond is obliged to pay back.

Here are a handful of Web sites for investors who favor bonds:

✦ **Bond Buyer:** Go to this site to investigate municipal bonds. Address: www.bondbuyer.com

✦ **Bond Market Association:** This Web site tells you everything you need to know about bonds. It explains the different kinds of bonds, bond dealers, and bond indexes. Address: `www.investinginbonds.com`

✦ **Bonds Online:** Go to the BondSearch/Quote Center to get historical data about different bond investment yields. Address: `www.bondsonline.com`

Finding a Broker

A broker is a person or company that purchases and sells securities on your behalf. As you choose a broker, the first question to ask is what your broker charges in commissions and fees. Most charge a commission or flat fee for each trade they make on your behalf. Many also charge yearly maintenance fees. Some also charge transfer fees to move money from your investment account to another account, such as a checking or savings account. Others charge inactivity fees, which you incur if you don't trade securities on a regular basis.

Here are two Web sites that can help you select the broker who is right for you:

✦ **National Association of Securities Dealers:** Click the Investor Information link to investigate a broker. From there, you can check the background of any licensed broker in the United States. Address: `www.nasdr.com`

✦ **Yahoo! Finance:** Get tips and articles about choosing a broker from Yahoo!. Address: `http://biz.yahoo.com/edu/ed_broker.html`

Chapter 2: Monitoring and Tracking Investments

In This Chapter

✓ Introducing online portfolios

✓ Surveying online-portfolio Web sites

✓ Managing an online portfolio at Yahoo! Financial

✓ Looking at financial software management programs

*A*ll investment managers agree that keeping good, accurate records of your investments is the only way to know for certain how well or poorly the investments are performing. To tell how your investments are doing, you have to track them carefully. You need to know by what percentage your investments are growing or shrinking. You need to track your brokerage fees, your account-maintenance fees, and the other secondary costs of investing.

This chapter explains how you can monitor and track your investments by setting up an online portfolio or by using software such as Money or Quicken.

Introducing Investment Portfolios

An *investment portfolio* is a collection of investments held by an individual or institution. A portfolio tells which stocks, mutual funds, bonds, and other securities you own, and how much each security is currently worth. As well, most investment portfolios include cash from the sale of investments or cash that has yet to be invested.

To update a portfolio in the old days, you needed an account ledger and a magnifying glass or, at best, a good pair of spectacles. You had to peer into the *Wall Street Journal* or another newspaper that reports on securities, note the value of the securities you owned, and enter the values carefully into the account register. Updating a portfolio was a dreary, Dickensian activity.

Computers have made keeping an investment portfolio up to date much easier. You no longer have to update the value of the securities you own by hand because the computer does it for you. In the case of online portfolios (more on them in a minute), security prices are entered right into the portfolio almost as soon as they change. In the case of financial software-management programs (more on them in a minute, too), you can download up-to-date security prices from the Internet in a matter of seconds.

Tracking a portfolio by computer has another advantage — you can analyze the investments you own. You can generate charts that show how your securities are performing. You can compare your securities' performance to that of securities you don't own. You can see how your securities compare to indices such as the Dow Jones Industrial Average or the S&P 500.

You have three ways to enlist your computer's help in managing an investment portfolio:

✦ **Online portfolio management:** At Web sites such as Yahoo! Finance and Money Central, you can create an online portfolio, a page on the Internet that lists your securities and their current value. The value of the securities is updated automatically. You can also compare and analyze investments at Yahoo! Finance, Money Central, and the other online-portfolio Web sites.

✦ **Financial software management programs:** Users of Money and Quicken can track their investment portfolios in those programs. To update security prices, you just connect to the Internet and give a simple command. The programs also offer commands for analyzing and comparing investments. Money and Quicken are comprehensive financial management programs. Besides tracking investments, you can track your spending, formulate a budget, bank online, balance your checkbook, and do any number of things to make yourself healthier financially.

✦ **Online portfolio management with a broker:** Some brokerage houses offer Web sites where you can track your investments and see how they are performing. Call your broker and ask whether you are eligible for this service. And whatever you do, don't pay extra for it. If your broker wants you to pay to track your securities online, tell that so-and-so that you can track your portfolio for free on the Internet, thank you very much!

Comparing the Online Portfolio Web Sites

Table 2-1 compares the different Web sites where you can track your investments in an online portfolio. To track your portfolio at any of these sites, you must register. Most of the Web sites offer enhanced portfolio-tracking services for a fee.

Table 2-1	Free Online Portfolio-Management Web Sites	
Web Site	**Description**	**Address**
ClearStation	Generate performance charts as well as Schedule D tax forms for reporting capital gains and losses in your investments. Click the Portfolio link.	http://clearstation.etrade.com
Money Central	Track your stocks and mutual funds. The site also provides news articles that mention the securities you own. In the Investing section on the left side of the window, click the Portfolio link. You must have a .NET Passport to use this service (see Appendix B).	http://moneycentral.msn.com
Morningstar	Track stocks as well as mutual funds. At this Web site, you can also track brokerage fees and expenses. Click the Portfolio link.	www.morningstar.com
Wall Street Journal	Follow market indices and track up to five portfolios at this Web site. After you register, go to the Setup Center and click the Portfolio link.	http://online.wsj.com
Yahoo! Financial	Track stocks and mutual funds, as well as indices. You can generate reports and view company profiles for the securities you own (see the next section in this chapter).	http://finance.yahoo.com

Tracking Your Investments in a Yahoo! Portfolio

 In my opinion, Yahoo! Finance is the easiest place to keep an online portfolio. Entering security names and security prices is easy. You can view your investments in different ways. And the Portfolio window offers all kinds of amenities. For example, you can read news articles about securities you are tracking, generate charts, and get company profiles. Figure 2-1 shows an online profile at Yahoo! Finance.

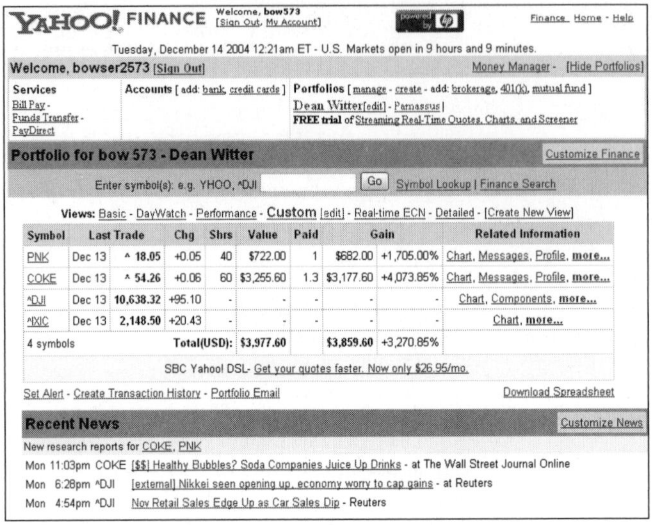

Figure 2-1:
The Portfolio window, where online portfolios appear.

To get to the Yahoo! Finance page and begin creating our online portfolio, do one of these things:

✦ Go to Yahoo! (www.yahoo.com) and click the Finance link.

✦ Go straight to the Yahoo! Finance page at this address: http://finance.yahoo.com.

Yahoo! offers four kinds of online portfolios:

✦ **Watch List:** For tracking stocks and mutual funds that you don't own but are considering purchasing. After you enter the securities on the watch list, you can research them easily.

✦ **Current Holdings:** For tracking stocks and mutual funds you have purchased and already own. Figure 2-1 shows a Current Holdings portfolio. It clearly shows how much your investments have gained or lost.

✦ **Transaction History:** For tracking each transaction in an investment account — all purchases, sales, disbursements, short sells, stock splits, and so on. I don't cover transaction portfolios in this book. If you want to track your investments that closely, you are better off with a program such as Money or Quicken (see "Financial Software-Management Programs," later in this chapter).

✦ **Online Brokerage Account:** For viewing account information from a brokerage account in Yahoo! Finance. This is for people who have accounts with many brokerage houses and want to view them all at once. Only a handful of brokerages allow you to view your accounts in Yahoo!.

To set up an investment portfolio at Yahoo! Finance, you must have a Yahoo! account and be signed in to your account. Appendix A explains how to do all that.

Before you begin . . .

Before you put together an online portfolio at Yahoo! Financial, get the paperwork in order:

+ Make a list of the ticker symbols for all the stocks and mutual funds you own. A *ticker symbol* is a one- to five-letter abbreviation that is used for tracking the performance of stocks and mutual funds. As you create your portfolio, you can look up these symbols, but doing it beforehand is easier and saves you time. You can look up ticker symbols at the Yahoo! Finance page.

+ Get the latest statement from your broker and lay it flat on your desk. Very shortly, you will plug the share-price information from the statement into your online portfolio.

Setting up an online portfolio

You can create more than one portfolio. Portfolio names appear in the upper-right corner of the Portfolio window (refer to Figure 2-1). Follow these steps to create an online portfolio at Yahoo! Finance:

1. **On the Yahoo! Finance page, click the Create link (refer to Figure 2-1).**

If you don't see this link, click the Show Portfolios link in the upper-right corner of the window. After you click it, you see the word *Portfolios* and links for managing and creating portfolios (refer to Figure 2-1). You come to the Create New Portfolio window after you click the Create link.

2. **Click the Track a Symbol Watch List link or the Track Your Current Holdings link.**

As I explain in "Tracking Your Investments in a Yahoo! Portfolio," earlier in this chapter, a watch list is a "pretend portfolio" for monitoring stock and mutual funds you have your eye on. Click the Track Your Current Holdings link if you have a real-life portfolio and you want to track it at Yahoo! Finance.

You come to the Create Your Portfolio window, where you describe what is in your portfolio.

3. **Enter a name for your portfolio in the Portfolio Name text box.**

You can create as many online portfolios as you need. Choose a descriptive name that says right away what you are tracking in this portfolio.

4. **In the Ticker Symbols text box, enter the ticker symbol of each security you want to track, separated by a blank space.**

You can click the Look Up Symbol link to look up a security's ticker symbol. Select a check box in the Example Market Indices section to track an index as well as securities.

5. **In the Basic Features section, select the Sort Symbols check box if you want to arrange security names alphabetically by symbol instead of by name in your portfolio.**

6. **Select the Don't Show Portfolio Total Value check box if, for some reason, you prefer not to see the total value of the securities you are tracking in this portfolio.**

You may be checking your portfolio while you're at work, and you don't want your coworkers to know how wealthy you really are.

7. **In the Advanced Features section, select check boxes to determine how thoroughly you want to track your securities in the portfolio.**

If you are creating a watch list, you needn't choose any check boxes. But if you want to track the changing value of securities that you already purchased, start checking away. Figure 2-1 shows what a portfolio looks like when all check boxes are selected. You can track these attributes:

- **Shares Owned:** Tracks the number of shares you purchased.

- **Purchase Price/Share:** Tracks the price per share so that you can calculate gains and losses.

- **Trade Date:** Tracks the value of your securities over time for analysis and tax purposes.

- **Commissions:** Tracks commissions paid to brokers so that you can figure these fees into profit and tax calculations.

- **Upper Limit/Lower Limit:** Permits you to be reminded by e-mail when a security reaches a certain low or high. The e-mail alert is sent to your Yahoo! e-mail address.

- **Notes:** Permits you to keep notes about your securities.

8. **Click the Continue button to go to the next window.**

You see the Portfolio Details window shown in Figure 2-2.

9. **For each security you are tracking, enter as much detail as you are asked for in Step 7.**

10. **Click the Finished button.**

The first time you create a portfolio, you are asked to okay the Yahoo! privacy policy for keeping portfolios at Yahoo! Finance.

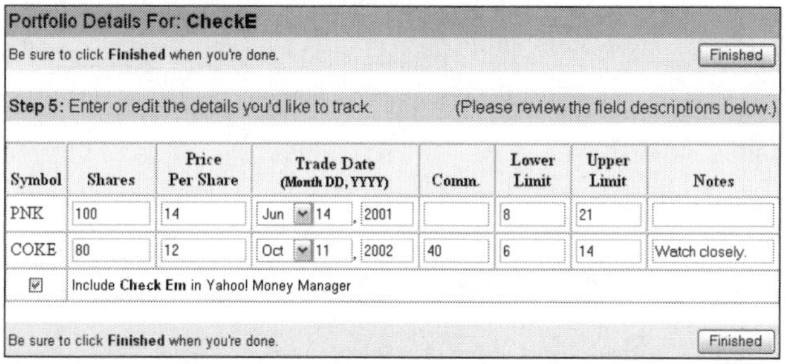

Portfolio Details For: **CheckE**

Be sure to click **Finished** when you're done. [Finished]

Step 5: Enter or edit the details you'd like to track. (Please review the field descriptions below.)

Symbol	Shares	Price Per Share	Trade Date (Month DD, YYYY)	Comm.	Lower Limit	Upper Limit	Notes
PNK	100	14	Jun 14, 2001		8	21	
COKE	80	12	Oct 11, 2002	40	6	14	Watch closely.

☑ Include **Check Em** in Yahoo! Money Manager

Be sure to click **Finished** when you're done. [Finished]

Figure 2-2: The Portfolio Details window.

To delete a portfolio you created, click the Edit link beside its name. Then, in the Edit Your Portfolio window, click the Delete This Portfolio link.

Examining and updating your investments

Security prices in your online portfolio are updated automatically. You don't have to be concerned about keeping prices up to date. You may, however, tinker with your portfolio in these ways:

- **Updating your holdings:** When you buy or sell a security, update your portfolio to make it show exactly what you own. Display the portfolio in the Portfolio window and then click the Edit link beside the portfolio's name (its name is in the upper-right corner of the window). You go to the Edit Your Portfolio window, which looks and behaves exactly like the window you used to create the portfolio. Update your holdings and click the Finished button.
- **Investigating a security:** Click a security's Chart link to see a performance chart, its Profile link to read about it, its Messages link to read what others have said about it on a message board, or its More link to read news articles about it.
- **Changing your view of the Portfolio window:** Experiment with views — Basic, Daywatch, Performance, and others — to get a different take on your investments' performance. You can click the Create New View link to create a customized view of your own.
- **Comparing a security to a potential investment:** Click the Chart link and, in the Basic Chart window, enter a ticker symbol to make the comparison. Figure 2-3 compares Coke to Pepsi over a one-year period.

Playing the investment game

Investing isn't a game, of course, but you can make a game of it. These Web sites offer investment games to sharpen your strategies and skills. Here, you can play the game for a few months before graduating to the real thing:

✔ **EduStock:** Read the tutorial and then test your skill by buying and selling stocks at up-to-date prices. Players start with 100,000 fantasy dollars with which to build a portfolio. You can practice researching stocks and securities from the Web site. Address: `http://library.thinkquest.org/3088`

✔ **Fantasy Stock Market:** Start with the requisite $100,000 in play money, and try to best the other players in building a healthy portfolio. Players are ranked, and a new game starts each month. You can also research stocks from this Web site. Address: `www.fantasystockmarket.com`

✔ **Investment Challenge:** "The most realistic stock market simulation for students," boast the makers of this site. Here, you start not with $100,000, but with 500,000 fantasy dollars (students always need extra money, don't they?). Different games are designed for middle school, high school, and college students. Address: `www.ichallenge.net`

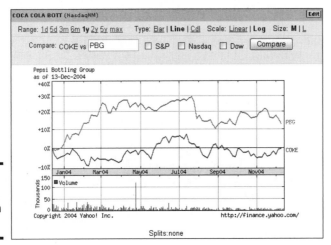

Figure 2-3:
Comparing
securities in
a chart.

Financial Software Management Programs

Another way to track your investments is to use a financial software management program. The two most popular programs are Microsoft Money and Quicken. These programs have tools for recording and analyzing investments that are superior and easier to use than the tools found in online portfolio-management Web sites. What's more, Money and Quicken are the whole package. You can analyze your spending very closely in Money and Quicken. You can formulate budgets, print checks, bank online, and plan ahead for your retirement. Figure 2-4 shows a window in Money for comparing investments.

Figure 2-4:
Comparing
investments
in Microsoft
Money.

To investigate Money, may I recommend *Microsoft Money 2005 For Dummies* (Wiley Publishing), written by yours truly? The *For Dummies* book about Quicken, *Quicken 2005 For Dummies,* by Stephen Nelson, isn't bad either. At the risk of sounding immodest, because I'm the author of the Money book, I think Money is superior to Quicken. I've used both programs. They're similar, but Money is better integrated with the Internet, which makes tracking investments online and banking online easier.

By the way, did you buy a lottery ticket this week? You can find out if your ticket is a winner by going to this Web site: http://lottery.yahoo.com. I hope you won the lottery. You won't have to work anymore, although, come to think of it, you'll have to invest your winnings, and tracking all that money could turn out to be a lot of work.

Chapter 3: Banking and Paying Bills Online

In This Chapter

✔ Doing your banking chores online

✔ Paying bills online

✔ Banking and paying bills online with Microsoft Money or Quicken

✔ Finding a credit card that is right for you

This chapter is dedicated to Buck Rogers, that citizen of the future who banks online and pays all his bills in digital cash. You won't catch Buck Rogers standing in line at a bank or ATM. You won't see him waiting for the bank statement to arrive in the mail to find out what his balance is or which checks have cleared his bank.

Buck Rogers does his banking and bill paying online. This chapter explains how you can join Buck Rogers. It demonstrates how to bank online and pay your bills online without writing checks, licking stamps, or putting envelopes in the mail. It looks into banking online with two software programs, Money and Quicken, and shows you how to search for the ideal credit card on the Internet.

Banking Online

Online banking means to do the chores associated with banking at your computer instead of inside the hallowed halls of a bank. Banking online saves you the trouble of visiting the brick-and-mortar bank. It also spares you from having to fill in paper forms and shuffle papers. You will be glad to know that banking online keeps getting easier because banks prefer their customers to bank online. It spares banks the expense of paying tellers and the trouble of managing paper records. Banking online is free at most major banks. I venture to say it is one of those things that people will do and take for granted in the future, much as we now take the ATM for granted.

At a bare minimum, most banks offer these online services:

✦ **Find out your account balances.** As shown in Figure 3-1, you can see an account overview page that lists how much money is in your accounts.

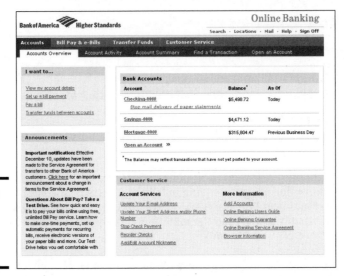

Figure 3-1:
Getting account balances online.

✦ **Examine recent deposits and payments.** This includes whether checks you wrote have cleared the bank, as shown in Figure 3-2. In effect, you can view your bank statement online, but you don't have to wait till the end of the month to see it. You can view recent transactions whenever you find it necessary to do so.

Figure 3-2:
Examining bank transactions.

Posting Date ↓	Transaction		Debit(-)	Credit(+)	Balance
12/13/2004	CHECK #2557	View Check	$80.00		$4,998.72
12/10/2004	CHECK #2558	View Check	$105.00		$5,078.72
12/10/2004	BKOFAMERICA ATM WITHDRWL 12-10 #000000 CUSTOMER 222222222 BANK OF AMERICA, SAN FRANCISCO, CA		$200.00		$5,183.72
12/10/2004	BKOFAMERICA ATM TRANSFER 12-10 #000000 CUSTOMER 222222222 FROM SAVINGS 00001-001001 BANK OF AMERICA, SAN FRANCISCO, CA			$3,000.00	$5,383.72
12/08/2004	CHECK #2556	View Check	$1,490.29		$2,389.67
12/07/2004	CHECK #2544	View Check	$34.80		$3,879.96
12/07/2004	CHECK #2549	View Check	$102.00		$3,914.76
12/07/2004	CHECK #2543	View Check	$169.00		$4,016.76

✦ **Transfer money between accounts.** For example, you can transfer money from your savings to your checking account to make sure that checks don't bounce. If you have a mortgage or loan from the same bank where you keep your checking account, you can transfer money from your checking account to your mortgage or loan account and, in so doing, make your monthly mortgage or loan payment.

✦ **Take care of routine banking chores.** You would normally have to call your bank to get these chores done. For example, you can order more checks, stop a check payment, or update your address and phone number.

Some banks go the extra mile and offer these online services as well:

✦ **Pay bills online.** Later in this chapter, "Paying Your Bills Online" looks into this topic. The amount of each bill is deducted from your savings or checking account as you pay it.

✦ **Schedule future money transfers between accounts.** Rather than give the order to transfer money each month, you can schedule transactions so that the transfers occur automatically. For example, to put a portion of your monthly paycheck into a savings account each month, you can schedule this money transfer to occur automatically.

✦ **View scanned images of checks you've written, deposit slips, and bill statements.** Online bank statements don't list the names of people to whom you wrote checks, but by clicking a View Check link, you can see a scanned image of your check, as shown in Figure 3-3. You can see to whom you wrote the check and compare your records to the bank's to make sure that your records are accurate.

Figure 3-3:
A scanned
image of a
check.

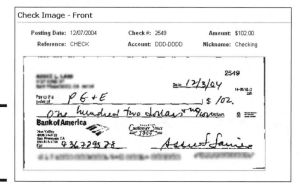

✦ **Download transaction information into Microsoft Money or Quicken.** As "Online Banking and Bill Paying with Money and Quicken" explains later in this chapter, you can download transactions into your Microsoft Money or Quicken software as well as pay bills with these programs.

✦ **Be alerted by e-mail when something untoward occurs.** For example, you can be alerted when your account balance rises above or drops below a certain level, when a check clears, or when a check bounces.

When you sign up for online banking, your bank will ask which accounts you want to make online accounts. You are asked to select a user ID. And you are given a temporary password that you change to a password of your own the first time you bank online.

Is online banking safe?

Occasionally you read in the newspaper about an evil, twisted computer genius who crashes into others' computers and steals bank account numbers and so on. And stories like that make you wonder whether banking online is safe.

Online banking *is* safe from the bank's side. The chances of anyone breaking into a bank's computers and stealing from bank accounts is nil because of encryption technology. This technology encodes — maybe the better word is *scrambles* — data so that only computers with the encryption key can decode it. No hacker, however bold or intelligent he or she is, can get an encryption key.

All the danger of an online bank account being robbed lies on the customer's side. Conceivably, a spyware program could (so to speak) look over a customer's shoulder, note which keys are being pressed on the keyboard, and in so doing, acquire the user ID and password to an online bank account. Book I, Chapter 4 looks at spyware.

A more likely way for a criminal to obtain a user ID and password, however, is by means of a fraudulent e-mail solicitation like the one shown here. This e-mail message looks like it comes from a bank. It looks authentic. Clicking the link in the message takes you to an authentic-looking Web site that asks for your user ID, password, and Social Security number.

Never reply to e-mail messages like this. Banks do not solicit personal information this way. Fraudulently obtaining personal information by e-mail or at a phony Web site is called *phishing*. Phishing, like spyware, is explained in Book I, Chapter 4.

Paying Your Bills Online

It's hard to go back to fumbling with paper checks, not to mention sealing envelopes and licking stamps, after you've paid bills online. Paying bills online is mighty convenient. Bills get paid faster when they are paid over the Internet. In most cases, the bill-payment service pays your bill right away by deducting the amount of the bill from your bank account and transferring the money over the Internet to the biller. If the service can't pay the biller directly, a computer-generated paper check is sent through the mail on your behalf.

Check with your bank to see whether it offers online bill paying for free. Some banks offer it for free as part of their online banking services. If your bank doesn't offer online bill paying, check out Table 3-1, which lists online bill-payment services and indicates how much they charge. The majority of services charge a flat monthly rate for paying a certain number of bills. If you exceed that number, you are charged for each additional bill you pay during the month. Usually the charge is 50 cents for each additional bill. If you do the math, you can see that paying bills online, even if you have to pay a fee, costs about the same as mailing checks, when you take into account postage costs.

Table 3-1	Online Bill-Payment Services	
Service	*Monthly Cost/ No. Payments*	*Web Address*
AOL Bill Pay	Free*	www.aol.com/product/ billpay.adp
Bills	$6.95 for 20	www.bills.com
CheckFree	Free**	www.checkfree.com
MSN Bill Pay	$5.95 for 15	https://billpay.msn.com
Paytrust	$4.95 + $0.50 per payment	www.paytrust.com
Quicken Bill Pay	$9.95 unlimited	www.quicken.com
Status Factory	$11.30 for 15	www.statusfactory.com
Yahoo! Bill Pay	$4.95 for 12	http://finance.yahoo. com/bp

AOL Bill Pay is free to America Online subscribers.

** *Individual banks offer CheckFree for free or for a small monthly fee.*

You are asked for the following information when you sign up with an online bill-payment service. The service needs this information to identify you and to successfully withdraw money from your bank account to pay your bills.

- ✦ **Social Security number:** You know what that is, I hope.

- ✦ **PIN:** The personal identification number with which you sign in to your bank.

- ✦ **Account name:** The name of the account from which payments are to be made.

- ✦ **Routing number:** The *routing number* is comprised of the first nine numbers in the lower-left corner of checks. On either side of the routing number is a colon (:).

As part of paying a bill through a service, you provide your account number or other identifying number. To pay a utility bill, for example, you provide your account number with the utility company. You can find these account numbers on your bills. If the biller hasn't assigned you an account number, you may have to provide a telephone number or other identifying number that is yours and yours alone when you pay the bill.

Online bill-payment services that are worth anything offer these amenities:

- ✦ **Confirmation when bills have been paid:** You are notified online by the biller when a payment has been received.

- ✦ **Records of past payments:** You can dig into your past history with a biller to see how much you've paid over the past months or years and when payments were made. Being able to review past payments is a great way to examine your spending habits.

Some services offer the opportunity to schedule bill payments and be billed by e-mail. Schedule a bill payment if the payment is one you make every month for a fixed amount. A rent payment, for example, is a good candidate for scheduling. Electronic bills can be sent to your bill-payment service instead of your home. Paying these "e-bills" is especially easy, because you don't even have to open an envelope, much less write or mail a check. The problem with e-bills, however, is that most don't contain details about what you are being charged for. A typical phone bill, for example, includes charges for long-distance calling, local calling, and various taxes. Sometimes it pays to look over the details in a bill to find out how you are being charged, but you can't do that very well in an e-bill. Figure 3-4 shows some e-bills.

Occasionally billers change their customers' account numbers or the biller's payment address without informing their customers. Online bill payments can't be completed if this information is submitted incorrectly. If you pay bills online, be alert to changes in your account numbers and payment addresses.

Payee	Amount	Send On	Deliver By	Confirmation Number	
American Express American Express -7530	$ 100.00	02/12/2004	02/14/2004	28C89-VC33L	Edit • Cancel
Bank of America Credit Card Personal BofA Credit Card -4193	$ 50.00	02/12/2004	02/13/2004	28C89-VFCM5	Edit • Cancel
MACY'S MACY'S Credit Card -1-632	$ 40.00	02/12/2004	02/17/2004	28C89-VFUH0	Edit • Cancel
SBC Phone Bill SBC e-bill -7432	$ 85.00	02/12/2004	02/13/2004	28C89-VGDC0	Edit • Cancel

This payment was applied to the e-Bill due on 2/13/2004. The e-Bill status has been changed to Paid and the e-Bill has been moved to Paid and Filed e-Bills.

Figure 3-4:
Paying
some e-bills.

Online Banking and Bill Paying with Microsoft Money and Quicken

The other way to bank and pay bills online is to enlist the help of Microsoft Money or Quicken. These programs include commands for banking online and paying bills online. Money and Quicken are equipped to connect to 800 different banks so that you can download transactions right into your account registers, the ledgers where you track your income and expenses. You can compare your online bank statement with the transactions you entered in Money or Quicken to make sure that your records are in sync with the bank's. Users of Money can pay bills online through MSN Bill Pay, Microsoft's online bill-payment service. Users of Quicken can pay bills with Quicken Bill Pay.

Figure 3-5 shows a Money account register with transactions downloaded from a bank. In the figure, downloaded transactions are being compared to previously entered transactions to find discrepancies. Balancing a bank account this way in Money or Quicken is considerably easier than balancing a bank account by hand. To learn more about Money or Quicken, check out *Microsoft Money 2005 For Dummies,* by Peter Weverka (that's me!), or *Quicken 2005 For Dummies,* by Stephen Nelson (both published by Wiley).

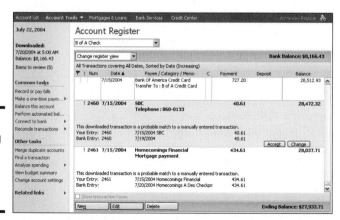

Figure 3-5:
Reconciling
a bank
account
online in
Money.

Searching for a Credit Card Online

If you are like me, you get six or seven offers every week from credit card companies asking you to please, please use their credit card. Sometimes telemarketers call asking me to use their credit card, not the other guy's. Sometimes they call me during dinner. Why not turn the tables on the credit card companies? Instead of them asking you to use a credit card, why not ask them? Go online, find a credit card that suits you — a card that offers frequent-flier miles or gifts or a low interest rate — and start using it.

Here are some Web sites where you can compare different credit cards and find the one that meets your needs:

✦ **123Debt:** A Web site devoted to helping you lower or consolidate your credit card debt. Address: www.123debt.com

✦ **Card Ratings:** Rates the different credit cards and credit card reward plans. Address: www.cardratings.com

✦ **Credit Card Goodies:** Looks into rebate cards, airline miles cards, and gas cards. Says the Webmaster, "Too few reports address the segment that I belong to — people who pay off their balances every month. Hence, I threw together this page dedicated to finding the best possible deals for people like me." Address: www.creditcardgoodies.com

✦ **Choosing a Credit Card:** Advice for shopping for credit cards from the Federal Reserve Board, the organization that oversees credit card companies. Address: www.federalreserve.gov/pubs/shop/default.htm

Book VI

Bargain Shopping

The 5th Wave   By Rich Tennant

"So, someone's using your credit card info to buy stylish clothes, opera tickets and exercise equipment. In what way would this qualify as `identity theft'?"

Contents at a Glance

Chapter 1: Searching for Bargains

In This Chapter

✔ Buying by the rules

✔ Searching with shopping search engines

✔ Doing product comparisons on the Internet

✔ Finding and reading online catalogs

✔ Visiting stores for bargain hunters

✔ Finding product reviews and consumer reports

The Internet, among other things, has become a giant shopping mall. Not that shopping malls will go the way of the dinosaur, but many people prefer shopping online to shopping at the mall. Who wants to deal with crowded parking lots and long lines? Some predict that basic goods such as groceries and drugstore items will be purchased online and that streets and highways everywhere will soon be filled with trucks delivering these online bargains.

This chapter is dedicated to the idea that, if you want it, you can buy it online. It explains the pitfalls of buying online and describes how to search the Internet for items you want. You discover shopping search engines — special search engines designed for finding things to buy. You also look at tools for comparison shopping. With these tools, you can compare prices for the same items being sold on different Web sites and buy items at the lowest price. This chapter looks at reading catalogs online, shows you the way to some online stores for bargain hunters, and steers you to Web sites where you can read product reviews and consumer reports.

Some Rules for Buying Items Online

Somewhere, somebody is trying to figure out a way to make odors travel over the Internet. Somebody else is working on technology that permits you to reach into your computer monitor and touch an item that you want to buy. Until these mad scientists complete their work — and they aren't likely to complete it soon — buying items online holds the same risks as buying items from a catalog. You can't smell, taste, or touch the item. Practically speaking, you can't tell what you've purchased until it arrives on your doorstep.

Items such as perfume, clothing, and jewelry are hard to judge online. Maybe the most important rule for shopping online also happens to be the most important rule for shopping: Let the buyer beware. Other than that, here are some rules for buying items online. Disregard these rules, and you do so at your peril:

✦ **Know what the shipping and handling charges are.** Some companies that sell items at a discount make up the lost revenue by charging exorbitant fees for shipping and handling.

✦ **Don't do business with a company that doesn't have a refund and return policy.** The terms of the policy should be stated somewhere on the Web site. What happens if you are unhappy with an item you purchased? Can you return it? How soon must you return it? Who pays for returning the item if returning it is an expensive proposition?

✦ **Take note of what the seller offers in the way of customer service.** Will the seller pay for repairs if any are needed? For high-tech products, does the seller offer technical and setup assistance?

✦ **Ask yourself how difficult the item is to assemble, if it needs assembling.** Not everyone can interpret the complicated directions that come with items you have to put together yourself. Not everyone can wield a screwdriver. Because online purchases are delivered by mail, they need assembling more often than other purchases. If you're not good at assembling things, make sure that the items you buy are already assembled.

✦ **Keep a well-documented paper trail of your dealings with the seller.** After you have filled out the order form, print it. When the seller sends you a confirmation notice by e-mail, print that, too. Keeping a paper trail is a hassle, but if you lose your customer order number or aren't sure when the package arrives whether everything you ordered is inside it, you will be glad you kept the papers. For that matter, print the Web page that describes the item. That way, you can be sure that you purchased what you thought you were purchasing.

✦ **Know the company's privacy policy.** Does the company intend to sell your name to spammers? Can you request that your name and personal information be kept private? As a matter of principle, I don't do business online with any company that doesn't post its privacy policy on its Web site.

✦ **Inspect your purchase as soon as it arrives.** Is this what you ordered? Some online retailers, especially during the holiday season, are so hurried that they fill orders incorrectly.

✦ **Trust your instincts!** If you are uncomfortable purchasing an item over the Internet, don't do it. If "supplies are running out," you are being pressured to buy an item, or you feel uneasy about it, don't buy. Make a cup of tea or putter in the garden instead.

How safe is online shopping?

Naturally, people have concerns about shopping online. Sending a credit card number across the Internet can be disconcerting. Is the number going to end up on a computer somewhere for anyone to see and steal?

You don't need to worry. Buying items with a credit card *is* safe. Online merchants have gone to great lengths to make sure that credit card information is kept private:

✔ Sensitive information is scrambled and encrypted on merchants' Web servers so that outsiders can't read it.

✔ Encryption technology is used to establish the identity of the buyer so that no one can pose as someone else.

If you're not sure whether a company has secured its site, just look on the right side of the status bar in your Web browser. Secure sites show a lock icon, while unsecure sites do not.

What's more, as an online buyer, the same federal laws that protect mail orders and telephone orders also protect you. You have the right to return an item if it is broken or not what you thought you ordered.

The American Bar Association maintains a Web site called Safe Shopping (www.safeshopping.org) that explains, from a legal point of view, everything you need to know about online shopping, including your rights as an online customer.

Shopping Search Engines

A shopping search engine works like a standard search engine, except it is trained to look for items that are for sale online (Book II, Chapter 3 explains how search engines work). Like other search engines, shopping search engines send automated spiders onto the Internet to index and describe Web pages, but shopping search engines focus on merchandise. Use a shopping search engine to find an item for sale online, and then check out the comparison-shopping Web sites in the next section of this chapter to compare prices for the item.

Table 1-1 describes shopping search engines. Some of these search engines can compare prices for the same item at different Web sites. If the search engine offers one, click the Advanced Search link and describe your search as pointedly as you can. Broad searches yield far too many results. Figure 1-1 shows the Advanced Search page at Froogle, Google's shopping search engine. Notice all the options for narrowing the search.

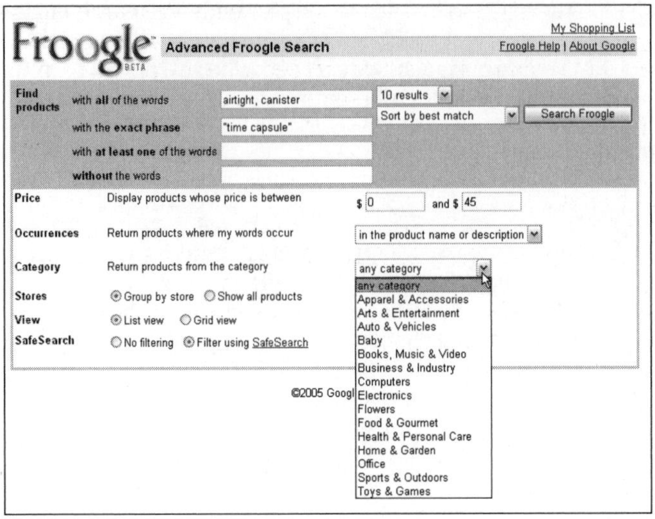

Figure 1-1:
Froogle is Google's shopping search engine.

Table 1-1		Shopping Search Engines	
Search Engine	*Web Address*	*Description*	*Advanced Search?*
Bizrate	www.bizrate.com	Choose an option from the Departments drop-down menu to narrow your search.	
Froogle	www.google.com/froogle	On the Advanced Search page, choose an option from the Category drop-down menu to narrow your search to a category. To comparison-shop, select the Grid View option to be able to see several items at once. "Froogle" is a play on the word *frugal*. (Click the Froogle link on the Google home page at www.google.com.)	✔
My Simon	www.mysimon.com	Click the Compare All Prices link in search results to compare prices from different vendors in a chart.	
Yahoo! Shopping	http://shopping.yahoo.com	On the Advanced search page, you can search by price range and use Boolean search techniques. (From the Yahoo! home page at www.yahoo.com, click the Shopping link.)	✔

Surprise.com (www.surprise.com) is an unusual search engine designed to help you find the perfect gift for someone you know or love. Click the Get Started button and take a survey to describe the person. On the basis of your answers, the Web site presents you with gifts in different categories. Select a category to see gift suggestions. Click the name of a gift and you go to a Web site where you can buy it.

Looking at Some Price-Comparison Web Sites

Comparison-shopping Web sites give you the opportunity to search the Internet for an item and compare its selling price at different online vendors. Table 1-2 lists price-comparison Web sites. Of course, the Internet being what it is, you can also buy items from one of these Web sites. Some of them also do double duty as shopping search engines. And some also offer product reviews and reviews of online stores. Figure 1-2 shows what a product comparison table looks like. You can see at a glance which store offers the lowest price.

**Book VI
Chapter 1**

Searching for Bargains

Table 1-2	Comparison Shopping Web Sites	
Web Site	*Web Address*	*Description*
Aim Lower	www.aimlower.com	Focuses on computers and electronics.
Best Web Buys	www.bestwebbuys.com	Compare prices for books, music, videos, electronic equipment, and bicycles.
Buy Path	www.buypath.com	Read product reviews as well as compare prices.
Froogle	www.google.com/froogle	Click the Advanced Froogle Search link and, on the Advanced Search page, click the Grid View option to use this search engine for comparison-shopping purposes.
Next Tag	www.nextag.com	Price comparisons factor in sales tax and shipping. Includes seller reviews.
Price Grabber	www.pricegrabber.com	Considered the best comparison shopper; enter your zip code to include the sales tax in an item's price.
Shopping	http://shopping.com	As well as shop, you can read product reviews from e-pinions.
Shopping Aisles	www.shoppingaisles.com	Specializes in books, magazines, videos, and video games.
Street Prices	www.streetprices.com	Specializes in electronics.

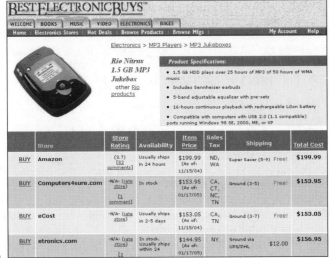

Figure 1-2:
Comparison-
shopping at
Best Web
Buys.

For die-hard online shoppers, the Shelron Group makes a toolbar called ActivShopper that fits into the Internet Explorer window. When you come to a product description page at an online store, the toolbar automatically searches the Internet for other Web sites where the product is sold. ActivShopper generates a comparison table so that you can compare prices. To download ActivShopper, go to this Web site: www.activshopper.com.

Reading Online Catalogs

If you're the kind of person who likes getting product catalogs in the mail, you'll be glad to know that now you can search for Web-page replicas of catalogs and read them online. Catalogs appear in the Google Catalog viewer, shown in Figure 1-3. Click a catalog page to enlarge and read it on-screen. You can also find commands for zooming in and out of pages and displaying pages in different ways. These are the same catalogs you get in the mail. Companies submit their catalogs to Google so that you can find them online.

To search for a catalog, open the Google Catalogs Search page and enter keywords for your search. You can click the Advanced Catalog Search link to search more thoroughly for a catalog. To get to the Google Catalogs Search page, do one of the following:

✦ Go to the Google home page (www.google.com), click the More link, and on the More page, click the Catalogs link.

✦ Open your Web browser to this address: http://catalogs.google.com.

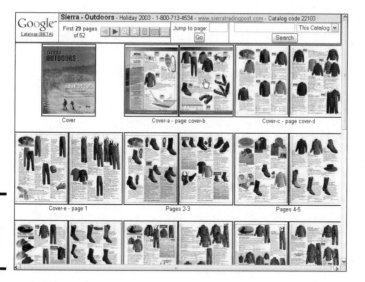

**Book VI
Chapter 1**

Searching for Bargains

Figure 1-3:
The online
replica of a
catalog.

Hunting for Bargains at Online Stores

Chapter 4 of this mini-book describes numerous online stores in different shopping categories. These stores sell all manner of things, and they sell them at bargain-basement prices. You never know what you'll find in these stores. The stores that follow are worth rummaging through when you're in the rummaging mood:

✦ **Deal Catcher:** This Web site is for coupon clippers, but instead of clipping coupons out of the newspaper, you can get them at this Web site, print them, and use them when you're shopping at a genuine brick-and-mortar store. Address: www.dealcatcher.com

✦ **Good Bazaar:** Use this Web site to take advantage of online sales and free shipping at different stores. Good Bazaar steers you to Web sites that are currently having sales. Address: www.goodbazaar.com

✦ **Half.com:** This Web site sells new and used books, music, movies, electronics, sporting goods, computer stuff, and video games for, at most, half of their original price. Goods are often sold at a quarter of their original price. Address: http://half.ebay.com

✦ **Overstock:** Excess inventory has to be moved out of the warehouse to make room for items that are selling. How to move this excess inventory? One way is to sell it at Overstock.com. You can find many bargains here as long as you aren't in a hurry. Address: www.overstock.com

✦ **Smart Bargains:** Clothing, bedding, jewelry, and electronics are offered at this Web site. When fewer than ten pieces of an item are left, the Web site tells you as much. Address: www.smartbargains.com

On the subject of bargains, take a look at Ugly Dress (www.uglydress.com), "the archive of the world's ugliest bridesmaid dresses," and ask yourself how many of these dresses were purchased for a bargain. You can also find a frightening collection of ugly shoes. Woot (www.woot.com) is an unusual Web site. It only sells one item at a time and offers a new item each day. And the item, whatever it is, is sold at a very low price.

Product Reviews and Consumer Reports

Before you buy that digital camera or that watch, find out what people who already bought it think about it. You can do that very easily on the Internet at one of the Web sites listed in Table 1-3. Most of these Web sites have a rating system similar to the five-star system BizRate uses, as shown in Figure 1-4. You can register at most of these Web sites and write product reviews. You, too, can be a critic-at-large.

Table 1-3	Product Review and Consumer Report Web Sites	
Web Site	*Web Address*	*Notes*
Amazon	www.amazon.com	The place to go to read book reviews (click the Books tab).
Audio Review	www.audioreview.com	Click the Reviews link to read what audiophiles think of their audio equipment and TVs.
BizRate	www.bizrate.com	As the name implies, you can read reviews of online businesses as well as the products they sell.
Cnet	www.cnet.com	The place to go for software reviews and reviews of computer equipment.
Consumer Reports	www.consumerreports.org	The online version of the highly regarded magazine, this Web site tests products in all areas.
Consumer Review	www.consumerreview.com	Read reviews of golf equipment and sporting goods, as well as consumer electronics.
Consumer Search	www.consumersearch.com	A comprehensive product review Web site; also ranks the best products in 100 different categories.

Web Site	Web Address	Notes
Epinions	www.epinions.com	Not as many reviews as other sites, but very friendly and easy to navigate.
Planet Feedback	www.planetfeedback.com/consumer	Starting at this Web page, you can write to a company to complain about its products or services.
Rate It All	www.rateitall.com	You can even rate politicians at this Web site!

Figure 1-4: Product ratings at BizRate.

Chapter 2: Buying at an Online Auction

In This Chapter

✔ Surveying online auction houses

✔ Looking at auction house search engines

✔ Registering and signing in to eBay

✔ Searching for stuff to bid on at eBay

✔ Designating favorite searches, categories, and sellers at eBay

✔ Keeping a watch list of items you are interested in

✔ Getting a winning bid at eBay

✔ Closing an auction transaction at eBay

Depending on your point of view, eBay is either the world's greatest auction bazaar or the world's greatest rummage sale. At any given time, about a half-million items are being auctioned on eBay. A recent *60 Minutes* story about the online auction house revealed that over 150,000 people earn an income selling items on eBay.

I'm not the kind of person who enjoys shopping, but I visit eBay three or four times a week because I enjoy looking at and occasionally purchasing folk art items. I have purchased about 20 folk art items on eBay in the past three years. Along the way, I became something of an expert on paño arte handkerchief drawings by prisoners in the American southwest, hand-knit sweaters made by the Salish Indians of British Columbia, sandpaper paintings from the 19th century, and West African barbershop art. I owe these peculiar fascinations to eBay. It's been a lot of fun.

The problem with eBay is that so many items are up for auction that finding what you're interested in can be difficult. Unless you know how to look for items that interest you or where to find these items, you can soon get lost.

This chapter starts with a look at several online auction houses and delivers some bad news about auction search engines (only one really works). Then the chapter explains how to search eBay and how to maintain a "My eBay" page, where you can save searches and the names of sellers you like. You also get strategies for bidding and discover the mechanics of eBay — how to place bids, research sellers, and close a sale.

Looking at the Online Auction Houses

eBay isn't the world's only online auction house, although it is the best by far. If buying by auction is your cup of tea, I suggest sticking with eBay but occasionally using the auction search engines to find items you hanker for at other auction houses (the next section in this chapter looks at auction search engines). Table 2-1 describes online auction houses, including eBay. To bid at these houses, you must register. Sellers decide the method of payment.

Table 2-1	Online Auction Houses	
Name	*Web Address*	*Notes*
Amazon	www.auctions.amazon.com	Amazon, the be-all-everything company, also offers online auctions. As you may expect, Books is the largest category.
Bidz	www.bidz.com	This auction house specializes in jewelry. Click the 3 Minute Auction link to eyeball auctions ending in three minutes or less.
eBay	www.ebay.com	eBay is the largest online auction house. Most of this chapter describes bidding and buying at eBay.
QXL	www.qxl.com	This online auction house is based in the United Kingdom.
Shop Goodwill	www.shopgoodwill.com	Browse items in 20 categories. All profits go to Goodwill Industries, a charity that helps the poor.
uBid Auctions	www.ubid.com	This house specializes in computer equipment and electronics.
Yahoo! Auctions	http://auctions.yahoo.com	Yahoo!'s is the second-largest auction house after eBay.

On the subject of auctions, check out Disturbing Auctions at this address: www.disturbingauctions.com. The Web site describes disturbing items that were auctioned on the Internet. The Terrifying Dolls category alone is worth a look.

Using Auction Search Engines

Auction search engines look at what's being offered at different online houses and report what they find so that you can compare prices or locate a hard-to-find item. Unfortunately, these search engines don't do their jobs very well. They are slow and, in my experiments, they didn't uncover items that I knew to be there. Only one auction search engine, Auction Beagle, passed the test in my experiments. You can find Auction Beagle at this Web address: www.auctionbeagle.com. It searches auctions being held at Amazon, eBay, and Yahoo!.

Use few keywords carefully and be very specific in your online auction searches. If you don't heed my advice, you will have to examine many items in the search results.

Book VI
Chapter 2

Registering with eBay

To bid on items at eBay, you must register. Registering costs nothing. Besides being able to bid, registered members get to keep a My eBay page for tracking items they are watching or bidding on. Registering also entitles you to a Favorites page, where you can save searches, save category names so that you can go to categories quickly, and save the names of eBay sellers whose goods you like.

To register, go to this address: www.ebay.com. Then click the Register link and fill in the form. You are asked the usual stuff — your name, address, and so on. Remember your password, because you must enter it whenever you sign in. Don't use your e-mail address for a User ID. Doing so makes you susceptible to all kinds of junk mail. If you need to change names, passwords, or other personal information, click the eBay Preferences link on the My eBay page (the next section in this chapter explains how to open this page).

Occasionally, eBay members get e-mail solicitations that look as though they are from eBay; the solicitations ask for personal information such as addresses and credit card numbers. These solicitations are fraudulent. Registering is the only time that eBay asks for personal information. If you get an e-mail that supposedly comes from eBay and asks you to update your personal information, go to the eBay Security Center at http://pages.ebay.com/securitycenter and report this false solicitation. You can also forward the e-mail to spoof@ebay.com. All messages that eBay sends to you land in the My Messages section of your My eBay page.

Signing in to Your My eBay Page

My eBay

To sign into eBay, go to www.ebay.com, click the My eBay link, enter your User ID and password, and click the Secure Sign In button. You land in your My eBay page, as shown in Figure 2-1. Every registered member gets one of these pages. Starting here, you can do just about anything a body can do in eBay. To return to your My eBay page at any time, click the My eBay link at the top of the screen.

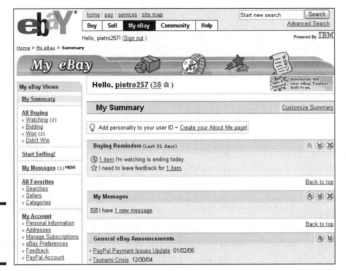

Figure 2-1:
The My
eBay page.

The left side of the My eBay page offers these links that you can click to track your activity in eBay:

✦ **All Buying:** A master list with items you're watching, items you're bidding on, items you've won, and items you didn't win because you were outbid.

✦ **Watching:** Items you've placed on your Watching list because you want to bid on them or you are curious how much they fetch (see "Keeping a Watching List," later in this chapter). Watching an item means to bookmark it so that you can click its name on the Watching list and revisit its Web page.

✦ **Bidding:** A list of items you have placed a bid on. For each item on this tab, eBay tells you its current price, how many bids have been made on it, and how much time is left before the auction closes (if it hasn't already closed).

✦ **Won:** A list of items you've won. Use this list to track whether you've received items.

✦ **Didn't Win:** A list of items you didn't win.

✦ **Selling:** A list of items you are selling or have sold (this one doesn't appear if you aren't selling items on eBay).

✦ **My Messages:** A list of messages you've received from from eBay. eBay does not send its members messages by e-mail.

✦ **All Favorites:** A master list with your favorite searches, sellers, and categories. (See "Saving searches, categories, and sellers," later in this chapter.)

✦ **Searches:** A list of saved searches. After you have carefully constructed a search (say, for Elvis 45s), you can save the search and instantly conduct it again by clicking its name on this list.

✦ **Sellers:** A list of eBay sellers whose merchandise consistently interests you. Click a seller's name on the list to see all of his or her online auctions.

✦ **Categories:** A list of your favorite categories. By clicking a category name, you can search a category instantly.

✦ **My Accounts:** A master list with your PayPal account information and feedback ratings from sellers.

✦ **Personal Information:** The personal information you gave eBay when you signed up. You can change the information here.

✦ **Addresses:** Your shipping address and address under which you are registered. You can change the information here.

✦ **Manage Subscriptions:** A list of services for eBay sellers.

✦ **eBay Preferences:** Options for changing how you sign in and how eBay pages are displayed.

✦ **Feedback:** Starting here, you can rate people who have sold you items and see how sellers have rated you. eBay maintains buyer and seller ratings so that buyers can buy with confidence and sellers can sell with confidence.

✦ **PayPal:** If you use PayPal (see Chapter 3 of this minibook), you can view account transactions here.

Searching for Items of Interest

What are you interested in? Stereo equipment? Antique cowboy clothes? Bank vaults? The question is Where on eBay is your item of interest located? Unless the item you want to find has a very specific name — say, a Canon

S50 Powershot S-50 — you may have trouble finding it. You can't simply enter **camera** in the Search box, because you end up wading through thousands of auctions before finding the camera you want. As an experiment, I just entered **camera** in the search box and got 45,314 auctions pertaining to cameras! You would need a lot of stamina and time to look into that many auctions.

To help you find your diamond in the rough, the following pages explain how to search eBay. All searches begin on the My eBay page (refer to Figure 2-1).

A straight search

As I just explained, a straight search is useful if the item you are looking for has a very specific name. For example, I entered **Canon S50 Powershot S-50** in the Search text box, and I found 67 auctions rather than the 45,314 I got when I entered **camera**.

eBay offers two ways to conduct a straight search:

✦ **Simple search:** Enter the term in the Start New Search text box on any eBay page and click the Search button.

✦ **Basic or Advanced search:** Click the Advanced Search link on any eBay page. You see a Search form. From here, you can fill in a form and conduct a Basic Search or an Advanced Search (by clicking the Advanced Search link). These forms offer many criteria for narrowing a search and finding what you want. Figure 2-2 shows the Advanced Search form.

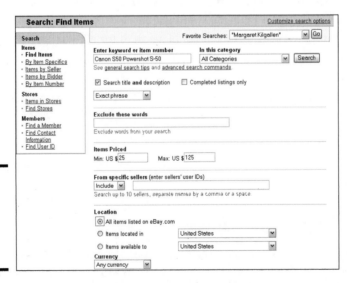

Figure 2-2:
An advanced search of eBay auctions.

To get more search results, select the Search Title and Description check box. This tells eBay to look for your search terms in item descriptions as well as titles.

The Advanced search page offers a Favorite Searches drop-down menu. The menu has searches you deemed as favorites (see "Saving searches, categories, and sellers," later in this chapter). You can choose an option from the menu and quickly run a search.

Browsing eBay categories

eBay auctions are classified by category, subcategory, sub-subcategory, and so on. In the browsing search method, you locate a category or subcategory that describes items you are interested in, you get a list of items in the category or subcategory, and you then click items one at a time to look them over. The browsing technique requires a fair amount of free time. For every gem you discover, you have to look at about 300 pieces of dross. Oh well, browsing can be fun. Follow these steps to browse different eBay categories:

Buy

1. **On your My eBay page, click the Buy link.**

   You see the Browse Categories list shown in Figure 2-3.

2. **Scroll down to see the complete category and subcategory list.**

3. **Click a category or subcategory and start browsing different items.**

**Book VI
Chapter 2**

Buying at an Online Auction

Browse Categories

Antiques Furniture | Rugs, Carpets | Silver...	**Gift Certificates**
Art Paintings | Prints | Posters...	**Health & Beauty** Bath & Body | Skin Care | Fragrances...
Books Antiquarian & Collectible | Children's Books | Education & Textbooks...	**Home & Garden** Baby | Dining & Bar | Home Decor...
Business & Industrial Construction | Manufacturing & Metalworking | Office, Printing & Shipping...	**Jewelry & Watches** Bracelets | Earrings | Necklaces & Pendants...
	Music Cassettes | CDs | Records...
Cameras & Photo Camcorders | Digital Camera Accessories | Digital Cameras...	**Musical Instruments** Guitar | Keyboards, Piano | Percussion...
Cars, Parts & Vehicles Motorcycles | Parts & Accessories | Passenger Vehicles...	**Pottery & Glass** Glass | Pottery & China...
Clothing, Shoes & Accessories Boys | Girls | Men's | Women's...	**Real Estate** Commercial | Land | Residential...
Coins Bullion | Coins: US | Coins: World...	**Sporting Goods** Cycling | Exercise & Fitness | Fan Shop...
Collectibles Advertising | Casino | Comics...	**Sports Mem, Cards & Fan Shop** Autographs | Baseball | Basketball...
Computers & Networking Desktop PCs | Laptops | Monitors...	**Stamps** Asia | Europe | United States...
Consumer Electronics Car Electronics | Cell Phones | Home Audio...	**Tickets** Event Tickets | Experiences...
	Toys & Hobbies Action Figures | Diecast, Toy Vehicles | Games...
	See all categories...

Figure 2-3: Browsing by category and subcategory.

Want to see detailed category lists with the names of many sub-subcategories? Click the See All Categories link at the bottom of the Browse Categories window (refer to Figure 2-3). From here, you can select a category and get a detailed list with many subcategories. Finding a subcategory like this is a great way to pinpoint what you are interested in.

Browsing to and searching a single category

A browse/search permits you to search exclusively in a single eBay category or subcategory. Under this searching method, you browse to the category you are interested in and then you conduct a search exclusively in that category. In my experience, this is the most efficient way to search eBay.

In Figure 2-4, for example, I browsed to the Westerns sub-subcategory (using techniques I describe in the previous section of this chapter). In the Basic Search form at the top of the page, I entered **Randolph Scott** to search for western movies starring that golden-haired box office idol of yesteryear. Only 37 items showed up in the search.

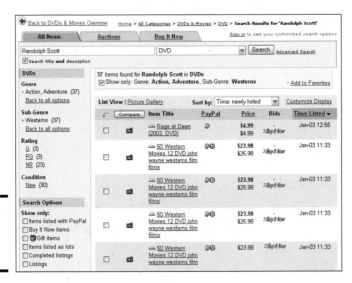

Figure 2-4: Searching one category.

Saving searches, categories, and sellers

After you hang around eBay a while, you find yourself (depending on your interests) revisiting the same categories, conducting the same searches, and looking at wares offered by the same handful of sellers. Rather than construct the same searches or browse the same categories repeatedly, you can put these searches and categories on the All Favorites portion of your My eBay page. Then, to conduct a search or visit a category, you just click its name on a Favorites page.

Putting the name of a seller or eBay store on the All Favorites list is a great way to see a seller's items. I have identified four sellers on eBay who consistently offer items I am interested in. I can see these items merely by clicking the Sellers link on the My eBay page and then clicking a seller's name.

Follow the instructions in the next three sections of this chapter to be able to quickly conduct searches for your favorite items, visit your favorite categories, conduct searches, or see what is being offered by your favorite sellers.

Book VI
Chapter 2

Buying at an Online
Auction

Favorite searches

On your My eBay page, click the Searches link and, on the My Favorite Searches page, click the Add New Search link. You see a Basic Search form. Describe the search and click the Search button. If the search results are to your liking, click the Add to Favorites link. Now you can run the search starting from your My Favorite Searches page.

Favorite categories

On your My eBay page, click the Categories link and, on the My Favorite Categories page, click the Add New Category link. Then click the names of categories and subcategories till you come to a category you like to visit often. Click the Submit button at the bottom of the page.

Favorite sellers

On every auction page is a link called View Seller's Other Items. By clicking this link, you can see a list of other items that the seller is offering. When you find a seller who consistently offers items you find interesting, jot down his or her name or store name. Then follow these steps to add the seller's name to your My Favorite Sellers page:

1. **On your My eBay page, click the Sellers link to go to the My Favorite Sellers page.**

2. **Click the Add New Seller or Store link.**

3. **Enter the seller's name or store name in the Seller's User ID or Store Name text box and click the Continue button.**

4. **Select the check box if you want to be notified by e-mail when the seller is offering a new item.**

5. **Click the Add to Favorites button.**

Managing your All Favorites list

To change around your All Favorites list, follow these instructions:

✦ **Rearranging the lists:** To change the order of lists on the All Favorites page, click a list's Move This View Up or Move This View Down button.

✦ **Removing a search, seller, or category:** Select the check box next to the search, seller, or category name and click the Delete button.

✦ **Refining a search:** Click the button next to "Edit Preferences" and choose Refine Search on the pop-up menu, as shown in Figure 2-5. The Search page opens. Choose new search options and click the Search button to run the search. If the search is satisfactory, click the Add to Favorites link.

✦ **Changing a search/seller name or requesting e-mails:** Click the Edit Preferences link. On the Edit Favorites page, change the name and change how you want to be alerted by e-mail.

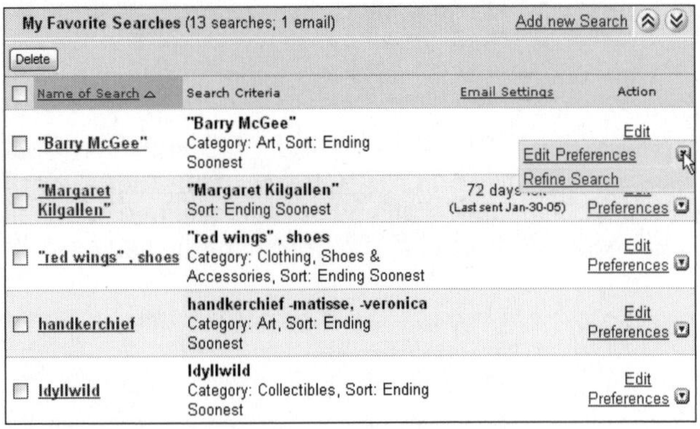

Figure 2-5:
Use the buttons on the right side of the screen to manage the All Favorites list.

My Favorite Searches (13 searches; 1 email)		Add new Search	
Delete			
☐ Name of Search △	Search Criteria	Email Settings	Action
☐ "Barry McGee"	**"Barry McGee"** Category: Art, Sort: Ending Soonest		Edit Edit Preferences Refine Search
☐ "Margaret Kilgallen"	**"Margaret Kilgallen"** Sort: Ending Soonest	72 days ... (Last sent Jan-30-05)	Preferences
☐ "red wings" , shoes	**"red wings" , shoes** Category: Clothing, Shoes & Accessories, Sort: Ending Soonest		Edit Preferences
☐ handkerchief	**handkerchief -matisse, -veronica** Category: Art, Sort: Ending Soonest		Edit Preferences
☐ Idyllwild	**Idyllwild** Category: Collectibles, Sort: Ending Soonest		Edit Preferences

Keeping a Watching List

When you come upon an item in eBay that piques your interest, either because you want to bid on it later or you're curious how much it will sell for, click the Watch This Item link. You can find this link in the upper-right corner of an item's eBay page. Clicking the link places the item on theWatching list. Figure 2-6 shows an Watching list. You can bid on items from this list, see how much items are selling for, and see how much time is left to bid on items.

To get to your Watching list, click the Watching link on your My eBay page.

Book VI
Chapter 2

Buying at an Online
Auction

Figure 2-6:
An Items I'm
Watching
list.

Knowing the Rules of the Road

Observe these rules as you bid on eBay items:

✦ **Avoid impulse bidding.** Yes, the beanbag chair is being offered at a good price, but do you really need a beanbag chair?

✦ **Investigate the price.** Just because an item is being auctioned at eBay doesn't mean that it's a good buy. Many people who auction at eBay are merely reselling items that they purchased at a discount. Sometimes you can purchase these items straight from the manufacturer and buy them cheaply. After all, all kinds of stuff is for sale on the Internet. The previous chapter in this minibook explains how to search for and investigate merchandise on the Internet.

✦ **Know what the shipping and handling charges are.** Some sellers who auction items cheaply make up the lost revenue by charging exorbitant fees for shipping and handling.

✦ **Contact the seller if you have any questions.** eBay makes it easy to contact a seller. On the item's eBay page, click the Ask Seller a Question link. A message form appears so that you can send an e-mail to the seller. The reply will be sent to the e-mail address you gave eBay when you registered.

✦ **Investigate the seller.** On the item's eBay page, you can click the Read Feedback Comments link to see a summary of the seller's transactions and ratings, as shown in Figure 2-7. Scroll down the page to see what buyers have said about the seller.

✦ **Ask yourself how difficult the item is to assemble, if it needs assembling.** Not everyone can interpret the complicated directions that come with items you have to put together yourself. Not everyone can wield a screwdriver. Because purchases are delivered by mail, they need assembling more often than other purchases. If you're not good at assembling things, make sure that the items you buy are already assembled.

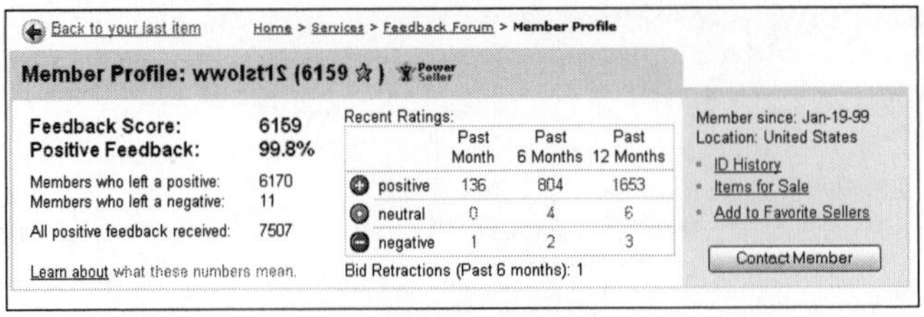

Figure 2-7:
Investigat-
ing a seller.

Bidding on Items

When you find an item you just gotta have, the next step is to bid on it. Go ahead. Don't be shy. eBay bidding is slightly different from conventional auction bidding, as I explain shortly. I also explain how to place a bid and close a sale.

How bidding works

Each auction page tells you how many days, hours, and minutes are left till closing time. The person who submits the highest bid before closing time, of course, wins the item, but it's not quite that simple. eBay auctions are not live auctions. Because not everyone who wants to bid can be online and signed in to eBay at closing time, eBay buyers make what are called maximum bids. Only the bidder knows what his or her maximum bid is. As long as your maximum bid — the maximum amount you are willing to pay for an item — exceeds other buyers' maximum bids, you are the high bidder. But if you make a maximum bid and someone who bid before has made a maximum bid that is higher than yours, you are not the high bidder. Instead the stated price of the item rises to the amount that you submitted in your maximum bid.

Confusing, huh? To see how it works, imagine an auction for a Chippendale mirror. The bidding starts at $50. The bid increment — the amount by which each bid must exceed the previous bid — is $2.50.

Dave, the first bidder, enters a maximum bid of $75. On the auction page, however, the price remains at $50. Dave has merely stated how high he is willing to go to win the item. Remember: Only Dave knows what his maximum bid is.

The next bidder, Sally, enters a maximum bid of $60, but because her $60 doesn't exceed Dave's maximum bid of $75, eBay informs Sally that she is not the high bidder. In the meantime, the price of the item rises to $60, the amount of Sally's maximum bid. If no one else bids, Dave can buy the mirror for $60.

Sally, still keen to own the mirror, enters a maximum bid of $65, but eBay informs Sally that she is still not the highest bidder. At $75, Dave remains the high bidder. The price of the item rises to $65, the amount of Sally's second bid.

Sally just has to have that beautiful Chippendale mirror. She enters a maximum bid of $85. Now she is the high bidder and the stated price of the item is $77.50, Dave's original maximum bid ($75) plus the bid increment ($2.50).

eBay informs Dave by e-mail that he has been outbid. Dave clicks the Bidding link on his My eBay page, goes to his Items I'm Bidding On list, selects the Chippendale mirror auction, and goes to the Chippendale mirror auction page. He sees that the item now costs $77.50. He has been outbid. He enters a maximum bid of $90. eBay tells Dave that he is the high bidder. The price of the mirror is now $87.50, the amount of Sally's maximum bid ($85) plus the bid increment ($2.50). Dave will win the mirror for $87.50 as long as no one outbids his maximum bid of $90.

Because you never know what the current maximum bid is, you never know whether a maximum bid you submit will make you the high bidder. The maximum bid formula is designed to keep one person from outbidding another by a few dollars at the last minute. It also gives you a chance to participate in auctions without having to be present at your computer at bid closing time.

Placing a bid

To place a bid and declare the maximum amount you will pay for an item, scroll to the bottom of the item's eBay auction page and look for the words *Ready to Bid?* As shown in Figure 2-8, enter your maximum bid and click the Place Bid button. You see the Review and Confirm Bid window, where you have a last chance to review your bid before clicking the Confirm Bid button.

Figure 2-8:
Making
a bid.

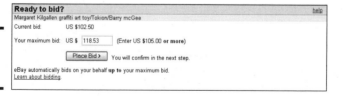

Ready to bid?   help
Margaret Kilgallen graffiti art toy/Tokion/Barry mcGee
Current bid: US $102.50
Your maximum bid: US $ 118.53   (Enter US $105.00 or more)
          [Place Bid >] You will confirm in the next step.
eBay automatically bids on your behalf **up to** your maximum bid.
Learn about bidding.

As soon as you submit a bid, eBay tells you whether you are the high bidder. The item you are bidding on is placed on your Items I'm Bidding On list. You can see this list by clicking the Bidding link on your My eBay page. If someone outbids you, eBay sends you an e-mail telling you as much. The e-mail is sent to the address you entered when you registered. To change this address, click the Personal Information link on your My eBay page.

Strategies for successful bidding

To be a successful bidder, be coy. When you see an item you really like, don't bid on it right away. Click the Watch This Item link to enter the item on your Watching list, a list you can see by clicking the Watching link of your My eBay page. From the Watching list, you can click the item's name and go to its auction page to find out whether others have placed a bid.

Ideally, bids should be placed at the last minute, but forgetting to bid on an item is easy. One strategy for remembering to bid is to enter a low bid in the early going. Each time you are outbid, eBay sends you an e-mail telling you so. The e-mail message includes a link that you can click to go directly to the auction page and up your bid.

Setting aside what I just said about being coy, if you really, really want an item, make a large bid for it. This way, you can scare off other bidders and decrease your chances of being sniped.

Auction sniping

Auction sniping means to outbid competitors at the last possible moment in an eBay auction. If the auction ends at high noon, the successful auction sniper makes the final, highest bid at 11:59:59. If you spend any time on eBay, you are bound to be sniped sooner or later. eBay maintains an article about auction sniping at this address: http://pages.ebay.com/help/basics/g-sniping.html.

Most people don't have the spare time to be an auction sniper, but several Internet services can do it for you — for a fee, of course. After registering for these services, you tell the service which eBay item you are bidding on, set your price, and let the auction sniper place the bid for you at the last moment. Here are some auction-sniping services and the Web-site addresses where you can find out more about them:

✔ **AuctionSniper:** The cost is 1 percent of the auction price, with a minimum fee of $0.25 and a maximum fee of $5. Address: www.auctionsniper.com

✔ **AuctionStealer:** The cost is $9 to $10 per month, depending on how long you enroll. Address: http://auctionchief.auctionstealer.com/home.cfm

✔ **Bidnapper:** The cost is between $4 and $10 per month, depending on how long you enroll. Address: www.bidnapper.com

✔ **HammerSnipe:** The cost is $6 to $9 per month, depending on how long you enroll. Address: http://hammertap.auctionstealer.com/home.cfm

Making the Purchase

When you win an auction, eBay sends you an e-mail telling you how much the item costs, including shipping and handling. At that point, it is up to you to pay for the item. If you did your homework, you know how the seller prefers to be paid. You can usually pay by check, a credit card, or PayPal (see the next chapter in this minibook).

When the transaction is complete and you have the item in hand, be sure to describe the seller to eBay. You can do this by clicking the Feedback link on your My eBay page. Click the Leave Feedback link to see a list of people who sold you items. Click a seller's name and enter a rating and brief description of the transaction. Other buyers depend on this information to decide whether a seller is trustworthy.

Chapter 3: Using PayPal

A s you know if you've purchased items on eBay, PayPal is a very convenient way to make a payment. More than 40 million people have signed up with PayPal. Payment information is encrypted so that the seller's and buyer's credit card and checking account information remains private. This chapter looks at PayPal, how to sign up with the service, and how to send and receive payments.

Discovering PayPal

PayPal is a convenient online system for sending and receiving payments over the Internet. If you've bought anything at eBay, you probably already know what PayPal is. Most eBay sellers prefer to receive payments by PayPal (eBay, in fact, owns PayPal). Apart from the cost of items they purchase, buyers pay nothing to send payments through PayPal. The money to purchase items is deducted from their credit card accounts or checking accounts and sent to the seller. For the convenience of receiving payments through PayPal, sellers pay a fee amounting to about 3 percent of the purchase price.

For buyers, using PayPal offers the advantage of getting the items they purchased that much sooner because sellers don't have to wait for checks to clear the bank before sending items. What's more, PayPal offers eBay buyers its buyer protection program. The cost of purchasing an item can be refunded if the item was never delivered or if it is significantly different from what the buyer thought he or she was getting. And using PayPal spares you trips to the post office because purchases are made by e-mail. You can pay for an item and deliver the payment to the seller without leaving your computer.

For sellers, using PayPal means receiving payments very quickly. And online stores can use PayPal in place of expensive checkout procedures that they would otherwise have to develop and maintain on their own. Your customers can click a PayPal button to make a purchase. They don't have to negotiate a hard-to-follow checkout rigmarole.

For sellers and buyers, PayPal tracks all purchases and sales in an account ledger similar to a bank statement. At any time, you can go online to review purchases and sales you have made with the help of PayPal.

Types of PayPal accounts

PayPal offers three kinds of accounts. If you run an online business, sign up for a Premier or Business account:

✦ **Personal account:** Send and receive payments for free. Funds to pay for items are withdrawn from a credit card you register with PayPal. You can't, however, receive credit- or debit-card payments with this kind of account.

✦ **Premier account:** Send payments for free, but pay a small fee to receive payments. You can receive payments from a customer's credit or debit card with this kind of account. You can also use the PayPal checkout tools — the Buy Now buttons and the Shopping Cart. This account is for individuals running small businesses.

✦ **Business account:** Same as a premier account, except more than one person can access the account. This account type is for small businesses with more than one employee.

For a complete explanation of PayPal features that are available to businesses, go to this Web address:

```
www.paypal.com/en_US/pdf/merchantOverview_interactive.pdf
```

Costs of using PayPal

PayPal operates a two-tiered fee structure. The standard rate charged for transactions is 2.9 percent plus 30 cents for each transaction taking place in the United States. A payment of $50, for example, costs the seller $1.75:

```
($50.00 × 2.9%) + 0.30 =  $1.75
```

For a transaction in which one of the parties is *not* in the United States, the standard rate rises to 3.9 percent plus 30 cents for each transaction. A payment of $50 costs the seller $2.25:

```
($50.00 × 3.9%) + 0.30 =  $2.25
```

To reward merchants who receive more than $3,000 per month, PayPal offers a cheaper merchant rate. This rate varies from 1.9 percent to 2.5 percent per transaction, depending on how much sales volume your business shows each month. For example, the per-transaction rate drops below 2.2 percent if your monthly sales exceed $10,000.

Go to this Web address for a complete explanation of the fees that PayPal charges:

```
www.paypal.com/us/cgi-bin/webscr?cmd=_display-fees
```

Signing Up for a PayPal Account

Signing up for a PayPal account is free. When you sign up for an account, PayPal asks for your name, address, phone number, and e-mail address, as well as a credit or debit card number and bank account information. Follow these steps to sign up for a PayPal account:

1. **Open your Web browser and go to this address:** `www.paypal.com`.

   You come to the PayPal home page.

2. **Click the Sign Up link.**

3. **Choose the kind of account you want and the country you live in; then click the Continue button.**

4. **Fill in the Sign Up form and click the Sign Up button.**

5. **Open the e-mail account whose address you gave to PayPal.**

6. **Open the e-mail message from PayPal.**

7. **Click the PayPal confirmation link in the e-mail message.**

   You go to the PayPal Welcome page. Starting here, you can log in and start using PayPal.

Logging in to the PayPal Window

To log in to PayPal, go to the PayPal home page (`www.paypal.com`), enter your e-mail address, and enter your password. You land on the My Account tab of the PayPal window, as shown in Figure 3-1. This is the starting point for all your activity in PayPal. Click one of these tabs to get going:

✦ **My Account:** Add or withdraw money from your PayPal account, as well as see a history of your account transactions with PayPal, resolve a dispute with a buyer, and change the personal information you filed with PayPal.

✦ **Send Money:** Send money to a seller.

✦ **Request Money:** Request a payment from a buyer.

✦ **Merchant Tools:** For merchants, include PayPal checkout mechanisms on your Web site.

✦ **Auction Tools:** Take advantage of PayPal features designed especially for people who sell items on eBay.

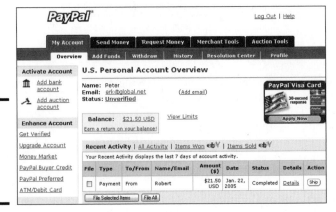

Figure 3-1:
The My Account tab of the PayPal window.

Sending a Payment through PayPal

Paying for an item you purchased at eBay with PayPal is a cinch. After you win the auction, click the Pay Now with PayPal button on the Congratulations, You Are a Winner page. Then sign in to PayPal, if you haven't already done so, and process the payment.

You can make a payment through PayPal to anyone in the United States, as long as the person has an e-mail address and is either already a PayPal member or is willing to be a PayPal member to collect the money. Log in to PayPal and follow these steps to send a payment:

1. **Select the Send Money tab.**

2. **Click the Pay Anyone tab.**

Figure 3-2 shows the Pay Anyone tab.

3. **Enter an e-mail address, the amount of the payment, the payment type, a subject for your e-mail message, and a note explaining what the payment is for.**

4. **Click the Continue button.**

5. Make sure that your address is listed correctly and click the Send Money button.

The e-mail message is sent to the recipient. It tells the recipient that you have sent a payment through PayPal. If the recipient is a PayPal member, he or she can log in to PayPal and receive the money. Otherwise, the recipient must register with PayPal to receive the money you sent.

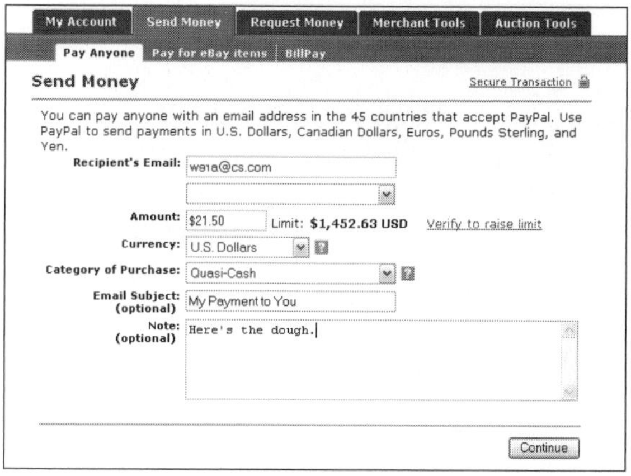

Book VI Chapter 3

Using PayPal

Figure 3-2: Making a payment through PayPal.

You can see a complete history of all payments you've sent and received through PayPal by going to the My Account tab of the PayPal window and clicking the History tab.

Receiving a Payment

You'll know when someone has sent you a payment through PayPal because the notice arrives by e-mail, as shown in Figure 3-3. The notice tells you who sent the payment and how much the payment is for. The payment is deposited immediately into your PayPal account. You can see it in the My Account tab of the PayPal window (refer to Figure 3-1).

Log in to PayPal and follow these steps to withdraw funds from a PayPal account:

1. Select the My Account tab in the PayPal window, if it isn't already selected.

2. Select the Withdraw tab.

3. **Click the Transfer Funds to Your Bank Account link or the Request a Check from PayPal link, and follow the instructions.**

4. **Click the Submit button.**

   The money will appear in your bank account in four to seven business days, depending on which country you live in. You incur no charge if you elect to have funds electronically sent to your bank account, but it costs $1.50 to receive a check from PayPal.

Figure 3-3: Receiving a payment through PayPal.

Chapter 4: Taking a Stroll through the Cyberbazaar

In This Chapter

✔ Antiques

✔ Apparel

✔ Art

✔ Computers and Electronics

✔ Furniture

✔ Gift Ideas

✔ Health and Beauty

✔ Jewelry

✔ Kitsch

✔ Sporting Goods

✔ Toys

This chapter describes online shops that are worth visiting. Any list of this kind is bound to reflect the bias of the person who put it together. I am biased toward shops that offer exceptional goods or goods that you can't find anywhere else on the Internet. I am interested in the weird and wonderful. I am interested in one-of-a-kind items that are made by hand. I am interested in online shops that are fun to browse in.

If you are looking for a particular item, try using a shopping search engine or a comparison-shopping Web site (Chapter 1 of this minibook explains what those are). This chapter is strictly for people who want to browse and have the time to do it.

Antiques

Antiques Company	"We are proud of our diverse collections of Samplers, Majolica, Steins as well as the other antique accessories that we stock for designers and homeowners."	`www.theantiquescompany.com`
Antiques on Old Plank Road	Many lovely antiques are presented on this Web site.	`www.oldplank.com/`
Castle Bryher	Antique porcelain and figurines from the U.K.	`www.castle-bryher.co.uk`
Fleur	French and English stone statuary and garden antiquary.	`http://fleur-newyork.com`
Woto and Wife Antiques	Unusual Victorian antique porcelain, glass, silver, and other eclectic items collected in British Columbia.	`http://wotoandwife.bc.ca`

Apparel

1 World Sarongs	Sarongs from Indonesia, as well as other Indonesian folk arts and crafts.	`http://1worldsarongs.com`
Attivo	Every kind of men's underwear found on Earth.	`www.attivousa.com`
Beau Ties Ltd.	"We exist to meet the bow tie needs of the world's bow tie wearers."	`www.beautiesltd.com`
Blue Fly	"Designer clothing sold at a discount. Over 350 designers; up to 75 percent off."	`www.bluefly.com`
China Bridal	Traditional Chinese wedding gowns and clothing for men, women, and children.	`http://chinabridal.com`
Coolibar	Special, UV-protection clothing, hats, sunglasses, and swimwear from Australia.	`www.coolibar.com`
Dad's Hats	Great collection of hats at modest prices.	`www.dadshats.com`
Delias	Hula-board shorts, asha skirts, and other items for teenage girls.	`www.delias.com`

Apparel *(continued)*

Designer Outlet	Shop for low-priced designer clothing in different categories.	www.designeroutlet.com
eLuxury	Marked-down designer-name clothes and handbags.	www.eluxury.com
Ex Officio	Special bug-resistant clothing for men, women, and children.	www.exofficio.com
Fashion Dig	Shop for vintage clothing by decade, from the 1920s to the present.	www.fashiondig.com
Flip Flop Trunk Show	Mules, slides, thongs, flip-flops and other unusual footwear.	www.flipfloptrunkshow.com
Frames Direct	Buy glasses frames straight from the manufacturer. Over 100,000 frames and styles are available.	www.framesdirect.com
Gempler's	Rugged clothes for people who work outdoors.	www.gemplers.com
Hong Kong Silk Company	Silk clothing — scarves, lingerie, pajamas — imported from Hong Kong.	www.hksilk.com
Just My Size	Clothing for full-figured women.	www.justmysize.com
Leg Wear Direct	Brand-name hosiery, tights, and socks sold at discount.	www.legweardirect.com
NetStage	Islamic clothing, jewelry, and daggers and Muslim décor.	www.desertstore.com
Norway Sweaters	Volund and dale sweaters imported from Norway.	www.norwaysweaters.com
Pendleton	Classic Pendleton clothes — the real thing — made in Pendleton, Oregon.	www.pendleton-usa.com
Prison Blues	Sturdy prison blues — that's clothes to the rest of us — made by prisoners in Oregon. Some of the proceeds fund rehabilitation and victim-restitution programs.	www.prisonblues.com
Sheplers	Clothes for cowboys, would-be cowboys, and plain-old dudes.	www.sheplers.com

Apparel (continued)

Name	Description	URL
Stockings HQ	Lots of stockings, some shocking and some not.	www.stockingshq.com
Ties	Ties, ties, and more ties, including a tie museum and instructions for tying different tie knots.	www.ties.com
Travel Smith	Unusual, easy-to-clean, sturdy clothes for travelers.	www.travelsmith.com
Underneath	Underwear for all occasions.	www.underneath.com
Village Hat Shop	Regardless of whether you wear hats, check out the variety at this Web site.	www.villagehatshop.com
Zenni Optical	Prescription eyeglasses for $19. It's hard to beat that.	http://19dollareyeglasses.com
Zoot Suit Store	Warning: Not everyone looks supercool in a zoot suit; the store also sells retro shoes and hats.	www.zootsuitstore.com

Art

Name	Description	URL
All Posters	Movie, sports, fine-art, and vintage posters.	http://allposters.com
Bauer Boys	Fiesta ware pottery in all shapes and colors.	http://bauerboys.com
Cartoonbank	Buy framed *New Yorker* cartoons — or cartoons on T-shirts.	www.cartoonbank.com
Exotic India	Paintings, sculptures, jewelry, dolls, and textiles from India.	www.exoticindiaart.com
Global Crafts	Fair-trade arts and crafts from Africa, including jewelry, clothing, baskets, and glass.	www.globalcrafts.org
Good Orient	Clothing, home décor, and gifts from East Asia.	www.goodorient.com
Museum of Bad Art	I just had to stick this one in the book somewhere, and yes, this museum also has a store.	www.museumofbadart.org
Night Owl Books	Vintage movie posters from old to not so old.	http://nightowlbooks.com
Painting Direct	"The easiest way to find and buy original paintings."	www.paintingdirect.com

Art (continued)

Photowow	Submit snapshots of your family or friends and have the turned into hand-tinted pop-art prints.	www.photowow.com
Postergroup	Vintage posters from around the world.	www.postergroup.com

Computers and Electronics

Advanced Intelligence	This spy shop offers the world's smallest video camera, surveillance equipment, and "spy optics."	www.advanced-intelligence.com
As Seen on TV	The HoverCopter Deluxe Kit, the Shower Stick, the Bun and Thigh Roller, and every other weird invention you've seen advertised on late-night TV is available here.	www.asontv.com
Cambridge Soundworks	Lots of fun gadgetry at low prices.	www.cambridgesoundworks.com
Chumbo	Low-cost computer hardware and software.	www.chumbo.com
Custom Phones	Telephones of all shapes, sizes, and colors.	www.customphones.com
Dynamism	The latest electronic gadgets from the most gadgetized country on earth — Japan.	www.dynamism.com
Tweeter	The biggest, brightest, gaudiest, and most technologically advanced TVs are served up here.	www.tweeter.com
UBid	Bid on or buy factory seconds from electronics manufacturers.	www.ubid.com

Furniture

Furniture Find	Search by room for articles of furniture.	www.furniturefind.com
Ironworx Designs	Wrought-iron furniture for the garden or backyard.	www.ironworxdesigns.com

Furniture *(continued)*

Minerva Antiques	Antique furniture and gilded mirrors from the U.K.	www.minerva-antiques.co.uk
Shaker Furniture	Elegant, expertly crafted furniture from time-tested Shaker designs.	www.shakerworkshops.com

Gift Ideas

All Nautical	Nautical knickknacks for people who love the sea.	http://allnautical.com
Crutchfield	Look in the Car Products section for high-tech items for the car, including satellite radios and radar detectors.	www.crutchfield.com
Harry and David	Home of the "Fruit of the Month Club."	www.harryanddavid.com
Interactive Russia	Unusual items from the old Soviet Union, including propaganda posters and military collectibles, including arts and crafts.	www.in-russia.com/store
Mama's Minerals	"Discover planetary magic and unusual gift ideas. Mama's Minerals has rocks, gems, minerals, geodes, quartz crystals, and more."	http://mamasminerals.com
Patent Museum	Order reproductions — most with illustrations — of patents issued by the U.S. Patent Office.	www.patentmuseum.com
Saigoniste	Exotic items imported from Vietnam.	http://saigoniste.com
ThinkGeek	Uber orbs, lasers, and other exotic gadgetry for the nerd or the geek.	www.thinkgeek.com
Year Box	Custom-made calendars with pictures of family members and pets.	http://www.yearbox.com

Health and Beauty

eBubbles	Bubble-bath powders, creams, lotions, massage oil, and other products to make you feel scrumptious.	`http://ebubbles.com`
Medichest	This rather unusual Web site combines medicine with nostalgia for times past. It offers "brands you grew up with" — antiseptics and beauty products from your childhood medicine cabinet.	`www.medichest.com`
Paula Young Wigs	Devoted to wigs and wig products.	`www.paulayoung.com`
Sephora	Hair-care, makeup, and skin-care stuff.	`www.sephora.com`
Travel Medicine	Medicinal products for travelers — mosquito repellants, jet-lag remedies, and more.	`www.travmed.com`
Urban Decay	Garish makeup in unusual colors, some of them found in nature.	`www.urbandecay.com`

Jewelry

Italian Bracelet Charms	Charm bracelets from Italy at very affordable prices.	`www.italianbraceletcharms.com`
Absolutely Vintage	Victorian, Edwardian, art nouveau, art deco, and retro jewelry.	`http://absolutelyvintage.net`
Antique Jewelry Exchange	Enjoy the jewelry of yesteryear.	`http://antiquejewelryexch.com`
Cufflinks	An entire Web site devoted to this slowly disappearing piece of men's attire — the cufflink.	`www.cufflinks.com`
Love Joy Jewelry	Antique jewelry collected from estate sales.	`www.lovejoyjewelry.com`

Kitsch

Archie McPhee	Check out the Mozart Action Figure and other tacky but wonderful gifts.	`www.mcphee.com`
Retro Junction	Retro clocks, radios, and other items, most from the 1950s.	`www.retrojunction.com`
Stupid	All things stupid — gifts, candy, toys.	`www.stupid.com`
Vintage Vending	Reproductions of 1950s items, including furniture, clocks, signs, and kitchenware.	`www.vintagevending.com`

Sporting Goods

AA Outfitters	Rods, reels, flies, wading gear, and everything else fishermen and fisherwomen need.	`www.aaoutfitters.com`
Army Surplus	Army and Navy surplus items, including camouflage face paint and water-treatment gear.	`www.armygear.net`
Baby Jogging Strollers	Get in your morning run and air out the baby at the same time.	`www.baby-jogging-strollers.com`
Cactus Juice	Buy all-natural bug repellant made from cactus juice.	`www.cactusjuicetm.com`
Outdoor Gear Exchange	New gear, used gear, and closeout camping gear.	`www.gearx.com`
Sierra Trading Post	You can find a huge selection of inexpensive hiking, backpacking, and camping gear, as well as outdoor clothing.	`www.sierratradingpost.com`

Toys		
Big Fun Toys	Unusual toys for children of all ages.	`www.bigfuntoys.com`
Catch the Wind	Exotic kites, windsocks, and other items that dance in the sky.	`www.catchthewind.com`
Copernicus Toys & Gifts	Educational toys for bright kids and kids whose parents think they're bright.	`www.copernicustoys.com`
Land of Marbles	Marbles of all shapes, colors, and sizes.	`http://landofmarbles.com`
Mobileation	Offers wagons, go-carts, and other items that kids can ride.	`www.mobileation.com`

Book VII

Selling on the Internet

The 5th Wave   By Rich Tennant

Contents at a Glance

Chapter 1: Selling Items on eBay

In This Chapter

✔ Examining the costs of selling on eBay

✔ Signing up to be a seller

✔ Getting ready to sell an item

✔ Posting an item for sale on eBay

✔ Monitoring the progress of an auction

✔ Closing the sale

*F*rom the seller's point of view, eBay presents a convenient way to empty the attic or garage of unwanted items, or a way to make a living. You may be interested to know that some 150,000 Americans make a living by selling items on eBay. Most eBay sellers, however, use the service to sell the occasional item — a piece of jewelry that isn't wanted, an old painting, or some used stereo equipment.

eBay understands that more sellers using the service necessarily attract more bidders and buyers, because more goods are available for them to choose from, and that more bidders and buyers, in turn, increase the cost of items at eBay and make the service more attractive to sellers, too. To speed this vicious cycle of sellers attracting buyers and buyers attracting sellers, eBay has done its best to please both parties. It has made selling items on eBay pretty easy.

This chapter explains how much it costs to sell items on eBay and describes the background work you must do to sell an item successfully. It shows how to sign up to sell an item and put up an item for auction. You also discover how to monitor an auction and close a sale.

By the way, don't attempt to sell anything at eBay until you are familiar with online auctions and, preferably, have purchased some items from eBay. Book VI, Chapter 2 explains how to buy items at an eBay auction.

Figuring the Costs of Selling on eBay

Before you consider selling an item on eBay, I bet you want to know the costs of selling. The costs, I'm happy to report, are low. How much it costs to sell an item on eBay depends on how much the item is sold for and whether you want amenities such as including more than one picture on your auction page. Fees break down like this:

✦ **Insertion Fee:** A fee each seller must pay regardless of whether the item sells. The amount of the insertion fee is based on the starting or reserve price. As of this writing, fees range from 30 cents for items with a starting or reserve price under $1 to $4.80 for items with a starting or reserve price over $500.

✦ **Final Value Fee:** The fee each seller pays if the item sells. The fee is not paid if the item doesn't sell. For an item that sold in the $25 to $1,000 range, the final value fee is 5.25 percent of the initial $25, plus another 2.75 percent for the remaining balance. For example, for an item that sold for $40, the final value fee is calculated like so:

```
       Initial $25: $25 × 5.25% = $1.31
Remaining balance: $15 × 2.75% = $0.42
                        Total  = $1.73
```

✦ **Optional Reserve Price Fee:** eBay charges you if you list a reserve price for an item you sell. For items that sell for below $50, the fee is $1; for items between $50 and $200, the fee is $2; after that, the reserve fee is 1 percent of the reserve price.

✦ **Optional Picture Service Fees:** The first picture you post on an auction page is free; after that, pictures cost 15 cents each. A super-size picture costs 75 cents.

eBay charges other fees as well if you want fancy stuff on your auction pages. Go to this Web page to get complete, up-to-date fee rates for selling items on eBay:

```
http://pages.ebay.com/help/sell/fees.html
```

Signing Up to Sell on eBay

In addition to what you told eBay when you signed up to buy items at the online auction house, eBay needs to know one or two things about you. Chiefly, eBay needs your credit card number and checking account number. The checking account number confirms that you are who you say you are. eBay charges your credit card when you put up an item for bidding and complete a sale.

Sign in to eBay and follow these steps to start signing up as an eBay seller:

1. **Click the My eBay button to go to your my eBay page.**

As Book VI, Chapter 2 explains, every registered eBay member gets a My eBay page for tracking items that he or she is watching and bidding on. If you have not yet signed up to sell items on eBay, a Start Selling link appears on the left side of the window (this link is called All Selling if you have signed up already).

2. Click the Start Selling link.

You come to the How to Sell Items window.

3. Click the Set Up a Seller's Account link.

You land in the Create Seller's Account window.

4. Click the Create Seller's Account button.

Now you're getting somewhere. You see the Create Seller's Account window shown in Figure 1-1. It's time to start entering credit card and bank account information.

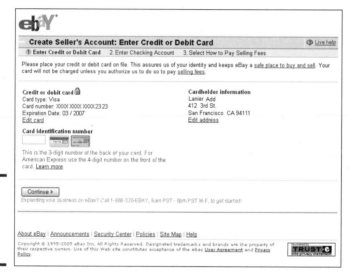

**Book VII
Chapter 1**

Selling Items on eBay

Figure 1-1:
Creating a seller's account at eBay.

In the next several windows, eBay asks for this information:

+ **Credit or Debit Card:** Enter your credit or debit card number.

+ **Expiration date:** Use the drop-down menus to enter the card's expiration date.

+ **Card Identification Number:** You can find this three-digit number on the back of your card.

+ **Account holder:** The name of the person who is listed on your checking account (that's probably you).

+ **Bank Name:** Your bank's name.

♦ **Bank Routing Number:** You can get this number by looking at a check. It's the first nine digits in the lower-left corner, the ones between the first and second colons (:).

♦ **Checking Account Number:** You can also get this from a check. It's the last nine or ten digits, the ones to the right of the second colon.

♦ **Pay selling fees:** Tell eBay whether to take fees from your checking account or credit card account.

♦ **Password:** Enter your eBay password.

To change anything about the seller information you entered, go to your My eBay page and click the Personal Information link. You can find this link under the My Account link. Click the Change link next to the words *Checking Account* or *Credit Card* to change the information you entered.

Doing the Background Work

Before you attempt to sell an item on eBay, do the background work. Find out how much you can realistically get from the item on eBay, take a photograph of the item, and write its description. Sure, you can write the description as you put the item up for bid, but I suggest thinking it over carefully beforehand and writing a good description in your word processor. You can paste the description into your auction page later.

Researching the cost of the item

Obviously, you want the highest price you can get for your item without running the risk of failing to sell it. Here are ways to gauge how much to charge for an item:

♦ **Search eBay:** Book VI, Chapter 2 explains how to conduct a search of eBay for an item. Find out whether anyone is currently selling the item you want to sell. For that matter, find out how much similar items are selling for. You can also find out how much similar items have sold for in previous auctions.

♦ **Search the Internet:** Search the Internet to see how much online stores are charging for the item, if the item is sold at online stores. Book VI, Chapter 1 lists shopping search engines and comparison-shopping Web sites where you can find out how much an item is selling for.

By the way, some items can't be sold on eBay. These items include firearms, pesticides, and tobacco. For a complete list of items that can't be sold on eBay, go to this Web page:

```
http://pages.ebay.com/help/sell/item_allowed.html
```

Writing your item description

Along with taking a photograph, writing an item description is the most important task you can do to make an item enticing to bidders. Be sure to list the specifics of the item — its size, brand name, the year in which it was made, and the materials it is made of. If it has any blemishes, include them in your description. Bidders trust you more if you do, and no one will be able to complain later that you didn't list the blemishes.

In your description, declare as well what makes the item special. Try to appeal to the inner shopper in everyone and suggest why the item is perfect, useful, or necessary. Make the bidder feel enthusiastic about buying the item. End your description by wishing the bidder good luck in the auction.

Taking the photograph

eBay does not charge for including a photograph on an auction page. After the initial photograph, photographs cost a paltry 15 cents each. Because a picture is worth a thousand words, you would do well to include a photograph of the item.

Digital cameras have made it easy to take photographs that can be posted on the Internet. As you take your photograph, consider these pointers:

**Book VII
Chapter 1**

**Selling Items
on eBay**

+ **Use good lighting.** Put the item near a window and photograph it in natural light. If you have to use artificial light, illuminate the item from two directions so that shadows don't appear.

+ **Shoot from different sides.** If you plan to post more than one photo, shoot the item from different angles to give bidders a better idea what it looks like.

+ **Use a contrasting background.** Use a neutral background that contrasts with the color of the item. This shows off the item's appearance.

+ **Show some indication of size.** If necessary, place a ruler or other familiar object next to the item so that bidders can clearly measure its size.

Putting Up an Item for Bidding

Putting up an item for bidding is a matter of completing five tasks:

+ Choosing a category

+ Entering the title and description

+ Uploading a photograph

+ Declaring how you want to be paid and how you will ship the item

+ Submitting your item for bidding

These five tasks are described in the pages that follow.

To put up an item for bidding, you must have registered to sell on eBay as well as buy on eBay (see "Signing Up to Sell on eBay," earlier in this chapter).

Choosing a category

To put an item up for bidding, start by signing in to eBay and following these steps:

1. **Click the Sell button along the top of the screen.**

   You come to the Sell window.

2. **Click the Sell Your Item button.**

   You see the Choose a Selling Format window.

3. **Select the Sell Item on Online Auction option button; then click the Continue button.**

   You land in the Select Category window.

4. **Select a category for the item you want to sell; then click the Continue button.**

   Choose a category carefully. Buyers sometimes browse through categories looking for items to buy.

5. **Select a subcategory for the item; then click the Continue button.**

   You can place your item in more than one category. To do so, select the List in Second Category for Greater Visibility option button, click the Continue button, choose another category, and click the Continue button again.

   Now you're ready to describe the item.

Describing your item

Which windows you see next depends on the category in which your item is placed. For all items, however, you are asked for the following, as shown in Figure 1-2:

✦ **Item Title:** The name of the item. What you enter here appears along the top of the auction page and in search results. Name the item as clearly and concisely as you can. Use the adjective *rare* in the title if the item is indeed rare. By using a common name, you increase the chances of the item coming up in an eBay search.

✦ **Subtitle:** A subtitle is optional and costs 50 cents. Spending the extra money is worth it if you can make the item seem a little more enticing.

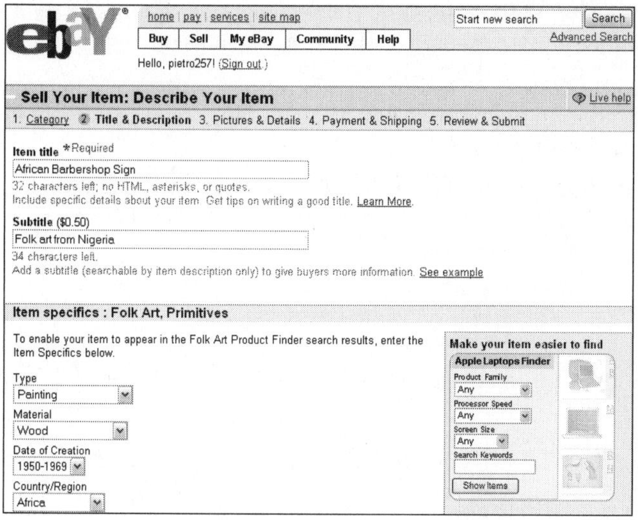

Figure 1-2:
Describing
an item.

✦ **Item Description:** On the Standard tab, paste the description you wrote
earlier (see "Writing your item description," earlier in this chapter). You
can click the Enter Your Own HTML tab and paste HTML code and text
as well, if you know your way around HTML coding.

Providing the pictures and item details

Now comes the important part — the pricing and the pictures:

✦ **Starting Price:** Enter your starting price in the text box. eBay recommends a low starting price, even if it means running the risk of selling
the item below value. Low starting prices encourage people to bid.
Studies show that once a bidder makes an initial bid, he or she is likely
to get the competitive spirit and keep bidding if others bid higher.

✦ **Reserve Price:** A reserve price is the price that must be met for the item
to be sold. Enter a reserve price if you can't part with the item for anything less than a certain amount. However, reserve prices discourage
bidders who think that a reserve price means an item is not a bargain.

✦ **Buy It Now Price:** By paying this price, you offer buyers the chance to
bypass bidding and acquire the item right away. As soon as someone
makes an initial bid, however, the Buy It Now price disappears, and the
auction is conducted like other auctions.

✦ **Duration:** From the drop-down menu, choose how long you want the auction to last: 1, 3, 5, 7, or 10 days. Choose 1 day for "hot" items that bidders
may snatch up immediately. If you expect bidders to run up the price,
choose 7 or 10 days to give them time to run the price especially high.

**Book VII
Chapter 1**

**Selling Items
on eBay**

✦ **Quantity:** If you are selling more than one copy of the item, enter the number you are selling in the Number of Items text box.

✦ **Adding Pictures:** Click the Add Pictures button and select your picture in the Open dialog box. For 15 cents more, you can place more than one picture on your auction page.

✦ **Selecting a Layout:** Choose a layout option to tell eBay how to arrange text and photos on your auction page. The preview box shows precisely what your choices are.

✦ **Selecting a Theme:** Using the drop-down menu and option choices, choose a theme for your auction page.

Click the Continue button to move ahead to the Payment & Shipping page.

Choosing the payment and shipping methods

Select check boxes to declare how you will accept payments and ship the item. If you are signed up with PayPal (see Book VI, Chapter 3), you can accept payments by PayPal. Make sure that the correct e-mail address is shown to the right of the PayPal check box so that notification that you've been paid is sent to the correct e-mail address.

Select the check boxes to declare where you will ship the items. In the Shipping Costs section, state how much you plan to charge for shipping (Book VII, Chapter 3 has advice for calculating shipping charges). Declare your return policy as well by selecting options from the drop-down menus under in the Return Policy section.

The Payment Instructions text box can be very useful for clearing up ambiguities in your payment and shipping policies. Buyers should clearly understand your policies before they bid. State the policies plainly in this text box, and you will spare yourself a lot of trouble down the road.

Reviewing and submitting

Before clicking the Submit Listing button at the bottom of the Review & Submit Listing page, take a last look at the options you chose for your item. If something needs changing, you can click a link on the right side of the window to go back to a page and make changes. Click the Save Changes button on the page to return to the Review & Submit Listing page.

After you click the Submit Listing button, eBay sends you an e-mail to confirm that your item is up for bid.

Monitoring the Auction

To find out whether anyone has bid on an item you are selling, go to your My eBay page and click the Selling link. For each item you are selling, the Selling page lists its current price, the number of bids, the ID of the highest bidder, the number of people who have put the item on their Watch lists, and the number of questions you have been asked about the item.

Questions arrive at the e-mail account you gave eBay when you signed up. Be sure to answer these questions promptly. Doing so greatly increases your chances of making a sale.

Closing the Sale

When the auction ends, eBay sends you an e-mail message saying as much. With a little luck, you get a "Congratulations" message because the item sold. The message tells you who the buyer is, the closing price, and the total owed you — including shipping and handling and insurance, if the buyer purchased insurance.

You can also go to your My eBay page and click the Sold link to find out how much an item sold for, as shown in Figure 1-3. The Sold page tells you the buyer's name, the selling price, and the total price.

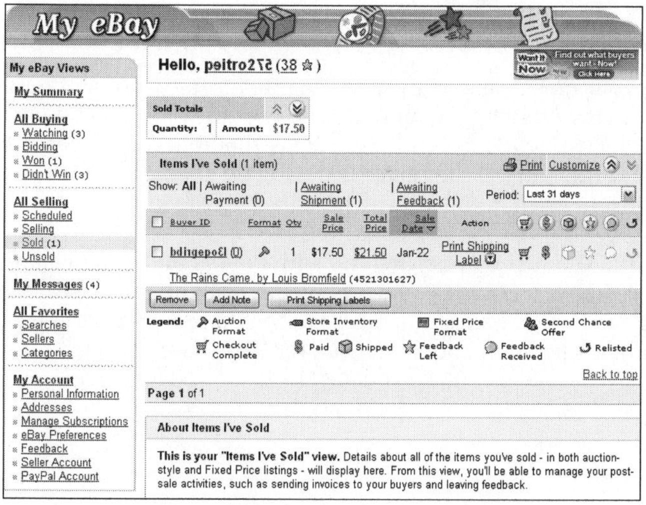

Figure 1-3: The Sold page tells you how much someone paid for your item.

At this point, it's up to you to communicate with the buyer about sending the package. You need to get the buyer's address and the sending instructions. Follow these steps to send the buyer an e-mail message:

1. **On the Sold page (refer to Figure 1-3), click the name of the item you sold.**

You go to the auction page. It tells you that your item sold and how much it sold for.

2. **Click the Contact the Buyer link.**

You can find this link next to the winning bidder's name. You land in the Contact eBay Member window, shown in Figure 1-4.

Figure 1-4:
Contacting
the buyer.

3. **Write the buyer an e-mail message and click the Send Message button.**

In your message, congratulate the buyer for winning the item. Be sure to state the winning bid amount, the cost of shipping and packing, and the total cost. Explain as well how long you hold on to checks before they clear the bank, if the buyer is paying by check. Ask for the buyer's address so that you know where to ship the item.

If you and the buyer are signed up with PayPal and you declared before the auction that you accept payments by PayPal, you may already have been paid. If so, PayPal has sent a message to your e-mail account explaining that a payment was made. Book VI, Chapter 3 explains PayPal.

Chapter 2: Selling Items Online

In This Chapter

✔ Settling into a niche market

✔ Setting up a commerce Web site

✔ Looking at e-commerce software programs

First, some bad news. Starting a business on the Internet really isn't very different from starting a conventional business. You still have to find customers. You still have to deliver a product that sets you apart from the competition. You still have to work hard and think innovatively to succeed. The good news is that the Internet levels the playing field somewhat. You have a direct connection to the millions of people who surf the Internet daily. You don't have to rent a storefront or send out hundreds of thousands of catalogs. You don't have to lay out hundreds of thousands of dollars to get started. You have a direct line to customers, and not just to customers in one geographic area. Your customers are potentially everywhere that people can connect to the Internet.

This chapter introduces you to selling online. Entire books have been written on this subject, and one chapter can't really do it justice, but this chapter lets you know what you're getting into and gives you ideas to consider as you set up an online business. You discover how to serve a market on the Internet, what is involved in setting up an e-commerce Web site, and which e-commerce software is available to you.

Choosing the Right Market

Generally speaking, the type of goods that sell on the Internet are the same type of goods that sell in catalogs — clothing, electronics, sporting goods. If a potential buyer has to feel it, taste it, or see it in person in order to buy it, it's hard to sell it online.

The trick is to find a niche market and become the official Web site for customers in that niche. It would be a mistake to try to sell backpacking equipment because you would have to compete with brand-name online retailers whose resources far exceed yours. But what if you were to specialize in

German-made hiking boots or Swiss rock-climbing equipment? Instead of selling sports memorabilia in general, you could specialize in one sport, such as baseball.

Here are some examples of online businesses that have been successful. If these businesses have anything in common, it is that they discovered a market niche and made it their own:

+ **FlightSimCentral:** This Web site specializes in selling flight-simulation games. The games are described in great detail so that hobbyists can find one just right for them. Address: `http://stores.yahoo.com/fsc`

+ **FridgeDoor:** This Web site is the be-all and end-all of refrigerator magnets. Address: `http://stores.yahoo.com/fridgedoor`

+ **Gun Dog Supply:** This Web site offers supplies for training hunting dogs. Talk about a market niche! Address: `www.gundogsupply.com`

+ **MyVitaNet:** Selling vitamins is nothing new, but this Web site has made a success of it by offering information about vitamins as well as selling the pills themselves. Address: `www.myvitanet.com`

Setting Up Your Web Site

Normally, if a Web site is to attract visitors, it has to present a good appearance and offer something special or something of value. An online business's Web site has to do even more than that. It has to present the items or services that are for sale in a good light, assure customers that they can buy with confidence, and be easy to navigate.

On the Internet, customers tend to judge a book by its cover. A comfortable, easy-to-use Web site is considered the sign of a good company, one worth buying items from. A good Web site inspires customer confidence. To be easy to navigate, a Web site needs tabs or buttons so that visitors can get quickly from place to place and always know where they are.

As shown in Figure 2-1, Amazon.com (`www.amazon.com`) has perfected the art of keeping customers from getting lost. You can tell at a glance how this Web site is structured and where you need to go to find the item you're interested in. In fact, Amazon.com's success can be attributed largely to its Web-site design. Customers are comfortable at Amazon.com and they make many purchases there, although the goods that Amazon.com sells can be purchased for less money at other Web sites. Another example of a Web site that is well structured is Barnes & Noble (`www.barnesandnoble.com`), shown in Figure 2-2. The tabs along the top of the window make it very easy to get from place to place.

Figure 2-1: The popularity of Amazon.com can be attributed to its user interface.

Figure 2-2: It's easy to get around at the Barnes & Noble Web site.

At the top of Figure 2-1, notice that Amazon.com has a shopping-cart mechanism. This is standard procedure at e-commerce Web sites. Customers need to be able to select items for purchase easily and be able to tell which items they have selected for purchase. They ought to be able to examine the items in the shopping cart and remove one from the list if they so choose.

On the subject of earning the confidence of your customers, one way to do that is to include a phone number and street address on your Web site. This ensures customers that yours is a real, three-dimensional company, not just a presence in cyberspace.

The next section in this chapter describes some software that you can use to set up commercial Web sites with shopping carts and customer checkout procedures. If you decide to create your Web site on your own without using e-commerce software, be prepared to spend $75 to $150 per hour on Web-site developers. Past work can give you an idea of how good a designer is, but just as importantly, take note of how curious designers are about your business as you interview them. Every company is different, and therefore every company's Web site should be different as well. A designer who understands this should ask about your company as he or she contemplates how to make your Web site.

E-Commerce Software

Setting up a Web site for an online business is no piece of cake. This is not something you should try at home unless you are a good hand with computers. Besides presenting the products you want to sell, the Web site has to be able to process payments from customers. In other words, it requires a shopping-cart mechanism so that customers can buy items and understand how much they cost, including tax and shipping charges. The Web site also has to process credit card payments.

A handful of software is available to help entrepreneurs run their businesses on the Internet. Table 2-1 describes these programs. Good e-commerce software can help you create a Web site and handle credit card transactions. Some programs also generate reports so that you can find out which products are selling and what your expenses and profits are.

Table 2-1	Software for Online Businesses			
Software	Web Address	Setup Fee	Monthly Fee	Notes
bCentral Commerce Manager	www.microsoft.com/ smallbusiness/bc/ default.mspx	-	$25	Build a catalog-style Web site; order-processing and management tools are excellent; support costs an extra $10 per month.
Bigstep	www.bigstep.com	-	$30	Build a Web site from templates; has limited reporting capabilities.

Software	Web Address	Setup Fee	Monthly Fee	Notes
FreeMerchant	www.freemerchant.com	$25	$50	Few reporting features; basic Web-site tools.
Interland Online Marketing	www.interland.com	$50	$50	Uses PayPal to handle payment processing; good Web-site tools.
SimpleNet Commerce	www.simplenet.com	$50	$35	Step-by-step site-building tools; commerce features are hard to set up.
StoreSense	www.storesense.com	$100	$50	Good site-building tools; good administrative tools for commerce.
Yahoo! Merchant	http://smallbusiness.yahoo.com/merchant	$40	$50+	Offers many e-commerce options; charges 1.5% for transactions.

Chapter 3: Sending It to the Buyer

*Y*ou sold it, which means now you have to ship it. And if you want repeat customers, you have to ship it in a timely fashion and make sure it gets there in one piece.

The responsibility for sending items undamaged and making sure they arrive on time rests with the seller. Even if your customer purchases insurance or your item listing says that you are not responsible for goods being damaged in transit, you *are* responsible. It's the law. If the item is damaged, the customer has the right to a refund.

This brief chapter looks at how to decide how much to charge your customers for shipping an item, packing items, buying postage online, and tracking items to their point of delivery.

Determining the Shipping Costs

Telling your customers what the shipping costs of an item are up front is essential. Customers consider the shipping costs as they decide whether to purchase or bid on an item. And they can tell when the shipping costs are too high. Many sellers pad the shipping costs to earn extra income from a sale, but the extra income gained from padding is lost when you consider how many customers turn down a purchase because they don't want to pay the extra shipping costs. By stating the shipping costs up front, you make it the buyer's responsibility to pay these costs. The buyer can't quarrel with the shipping costs after the purchase.

If the item weighs more than a half-pound, is fragile, or has an unusual shape and requires special care in packing, determining the shipping and packaging costs can be a chore. Here are things to consider as you tabulate the shipping costs of an item:

✦ The postage costs

✦ The cost of all packing materials

✦ The time you spend packaging the item

✦ The time you spend delivering the item to the post office or other service you use for shipping, if the carrier doesn't come to your door

As you consider these costs, remember that postage and packing materials are tax deductible. You recoup some of these costs if you itemize them on your tax return.

Whether you charge a flat rate or a variable rate for shipping depends on whether you want to gamble on making lower shipping rates an incentive for buyers who live near you. Obviously, declaring a flat rate is simpler. With a variable rate, you count on bidders and the buyer to make the extra effort to find out what the shipping charges are. eBay sellers can include a shipping calculator on their Web pages. A bidder can enter a zip code in the calculator to see precisely what his or her shipping charges are. To look into the eBay shipping calculator, go to this Web page:

`http://pages.ebay.com/services/buyandsell/shippingcenter7.html`

Go to these Web sites to calculate the cost of sending a package:

✦ **FedEx:** Click the Ship tab and choose Get Rates on the drop-down menu. Address: `www.fedex.com/us`

✦ **UPS:** Click the Calculate Time and Cost link. Address: `www.ups.com/content/us/en/shipping/index.html`

✦ **USPS:** Click the Calculate Postage link, as shown in Figure 3-1. Address: `www.usps.com`

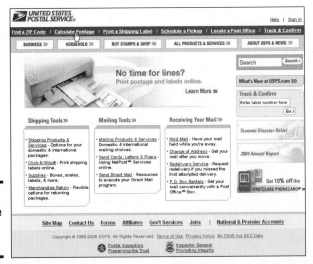

Figure 3-1:
A visit to the online post office.

If you buy stamps from Stamps.com, you can hide your postage costs. The postage costs don't appear on the label. Some buyers are resentful when they see that the cost of postage is lower than the shipping cost, but you can get around this problem by buying stamps at Stamps.com (see "Buying Postage Stamps Online," later in this chapter).

Packing It

It's no coincidence that the first online seller to make a name for itself was Amazon.com. Amazon.com started by selling books, and books are easy to package. They're durable and impossible to break. Nothing is easier than packing a book because its pages serve as packing material. Unless the box is oversize, you don't have to wrap a book in bubble wrap or popcorn. An old folded newspaper suffices.

Packing some items can be difficult, but going to extra trouble when packing pays dividends. It encourages customers to come back for more. On eBay, buyers often mention how items were packed in their seller assessments. When you pack an item, pack it as though you were going to purposefully damage it after you finish packing. For that matter, pack it as you would like it to be packed if it were being sent to you.

The cost of packing materials can add up. Here are some free or low-cost sources of packing materials:

+ **Delivery services:** If you are a steady customer, you can get free boxes and labels from delivery services.

+ **Shredded paper:** If you live near an industrial park or other place where offices run paper through shredders, you may be able to convince an office to let you have first dibs on its shredded paper. Or, if you generate a lot of paper, get your own paper shredder. Electronic paper shredders cost $150 and up.

+ **Bulk purchases:** If you buy boxes in bulk, they cost less. Buying boxes in bulk is an option if the items you send are roughly the same size. (And don't forget, you can recycle boxes that others send you.)

Be sure to enclose an invoice in the package so that the customer understands clearly what is in the package and where it came from. If the package is damaged in the mail, the carrier can open it and find out from the invoice who sent it and where it is meant to go.

What about delivery confirmation?

Whether to use delivery confirmation depends on the items you sell. If the items are inexpensive and easy to replace in the event they are lost, delivery confirmation isn't really necessary. But delivery confirmation offers advantages if you sell items worth $20 or more. You know when the package was delivered and that it was delivered. Delivery confirmations are a defense against scam buyers, the people who order an item and then claim it wasn't delivered. And customers like being able to track deliveries online. After you send a customer a tracking number by e-mail, the customer can go online to find out where the item is and how close it is to being delivered.

Buying Postage Stamps Online

Thanks to the miracle of the Internet and Stamps.com (`www.stamps.com`), you no longer need to wait in line at the post office to buy stamps. You can buy them online with a credit card, print postage at any amount, affix the postage to the package, and drop off the package at the post office without having to wait in line. The Web site also offers postage-rate calculators and a means of tracking your packages through the mail. Figure 3-2 shows Stamps.com.

Figure 3-2:
Buy stamps online at Stamps.com.

Tracking It

Go to one of these Web sites when you want to track the progress of a package:

+ **FedEx:** Click the Track tab. Address: `www.fedex.com/us`

+ **UPS:** Click the Tracking tab. Address: `www.ups.com/content/us/en/index.jsx`

+ **USPS:** Click the Track and Confirm link. Address: `www.usps.com`

At Pack Track (`www.packtrack.com`), you can track the progress of a package mailed with UPS, FedEx, Airborne, or 55 other carriers. Enter the tracking number, choose the carrier, and click the Track button.

Book VIII

Hobbies and Pastimes

The 5th Wave   By Rich Tennant

"Games are an important part of my Web site. They cause eye strain."

Contents at a Glance

Chapter 1: Playing Games Online

In This Chapter

✔ Playing card, arcade-style, casino, and board games

✔ Taking a look at some unusual games only found on the Internet

✔ Finding a good fantasy sports Web site

✔ Surveying Web sites for video-gamers

*W*hat with almost everyone being anonymous, and all the strange Web sites, and all the oddball opinions getting tossed back and forth, some would argue that the Internet is one big game to begin with. And they may be right. However, this chapter looks at games on the Internet, not whether the Internet is a game.

This chapter describes Web sites where you can play standard games and off-the-wall games that can only be found on the Internet, Web sites devoted to fantasy sports leagues, and Web sites for people who enjoy playing video games.

All-Purpose Game Sites

All-purpose game sites are Web sites that offer many different games — card games, casino-style games, board games, puzzles, and word games. At these sites, you can play against other players or a computer. I should warn you that the all-purpose game sites are addicting. The hands of the clock move faster when you're playing a game at one of these sites. You think 15 minutes have passed, but you glance at the clock to discover you wasted the entire afternoon!

You can download card and puzzle games for free or very inexpensively at Download Free Games. The Web site is located at this address: www.download-free-games.com.

MSN Zone

The mother of the all-purpose game sites is MSN Zone (http://zone.msn.com). As Figure 1-1 shows, The Zone (as it is known to its habitués) offers card games, trivia games, puzzles, casino-type games, and board games. You can play against a computer or against one of the 150,000 people who on average are signed in to The Zone. You can chat with other players as well.

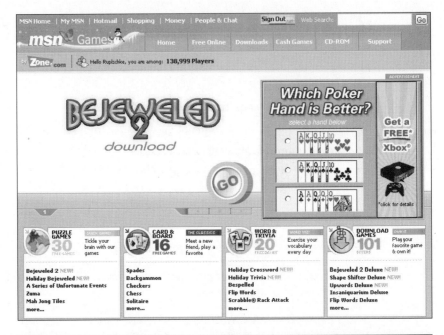

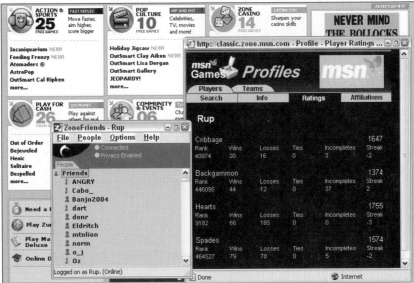

Figure 1-1:
The MSN
Zone home
page.

To play games at MSN Zone, you must have a .NET passport. Appendix B explains how to get one of those. Click the Sign In button to enter The Zone and start playing. You are asked to choose a nickname the first time you sign in. The Zone keeps track of your play and assigns you a rating for the different games you indulge in, as the lower-right corner of Figure 1-1 shows.

While you are signed in, you can right-click the nickname of a person you encounter in The Zone, choose Add to Friends on the shortcut menu, and place the person's name on your Friends list. (The Zone has more than its share of cheaters and curmudgeons. Many people use their Friends list to keep track of them.) The Friends list appears in the ZoneFriends dialog box, shown at the bottom of Figure 1-1. This dialog box appears while you are signed in to The Zone. Use it to maintain your privacy and send messages to other players:

✦ **Sending and receiving messages from friends:** Right-click a friend's name, choose Send Zone Message, enter a message, and click the Send button. When someone sends you a message, the Zone Message window appears. Read the message and enter a reply, if you dare.

✦ **Maintaining your privacy:** Open the Options menu and choose a Show Me option (Online, Away, Do Not Disturb) to tell your friends whether you want to be sent messages. The icon beside names on the list indicates which option a friend chose. Choose Options⇨Privacy to open the Privacy dialog box and be very clear about safeguarding your privacy. You can find options in the dialog box for being invisible to your friends or to everybody.

Yahoo! Games

Yahoo! Games is not nearly as sophisticated or smooth-running as MSN Zone (see the previous section in this chapter). Most of the games are Java applets — small applications that run on your computer. The applets are clunky, unappealing to look at, and unwieldy. You can find about a hundred games at Yahoo! Games. To play, you need a Yahoo! account and you must sign in to Yahoo! (Appendix A explains all that).

Use either of these methods to get to the Yahoo! Games page:

✦ Go to Yahoo! (www.yahoo.com) and click the Games link.

✦ Go straight to the Yahoo! Games page at this address: http://games. yahoo.com.

The only reason I include Yahoo! Games in this chapter is because the arcade-style games are kind of fun and can't be found elsewhere on the Internet. Look for downloadable arcade-style games in the Arcade & Other Games category.

Pogo

Like MSN Zone and Yahoo! Games, Pogo offers the usual array of card games, puzzles, word games, and casino-style games. You can chat with other players. You can play with other people or play against the computer. What makes this Web site a little unusual are the cash prize drawings and the jackpots. Win a game and you win some play money. Win enough play money and you get a chance to spin the jackpot wheel. Spin the wheel to the right spot and you win real money (or a gift certificate to Tower Records if you are under age 18), not play money.

You must register to play games at Pogo. Pogo's address is www.pogo.com.

ItsYourTurn

ItsYourTurn offers online versions of games in which players take turns — Chess, Checkers, Backgammon, Go, and others. What makes this site special is the ongoing games. You can leave ItsYourTurn in the middle of a game, come back a day later, see your opponent's latest move, and make your next move. The site tracks all games so that you can pick up or leave a game as you please.

Games begin in the Waiting Room, where you either accept someone's invitation to play or invite others to play. You must register and sign in to play games at ItsYourTurn. The address is www.itsyourturn.com.

Boxerjam

Boxerjam is also an all-purpose game site, but the games are not to be found anywhere else. Games include Atomica, where players turn atoms into molecules to score points, and Mah Jong Solitaire, a puzzle game in which players match tiles in pairs to eliminate them from the board.

You must register and sign in to play games at Boxerjam. Visit the site at this address: www.boxerjam.com.

Some Slightly Off-the-Wall Games

Wherever the Internet is, you can bank on finding a few off-the-wall items. The games I describe here defy categorization. They are off-the-wall, unusual, quirky, and just plain weird.

20 Questions

Welcome to the Internet version of 20 Questions, the old parlor game. This is your chance to find out how smart computers really are. In 20Q, you choose an animal, vegetable, mineral, other, or unknown, and you answer yea or nay as the computer tries to find out the thing you chose. Be careful, because according to the makers of this game, the computer keeps getting smarter: "20Q.net is an experiment in artificial intelligence. The program is very simple but its behavior is complex. Everything that it knows and all questions that it asks were entered by people playing this game. 20Q.net is a learning system; the more it is played, the smarter it gets." Go to this address to play 20 Questions against a computer: www.20q.net.

City Creator

In this little ditty of a game (it's for children and easily amused adults), you create a medieval, snowbound, or modern city by choosing and arranging buildings as you please. Just be sure to lay down the roads before putting the buildings up. Snaking the roads around the buildings is hard work. You can try your hand at city-building by going to this address: http://citycreator.com.

The ESP Game

In this game, two players who can't see the other's computer screen are presented with an image collected at random from the Internet. As shown in Figure 1-2, each player types descriptive words about the image, being careful not to type a word on the Taboo list. When both players type the same word, they score points and are presented with another image. To play The ESP (extra sensory perception) Game, go to this address: http://espgame.org.

Book VIII Chapter 1

Playing Games Online

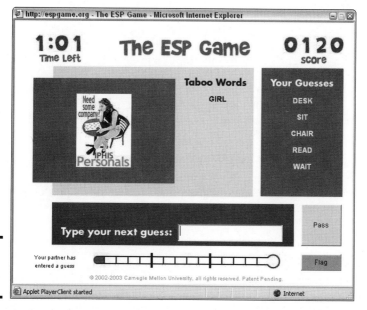

Figure 1-2: Playing The ESP Game.

This game has another purpose besides having fun and passing the time. Computer scientists at Carnegie Mellon University invented it as a way of labeling images on the Internet for search purposes. Here's how it works: Two players type the word *moon,* for example, to describe an image, and the image is assigned the keyword *moon.* Later, someone searching for images with the ESP search engine who types the word *moon* gets the image in the search results. The game is a way to accurately assign keywords to images. To test-drive the ESP search engine, click the ESP Image Search link on The ESP Game home page or go to this address: `www.captcha.net/esp-search.html`.

Geocaching

Geocaching calls itself a "sport." Not only that, it is, according to its inventors, "the sport where you are the search engine." Maybe Geocaching really is a sport. New sports develop as technology develops. The spear begat the javelin toss. The bow and arrow begat archery. The internal combustion engine begat auto racing. Geocaching is the child of two modern technological advances, the Internet and the GPS (global positioning system) device. A GPS device is a pocket-sized instrument that receives signals from satellites to pinpoint your location and mark it by latitude and longitude coordinates. You can buy a GPS device for less than $100. To see what Geocaching is about, go to this address: `www.geocaching.com`.

In Geocaching, a player hides or buries a cache (the word is pronounced "cash"), usually a plastic container with a few select objects and a logbook where you can write your name. The player measures the cache's coordinates with a GPS device and posts the coordinates at Geocaching.com along with directions for finding the cache, as shown in Figure 1-3. Players at Geocaching.com can find out where each cache is hidden or buried, visit a cache, add a little something to the cache or write their names in the logbook, and report on their excursion at the Web site. Cache hiders get the pleasure of reading reports from people who have found their cache. Caches are usually hidden in scenic or otherwise interesting places. Cache seekers enjoy discovering lovely new places they didn't know about.

Enter your zip code at the Geocaching home page to see whether any caches are hidden in your neighborhood. I was surprised to find nine caches within a mile of my home, and I live in San Francisco, a crowded city. It's kind of exciting to think of all that buried treasure just waiting to be found.

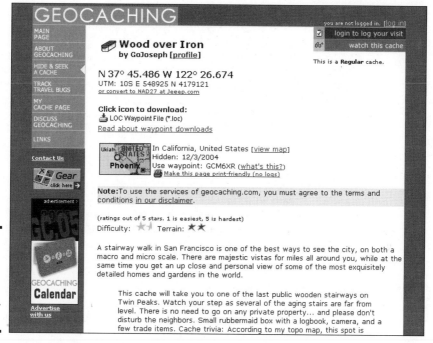

Figure 1-3:
A description of a cache at Geocaching.com.

Playing Fantasy Sports Online

In a fantasy sports league, players assemble teams composed of real athletes, and points are awarded according to how well the real athletes play. If Shaquille O'Neal scores 45 points in a game one week, the lucky manager who has O'Neal on his or her fantasy basketball team scores a lot of points, too. The Internet makes tracking fantasy sports that much easier because managers can get statistics about players in a matter of seconds. Managers can translate statistics into fantasy points in a matter of seconds, too. Table 1-1 describes some Web sites for fans of fantasy sports.

Table 1-1	Fantasy Sports Web Sites	
Web Site	*Sports*	*Address*
CBS SportsLine	Auto racing, baseball, basketball, football, golf, hockey, tennis	`http://fantasy. sportsline.com`
The Roto Times	Auto racing, baseball, basketball, football, hockey	`www.rototimes.com`

(continued)

Table 1-1 *(continued)*

Web Site	Sports	Address
USA Today Fantasy Leagues	Baseball, basketball, football, hockey	`www.usatoday.com/ sports/fantasy/ front.htm`
WhatIfSports	Baseball, basketball, football, hockey	`www.whatifsports. com`
Yahoo! Fantasy Sports	Auto racing, baseball, basketball, football, hockey	`http://fantasysports. yahoo.com`

WhatIfSports is the unusual one in the bunch. At WhatIfSports you can assemble a team with players from the past as well as the present. For the record, my all-NBA basketball fantasy team consists of Kareem Abdul-Jabbar at center, Rick Barry and Larry Bird at forward, and Magic Johnson and Oscar Robertson at guard.

Web Sites for Gamers

In case you don't know, a *gamer* is someone who loves to play video games. Here are a handful of sites for gamers:

✦ **Electronic Arts:** Sample EA games, get upgrades, and compete against other players online at this Web site. If you look carefully (the Web site is quite large), you can find free arcade games that unregistered users can try. Address: `www.eagames.com`

✦ **GameSpy:** Preview upcoming releases, sample new and old games, and see how games are rated at this Web site. You can also trade strategies and tactics with other gamers on the forums. Address: `www.gamespy.com`

✦ **Playstation Online Gaming:** At this Web site, you can play Sony Playstation games online. Or, you can trade tactics with other gamers on the message boards. You can also preview soon-to-be-released games. Address: `www.us.playstation.com/onlinegaming`

✦ **Xbox Live:** Play Xbox games with other enthusiasts over the Internet at this Web site. After you register, you get a Gamertag — a name you are known by in every game you play. This site includes a message board and the opportunity to download extras for your games. Address: `www.xbox.com`

Looking for a good video game? At Epinions, people express their opinions about all kinds of stuff, including video games. You can read what other gamers have to say about different games by going to this address: `www.epinions.com/game-Software-All`.

Chapter 2: Planning Your Next Vacation

In This Chapter

✔ Looking at travel-booking services and travel search engines

✔ Searching for travel bargains

✔ Finding a cheap airline ticket

✔ Looking for bargain hotel rooms

✔ Finding detailed maps of destinations

✔ Getting advice for making the most of your vacation

✔ Traveling in your armchair

✔ Seeking outdoor adventures

✔ Traveling by train

✔ Traveling abroad

✔ Taking a look at some eccentric Web sites for travelers

Most people, however tentatively, are planning their next vacation. You need something to look forward to. About 3:00, when the afternoon starts to wane, lunch is a distant memory, and two or three hours of work are still due at the office, most people dream of being on vacation: backpacking in the Sierra Nevada, partying at Mardi Gras in New Orleans, cruising up the Amazon in a steamer, or basking in the sun on a beach in Bali.

This chapter is dedicated to people who want to make their next vacation the best ever. It describes how to research a destination — how the Internet can help you find out where to stay and what to do while you're away. You find out how to obtain inexpensive airfares, hotel rooms, and rental cars. This chapter also presents Internet resources for traveling abroad.

Figuring Out Where to Begin

You know where you want to go. You've been dreaming about going there for some time now. The question is, "How do you make arrangements to get there?" Thousands of Web sites on the Internet are devoted to travel. Where do you start looking on the Internet to buy an airline ticket, book a hotel room, or rent a car?

The conventional answer to that question is this: Start looking at Expedia, Orbitz, or Travelocity, the Web sites listed in Table 2-1. The "big three" travel-booking agencies account for three-fourths of online bookings, according to PhoCusWright, a research firm that tracks the online travel industry. However, Expedia, Orbitz, and Travelocity aren't necessarily the best Web sites from which to make travel purchases. The "big three" only work on behalf of companies with which they have a contract. Because they don't have contracts to sell tickets for low-cost carriers such as Independence Air or JetBlue, for example, the "big three" don't sell tickets on behalf of those airlines. Expedia, Orbitz, and Travelocity are not all-inclusive when it comes to finding an airline ticket, hotel room, or rental car.

Table 2-1	The Big Three Travel-Booking Services					
Service	*Web Site*	*Flights*	*Hotels*	*Cars*	*Rail*	*Cruises*
Expedia	www.expedia.com	✔	✔	✔		✔
Orbitz	www.orbitz.com	✔	✔	✔		✔
Travelocity	www.travelocity.com	✔	✔	✔	✔	✔

A better way to search for travel bargains is to begin with a travel search engine, also known as an *aggregator*. These Google-like search engines scour many different Web sites, including JetBlue's and Independence Air's, for bargains. Table 2-2 lists the travel search engines. My favorite is Mobissimo (the word means "the ultimate in mobility" in Italian). It searches 81 travel sites, including Expedia and Travelocity, as well as other travel search engines. The results of the search appear in a list like the one shown in Figure 2-1. Travel search engines earn their daily bread from referrals. Clicking the Details button at the Mobissimo Web site, for example, refers you to an airline's Web site. If you buy a ticket there, Mobissimo makes a commission of $5.

Table 2-2	Travel Search Engines, or Aggregators	
Search Engine	*Description*	*Address*
Cheapflights	Searches 100+ sites for flights	www.cheapflights.com
FareChase	Searches 50 sites for flights, hotels, and rental cars	http://farechase.yahoo.com
Kayak	Searches 60+ sites for flights, hotels, and rental cars	http://kayak.com
Mobissimo	Searches 81 sites for flights, hotels, and rental cars	www.mobissimo.com
Opodo	Searches 9 large European carriers for flights	www.opodo.com
Qixo	Searches 50+ sites for flights, hotels, rental cars, and cruises	www.qixo.com

Figure 2-1: Search results at Mobissimo.

Travel search engine commissions are half of what travel-booking service commissions are, with the exception of Qixo, which charges a whopping $14 commission per ticket. The cheapest way to travel is to do some of the legwork yourself and avoid paying commissions. With a booking agency or travel search engine, find a bargain and then buy the ticket on your own. For example, find a cheap flight with Mobissimo, jot down the flight's departure time and number, call the airline, and buy the ticket directly. You can find a thorough list of airlines, their Web sites, and their toll-free telephone numbers at this Web address: www.cheapflights.com/agents. For hotels and car rental agencies, you'll have to look up phone numbers on the Internet. Book II, Chapter 3 explains how.

Finding a Travel Bargain

Besides checking out the travel-booking sites and travel search engines (see the previous section in this chapter), you would do well to look into these bargain travel sites. You never know what you will find here:

✦ **Cheaptickets:** This site's specialty is package tours — cheap ones. It also has a search engine for finding airline tickets, rental cars, hotel rooms, and cruises. Address: www.cheaptickets.com

✦ **Go-Today:** This site specializes in travel packages, some of them at cut-rate prices. You don't necessarily have to purchase a package today, but make your travel decision quickly, because offers come and go quickly on this Web site. Address: www.go-today.com

✦ **Johnnyjet:** This site, maintained by inveterate traveler John DeScala, offers links to hundreds of travel Web sites. What makes it useful to people looking for cheap airline tickets is "Today's Top Picks," a list of the best airline bargains of the day. Address: `www.johnnyjet.com`

✦ **Site59:** This site specializes in last-minute travel bargains. Travel services with airplanes to fill, hotels rooms that are empty, and rental cars to move off the lot advertise their wares here. Address: `www.site59.com`

✦ **Travelzoo:** "Outstanding deals handpicked daily" is the motto of Travelzoo. This site is a sort of bargain basement for travelers. You can find some great deals here. Address: `www.travelzoo.com`

Flying There

At the start of this chapter, the section "Figuring Out Where to Begin" explains how to use travel search engines and travel-booking services to buy airline tickets. Here are some other Web sites devoted to flying that you may find useful:

✦ **Airline Meals:** Yikes! Three thousand photos of airline meals. And check out the message boards, where visitors submit photos of awful meals and describe what they tasted like. Gag me with a spoon! Address: `www.airlinemeals.net`

✦ **Airliners:** If you are the kind of person who doesn't take the miracle of flying for granted, you may like this Web site and its thousands of pictures of commercial airplanes in flight. There is also a message board in which pilots talk the tricks of the trade. Figure 2-2 shows the Web site's home page. Address: `www.airliners.net`

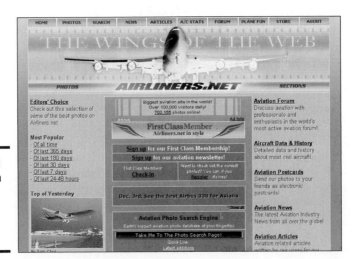

Figure 2-2: Airliners, a Web site for people who love airplanes.

✦ **AirSafe:** This Web site is devoted to helping people who are afraid to fly get over their fear of flying. Still, you have to wonder what the makers of this site were thinking when they included the Fatal Events and the Sole Survivors links. The Sole Survivors link takes you to a Web page that describes airplane crashes in which only one passenger survived. Grisly! Address: www.airsafe.com

✦ **Around the World Air Fare:** Suppose you were going to travel around the world by airplane, stopping in this or that country, of course, to shop for souvenirs. How much would it cost and which airlines would you take? You can find out at this Web site. Address: www.airtreks.com

✦ **Discount Airport Parking:** Make an online reservation to park at one of 65 airports in the United States. Address: www.discountairport parking.net

✦ **Flight Arrivals & Departures:** Is the flight leaving on time? Arriving on time? If the flight is a commercial flight in the United States or Canada, you can find out at this Web site. You can also get a weather report for 81 North American airports. Address: www.flightarrivals.com

Finding a Hotel or Motel Room

At the start of this chapter, "Figuring Out Where to Begin" explains how to use travel search engines and travel-booking services to find a hotel room. But if you are looking for something special — a romantic retreat or a cozy hideaway — look into these sites:

✦ **BedandBreakfast.com:** If you are turned off by impersonal hotel chains, this is the site to visit. Address: www.bedandbreakfast.com

✦ **Epinions:** At Epinions, people state their opinions about electronic devices, garden tools, beauty products — you name it. They also offer their opinions about hotels. This Web site is a great place to cut through the hype and find out whether a hotel is really worth staying in. Address: www.epinions.com/trvl

✦ **Hostelling International:** They don't call them "youth hostels" anymore, because hostels are for everybody, not just the budget backpacking crowd. Starting here, you can search for a hostel in the part of the world you want to visit. Address: www.iyhf.org

✦ **InnSite:** InnSite is "the bed and breakfast, lodging and accommodation guide to bed and breakfasts, country inns, and small luxury hotels throughout the world." This site is slow, perhaps because it indexes 50,000 pages of inn directories. But the wait is worthwhile. Address: www.innsite.com

✦ **Rentvillas:** Why stay in a measly hotel room when you can stay in a villa? This site offers villas — country estates — in England, Ireland, France, Spain, Portugal, and Italy. Address: www.rentvillas.com

**Book VIII
Chapter 2**

**Planning Your Next
Vacation**

✦ **Vacation Direct:** Owners list their vacation homes and condos at this site, where you can find descriptions of the vacation rentals and instructions for contacting the owners. Address: `www.vacationdirect.com`

Of course, you can also go the Web sites of the different hotel chains to book last-minute deals.

Exchanging Your Home with Another Family's

Exchanging your home with another family's home is an excellent way to lower the cost of traveling. You don't have to pay hotel bills. In some exchanges, parties borrow each others' cars. You can cook your meals and do your laundry in a private residence. Because you aren't staying in a hotel, you can make like a local and immerse yourself in the culture of the place you're visiting. Home exchanges make for a better travel experience.

Table 2-3 describes Web sites that arrange home exchanges. Sign up with one of these sites and you can post descriptions and photos of your home, and view others' homes. The Web sites don't arrange for the exchange of homes. That is up to you. Read home descriptions, see who wants to visit your town or city, and trade a few e-mail messages to make the exchange happen.

Table 2-3			Home Exchange Web Sites	
Name	*Listings*	*Cost Per Year*	*Notes*	*Address*
HomeExchange	6,000	$50	You can look at home listings without being a member, but you have to sign up to contact other members. Does not offer a printed directory of listings.	`www.home exchange.com`
HomeLink	14,000	$75	You must be a member to view listings and contact other members. For $45, HomeLink sends you a printed directory of listings.	`www.swapnow.com`
Intervac	11,000	$65	You must be a member to view listings and contact other members. For $120, Intervac sends you a color-printed directory of listings.	`http://intervac-online.com`

Letting strangers into your home can be a nerve-wracking proposition. Here are some guidelines to make home exchanges go smoothly:

✦ Make sure that both parties know the ground rules of staying in one another's home. For example, make a list of the household items and amenities — the washer and dryer, your car, your computer — that your guests can use.

✦ Check with your insurance agent to make sure that your policy covers home exchanges. If you intend to swap cars as well as homes, see whether your auto insurance policy covers guests driving your car.

✦ Start looking well in advance of your trip for a home to exchange so that you can get to know the other party well before your vacation starts.

✦ Leave the name of friend or neighbor that the other party can contact in the event of an emergency.

Driving There

The Web sites listed here are meant to keep you from getting lost and help you take the scenic route. These Web sites present online mapping tools to help you go from point A to point B (the next section in this chapter recommends advanced mapping tools). Still, before you look at the Web sites, consider the advantages of getting lost. Being lost quickens the senses. It makes you acutely aware of your surroundings. It makes you feel alive. Someday, a genius is going to put up a Web site with instructions for helping people get lost. Check out these driving Web sites:

✦ **America's Byways:** Since 1992, the United States Department of Transportation has been overseeing a collaborative effort with states and counties to recognize and preserve especially lovely stretches of the American highway. This Web site tells you where these byways are located and what you can expect when you drive them. Address: `www.byways.org`

✦ **AccuTraffic:** From here, you can get the latest report about road conditions on American highways. Click the Traffic link and select a state to go the official Web site of the state's Department of Transportation. Weather reports are also available from this site. Address: `www.accutraffic.com`

✦ **How far is it?:** As the crow flies, how far is Athens, Georgia, from Athens, Greece? The answer: 5,628 miles (or 9,058 kilometers). This very friendly Web site for crows and travel-planners calculates distances in no time at all. Address: `www.indo.com/distance`

✦ **Maps On Us:** The best of the mapping Web sites has less clutter than the others. You can enter your starting address and destination address, and this site creates a map for getting from one to the other, as shown in Figure 2-3. Address: `www.mapsonus.com`

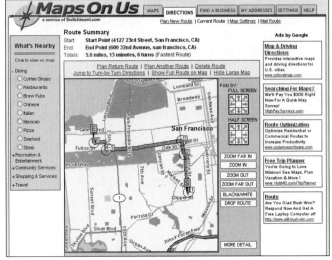

Figure 2-3:
Getting
driving
directions at
Maps On
Us.

✦ **MapQuest:** At this site for creating a map, you enter an address and click the Get Map button to get your map. Address: www.mapquest.com

✦ **MSN Maps & Directions:** Displaying a map is pretty simple, and the tools for zooming in, zooming out, and printing are easy to understand and use. You can also get driving directions here by clicking the Directions tab. Address: http://mappoint.msn.com

✦ **Speed Trap Exchange:** By definition, a *speed trap* is a stretch of highway where police trap unsuspecting motorists who are driving too fast and give them tickets. At this Web site for cross-country road-trippers, you can find out where speed traps are located and nominate speed traps of your own. Address: www.speedtrap.org

✦ **The Subway Navigator:** For several dozen cities around the world — about a dozen in the United States — plan a subway or light-train route from one station to the next. Address: www.subwaynavigator.com

Before you embark on a long car trip, visit the Radio-Locator at this Web address: www.radio-locator.com. You can find radio stations in various locales at this Web site and even listen to Internet radio. I don't want you to be lonely when you're driving deep into the hinterland.

Advanced Mapping

Cross-country backpackers, four-wheel-drive enthusiasts, and geocachers need sophisticated maps and navigation tools. When you really, really need to know the lay of the land, look into these Web sites:

✦ **Keyhole:** Keyhole is a satellite-imagery program that you can download from the Internet. The images are remarkably clear. I was alerted to this program by a friend who found his mother's house with her car clearly visible in the driveway! The cost is $29.95, although a seven-day free trial is available as of this writing. Address: www.keyhole.com

✦ **Terraserver:** View aerial and satellite imagery at a resolution of 8 meters and above. Subscription rates range from seven days ($9.95) to one year ($119.95). I remember when only the CIA and the KGB could see satellite images as sharp as these. You can also download and print topographical maps. Address: www.terraserver.com

✦ **TopoZone:** From this Web site, you can view topographical maps of the United States, as shown in Figure 2-4. The maps are generated from USGS (United States Geological Survey) maps. As a paid subscriber, you can download the maps and view aerial photos as well. Address: www.topozone.com

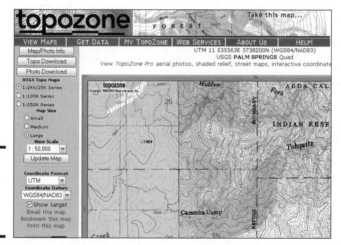

Figure 2-4: A topographical map at TopoZone.

How's the Weather?

Ants and mosquitoes can ruin a good picnic, but that's nothing compared to what a vigorous storm can do to a weekend at the beach. Before you leave for that dream vacation, check out these Web sites to see what kind of weather you will encounter:

✦ **AccuWeather:** While you are deciding whether to pack a sweater or a t-shirt, sunblock or an umbrella, pay a visit to AccuWeather. By entering a city or zip code, you can find out what meteorologists think the weather

**Book VIII
Chapter 2**

Planning Your Next Vacation

will be for the coming week at your destination. You can also choose a state and watch a satellite animation showing changes in the weather. Address: www.accuweather.com

✦ **Daily Tide Predictions:** Surfers, fisherfolk, and open-water swimmers in the western United States and Canada can go to this Web site to generate easy-to-read tide charts. Just choose a location from one of the drop-down menus. Address: www.duckcentral.com/daily_tideA.shtml

✦ **National Oceanic and Atmospheric Administration:** From this Web site, you can get long-term forecasts, eight days in advance. Address: www.noaa.com

✦ **USA Today Online Weather Almanac:** For travel planning, this site offers monthly climate data for cities the world over. Go here to find out what the average monthly high and low temperatures, rainfall, and snowfall are in a vacation spot that you are eyeing. Address: www.usatoday.com/weather/walm0.htm

Deciding What to Do When You Get There

Taping a map to the wall and throwing darts at the map to decide where to go next is one way of travel planning. However, mathematicians have determined that the amount of pleasure you derive from a vacation is directly proportional to the amount of time you spend planning it. The following Web sites can help you match your desires and interests with attractions and destinations:

✦ **Arthur Frommer's Budget Travel Online:** This site is the Internet companion to the famous *Frommer's Travel Guides.* Besides travel advice, you can look for hotel accommodations, nightlife, shopping, and dining opportunities in cities the world over. Address: www.frommers.com

✦ **Chowhound:** What's the best place to eat in Akron, Ohio? You can find out by running a search at this Web site. Or, go to Chowhound's message boards and post a question about a good place to eat. Address: www.chowhound.com

✦ **Citysearch.com:** This site currently offers comprehensive guides to several dozen U.S. cities and a handful of cities abroad. The guides are up to date, with detailed information about local restaurants, nightspots, clubs, and shopping. Address: www.citysearch.com

✦ **IgoUgo:** "Real travelers; honest advice" is the motto of I Go, You Go. To explore here, you have to register, but registering is worth it. The site offers 3,000 travel diaries and some 80,000 photos. Address: www.igougo.com

✦ **New York Times Travel:** Many *New York Times* readers turn first to the Travel section on Sundays to armchair travel and whet their appetite for traveling to faraway places. You can research a destination by clicking the map at this Web site. It presents travel articles from the *Times* dating back to 1996. Address: `www.nytimes.com/pages/travel/index.html`

✦ **Online City Guide:** From this site, you can pinpoint a city in the United States, find a list of hyperlinks with information about the city, and click a link to help plan your vacation. The links are to private Web sites and sometimes are not the greatest, but try your luck. Address: `www.olcg.com`

Armchair Traveling

If you can't go there in the flesh, you may as well go there in your armchair. Here are some worthy Web sites for armchair travelers:

✦ **GeoSnapper:** At this unusual Web site, travelers post photographs of their vacations. Nothing new there, except when they post each photograph, they list the latitude and longitude where it was taken, as shown in Figure 2-5. Knowing the coordinates, you could return to the very spot where these pictures were taken, if you wanted to. Address: `http://geosnapper.com`

✦ **Leonard's Worldwide Cam Directory**: A *cam* is a mounted camera that broadcasts pictures to the Internet at regular intervals. Starting at this Web site, you can find a cam to get a glimpse of a part of the world that interests you. Address: `www.leonardsworlds.com/camera.html`

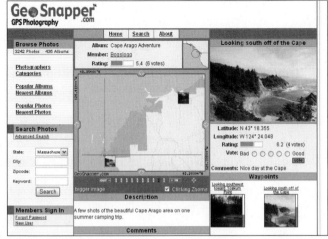

Figure 2-5:
A travel photograph at GeoSnapper.

✦ **Quiet American:** From this site, you can download one-minute recordings made in exotic locations. Says the site, "One-minute vacations are unedited recordings of somewhere, somewhen. Sixty seconds of something else. Sixty seconds to be someone else." You'll be surprised by how fascinating — and soothing — these one-minute auditory vacations are. Address: `www.quietamerican.org/vacation.html`

✦ **Ruavista:** At this Web site, you can travel in time as well as in space. This unusual site presents photos of cities taken far in the past. Last time I looked, you could stroll the streets of Moscow or Buenos Aires in the 1960s. Address: `http://ruavista.com`

✦ **Worldisround:** Traveler's post their diaries and travel photos at this excellent Web site. Search for a place and travel there vicariously. This is also a great place to research a trip. Address: `www.worldisround.com/`

Outdoor Adventuring

We are blessed in the United States with some of the most beautiful open country in the world. You are hereby invited to explore it starting from these Web sites:

✦ **The Backpacker:** Check out the hiking trail reviews on this Web site to get ideas for your next backpacking trip. You can also hook up with other backpackers from this Web site. Address: `www.thebackpacker.com`

✦ **iExplore:** For the adventurer, this is the place to search for fishing trips, kayak tours, and all manner of rugged outdoor fun. Address: `www.iexplore.com`

✦ **Info Hub:** This Web site offers numerous links to unusual travel offerings — barging, sea kayaking, and off-road adventure. You can even find ideas about where to go on a honeymoon. Address: `www.infohub.com`

✦ **National Park Service:** See maps and get information about all of America's National Parks. You can also reserve campsites online starting here. Address: `www.nps.gov`

✦ **Reserve America:** Reserve a campsite at this Web site. You can view maps of many of the campgrounds. Address: `www.reserveamerica.com`

✦ **SkiMaps:** Skiers will love this Web site. It shows three-dimensional maps of ski resorts and ski runs, as shown in Figure 2-6. You can also find a forum on which skiers discuss downhill skiing, cross-country skiing, and snowboarding. Address: `www.skimaps.com`

Figure 2-6:
A map of the Steamboat Springs ski runs and lifts.

Traveling by Rail

Traveling by rail offers the pleasures of traveling by car without the hassles. You can get up and stretch your legs. Instead of fast-food restaurants and highway clutter, the picturesque and the seedy roll past the window. Railroads cut through mountain passes and fly above wild rivers. The planet never looked as beautiful as it does from a railroad car.

Here are some Internet resources for traveling by rail:

✦ **Amtrak:** This, of course, is the United States passenger railway service. From this site, you can plan a trip by railroad and purchase tickets. Address: www.amtrak.com

✦ **European Railways:** This site offers planning tips and advice for traveling by rail in Europe. You can get information about the famous Eurail Pass as well as schedules of all European trains. Address: www.eurorailways.com

✦ **Via Rail Canada:** This is the official site of Rail Canada. Use it to purchase train tickets when traveling in the United States' winsome windswept neighbor to the north. Address: www.viarail.com

Resources for Traveling Abroad

Many people like to travel abroad. When you go to the expense and trouble of traveling, you may want to land in a place where things look different and no one speaks English. That way, you really feel like you've traveled somewhere! Here are some Internet resources for world travelers:

- ✦ **Centers for Disease Control — Traveler's Health:** This invaluable Web site offers advice for staying healthy during your vacation. It explains which vaccinations you need and presents health information about specific regions. Address: `www.cdc.gov/travel`

- ✦ **Crazy Dog Travel Guide:** This site offers tips, advice, and numerous hyperlinks to help budget travelers all over the world plan their adventures. Address: `www.crazydogtravel.com`

- ✦ **Foreign Languages for Travelers:** How do you say "excuse me" in Swedish? You say, "Ursakta," as this Web site so ably points out. What makes this site cool and useful is its sound capabilities. When you click a foreign-language phrase, the Windows Media Player comes on-screen, and you can hear the phrase. Address: `www.travlang.com/languages`

- ✦ **Lonely Planet Online:** From this superb Web site, you can research different destinations, get travel tips from others, or post a travel question that is bound to get an answer from Lonely Planet's legion of adventurers. Click the Search hyperlink to research a destination abroad or in the United States. Click the Thorn Tree hyperlink to see what others say about a destination, or post your own question about it. Address: `www.lonelyplanet.com`

- ✦ **Rough Guides:** Rough Guides are written for the kind of people who carry their belongings in a backpack as they travel. From this Web site, you can get information about traveling on the lowdown to all four corners of the world. Address: `www.roughguides.com`

- ✦ **Traveler's Telephone Search Engine:** This Web site gives you the calling-code instructions so that you can call from any nation to any other nation. To call Japan from the United States, for example, you must dial the prefix 011 81, as this Web site informs you. Address: `www.embassyworld.com/directories/global_telephone.html`

- ✦ **The Universal Currency Converter:** One United States dollar fetches how many Malaysian ringgits? The answer: 3.799 (as of this writing, anyway). Go to this easy-to-use Web site to see what happens when one currency is converted into another. Address: `www.xe.net/ucc`

- ✦ **U.S. Customs and Border Protection:** This very helpful Web site explains such matters as how to import a car and why you were charged for what you thought was a duty-free purchase. Address: `www.customs.ustreas.gov`

- ✦ **U.S. Department of State — Travel Warnings and Consular Information Sheets:** Here, you can find the visa and entry requirements that Americans must fulfill to travel to every country in the world. You can also find safety statistics, descriptions of medical facilities, and embassy addresses. Address: `http://travel.state.gov/travel/warnings.html`

World Currency Gallery

The World Currency Gallery (www.banknotes.com/images.htm) presents pictures of banknotes from the different countries of the world. Some of these banknotes are nothing short of beautiful. Scroll to the bottom of the World Currency Gallery page, click the name of a continent, and then click the name of a country to see examples of its banknotes. I was surprised to learn that Antarctica prints banknotes, and I was doubly surprised to find out how beautiful Antarctica's banknotes are.

Eccentric Sites for Eccentric Travelers

Finally, here are some eccentric sites for eccentric travelers. One of the drawbacks of getting travel information from the Internet is that much of the information was put there by corporate hotel chains that want to sell you something. These sites are devoted strictly to travel, its spontaneous joys, and its occasional apprehensions:

✦ **Bureau of Atomic Tourism:** This site is dedicated to the promotion of tourist locations worldwide that have witnessed atomic explosions or display exhibits about the development of atomic devices. It's hard to tell how far the creators of this site have thrust their tongues into their cheeks. At any rate, you can see many photos of nuclear devastation, and yes, detailed tour schedules and visitor information are available, too. Address: www.atomictourist.com

✦ **Dead Presidents:** Manus Hand, surely one of the most eccentric people on the Internet, has made it his hobby to take photographs of himself at the graves of the presidents of the United States. Writes Mr. Hand, "If you're into dead presidents (and gosh, who isn't?), you came to the right place. By simply clicking your mouse button, you can see pictures of me, Manus Hand, visiting the final resting places of every one of them (save three — I'm still working on it!)." This site is living testimony that any excuse will do when it comes to traveling. Address: `http://starship.python.net/crew/manus/Presidents`

✦ **Degree of Confluence Project:** A *confluence* is where latitude and longitude integer degrees intersect. The goal of the Degree of Confluence Project is to collect photographs from each of these intersections and, in so doing, construct a representative picture of the earth. At this Web site, you can view photographs taken at the intersections and submit photos for intersections that haven't been photographed yet. Address: `www.confluence.org`

✦ **National Caves Association:** This site is dedicated to spelunkers and their friends who enjoy exploring caves and caverns. Click the Caves & Caverns Directory link to go to the United States map. From there, you can click a state to look into its caves, caverns, and spelunking opportunities. Address: `www.cavern.com`

✦ **Roadside America:** This is unquestionably one of the very best sites on the World Wide Web. Where to begin? How about the Electronic Map. Click this link to go to a page with links to weird roadside attractions in 50 states (New Jersey, with the Uniroyal Giantess and Palace of Depression, seems to have more than its share). Check out the pet cemetery, the Travel Brain Trauma Center, or the Miraculous Virgin Mary Stump. The site is shown in Figure 2-7. Address: `www.roadsideamerica.com`

Figure 2-7: Go to Roadside America to find out where the roadside attractions are.

✦ **Robert Young Pelton's Dangerous Places:** Traveling to dangerous places can be exciting. Traveling vicariously to dangerous places can be exciting as well, as this site demonstrates. Here, you can read tales of dangerous locations and get advice for traveling to dangerous places if you feel like taking the plunge. Address: `www.comebackalive.com/df/dplaces.htm`

✦ **The Walking Connection:** Walking, if you have the time and you are in good company, is the best way to travel. This site is devoted to walking tourism. It offers a message board for walkers, news of upcoming walks, and plenty of advice about good shoes. Address: `www.walkingconnection.com`

✦ **The World Clock:** You're going to Uzbekistan and you want to arrive fit and refreshed. To do that, however, you have to put yourself on Uzbekistan time three or four days before departure. What time is it in Uzbekistan? You can find out at this Web site. Address: `www.timeanddate.com/worldclock`

Chapter 3: Let Me Entertain You

In This Chapter

✔ **Viewing made-for-the-Internet movies**

✔ **Visiting Web sites for movie fans**

✔ **Renting a DVD online**

✔ **Getting the local TV listings**

✔ **Playing Internet radio**

✔ **Finding a good book online**

*F*or many years now, pundits have predicted that the television, radio, DVD player, and computer will merge into a supersonic entertainment monster. Whether this hybrid creature will really come to pass remains to be seen. For the time being, however, you can treat your computer like an entertainment console. You can watch movies and listen to faraway radio stations by way of the Internet. This chapter explains how to do all that — or at least keep yourself occupied on a rainy day. Oh, and I also list some good sites for buying books online in case you're as old-fashioned as I am and you occasionally prefer reading a book to slaving over your computer.

Playing Internet Shorts Online

The Internet has given birth to a new movie genre that I call the "Internet short." These are short videos that were not made for the big screen or for television, but for the computer screen. Internet shorts are concise films, usually no longer than three or four minutes. Many are made at home on camcorders by amateur filmmakers. Some of the films available from these Web sites are quite remarkable for their artistic merit; others are downright goofy. If you have a broadband connection and a few minutes to spare, drop into one of these Web sites and watch an Internet short:

✦ **Albino Blacksheep:** Click the Video Files link or the Flash Files link to peruse the rather bizarre offerings at this sprawling Web site. If you look carefully, you can find many sketches from the Comedy Central network. Address: www.albinoblacksheep.com

✦ **IFilm:** Besides Internet shorts, you can find celebrities doing pratfalls, music videos, oddball commercials, movie trailers, and snippets from

Hollywood movies at this Web site. There is also a nice collection of *viral videos* — videos, usually political in nature, that people e-mail to one another. Address: `http://www.ifilm.com`

✦ **Kontraband:** You can find animations, movies, and humorous TV ads at this Web site (as well as a nice selection of games). On the Movie pages alone, you can find more than 400 different movies and sketches. Address: `www.kontraband.com`

Want to download a movie — the genuine Hollywood article — to your computer and watch it on-screen? Movielink is to movies what iTunes is to songs. You can download entire movies from Movielink and watch them, as long as you pay the fee ($1.99 to $4.99 per movie), you have a broadband connection, you have enough disk space on your computer to hold a movie (more than 120MB), and you agree to view the movie within a 24-hour period. Check out Movielink at this address: `www.movielink.com`.

Book I, Chapter 6 explains the plug-in programs that you need to watch videos and listen to Internet radio stations on your computer. It also describes how to make one program the default that starts automatically whenever you play a video or listen to the Internet radio.

Going to the Movies

Everybody loves a good movie, but these days, when you sometimes have to shell out $8 or $9 dollars for a ticket, going to the movies is a risky endeavor. Who wants to pay that much money to sit through a stinker? These pages are devoted to helping make your movie experience a better one. Here are Web sites for movie fans, sites where you can read movie reviews, and sites where you can find out what's playing in your neighborhood.

Sites for movie fans

Here are a handful of sites for people who love movies and the people who make them. Some of these sites fall in the "gossip" category. Dish the dirt, girl!

✦ **The Agony Booth:** For those times when you want to watch a bad movie, the Agony Booth is here to help. Says this Web site, "The Agony Booth is an ongoing inquisition into some of the worst movies humanity has to offer, and is not for the weak of spirit or the easily disheartened. However, if you think you have the fortitude to completely immerse yourself in a truly awful film, withstanding in-depth commentary and analysis, then the Agony Booth is the place for you." Address: `www.agonybooth.com`

✦ **Ain't It Cool:** Ain't It Cool is Harry Knowles's personal take on Hollywood and the movies. Who is Harry Knowles? Just your average rabid movie fanatic gone berserk. At this Web site, Knowles picks and pans the latest releases. He also dishes out celebrity gossip. Interestingly, this Web site started out in 1996 as a mere blog, but it has since become a highly regarded source of insider Hollywood news. Address: `www.aintitcool.com`

✦ **The Internet Movie Database:** This Web site is indispensable if you are a movie fan. Starting here, you can rummage through a vast database with, as far as I can tell, everything there is to know about the movies. Search by title, name, or character name. Or just click one of the numerous hyperlinks and see what happens. For example, you can click an actor's name to get a list of all the movies he or she was in, and by clicking a movie title, see a list of everybody who appeared in or worked on the movie. Be prepared to get pleasurably lost in the Internet Movie Database, which is shown in Figure 3-1. Address: `www.imdb.com`

Figure 3-1: The Internet Movie Database.

Book VIII Chapter 3

Let Me Entertain You

✦ **Nitpickers:** At this amusing Web site for movie and TV watchers with a discerning eye, fans point out mistakes and flubs in their favorite movies and TV shows — the car driving the wrong direction across the Bay Bridge *(The Graduate),* the Roosevelt dime appearing in 1912 *(Titanic),* the Roman soldier wearing a wristwatch *(Gladiator).* If you care to refute someone's idea of a flub, you may do so as long as you register first. Address: `www.nitpickers.com`

✦ **The Smoking Gun:** I'm not sure if The Smoking Gun is necessarily for movie fans, but more than a few actors wind up at The Smoking Gun. Besides, I had to fit The Smoking Gun into this book somehow. The Smoking Gun's motto is "Paving the Paper Trail." At this Web site, you can view public documents — court records, citations, and mug shots — that shine a very bright light on celebrities and famous people behaving badly. Address: www.thesmokinggun.com

Choosing a good movie

I'm not saying you have to agree with these movie critics, but if you are hungry for a good movie, you could do worse than look to these Web sites for a good one:

✦ **Film Critic:** At this Web site, a team of film critics, some members of the Online Film Critics Society, serve up their opinions about some 5,000 different movies from the past and the present. Films are rated on a five-star system. Address: www.filmcritic.com

✦ **Movie Review Query Engine:** This badly named Web site is quite marvelous. It's a search engine for movie titles. Enter the name of a movie you are curious about, click the Find Reviews button, and look in the search results for a critique of or essay about your movie. The "query engine" has mapped over 430,000 movie and DVD reviews. Address: www.mrqe.com

✦ **Roger Ebert.com:** Roger Ebert's movie reviews are a pleasure to read, even when you disagree with him. At this Web site, shown in Figure 3-2, the chief critic of the TV show *At the Movies* offers a database of his own movie reviews. You can search by title, people's names, genre, or rating. You can also read interviews with famous directors at this Web site. Address: www.suntimes.com/ebert

Getting your local movie listings

The best place to find local movie listings is your hometown newspaper. If its editors know anything about the 21st century, they know that publishing an online edition of the newspaper with movie listings is a great source of ad revenue. Whether your local newspaper has online movie listings, you can find listings for your area at these Web sites:

✦ **MSN Entertainment Movie Listings:** Enter your zip code or the name of the city where you live and click the Go button to get local movie listings. By clicking the Buy Tickets button and brandishing your credit card, you can purchase movie tickets through this Web site. Address: http://movies.msn.com

✦ **Moviefone:** Select the Zip or City option button and, in the Movie Search text box, enter your zip code or the city were you live and click the Go button. You'll get a list of local theaters and the movies that are playing in each one. Address: http://movies.channel.aol.com

Figure 3-2:
Movie
reviews
from the
great Roger
Ebert.

Renting DVDs over the Internet

For a subscription rate of about $18 per month, you can rent DVDs over the Internet. The DVDs are sent to you in the mail, and you return them by mail. If $18 per month for renting DVDs seems expensive to you, consider how much most people pay each month in late fees to their local video rental store. Industry studies show that one-third of the income movie rental companies make comes from late fees. The advantage of renting DVDs over the Internet is never having to pay late fees. And you don't have to pay postage for sending the DVDs back, either. When the DVD arrives, it comes with a self-addressed stamped envelope. All you have to do is pop the DVD in the envelope and put it in the mail when you are finished viewing it. You order the DVDs online.

Table 3-1 lists companies that rent DVDs over the Internet. These companies offer many more videos than can be found in a video rental store. From my point of view, that's the advantage of renting DVDs over the Net. I have exhausted the video rental stores in my neighborhood, and it's not necessarily the stores' fault. It would be impossible for the locals to satisfy my hunger for westerns and obscure *film noir* movies. I have to go on the Internet to satisfy my craving.

Table 3-1	Online DVD Rental Companies	
Company	*Web Address*	*Cost*
Amazon	www.amazon.com	As of this writing, Amazon has announced it will rent DVDs, but the company has not announced rental prices.
Blockbuster	www.blockbuster.com	Rent three videos at any given time for a $17.50-per-month flat rate.
netflix	www.netflix.com	Rent three videos at any given time for an $18-per-month flat rate.
Wal-Mart	www.walmart.com	Rent two videos at any given time for a $15.54-per-month flat rate; three for $17.36; or four for $21.94.

DVD Price Search (www.dvdpricesearch.com) is a comparison-shopping search engine for finding inexpensive DVDs at Internet stores. Search for a title, and when you find it, click the Check Prices link to see how much different online stores charge for the DVD.

Getting Your Local TV Listings

I'm sure you've heard it said before: There are five hundred TV channels, but nothing's on. Actually, one or two shows are usually worth watching on television's 500 channels. These Web sites can help you find the one or two:

✦ **MSN Entertainment TV Listings:** Enter your zip code, click the Go button, and declare whether you want antenna, cable, or satellite listings for your area. This fast, sleek, well-designed Web site is a big improvement over *TV Guide.* Address: http://tv.msn.com

✦ **SpoilerFix:** Want to know what happens next week on your favorite TV show? This Web site is for people who simply can't wait till next week and have to know *right now.* It spoils a dozen different TV shows, and you've been warned: Visiting SpoilerFix removes much of the suspense from watching TV. Address: www.spoilerfix.com

✦ **Television without Pity:** At this aptly named Web site, critics skewer reality shows and TV dramas, all in the name of good fun, mind you. Address: www.televisionwithoutpity.com

✦ **TV Guide:** This is the online version of *TV Guide,* the bestselling magazine in the United States. You have to register to look up TV listings at this Web site. Click the name of a TV show to read its description on the left side of the screen, as shown in Figure 3-3. Unfortunately, this site is run by a very slow Java applet, although it is thorough. A faster way to look up TV listings is to go to MSN Entertainment TV. Address: www.tvguide.com

Figure 3-3:
TV Guide
Online.

✦ **TV Tome:** This Web site is an all-volunteer attempt to document and describe every TV show that ever appeared on American television, from the *Donna Reed Show* to *The Mod Squad* to *Everybody Loves Raymond.* Not all the shows have been "adopted" by a volunteer yet, so you can't get information about all of them, but for the majority of shows, you can find out basic facts, such as when they aired and who starred. Some shows offer an "episode list," with detailed descriptions of each episode. Address: www.tvtome.com

Listening to Internet Radio

I can't imagine anything more cosmopolitan than Internet radio. You can listen to broadcasts from Borneo to Bogotá. Because the cost of broadcasting is considerably less than broadcasting a traditional radio show, producers can devise shows for narrow-range audiences. You may be able to find an Internet radio show devoted to your favorite music genre or your favorite pastime, no matter how obscure it is. Some radio stations only broadcast on the Internet. The number of Internet radio broadcasts is likely to grow in the coming years because of advances in cell phone technology. For now, you can only listen to the Internet radio while sitting at your computer, but soon, cell phones will be able to get Internet radio. You will be able to listen to Internet radio in your car. Maybe we are about to witness a rebirth of interest in the radio — another Radio Golden Age.

**Book VIII
Chapter 3**

**Let Me
Entertain You**

One way to play Internet radio is to go to a radio station's Web site, click the Play link (or whatever it's called), and start listening. The other way is to keep track of the radio stations you know and love with an audio player, a computer program capable of playing Internet radio, and play music from there. Better read on.

Finding an Internet radio station

After you find an Internet radio station and go to its Web site, you can find a link of some kind that you can click to start receiving the broadcast. Use these Web sites to find Internet radio stations:

✦ **Live 365.com:** Click the Listen tab to search by genre or review the editors' picks of the best online radio stations. For $3.95 a month, you can buy a VIP membership and listen to stations without being bothered by commercials. Address: www.live365.com

✦ **MSN Radio:** Click the name of a radio station on the list to start receiving it. Names that are grayed out are only available by subscription. Subscribing to MSN Radio costs $29.99 per year or $4.99 per month. Address: http://radio.msn.com

✦ **Radio Free Virgin:** Click the Listen tab and then the Channel Guide to see a list of 60 online music stations. Click a Listen Now link to start listening to a station. Address: www.radiofreevirgin.com

✦ **Radio-Locator:** Under "Find Internet Streaming Audio," select a format or a country and click the Go link, as shown in Figure 3-4. You see a list of radio stations. Stations with a lightning bolt next to their names offer online broadcasting. Address: www.radio-locator.com

✦ **Radio Lovers:** Now this is my idea of an interesting radio station. From here, you can listen for free to old radio shows — Dick Tracy, Hopalong Cassidy, Al Jolson, Buck Rogers, Flash Gordon, and others. Address: www.radiolovers.com

✦ **ShoutCast:** Click the Listen tab to see the list of online radio stations. What makes this Web site a little out of the ordinary is being able to search not only by genre but also by bit rate. High-quality online radio stations broadcast at 128 Kbps or higher. You can find those stations at this Web site. Address: www.shoutcast.com

✦ **Web Radio Directory:** Search for radio stations by call letters, format, state, or country. Address: www.radio-directory.fm/it_list.cfm

Be sure to bookmark the Web site of a radio station you like so that you can visit it later. Finding a station all over again can be a difficult task unless you bookmark it the first time around. Book II, Chapter 1 explains bookmarking.

**Book VIII
Chapter 3**

Let Me
Entertain You

Figure 3-4:
Find a radio
station at
Radio-
Locator.

Receiving an Internet radio station

To listen to the Internet radio, you need a program that's capable of playing
streaming audio. *Streaming* means that you don't download a file to listen to
audio, but you listen as the audio arrives in your audio player. Table 3-2 lists
audio players that are capable of receiving and playing Internet radio stations. All of these audio players are free.

Table 3-2	Programs That Play the Internet Radio
Audio Player	*Web Site*
Musicmatch Jukebox (Musicmatch)	www.musicmatch.com
QuickTime (Apple)	www.apple.com/quicktime
RealPlayer (RealNetworks)	www.real.com
Winamp (Nullsoft)	www.winamp.com
Windows Media Player (Microsoft)	www.microsoft.com/windows/ windowsmedia/default.aspx

Introducing Windows Media Player

If your computer runs Windows, you already have a very good audio player —
Windows Media Player, shown in Figure 3-5. This program is superb for listen-
ing to the Internet radio. Searching for stations and bookmarking your favorite
radio stations in Windows Media Player is pretty simple. The program is also a
CD player, MP3 player, and CD burner. Use one of these methods to open
Windows Media Player:

✦ Click the Windows Media Player icon on the Quick Launch toolbar.

✦ Choose Start⇨All Programs⇨Accessories⇨Entertainment⇨Windows
   Media Player.

Click the Radio tab to listen to the Internet radio. Here are the basics of listening to the Internet radio with Windows Media Player:

✦ **Searching for a station:** Either search by category or enter a search term
   in the Radio Search text box and click the Go button. You see a list of
   radio stations brought to you by MSN Radio (http://radio.msn.com).
   Click a radio station name to start receiving the station. Radio station
   names that are grayed out are only available if you subscribe to MSN
   Radio (subscriptions cost $29.99 for a year or $4.99 for a month).

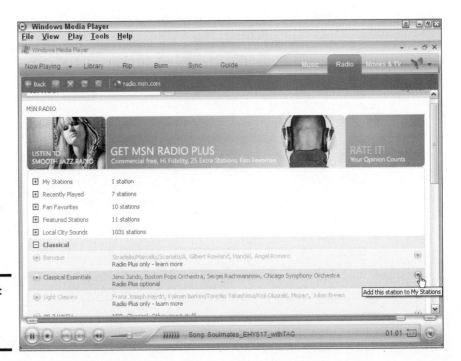

Figure 3-5:
Windows
Media
Player.

✦ **Controls:** Controls for playing the radio are found at the bottom of the window. These controls work like the ones on a tape player or video player. Click the Stop button, for example, to turn off the radio. Click the Play button to resume playing songs.

✦ **Bookmarking stations:** If you have a .NET passport (see Appendix B), you can bookmark stations in Windows Media Player and be able to revisit them easily. Click the Radio tab and then the Sign In link to sign in with your .NET passport. Click the Add This Station to My Stations button (refer to Figure 3-5) to place a station's name on your My Stations list. This list is found at the top of the station categories.

Finding Books Online

Books? Why, I remember them. Big bundles of paper all bound together. You read them, right? You curl up in bed with one. Or you take one to the beach for some "summer reading." In case you enjoy the old-fashioned pleasures of reading, Table 3-3 lists Web sites that specialize in selling books and search engines that are designed especially for searching for books on the Internet. Table 3-4 lists Web sites that offer books online; you can either read these books on-screen or download them to your computer.

Table 3-3	Online Booksellers and Book Search Engines	
Web Site	*Address*	*Notes*
Abe Books	www.abebooks.com	Specializes in rare and out-of-print books.
Add All	www.addall.com/used	Search engine for used and out-of-print books.
AKA Book	www.akabook.com	Excellent comparison-shopping search engine for books.
Alibris	www.alibris.com	Largest seller of used books (as well as videos and CDs) on the Internet.
All Search Engines	www.allsearchengines.com/books.html	Lists search engines that specialize in finding books.
Amazon	www.amazon.com	The granddaddy of booksellers, useful for its online book reviews.
Barnes and Noble	www.bn.com	Specializes in new books; easiest bookseller site to navigate.
Best Book Buys	www.bestwebbuys.com/books	Search engine for used books on the Internet. Click the Compare Prices button to find copies of a book at different prices.

Book VIII
Chapter 3

Let Me
Entertain You

(continued)

Table 3-3 *(continued)*

Web Site	Address	Notes
Book Finder	www.bookfinder.com	Search engine for used books for sale at different Web sites.
Which Book?	www.whichbook.net	Get a book recommendation by choosing adjectives that describe what kind of book you want to read.

Table 3-4   **Web Sites That Offer Online Books**

Web Site	Address	Notes
Bartleby	www.bartelby.com	Literature, reference books, and verse that you can read online.
Blackmask	www.blackmask.com	Books in many different categories that you can download for free.
Magazine Boy	www.themagazineboy.com	Search for magazines that you can read online.
Online Books Page	http://digital.library.upenn.edu/books	Provides links to books that you can download or read online for free.
Project Guttenberg	http://promo.net/pg	Offers 6,000 classic books that you can download for free.

Regarding the online booksellers listed in Table 3-3: Most of these sellers don't keep books in their inventories. They merely list used books that other booksellers have. When you order a book, the word goes out to the bookseller who actually has the book, and that bookseller sends the book to you. Some booksellers, however, don't keep their inventories up to date, and sometimes the book you ordered has already been sold.

Chapter 4: The Internet for Music Lovers

In This Chapter

✔ Exploring Web sites for music lovers

✔ Buying songs from online music stores

✔ Trading music files with others on the Internet

*W*ho isn't a music lover? Music soothes the soul and tames the savage beasts. This chapter is devoted to Web sites and Internet services for music lovers. Read on to discover Web sites for music lovers, find online stores where you can buy music files, and get instructions for trading music files online with others over the Internet. (The previous chapter explains how to listen to Internet radio.)

Web Sites for Music Lovers

Any collection of Web sites for music lovers is bound to reflect the tastes of the person who put the collection together. My apologies if your favorite Web site didn't make it in my collection. If you know of a good Web site devoted to music, I would like to know about it, too. Please e-mail me at weverka@sbcglobal.net with the name of the Web site. If you're a music lover, check out the following Web sites:

✦ **All Music:** Go to All Music to read about your favorite singers and musicians. As shown in Figure 4-1, you can find biographical information, discographies, and song lists at this Web site. Address: www.allmusic.com

✦ **Country Music Hall of Fame:** I know that country music isn't to everyone's taste, but if it's to yours, check out the Country Music Hall of Fame. You can read about inductees and view online exhibits. Plus, the Web site plays snippets of country music songs just for you. Address: www.countrymusichalloffame.com

✦ **Gramophone:** This site bills itself as "The Classic Music Web Site." You will find CD reviews, articles, and composer biographies, all well written and researched. Address: www.gramophone.co.uk

Figure 4-1:
Checking up
on Little
Walter at All
Music.

✦ **KissThisGuy – The Archive of Misheard Lyrics:** In his song "Purple Haze," did Jimi Hendrix sing, "Excuse me while I kiss the sky" or "Excuse me while I kiss this guy"? You can find out at this Web site, which offers numerous funny examples of misheard song lyrics. By the way, misheard song and poetry lyrics are called *mondegreens*. The expression originated with a British writer who misheard the last lines of a poem called "The Bonny Earl of Murray." The real lines are *They ha'e slain the Earl of Murray, and they laid him on the Green,* but she heard *They ha'e slain the Earl of Murray, and Lady Mondegreen.* Address: www.kissthisguy.com

✦ **Oddmusic:** Do you know what an Aeolian wind harp sounds like? How about a beer bottle organ? You can find out at this Web site by going to the Oddmusic Gallery and clicking the speaker icon next to an instrument's name. Click the name itself to find out the history of the instrument. Address: http://oddmusic.com

✦ **Wilson & Allroy's Record Reviews:** David Wilson and John Allroy are a couple of opinionated but also very witty music reviewers. They focus mostly on rock and roll from the '60s, '70s, and '80s. If you're looking to explore new musical territory, you could do worse than check out this site. Address: www.warr.org

✦ **WWW Sites of Interests to Musicologists:** I stumbled upon this eccentric Web page one day and couldn't believe my good luck. It has hyperlinks to hundreds of Web sites of interest to the people who study music. Some of the items on this list are downright bizarre — for example, The Gregorian Chant Page, Hurdy-Gurdy: A Brief History, and The Lute Society of America. Address: `www.sas.upenn.edu/music/ams/ musicology_www.html`

Buying Music Online

It appears that buying music online, not downloading it for free (a subject taken up later in this chapter), is really catching on. The Apple iTunes online music store has proved to be a resounding success. Music lovers like knowing that a song they are getting online is the real thing. At 99 cents a pop, the songs are relatively inexpensive. And many online music stores offer special software that you can use to play and organize the songs you purchase. The software includes commands for burning songs to a CD and loading songs onto an iPod or other portable music player.

Table 4-1 describes online music stores. At all these stores, you can preview a song before you buy it. My favorite store is Apple iTunes. In fact, I like this store and its iTunes music player so much, I devote an entire chapter to it — the next chapter of this mini-book. In my opinion, being able to play and organize the songs you buy from an online music store with software from the store is a big plus. It makes downloading the songs and playing the songs — not to mention burning CDs or loading songs onto a portable music player — that much easier.

Table 4-1	Online Music Stores	
Site	*Web Address*	*Notes*
Apple iTunes	`www.apple.com/itunes`	Songs cost 99 cents; albums $9.99. Offers 700,000 songs. Includes the superb iTunes software program for playing and organizing songs, as well as burning CDs. Although the store is managed by Apple, its iTunes software is also available for PC users. (iTunes is the subject of the next chapter in this minibook.)
BuyMusic	`www.buymusic.com`	Songs cost 79 cents to $1.14; albums, $7.95 to $12.95. Does not include software for playing and organizing songs.

(continued)

Book VIII Chapter 4

The Internet for Music Lovers

Table 4-1 *(continued)*

Site	Web Address	Notes
Connect	http://musicstore.connect.com	Songs cost 99 cents. Includes the Connect Player for playing and organizing songs, as well as burning CDs.
MSN Music	http://music.msn.com	Songs cost 99 cents. You can play songs on Windows Media Player, but this software is unstable and is not the best, either for organizing songs or burning CDs.
Musicmatch	www.musicmatch.com	Songs are 99 cents; albums $9.99. You can download the MusicMatch Jukebox, a software program for playing and organizing songs.
MusicNow	www.musicnow.com	Songs cost 99 cents; for a $9.95 monthly fee, you can listen to complete songs and albums before buying. Does not include software for playing and organizing songs.
Napster 2.0	www.napster.com	Songs cost 99 cents; albums $9.99. Does not include software for playing and organizing songs.
Rhapsody	www.listen.com	Songs cost 79 cents; for a $9.95 monthly fee, you can listen to complete songs and albums before buying. Includes the Celestial Jukebox for playing and organizing songs, as well as burning CDs.
Wal-Mart	http://musicdownloads.walmart.com	Songs cost 89 cents; albums $9.44. Only offers 300,000 songs, half the number of other stores. Does not include software for playing and organizing songs.

Trading Free Music Files on the Internet

Table 4-2 describes programs for trading files on the Internet. Most of these programs are used for trading MP3 music files, although movies, images, games, and computer programs are being shared with increasing regularity. To share files with one of these programs, you download the program to your computer, sign in to a network of file sharers, and search the network for the song you're looking for. The majority of file-sharing programs plug into one of these four networks: eDonkey, FastTrack, Warez, or Gnutella. When you find a song or file you want, you download it to your computer from the network. Meanwhile, others on the network can download songs and files on your computer to their computers.

Table 4-2	File-Sharing Programs	
Program	*Web Address*	*Notes*
Bearshare	www.bearshare.com	Connects users to the Gnutella network.
eDonkey	www.edonkey.com	Now the most popular file-sharing software with 230 million downloads.
EMule	www.emule-project.net	An open-source software product that connects users to the eDonkey network.
Gnucleus	www.gnucleus.com	An open-source software product for accessing the Gnutella network.
Gnutella	www.gnutella.com, www.gnutelliums.com	An open-source file-sharing software product; the parent network of Bearshare, Limewire, and others.
Kazaa	www.kazaa.com	This is the second-most popular software for online file trading; 215 million people have downloaded it.
Kazaa Lite	www.kazaalite.nl/en	Kazaa without the spyware; this software is not authorized by Kazaa.
Limewire	www.limewire.com	A software product that connects users to the Gnutella network.
Shareaza	www.shareaza.com	Searching multiple networks, this open-source client lets you preview songs as you download them (refer to Figure 4-2).
Warez P2P	www.warezclient.com	The fastest-growing file-sharing network.
Xolox	www.xolox.com	Another Gnutella client.

Figure 4-2 shows the Search window in Shareaza. The important thing to note when you search for files is the number of sources — the number of computers on the network where the file you want to download resides. Files download faster when many sources are available. Shareaza is typical in that it gives you the opportunity to search by file type (audio, video, games, computer programs, or images). When you see a file you want to download, you select it and click the Download button. Like most file-sharing programs, Shareaza has a media player for playing the files you downloaded.

The first file-sharing program was Napster. This program revolutionized the Internet in the late 1990s. All of the sudden, millions of people around the world were exchanging MP3 music files with Napster. Obscure songs that were well-nigh impossible to find at the local music store could be plucked for the taking off the Internet. Not-so-obscure songs could be acquired for free as well. From the perspective of music lovers, it was too good to be true, but music-industry executives grumbled because CD sales started falling. Musicians and songwriters complained as well, because they weren't being compensated for their recordings. The Recording Industry Association of America (RIAA) hit Napster with a series of lawsuits that ran the company out of business (it has since been revived as a legitimate seller of online music).

Napster was a registered company, with headquarters in California's Silicon Valley, but the next generation of file-sharing software manufacturers did not have headquarters. Morpheus, Kazaa, Grokster, and the others were managed from small offices throughout the world. These companies weren't registered in any country or state. They used peer-to-peer technology (more about that in a minute) so that the sharing of files wasn't managed from a central point, but was managed all across the network of file sharers. The decentralized structure of second-generation file-sharing was such that the RIAA couldn't sue the companies who manufactured the software. It had no company to sue, so the RIAA did the next best thing — it sued registered users of Kazaa for sharing copyrighted songs. "Our goal is not to be vindictive or punitive," RIAA President Cary Sherman said in 2003 when the RIAA issued lawsuits against 216 Kazaa users. "It is simply to get peer-to-peer users to stop offering music that does not belong to them."

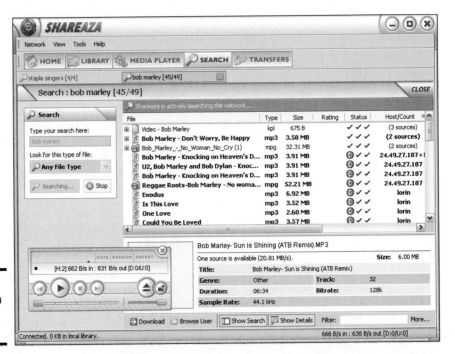

Figure 4-2:
The Search window in Shareaza.

In peer-to-peer (P2P) file sharing, files are stored on users' computers, and no central computer manages the sharing of files. In effect, each member's computer is a "mini-server," with music files for all the members. As members sign in to the service, the service records the names of music files stored on their computers. When a member asks for a music file, the service merely points to where it's located on members' computers. What's more, to make downloading go faster, a music file can be cobbled together from files on different computers. For example, if I ask for "Battle Hymn of the Republic" and the service tells me that the same "Battle Hymn of the Republic" file is on five members' computers, I can download the file from all five computers simultaneously and get the file that much faster. And because files are broken into tiny pieces and reassembled as they are shared, my computer can distribute a file at the same time as it downloads the file, which makes for faster file sharing.

No one can say for certain how much the RIAA lawsuits slowed file sharing on the Internet, but file sharing has been slowed. I suspect that the real reason for the slowdown has to do with spyware and the fact that the legitimate online music stores do such a good job of delivering music files. Most file-sharing software contains harmful spyware. Kazaa, the second most popular file-sharing program, with 215 million users, is notorious in this regard. In November 2004, Computer Associates International, an Internet security company, officially declared Kazaa a spyware program, not a file-sharing program! Computer Associates International put Kazaa at the head of its Top 5 list of spyware threats. Install Kazaa on your computer and you will notice your computer slowing down almost immediately, as your computer devotes processing time to spying on you and reporting back to spyware manufacturers. Figure 4-3 shows the Kazaa home page. (Computer Associates International maintains a Spyware Information Center at this address: www3.ca.com/securityadvisor/pest).

Another drawback of file-sharing services is the quality of the music files. You never know what you've downloaded until it arrives on your computer and you play it. Music companies have been known to flood peer-to-peer file-sharing networks with inferior, purposefully damaged files. Many files are incomplete or of low quality. Sometimes the file you think you're getting turns out to be something else altogether.

As to copyright issues, and speaking as someone who makes part of his living from book royalties, I think it's dishonest to skirt the copyright issue and claim that file-sharing doesn't violate the copyright laws. Songwriters and performers own the songs being shared. They are entitled to royalties for their creative work. The people who make their living by earning income or collecting royalties from the sale of music and video being copied on the Internet deserve our consideration and respect.

Book VIII
Chapter 4

The Internet for
Music Lovers

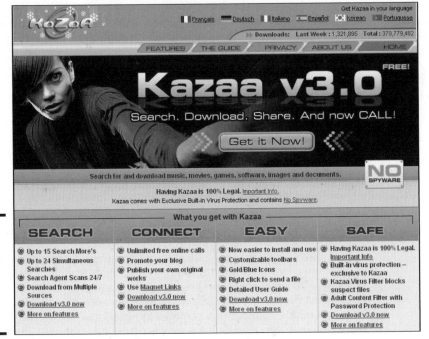

Figure 4-3:
Kazaa the
Notorious.
Disregard
the "No
Spyware"
claim.

Why not download music legally with iTunes or another service? You can listen to 15 or 20 seconds of a song before you download it. The files you get are sure to be of high quality. You can rest assured that you are not inviting spyware into your computer. The musicians and songwriters receive their royalties. All things considered, the cost of downloading songs from iTunes or another online music seller isn't very great. It costs a dollar to play a song on a jukebox these days. For 99 cents, you can download a song from iTunes, play it over and over, and burn it to a CD. That's a bargain, I think.

Slyck News, a Web site devoted to file sharing and file-sharing programs, offers the latest news, fix-its, and rankings for fans of file sharing on the Internet. You can visit Slyck News at this address: www.slyck.com.

Chapter 5: Buying and Playing Music with iTunes

In This Chapter

✔ Getting acquainted with iTunes

✔ Downloading iTunes software to your computer

✔ Purchasing songs from the Apple Music Store

✔ Playing songs in iTunes

✔ Organizing songs in the Library

✔ Adding songs you didn't purchase from Apple to the Library

✔ Burning a CD with your favorite songs

*I*f Academy Awards were given out for software, I would nominate iTunes for Software of the Year. The program is easy to use. You can buy songs from the Apple Music Store with the software as well as play songs, burn CDs, and organize your music collection. You can even play online radio and copy songs from CDs to your computer. All these pleasurable tasks are described in this chapter.

iTunes is free. Although iTunes is made by Apple Corporation, Windows users are invited to the party, too. Apple makes a version of iTunes for Macintosh computers and Windows computers. iTunes does not work with Windows 98 software; you must have Windows XP or 2000.

Introducing iTunes

iTunes is a software program that serves many purposes. Use it to buy music files from the Apple iTunes online music store. Rather than open a browser and find your way to the store, open iTunes and search the store's 700,000 songs with the iTunes program. Songs cost 99 cents each. After you buy songs, you can play them with iTunes. For that matter, you can play songs you didn't buy from the Apple Music Store. You can burn a CD and download music to an iPod with iTunes. You can arrange your songs into playlists to make locating and playing songs easier. You can copy songs from CDs you own to your computer. You can even listen to Internet radio with iTunes.

Figure 5-1 shows the iTunes window in Library view. This view is for locating and organizing songs in your music library so that you can play songs. Notice the Source box on the left side of the window. By clicking items in the Source box, you can do different things in iTunes:

✦ **Library:** Locate songs you want to play or collect in a playlist. A *playlist* is a collection of songs you gather so that you can play them more easily or burn them to a CD.

Figure 5-1:
The iTunes window in Library view.

✦ **Party Shuffle:** Play songs at random. On the Source menu, choose where to get the songs — from a playlist or the Library, for example.

✦ **Radio:** Find and play an online radio station.

✦ **My Top Rated:** List songs by rating. To rate a song, right-click its name, choose Rating, and choose a rating.

✦ **Recently Played:** List the last three dozen songs you played.

✦ **Top 25 Most Played:** List the 25 songs you play most often — in other words, your favorite songs.

✦ **Playlists:** Display a list of songs you collected and named.

If you prefer not to have the Party Shuffle and Radio items in the Source box, choose Edit➪Preferences and, on the General tab of the iTunes dialog box, deselect the Party Shuffle and Radio check boxes. Choose Large on the Source Text drop-down menu if you want to make the text bigger in the Source box.

To remove the artwork at the bottom of the Source box and get more room for playlist names, click the Show or Hide Song Artwork button.

Downloading iTunes Software

The first step in running iTunes is to download the software. Download iTunes starting at this Web page:

```
www.apple.com/itunes/download
```

Downloading the software costs nothing. Well, if you have a slow Internet connection, it costs a certain amount of time. At 20MB, the installation file is fairly large.

During the installation, you are asked whether you want iTunes to be the default player for audio files and QuickTime to be the default player for video files (QuickTime is installed on your computer as part of the iTunes installation). What this question really asks is, "Do you want iTunes to play music files automatically or QuickTime to play video files automatically when you open a music or video file on the Internet or on your computer?" Maybe you prefer to watch videos with Windows Media Player. If so, deselect the Use QuickTime as the Default Player for Media Files check box. I suggest leaving the Use iTunes as the Default Player for Audio Files check box intact. iTunes is the best program for playing audio files that I know of.

To tell your computer which program to open a file with by default, find an example of the file in Windows Explorer or My Computer, right-click the file, and choose Open With➪Choose Program. In the Open With dialog box, select the name of the program that you want to open the file type automatically. Then select the Always Use the Selected Program to Open This Kind of File check box and click OK.

Buying Songs from the Apple Music Store

Songs cost 99 cents at the Apple Music Store, and you have some 700,000 songs to choose from. The songs you buy can be copied and played on three computers besides the one to which you download a song from the music store. Them's the rules. (If you want to copy a song to a fifth computer, connect to the Internet and deauthorize one of your computers by choosing Advanced➪Deauthorize Computer.) These pages explain how to purchase songs from the Apple Music Store and how to register your credit card with the store so that you can purchase songs.

To get to the Apple Music Store, open iTunes and click the Music Store item in the Source box, as shown in Figure 5-2.

Figure 5-2:
Visiting the
Apple
Music
Store.

Starting an account with Apple

The first time you visit the Apple Music Store online and attempt to purchase a song, you are asked to create an account. Creating an account entails entering your e-mail address, entering your name, choosing a password, and entering your credit card number. Your credit card is billed 99 cents each time you buy a song. To create an account at any time, click the Sign In button and click the Create New Account button in the iTunes dialog box. Instead of an account name, you are identified by the e-mail address you give Apple. It appears in the upper-right corner of the window (refer to 5-2).

Searching for a song to buy

Here are the different ways to search for that special song you used to dance to in your flowering youth:

+ **Searching by keyword:** In the Search Music Store text box, as shown in Figure 5-3, enter an artist's or composer's name, the name of a song, or the name of an album, and press Enter. You see a list of song titles that match your search criteria.

+ **Conducting a more-thorough keyword search:** Open the drop-down menu in the Search Music Store text box and choose a category to search in, as shown in Figure 5-3. Choose Power Search to look in several categories — Song, Artist, Album, Genre, and Composer — at once.

+ **Searching for songs in record albums:** Click the Browse Music link (refer to Figure 5-2) and select a genre, an artist, and an album to see a list of songs in the album.

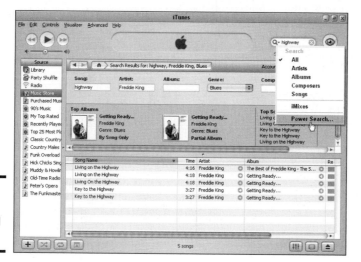

Figure 5-3:
Searching
by keyword
for a song.

As you go from place to place in the Music Store, you can retrace your steps by clicking the browser buttons — Back, Forward, and Home (refer to Figure 5-2). These buttons work exactly like the buttons in a Web browser. Clicking the Home button takes you to the home page of the Apple Music Store.

Buying a song

Before you buy a song, preview it. Listen to a few bars and decide whether you like it. To preview a song, double-click its name in a song list. Previews last about 30 seconds.

To buy a song, click the Buy Song button (you may have to scroll to the right to see it). A dialog box appears so that you can enter your password. Enter it and click the Buy button. The song is downloaded to your computer.

Here are a few things worth knowing about buying songs:

✦ Click the Purchased Music item in the Source box to see a list of songs you purchased from the Apple Music Store.

✦ Instead of buying songs one at a time, you can buy them in bunches. Choose Edit⇨Preferences, select the Store tab in the iTunes dialog box, and select the Buy Using a Shopping Cart option button. To see a list of all the songs in your shopping cart, choose Advanced⇨Check for Purchased Music.

Book VIII
Chapter 5

Buying and Playing
Music with iTunes

✦ On your computer, songs you purchase land in subfolders of this folder: `C:\Documents and Settings\`*Your Name*`\My Documents\My Music\ iTunes\iTunes Music`. In that folder, songs are filed away even deeper by artist name and album name. If you prefer to keep incoming files in a more convenient folder, choose Edit⇨Preferences, select the Advanced tab in the iTunes dialog box, and click the Change button to select a different folder.

Playing Songs

To play a song, double-click its name in the song list. You can tell which song is playing because the Play icon appears beside its name. As shown in Figure 5-4, use the controls along the top of the screen to pause or play the song, play the previous or next song on the song list, change the volume, rewind, or fast-forward.

Figure 5-4:
Controls for playing songs.

You can also take advantage of these commands to make your listening experience more pleasurable:

✦ **Shuffling:** Shuffling plays the songs on the song list in random order. Click the Turn Shuffle On or Off button, or choose Controls⇨Shuffle to shuffle songs on the list.

✦ **Repeating songs:** Choose a Controls⇨Repeat command to repeat the song list when it has finished playing (Repeat All), repeat the song that is currently playing (Repeat One), or stop playing songs when the song list has played through (Repeat Off). You can also give these commands by successively clicking the Repeat button.

✦ **Experimenting with sound distribution:** Click the Open the Equalizer Window button to see the Equalizer, shown in Figure 5-5. By dragging the sliders or choosing an option from the menu, you can experiment with how sound is distributed between the treble and bass register in the songs you play.

✦ **Watching the visual fireworks display:** Click the Turn Full Screen Visual Effects On button if you are easily entertained by computerized visual effects displayed to the accompaniment of music. Press Esc or click the screen to see the song list again.

Making sure the song information is correct

The song list tells you each song's name, the artist who performs it, the name of the album it is found on, and its genre, among other things. But sometimes this information isn't correct. You may decide that a song has been placed in the wrong genre. Especially if you acquired the song from a source apart from the Apple Music Store, the artist and title may be wrong.

To change the information by which a song is categorized in the Library, select the song and press Ctrl+I or right-click and choose Get Info. A dialog box named after the song appears. On the Info tab, enter the correct name, artist, composer, and genre. If you own a lot of songs, making sure this information is accurate is essential for finding songs in the Library.

Figure 5-5:
The
Equalizer.

TIP

Song lists tell you the name of each song, its length, the artist's name, the album name, and when you last played the song, among other things. To decide what appears on a song list, choose Edit⊅View Options (or press Ctrl+J) and make selections in the View Options dialog box. You can sort, or rearrange, songs in a list by clicking a column heading. For example, clicking the Artist column heading arranges the song list in alphabetical order by artist name.

Organizing Your Songs with Playlists and the Library

How do you find a song you want to listen to? Start by clicking the Library item in the Source box. The Library lists all the songs you purchased from the Apple Music Store and well as songs you imported into iTunes (see "Adding songs you didn't get from Apple to the Library," later in this chapter). Starting in the Library window, iTunes offers several different ways to organize songs so that you can find them quickly:

+ **The Library:** Click an artist's name in the Artist list, and you see only songs by the artist whose name you clicked. By clicking an album name as well, you see songs from one album.

You can make Genre another category for arranging songs in the Library (refer to Figure 5-1). Choose Edit⇨Preferences and, on the General tab of the iTunes dialog box, select the Show Genre When Browsing check box.

+ **Playlists:** Playlists are the best way to organize music. To see the songs in a playlist, click the playlist's name in the Source box. To burn a CD, you must create a playlist first with the songs you want to burn (see "Burning a CD," later in this chapter). Create playlists for your favorite songs in different categories. You give a playlist a name when you create it. iTunes offers two ways to create a playlist:

  • **Drag songs to the list:** Choose File⇨New Playlist (or press Ctrl+N) and type a name for the playlist in the Source box. Then drag the names of songs you want for the list onto the playlist name.

  • **Select the songs first:** Select the songs by Ctrl+clicking their names and choose File⇨Create Playlist from Selection. Then type a name for the playlist in the Source box.

+ **Smart Playlists:** A *smart playlist* is one that iTunes creates for you based on parameters you choose. Choose File⇨New Smart Playlist. In the Smart Playlist dialog box, describe which songs you want for the playlist. The list is named after the words you enter in the text box. To change a smart playlist, right-click its name and choose Edit Smart Playlist. The Smart Playlist dialog box opens so that you can change parameters.

+ **The Search text box:** Enter a keyword in the Search text box in the upper-right corner of the window. Entering the word *blue,* for example, brings up a list of all songs with that word in their title.

To delete a playlist, right-click its name in the Source box and choose Clear. Deleting a playlist in no way, shape, or form deletes any song files from your computer. You merely remove the playlist from the Source box. To remove a song from a playlist, select it and press the Delete key. The song is removed from the list, not deleted from your computer.

Adding Your Own Songs to Your iTunes Collection

You can make iTunes the means of organizing your entire music collection, not just the songs you bought online from the Apple Music Store. Perhaps you have MP3 files you got from other sources and you want to be able to find and play them with the iTunes software. Or, you want to copy songs from CDs you own to your computer and play them there. Better read on.

Copying songs from your CD collection

Copying a song from a CD to a computer is called *ripping* a song. Why ripping? I don't know. Maybe the person who invented the term was feeling macho that day. Maybe he was the kind of guy who likes to rip telephone books in half. At any rate, the first step in ripping a song from a CD is to choose how to encode the song files as you take them from your CD. Choose Edit⇨Preferences and, on the Importing tab of the iTunes dialog box, select an Import Using Option:

- ✦ **AAC Encoder:** This is high-quality format is native to songs you get from the Apple Music Store. Only Apple supports this format. MP3 players apart from the iPod can't play AAC-encoded songs.

- ✦ **AIFF Encoder:** This is the standard for sound on Macintosh computers. Choose this one only if you have a Macintosh computer.

- ✦ **Apple Lossless Encoder:** Another standard for the Macintosh, this format features slightly higher sound quality than AIFF.

- ✦ **MP3 Encoder:** MP3 is the most widely supported standard, but not the highest-quality standard. This option is recommended for Windows computers and portable music players other than the iPod.

- ✦ **WAV Encoder:** This is also a Windows standard, but it's of higher quality than MP3.

Follow these steps to copy songs from a CD to your computer with iTunes:

1. **Put the CD in your CD player or DVD player.**

A list of songs on the CD appears.

2. **Deselect the songs that you *don't* want to copy.**

   To deselect a song, click the check box beside its name to remove the check mark. Check boxes are found between song numbers and song names.

3. **Click the Import button.**

   You can find this button in the upper-right corner of the window. Songs are played as soon as they are successfully copied to your computer. To stop copying a song, click the Close button (the *X*) in the Time Remaining box at the top of the window.

Adding songs you didn't get from Apple to the Library

Chances are, your computer has more than a few music files that you acquired from friends or from here and there on the Internet. You can add these songs to the iTunes Library to make finding and playing them easier. The problem with adding foreign songs to the Library, however, is that song information — the song's official title, artist, and genre — is usually inaccurate, and you need song information to find and play songs in the Library. The Apple Music Store is very good about tagging songs with correct titles and artist names, but other programs and stores do it haphazardly. Bringing foreign songs into the Library isn't as simple as adding the songs, because you also have to update the songs' information.

Included in these instructions is a little trick for making sure that song information is updated as you add foreign songs to the Library:

1. **Choose Edit⇨View Options or press Ctrl+J.**

   The View Options dialog box appears. It lists categories you can put in the song list.

2. **Select the Date Added check box if it isn't already selected, and click the OK button.**

   Later, you will sort the song list on the Date Added category and, in so doing, be able to find foreign songs you added to the Library.

3. **Choose File⇨Add Folder to Library and, in the Browse to Folder dialog box, select the folder with the foreign songs you want to add; then click the OK button.**

4. **Click the Library item in the Source box to display all songs in the song list.**

   Make sure that all artists, albums, and genres (if genres are displayed) are shown in the list.

5. **Scroll to and click the words *Date Added* at the top of the Date Added column to arrange songs in the list according to the dates they were added to the library.**

6. **Scroll to the bottom of the list to the view the songs you just added to the Library.**

   You see the songs you just added.

7. **One by one, right-click each song you just added, choose Get Info, select the Info tab in the Song dialog box, and make sure that the information listed there is correct.**

   Earlier in this chapter, the sidebar "Making sure the song information is correct" explains what song information is and how to edit it.

All songs on iTunes song lists are actually shortcuts to the folder on your computer where the songs are stored. If you move one of these song files, the shortcut is rendered invalid, and you can't play the song by double-clicking its name in a song list. To find out where on your computer a song file is located, right-click the song's name and choose Show Song File. Doing so opens My Computer to the folder where the song is stored.

To find out whether a song was entered more than once in the Library, choose Edit⇨Show Duplicate Songs. Duplicate copies of songs appear in the song list. You can right-click the duplicate copy and choose Clear to remove it from the library. Choose Edit⇨Show All Songs to see the complete list again.

Burning a CD

Burning a CD means to copy songs from a computer to a CD that you can play on a CD player in your car or your living room. Approximately 74 minutes of songs (about 650MB of data) can fit on an audio CD, although some discs allow 80 minutes (about 700MB). Roughly speaking, you can fit 20 songs on an audio CD. Before you attempt to burn a CD, assemble the songs for the CD on a playlist (see "Organizing Your Songs with Playlists and the Library," earlier in this chapter).

Start by declaring how you want to record the CD. Choose Edit⇨Preferences and, in the iTunes dialog box, select the Burning tab. Choose these recording options:

✦ **Preferred Speed:** iTunes is supposed to detect the speed rating of a CD. Choose Maximum Possible, unless you have trouble burning CDs. In that case, look on the package the CDs came in to see whether your CDs are rated for a slower speed, and choose that speed from the drop-down menu.

✦ **Disc Format:** Your choices are Audio CD, MP3 CD, and Data CD. Audio CDs are the ones that play on CD players in living rooms and cars.

✦ **Gap Between Songs:** From the drop-down menu, choose how many silent seconds to place between songs.

✦ **Use Sound Check:** Select this option to make all files on the CD play at a uniform volume.

Now you're ready to burn the CD by following these steps:

1. **In the Source box, select the playlist whose songs you want to burn to a CD, as shown in Figure 5-6.**

You can rearrange the order of songs in the playlist by dragging song names upward or downward.

Figure 5-6: Burning a CD.

2. **Click the Burn Disk button or choose File⇨Burn Playlist to Disc.**

3. **Insert a blank CD in the CD burner.**

4. **Click the Burn Disc button again when iTunes tells you to click it.**

The top of the window tells you when to click the button. Burning a CD takes about ten minutes. The program copies as many songs as will fit on the disc.

Printing a jewel case insert

Write the playlist name on the CD you burned to identify the CD. You can also print an insert and fold it into the jewel case. The insert lists the name of the playlist, artists' names, the name of each song on the playlist, and the playing time of each song. Follow these steps to print jewel case inserts:

1. **Select the playlist name if it isn't already selected.**

2. **Choose File⇨Print (or press Ctrl+P).**

   You see the Print dialog box.

3. **Select a theme from the Theme drop-down menu.**

   The dialog box clearly shows what your choices are.

4. **Click the OK button.**

   The printout shows you where to fold the page to make it fit in the CD case. I hope that you are a good folder and your origami skills are up to the task.

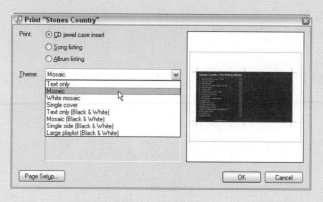

Chapter 6: Genealogy Online

In This Chapter

✔ **Doing the background research before you go online**

✔ **Searching from a comprehensive Web site**

✔ **Obtaining information from the Social Security Death Index**

✔ **Looking up vital records on the Internet**

✔ **Searching by surname**

✔ **Searching ships' passenger lists**

✔ **Searching within a locality**

✔ **Obtaining vital records about an ancestor**

*T*he Internet has given a powerful boost to genealogists. What used to require a trip to a Vital Records office can be done in minutes on the Internet. Genealogists, who used to practice their hobby in obscurity, have discovered one another. All across the Internet are sites where genealogists post their findings for others to see. A brisk trade in genealogical data goes on all day long. And a number of people, including me, have discovered long-lost relatives in the course of their genealogical research.

That's the good news. The bad news is that much of the genealogical data is in list form or on hard-to-find Web sites. Much of it is still on microfiche. To access most of it, you have to pay a few bucks to subscribe to a Web site. You can't just download your great-grandma's birth certificate from a site on the Internet, but you can find census data on an ancestor. You can find census indexes, property records, and immigrant records. You can quickly find out where data is kept and write to obtain the data. And your chances get better by the day of finding another genealogist who is working the same vein as you. We are, it appears, entering a golden age of genealogy.

This chapter explains a handful of ways to research your ancestors on the Internet. You find out how to search census records, search other vital records, scour the Internet to find information about a surname, and peer into the ghastly-sounding Social Security Death Index to locate your ancestors. This chapter also looks into researching ancestors who lived in a particular place and obtaining vital records. Before you start researching your ancestors, however, you have to do a little background work.

Doing the Detective Work

Before reaching into the misty past to connect with your ancestors, you need to make like a detective. Would Sam Spade (as played by Humphrey Bogart) search for the Maltese Falcon on the Internet without knowing what bird he was searching for? Of course not. The same goes for genealogical research. Before you jump in, take stock of what you already know, gather all the material records you can, interview your relatives, and devise a plan for storing all the data.

You probably already know the names and birthplaces of the previous one or two generations of your family. Start by writing down what you know about them. Why write it down? Because, like a detective, you can start putting the clues together after you have written them down. Write down your ancestors' names, birthdays, and places of residence. Write down their occupations and the names of clubs, groups, and institutions to which they belonged. Every scrap of evidence you have about an ancestor may be an important clue.

Next, assemble the material records about your family. Land titles, letters, diaries, certificates of birth and death, court records, family Bibles, and newspaper articles are examples of material records. These records can be invaluable. A birth certificate, for example, reveals not only when an ancestor was born but also in which county his or her parents lived at the time of the birth. Some birth certificates list the parents' occupations. Ask around for copies of material records that pertain to your family. Maybe you will get lucky and stumble upon a pack rat who has saved old newspaper articles, baptismal certificates, and so on.

On the subject of asking around, interview your relatives. They will be delighted to tell you about the past. And be sure to bring along a tape recorder and photographs. Photographs tend to jog people's memories. Here are some good questions to ask your relatives:

✦ When and where were you born?

✦ When and where were you married?

✦ Where did you go to school, and what clubs or institutions were you affiliated with?

✦ From which country or countries did our ancestors come?

✦ Can you tell me anything about other relatives? When and where were they born? Where did they go to school? What clubs or institutions were they affiliated with?

✦ Were you in the military? Do you know of anyone in the family who was in the military? To which units did you or other family members belong?

✦ Do you have any material records — birth certificates, photos, family letters — that I can borrow and copy?

Heritage Quest offers a Genealogy 101 primer for newcomers to genealogy at this Web address: `www.heritagequest.com/gen101/index.html`.

Organizing Your Genealogical Data

One task remains after you've determined what you know, assembled the material records, and interviewed your relatives: Think of a way to organize your genealogical data. Dropping scraps of paper in a desk drawer won't do the trick. Look at it this way: For each generation you research, the number of parents doubles. A search that goes back four generations requires tracking 30 different people. Go back five generations, and you are tracking 62 ancestors.

Some people make do with 3-by-5 index cards and manila folders. Others create a database and work from there. One way to tackle the problem of organizing the data is to enlist the help of software. Genealogy Software Review (`www.genealogy-software-review.com`) rates and ranks the ten leading programs. The programs cost from $20 to $76.

All-Purpose Searching Sites

Maybe the best way to get acquainted with all the different sites on the Internet that pertain to genealogy is to visit one or two all-purpose genealogy Web sites, click a few links, and see where the adventure takes you. Genealogists come in all stripes and colors. Your expedition will take you to online government offices, online graveyards, and everything in between. When you get stuck in the course of a genealogical exploration, try visiting these Web sites to get unstuck:

✦ **Cyndi's List:** You can't go wrong at Cyndi's List. This Web site lists hundreds, if not thousands, of links to genealogy Web sites. Bookmark this site. Its A-to-Z index is invaluable. Address: `www.cyndislist.com`

✦ **The Genealogy Home Page:** Click the links at this user-friendly Web site to sample the different resources on the Internet. The authors of this site have divided genealogy into a dozen or so clearly defined categories to get you started. Address: `www.genealogyhomepage.com`

✦ **Genealogy Resources on the Internet:** You can find a vast, eccentric A-to-Z index of genealogy Web sites here. This is another place to find out just how many types of genealogy Web sites there are. (In the address, notice that a hyphen, not a period, appears after www.) Address: `www-personal.umich.edu/~cgaunt/gen_web.html`

✦ **Helm's Genealogy Toolbox:** This Web site offers an eclectic blend of genealogical resources, including links to census, immigration, and military records. Address: `www.genealogytoolbox.com`

Obtaining Vital Information from the Social Security Death Index

The Social Security Death Index, also known as the Death Master File (how do you like these macabre names?), contains the names of people for whom a lump-sum Social Security benefit was paid at the time of death. Usually, a surviving family member, lawyer, or mortician requests the payment. Over 72 million names are in the index, and more importantly, you can find out a lot by looking in the index. You can find out when an ancestor was born, when he or she died, and where he or she died. Then, for $27, you can write the Social Security Administration to obtain a copy of your ancestor's Social Security application. The application includes this vital information:

✦ Place of birth

✦ Mailing address at the time the application was filed

✦ Father's full name

✦ Mother's full name, including her maiden name

✦ The name and address of the person's employer

The Social Security Index is perhaps the best, free way to get information about an ancestor. To search the index and obtain an ancestor's Social Security application, follow these steps:

1. **Open your browser and go to the following address:**

   ```
   http://ssdi.genealogy.rootsweb.com
   ```

2. **Fill in the form as best you can, as shown in Figure 6-1.**

   The more information you can enter on the form, the better. Common names, such as Smith and Martinez, can generate thousands of database entries. If you're looking for information about an ancestor with a common name, click the Advanced Search button and enter more search criteria on the Advanced Search page.

3. **Click the Submit button.**

   If the name can be found, it appears in the search record. Scroll down to see the name.

4. **Click the SS-5 Letter link to generate a prewritten letter asking the Social Security Administration to send you a copy of your ancestor's application.**

   If you click the link, you get a written copy of the letter that you can print and send. Don't forget to write your address on the letter and enclose the $27.

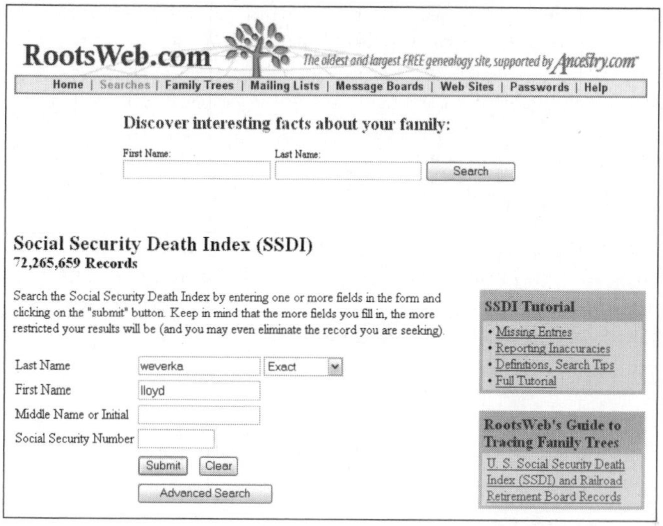

Figure 6-1:
Searching
for an
ancestor in
the Social
Security
Death Index.

Searching the Census and Other Vital Records

Article 1, Section 2, Clause 3 of the United States Constitution tells the Congress to carry out a census "every subsequent Term of ten Years, in such Manner as they shall by Law direct." And that is certainly good news for genealogists. Starting with the first census in 1790, the United States government has collected census records and maintained them at the offices of the National Archives and Records Administration (NARA). By law, census records can be made public only after 72 years have passed. As I write this, the 1930 census records are about to be made available for the first time.

But not all census records are available online. Nor are all the other vital records that have been indexed in databases — church records, military records, immigration and naturalization records, and land records. These vital records are not available from a central location. One way to look up vital records is to go to an all-purpose Web site (see "All-Purpose Searching Sites," earlier in this chapter), find a link that takes you to the state where your ancestor lived, for example, and see whether you can find a census database to search.

If you are willing to pay to look in vital records, Ancestry.com (`www.ancestry.com`) is the place to go. For $19.95, you can search the databases for three months (free two-week trials and other, more-expensive plans are available as well). According to Ancestry.com, the company's databases contain 543 million names. Besides census records, you can look in church records, military records, immigration and naturalization records, and land records.

Figure 6-2 shows the results of a search at Ancestry.com in the census records for my great-grandfather, Archibald McPhee. I found him in the 1920 census. By clicking the census image, I can see an enlarged version of the actual census ledger where his name was recorded by hand 85 years ago. I enlarged the image and discovered, written in the beautiful handwriting of yesteryear, below the names of my great-grandparents, the names of my great aunts (Ida, Mabel, Myrtle, and Winifred). I knew these illustrious old ladies when I was very young but had forgotten their names. Typical of a genealogical investigation, the handwritten census record shed light on my ancestry but also added to its mystery. The official census record says Archibald McPhee was born in Canada, but the ledger says he was born in Scotland. Anyhow, seeing this handwritten census record on my computer screen, I had one of those "the Internet really is amazing" moments.

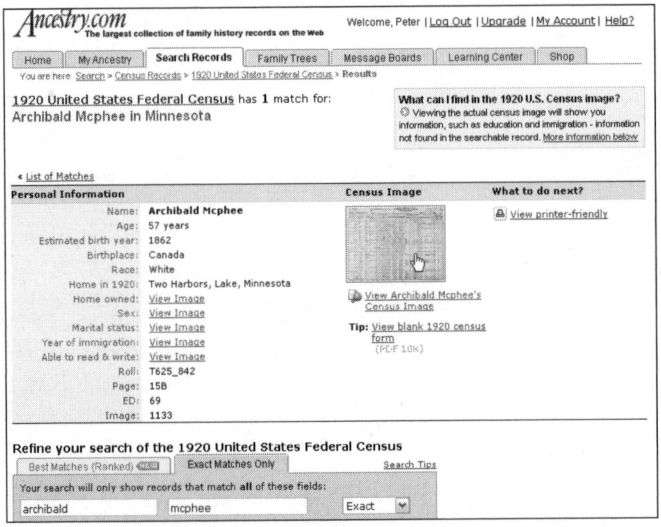

Figure 6-2:
A census
record at
Ancestry.
com.

Searching for Information about a Surname

You probably aren't the only person conducting a genealogical investigation of a surname. Others are also looking for Chaffees, Goughs, or whatever surname you happen to be looking for. Wouldn't it be great if you could connect with someone who is doing the same research as you?

From the Web sites that follow, you can look into a surname and perhaps swap data with another lonely soul who is looking down the same path you are. You can also list your e-mail address or Web page at these sites to make your research available to other genealogists:

✦ **Ancestry.com Message Boards:** To search for a message board with messages devoted to a surname, enter a surname in the Find a Message Board text box and click the Go button. To search across all the message boards, enter keywords in the Search All Message Boards text box and click the Go button. Address: `http://boards.ancestry.com`

✦ **RootsWeb Message Boards:** Ancestry.com purchased the RootsWeb genealogical Web site a few years ago, but the RootsWeb message boards remain from the old days. These message boards are different from Ancestry.com's, although the techniques for searching them are the same (see the previous paragraph for instructions in searching these message boards). Click the Message Boards tab to start searching. Address: `http://rsl.rootsweb.com`

✦ **SurnameWeb's Genealogy Search Engine:** From this site, you can search for variants of a name as part of the search. Address: `www.surnameweb.org/search/Search.cgi`

Sounding out the Soundex system

Occasionally, when you submit surname searches in genealogy databases, you are given the opportunity to submit a name under the *Soundex system*. The Soundex system is an attempt to account for surnames that sound the same or sound alike but are spelled differently. For example, instead of conducting four different searches for Christian, Christianson, Christiansen, and Christiani, you can conduct one search with the Soundex code C623.

Here is how the Soundex code works:

✔ Each name, no matter how long it is, comprises four alphanumeric characters, with one letter and three numbers.

✔ The first letter of the name is the first letter of the code.

✔ Each consonant in the name (vowels are excluded) is assigned a number using the

Soundex key: 1 = b, f, p, v; 2 = c, g, k, j, q, s, x; 3 = d, t; 4 = l; 5 = m, n; 6 = r. The following letters are not assigned a number, but are disregarded: a, e, h, i, o, u, y, w.

✔ Zeroes are used if the end of the name is reached prior to three digits.

Confused? Fortunately, a handful of Web sites have come to the rescue and can convert a name to a Soundex code in the wink of an eye. Soundex codes really are a more efficient way of searching databases. To convert a name to its Soundex code, visit one of these Web sites:

✔ Soundex Conversion: `http://searches.rootsweb.com/cgi-bin/Genea/soundex.sh`

✔ The Soundex Machine: `www.nara.gov/genealogy/soundex/soundex.html`

Are you interested in the old-world origins of a surname? In that case, you can pay a visit to an outfit called The Guild of One-Name Studies (www.one-name.org). Each member of the Guild is assigned a surname. The member's job is to identify the origins of the surname and track its distribution over the centuries. From the Web site, you can look up a surname, get the name and address of the person to whom it has been assigned, and e-mail or write the person to learn more about the name.

Searching the Passenger Lists

Chances are, some of your ancestors came to the United States by ship. And if they came by ship, they very likely arrived in New York's Ellis Island. Here are some Web sites for searching ships' passenger lists:

✦ **Ellis Island Passenger Arrivals:** By registering, you can search the database of immigrants who arrived in the United States at Ellis Island, as shown in Figure 6-3. The database tells you the immigrant's date of arrival, hometown, age upon arrival, port of departure, and ethnicity, as well as the name of the ship that carried him or her across the water. Address: http://webcenter.ellisisland.netscape.com

✦ **Olive Tree Ship Lists:** Search Canadian as well as American passenger lists at this Web site. Address: http://olivetreegenealogy.com/ships/index.shtml

Figure 6-3:
You can look into ships' passenger lists at Ellis Island Passenger Arrivals.

Obtaining Data from Localities

At some point, the search for your ancestors may take you to a state, country, city, or other locality. Now you're getting somewhere. You have pinpointed where an ancestor lived. Your next step is to look for resources on the Internet that are specific to different locales. Try starting from these sites:

✦ **Genealogy.com – Genealogy Toolbox:** Click the United States link. When you come to a list of states, click a state name to see a list of geographic resources. (Click the Helpful Web Sites link.) Address: `www.genealogy.com/links/c/c-places-geographic.html`

✦ **North American Genealogy Resources:** A comprehensive list of genealogical resources in each state and in Canada is found at this Web site. Address: `www.genealogyhomepage.com/northamerican.html`

✦ **USGen Web Project:** This Web site also organizes genealogical resources on the Internet by states. Click the States link. Address: `www.usgenweb.org`

Following the history of a surname

The Hamrick Software Surname Distribution Web site is fascinating. From this Web site, you can discover — in the 1850, 1880, 1920, or 1990 census — how common a surname was. Here, for example, the results of the 1920 census show that McPhee was a common name in the Dakotas, Washington, and Michigan, but not very common elsewhere in the United States.

Go to the Hamrick Software Surname Distribution Web site to trace the path of a surname across the United States from 1850 to 1880 to 1920 to 1990. Enter a surname in the text box, choose a census year, and click the Display button. Address: `www.hamrick.com/names/index.html`

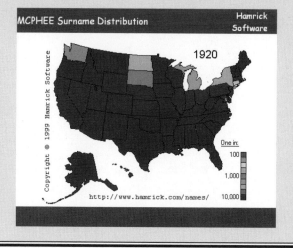

Book VIII Chapter 6

Genealogy Online

Don't be discouraged if none of these Web sites turn up anything. The Internet is full of genealogical societies, city directories, cemetery listings, and other places where long-gone ancestors' names may have been recorded. Refer to Book II, Chapter 3 for information on how to conduct an Internet search. Try running a search using your ancestor's name, a place name, and the word *genealogy* as the keywords. Maybe something will turn up.

Book IV, Chapters 3 and 4 describe mailing lists and newsgroups, respectively. Mailing lists and newsgroups are excellent places to conduct genealogical research.

Writing to Obtain Vital Records

In the United States and its territories, certificates of births, marriages, deaths, and divorces are kept on file in the Vital Statistics office of every city or county where the event occurred. Some states also maintain offices where the records are kept. As long as you know where and when an ancestor was born, married, died, or divorced, you can write to the Vital Statistics office to obtain a copy of a certificate.

To find out the address of the Vital Statistics office you are looking for, go to this Web address: www.vitalrec.com. Click the States & Territories link to see a list of states and U.S. territories. Then click a state name to find out how to obtain vital records there.

Book IX

Appendixes

The 5th Wave   By Rich Tennant

©RICHTENNANT

"Guess who found a Kiss merchandise site on the Web while you were gone?"

Contents at a Glance

Appendix A: Signing Up for a Yahoo! ID

In This Chapter

✔ Looking at the advantages of having a Yahoo! account

✔ Registering for a Yahoo! account

✔ Signing in to your account

✔ Creating a Yahoo! profile

✔ Changing your Yahoo! ID

✔ Closing a Yahoo! account

hroughout this book, I describe all the different things you can with Yahoo!, one of the oldest and most venerable services on the Internet. To take advantage of Yahoo!, however, you must be a registered Yahoo! member.

This appendix describes some of the advantages of being a Yahoo! member. It explains how to become a member, how to sign in to Yahoo!, and how to present yourself to other members in the form of a *profile*, a page on the Internet where your vital statistics and interests are laid bare for all to see. This appendix also shows how to change your Yahoo! ID and close a Yahoo! account, should you decide Yahoo! isn't the big deal everyone says it is.

By the way, the term *Yahoo* was coined by Jonathan Swift, the author of *Gulliver's Travels.* In Book 4 of that novel, Gulliver travels among the Houyhnhnms — noble, intelligent horses who are constantly being plagued by their enemies, the foul savage human Yahoos. The Houyhnhnms are pleasantly surprised to find in Gulliver a human as cultivated as themselves, but they soon discover that Gulliver has more in common with the hairy, dirty Yahoos than they realized at first. I just thought you'd like to know.

What You Get with a Yahoo! Account

Signing up for a Yahoo! account is free and takes about two minutes. For your trouble, here's what signing up for a Yahoo! account entitles you to:

✦ **Yahoo! Mail:** A Web-based e-mail account. (Book III, Chapter 4 explains Yahoo! Mail.)

◆ **My Yahoo!:** The ability to track an investment portfolio online (see Book V, Chapter 2) and bring together news items of interest to you (see Book II, Chapter 6) at a Web page you create on My Yahoo! (`http://my.yahoo.com`).

◆ **Yahoo! GeoCities:** A chance to create a Web site and present it online at Yahoo! GeoCities (`http://geocities.yahoo.com`). (See Book IV, Chapter 7.)

◆ **Yahoo! Auctions:** A ticket to bid on items at Yahoo! Auctions (`http://auctions.yahoo.com`). (See Book VI, Chapter 2.)

◆ **Yahoo! Groups:** The means to join and create a Yahoo! group (`http://groups.yahoo.com`), a discussion group for people with the same interest or hobby. (See Book IV, Chapter 5.)

◆ **Yahoo! Personals:** The possibility of making new friends and perhaps mending a broken heart (`http://personals.yahoo.com`). (See Book IV, Chapter 8.)

◆ **Yahoo! Travel:** An invitation to start planning your next glorious vacation (`http://travel.yahoo.com`). (See Book VIII, Chapter 2.)

◆ **Yahoo! Education:** An entrée to Yahoo! Education (`http://education.yahoo.com`), where you can research different topics, take sample SAT tests, and otherwise rummage for the information you need to get the term paper in on time. (See Book I, Chapter 7.)

◆ **Yahoo! Games:** A chance to engage others in games at the Yahoo! Games Web site (`http://games.yahoo.com`). (See Book VIII, Chapter 1.)

◆ **Yahoo! Messenger:** A free pass to Yahoo! Messenger (`http://messenger.yahoo.com`), an instant-messaging service. (See Book IV, Chapter 1.)

◆ **Yahoo! Chat:** An opportunity to chat with other Yahoo! members (`http://chat.yahoo.com`). (Book IV, Chapter 6 looks into chatting on the Internet.)

Getting a Yahoo! Account

To get a Yahoo! account, go to this Web page: `http://login.yahoo.com`. Then click the Sign In Now link to open the Yahoo! Registration window shown in Figure A-1. Starting here, answer these questions to get your Yahoo! account:

◆ **First Name:** Enter your first name.

◆ **Last Name:** Enter your last name.

◆ **Preferred Content:** Choose the country you live in.

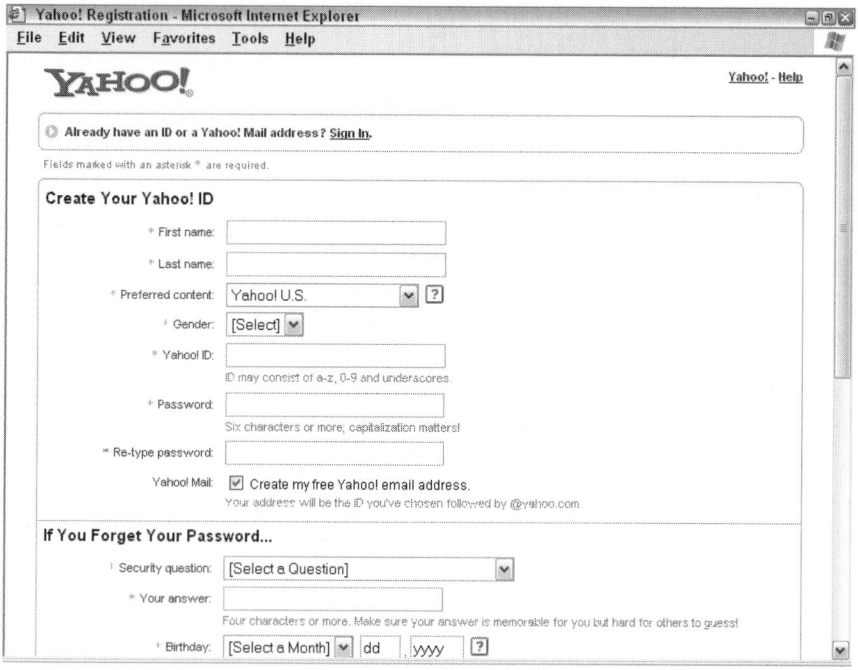

Figure A-1:
Describe
yourself in
the Yahoo!
Registration
window.

✦ **Gender:** If you don't know the answer to this question, look it up at Google.

✦ **Yahoo! ID:** Enter a descriptive name. This is the name you will go by in your dealings with Yahoo! If the name you enter is already taken, Yahoo! gives you a chance to choose a different one.

✦ **Password:** Enter your password. Passwords can be six characters long and are case sensitive. If your password includes capital letters, remember them well, because you will have to enter capital letters when you type in your password.

✦ **Re-Type Password:** Enter the password you chose a second time.

✦ **Yahoo! Mail:** For the moment, deselect this check box. Book III, Chapter 4 explains how to sign up for Yahoo! Mail if that is why you're getting a Yahoo! account.

✦ **Security Question:** Choose a question whose answer you can give right away without thinking. If you lose your password, you must answer this question to obtain your password.

✦ **Your Answer:** Enter the answer to the security question you chose.

✦ **Birthday:** Enter your date of birth.

+ **ZIP/Postal Code:** Enter the zip or postal code where you live.

+ **Alternate Email:** After you sign up, Yahoo! sends you a verification message to the e-mail address you enter here. To activate your account, you click a link in that message. If you lose your password, you can ask Yahoo! to send it to the e-mail address you enter here.

+ **Enter the Code Shown:** Enter the number-and-letter code shown in the box below. The purpose of this code is to prevent computer robots from signing up with Yahoo!.

Click the Submit button when you have finished answering the questions. If you entered the information completely and correctly, the next window tells you to check your mail at the alternate e-mail address you gave to Yahoo!. There you will find an e-mail message like the one in Figure A-2. To activate your account, click the Important link in the e-mail message. Your browser opens to an E-Mail Verification page at Yahoo!, where you enter your password and click the Verify button to activate your account. You land in your Front Page. This is where you land when you sign in to Yahoo!.

Figure A-2:
Yahoo!
sends an
e-mail
message so
that you can
activate
your
account.

Signing In and Signing Out

After you have obtained a Yahoo! account, and your Yahoo! ID and password are locked away safely in the dungeon of your memory, you can sign in to your Yahoo! account by following these steps:

1. **Open your browser to this Web page:** www.yahoo.com

2. **Click the My Yahoo! button or the My Yahoo! link.**

You can find the button and link along the top of the window. After you click the button or link, you land in the My Yahoo! Web page at http://my.yahoo.com.

3. **Enter your Yahoo! ID and Yahoo! password.**

4. **Click the Sign In button.**

   You go to your Front Page, the starting point for your adventures in Yahoo!

   Select the Remember My ID & Password check box if you want your sign-in information to be recorded on your computer. Next time you click the My Yahoo! button or the My Yahoo! link, you will be signed on right away without having to enter an ID or password.

   To sign out of Yahoo!, click the Sign Out link. You can find this link along the top of most Yahoo! pages.

All about Yahoo! Profiles

   Everyone with a Yahoo! account is given a Profile page like the one shown in Figure A-3. To begin with, your Profile page doesn't amount to much. All it contains is your Yahoo! ID name and the date you became a Yahoo! member. To describe yourself more thoroughly on the Profile page, be my guest. As I explain shortly, Yahoo! members can visit other members' pages and search the profiles for people with common interests.

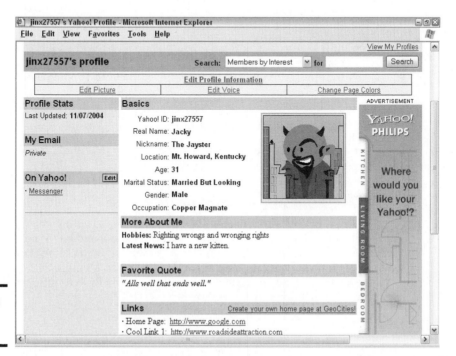

Figure A-3:
A Yahoo!
profile.

Describing yourself in a profile

After you sign on to Yahoo!, follow these steps to describe yourself in a profile:

1. **Go to the Yahoo! Member Directory at this Web page:**

   ```
   http://members.yahoo.com
   ```

2. **Click the View My Profiles link.**

   You can find this link in the upper-right corner of the window. After you click it, you go to the Public Profiles page.

3. **Click the Edit link, or, if you have created more than one profile to describe yourself, click the link named after the profile you want to change.**

   You come to your Profile page (refer to Figure A-3). This is the page others see when your profile turns up in a search.

Now you're getting somewhere. The Profile page offers four links for describing yourself to other Yahoo! members. Click one of these links to go to another Web page and paint yourself in profile:

+ **Edit Profile Information:** Enter your real name, age, marital status, and other personal-type stuff. If you want others to be able to find and contact you by way of the Member Directory, be sure to select the Add This Profile to the Yahoo! Member Directory check box.

+ **Edit Picture:** Click the Browse button and select an image file from your computer, or click the Our Gallery link and choose a cartoon character to represent you. The image appears on your Profile page.

+ **Edit Voice:** Enter the Web page address of a voice recording to make a recorded voice a part of your profile. Recordings can be in the following formats: AIF, MP3, MPEG, MIDI, MOV, RM, or WAV.

+ **Edit Page Colors:** Choose a color scheme that illustrates your character or disposition or temperament.

Checking out others' profiles

To view others' profiles and maybe make a friend with someone whose interests are the same as your own, sign in to Yahoo! and go to the Member Directory at this Web page: `http://members.yahoo.com`. Here you find tools for searching profiles. Click the Advanced Member Search link to search with many criteria. Click subjects in the Browse Interest section to look for members by interest group.

Changing Your Yahoo! ID

Unfortunately, you can't change your Yahoo! ID. If you want to abandon one Yahoo! persona and take up another, your only options are to create a second account with Yahoo! under a different ID name or create a second profile.

Operating under different profiles in Yahoo! is more trouble than it's worth, but if you want to try out having a second profile, go to the Yahoo! Member Directory at `http://members.yahoo.com`, click the View My Profiles link, and click the Create New Public Profile button. All you get from having another profile is a second portrait of yourself in the Yahoo! Member Directory.

Closing a Yahoo! Account

Sometimes it just doesn't work out. You and Yahoo! didn't get along. If that is the case, you can close your Yahoo! account by following these steps.

1. **Sign in to Yahoo!.**
2. **Go to this Web address:**

   `https://edit.yahoo.com/config/delete_user`

3. **Enter your password in the text box.**
4. **Click the Terminate This Account button.**

   Now wave good-bye to your Yahoo! account as it disappears into the ether.

Appendix B: Getting a .NET Passport

A *.NET passport* is a combination username and password that you establish when you register with the .NET passport service. This service, offered by Microsoft, is supposed to make entering user IDs and passwords easier. If you have a Hotmail or an MSN e-mail account, you already have a .NET passport.

This appendix explains precisely what a .NET passport is, how to get a passport, and how to sign in with Web sites and Web services that require a passport. Finally, you discover how to change your .NET passport and delete your passport account.

What Is a .NET Passport?

The mighty Microsoft Corporation invented the .NET passport in 1999 as a convenient way for people to sign in to Web sites without having to remember a dozen different sign-in names and passwords. Instead of all those names and passwords, they would simply enter the username and password that they registered with Microsoft when they got their .NET passport.

Microsoft hoped that Web-site developers would embrace the .NET passport idea, but it never caught on. Developers liked the idea of Web-site visitors not having to remember IDs and passwords, but they balked at the idea of Microsoft knowing who was visiting their Web sites. Web surfers disliked the prospect of Microsoft looking over their shoulders and knowing where they traveled on the Internet.

Now only Microsoft-owned Web services and a handful of others ask for .NET passports when you log in. Three such services are described in this book:

✦ **Hotmail:** A Web-based e-mail service (see Book III, Chapter 4).

✦ **MoneyCentral:** A financial-management Web site where you can build an online portfolio (`http://moneycentral.msn.com`). (See Book V, Chapter 2).

✦ **MSN Games:** A great Web site where you can play any number of games, including bridge and chess, with other people over the Internet (`http://zone.msn.com`). (See Book VIII, Chapter 1.)

Obtaining a .NET Passport

To obtain a .NET passport, start by going to this Web site: `http://register.passport.com`. You see the Passport Member Services Web page shown in Figure B-1. Enter information like so:

✦ **E-Mail Address:** Enter your e-mail address.

✦ **Password:** Enter a password no longer than six characters, without any spaces between characters.

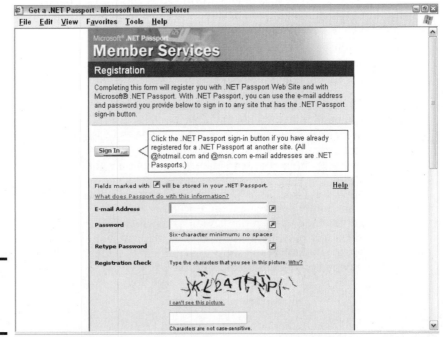

Figure B-1:
Signing up
for a .NET
passport.

Enabling cookies

When you visit a Web site, the site may deposit a small text file, called a *cookie,* on your hard drive. Cookies store information about you and enable the Web site to retrieve this information on visits subsequent to your first visit. The idea is for the Web site to serve you better. The cookie, for example, may store your preferences or user ID, which makes it unnecessary for you to state your preferences or enter your user ID on subsequent occasions when you visit the Web site. Perhaps you've had the experience of visiting a Web site, being asked to identify yourself, and discovering your user ID already entered on the Web page that asks for your ID. Your ID is already there because a cookie on your hard drive has identified you.

Some people believe that cookies violate their privacy because they leave a trail of the Web sites you have visited. For this reason, most Web browsers allow you to turn off cookies. However, you can't make use of the .NET passport if cookies are disabled in your browser.

Follow these instructions to enable cookies:

✔ **Internet Explorer:** Choose Tools⇨Internet Options, and select the Privacy tab in the Options dialog box. Make sure that the Settings slider isn't pushed to the topmost setting, Block All Cookies.

✔ **Mozilla:** Choose Edit⇨Preferences and, in the Preferences dialog box, select the Privacy & Security category and then the Cookies subcategory. Make sure that the Block Cookies option button is not selected.

✦ **Retype Password**: Reenter the password.

✦ **Registration Check:** Enter the letter-and-number code. This code prevents computer robots from getting .NET passports.

✦ **Share My E-Mail Address:** Select this check box if want Web sites that accept .NET passports to be able to collect your e-mail address. I strongly suggest deselecting this check box.

✦ **E-Mail Address:** Enter your e-mail address again.

Click the I Agree button when you have finished filling out the Web page.

Signing In and Signing Out

When a Web site or Web service wants you to provide your .NET password, the Sign In button appears. Click this button and you see the .NET Password Sign In form shown in Figure B-2. Enter your e-mail address and password, and good luck to you.

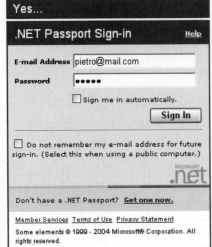

Figure B-2:
Entering
your e-mail
address and
password.

Look for the Sign Out button when you want to sever your connection to the Web site you are horsing around in. After you click the button, your .NET password no longer gives you free reign to frolic inside the Web site.

Managing Your .NET Passport Account

If somewhere down the line you want to change something about your .NET passport or close your account, start by going to this Web site: `http://memberservices.passport.net`. Then click the Sign In button, enter your e-mail address and password, and take care of business.

You find links on the page for changing your password, changing your profile information, and even closing your .NET password account. Click the I Forgot My Password link to recover a password that slipped behind the refrigerator and was never seen again.

Appendix C: Getting a Google Account

*T*his brief appendix explains how to sign up for a Google account — not a Google e-mail account, but an account that permits you to post messages in newsgroups and ask questions of Google experts. I wish all appendices were this short.

What You Get with a Google Account

An account with Google entitles you to the keys to the kingdom and these amenities:

✦ The opportunity to post messages to newsgroups with a Web browser (see Book IV, Chapter 4).

✦ The chance to submit questions to Google researchers (see Book II, Chapter 4).

✦ The opportunity to translate Google Web pages into foreign languages, if you want to volunteer to do that.

✦ The means to develop your own Google applications (admittedly, this one isn't for everybody).

Obtaining a Google Account

To obtain an account with Google, open your Web browser and go to this Web address: `www.google.com/accounts/NewAccount`. Then scroll down the screen and enter this information:

✦ **E-mail address:** Enter an e-mail address. Google sends a confirmation notice to this address when you finish setting up your account.

If you intend to post messages to newsgroups using your Google account, don't enter your primary e-mail address. Enter a secondary address instead. Spammers collect e-mail addresses from newsgroup posts. If you enter your primary address, you subject yourself to lots of junk mail. (Book III, Chapter 5 explains how to keep from getting spammed.)

✦ **Password:** Enter a password no longer than six characters.

✦ **Re-enter password:** Enter the password again.

✦ **Word verification:** Type the letters in the box below. The purpose of this code is to prevent computer robots from signing up with Google.

Click the Create My Account button. Immediately, Google sends an e-mail verification notice to the e-mail address you entered. The message is from accounts-noreply@google.com and its subject is "Google Email Verification." Open the message and click the link inside it to activate your account.

Glossary of Internet Terms

adjacent searching: *See* proximity searching.

adware: Software loaded surreptitiously on a computer that gathers information about the user's browsing habits and displays advertisements in the browser window tailored to the user's tastes and browsing patterns. Adware is a form of spyware. *See also* spyware.

aggregator: A software or Web-based program that collects and displays headlines and story summaries from Web sites and blogs. By clicking a headline in an aggregator, you can open a Web site and read a story. Also called a feed reader, news aggregator, news reader, and RSS aggregator. *See also* RSS *and* RSS feed.

airsnarf: A wireless device, attached to a network, designed to steal usernames and passwords from people who wirelessly connect to the Internet on their laptop computers or cell phones by way of a hotspot. *See also* hotspot.

algorithm: In Internet searching, a mathematical formula for scoring a Web page's relevance compared to other Web pages in search results. Web pages with more relevance are placed higher in the search results list.

antivirus program: A program that searches a computer's hard drive for viruses and removes any that are found.

applet: *See* Java applet.

article: A post, or contribution, to a newsgroup.

atom: A protocol for RSS feeds. *See also* RSS feed.

autoresponder: A computer program that responds automatically to e-mail messages with a prewritten reply.

bandwidth: The speed at which data is transmitted on a given path or medium. Bandwidth is expressed in bits per second (bps). In discussions about modems, refers to DSL and cable modems, not dialup modems. *See also* data transfer rate.

baud rate: The speed at which a modem transmits data. Named for J.M.E. Baudot, a French engineer who invented the teletype.

Bayesian filtering: A statistical analysis method used to identify spam e-mail messages. Bayesian filtering software looks at messages' content and properties to determine whether messages are spam. *See also* spam.

binaries: Refers to media files — music and video files — posted on a newsgroup.

blocking software: *See* filtering software.

blog: An online journal that includes frequent references to writings in other online journals. The term is short for *Web log.*

blogger: One who maintains a blog on the Internet.

blogosphere: All blogs on the Internet. Also, the community of people who write blogs and publish them on the Internet.

bookmark: To save a shortcut to a Web page so that you can click the short-cut and revisit the Web page quickly without having to enter the page's address. All Web browsers offer commands for bookmarking Web pages and visiting Web pages that you bookmarked. The term also refers to a shortcut to a Web page.

Boolean operators: Operators — AND, OR, NOT, and NEAR — that tell search engines how to use keywords in a search of the Internet. The operators are named for their inventor, George Boole, a 19th-century English logician. Also called search operators. *See also* keyword.

bot: *See* spider.

bounce: When an e-mail message is returned as undeliverable.

browser: *See* Web browser.

browsing: To go from Web page to Web page during an exploration of the Internet.

cable modem: A modem that connects a computer to the Internet by way of cable TV wiring.

cam: *See* Webcam.

channel: *See* chat room.

chat: Real-time communication between people at different computers. Chatters communicate by typing on their keyboards.

chat room: The metaphoric place on the Internet where chatters gather. Also called a channel.

cloaking: Placing keywords in a Web page that are invisible to Web-page visitors but can be indexed by spiders. Cloaking is a method of making a Web page appear more prominently in Internet searches. Because more keywords are indexed, more matches to the page are found in search results. *See also* keyword loading, link loading, *and* spider.

cookie: A text file that a Web page deposits on your computer so that the next time you visit, the Web site can identify you.

crawler: *See* spider.

cyberspace: The virtual reality of the Internet in which people communicate by computers without regard for physical distance. The term was coined by William Gibson in his 1982 novel *Neuromancer.*

cybersquatting: Registering a Web address name with the purpose of selling it later to a person or company with which it is rightfully associated.

data transfer rate: In measuring Web-server use, how much data, in gigabytes, a Web server has transferred in a month. Some Web-hosting services charge fees according to the data transfer rate.

dead link: A hyperlink that is no longer valid because the page to which it leads is either no longer available on the Internet or no longer available at the address to which the hyperlink points. When you click a dead link, you see a "Page cannot be displayed" message.

demilitarized zone: *See* DMZ.

dialup modem: A modem that sends data over the telephone lines rather than through a dedicated circuit.

dictionary attack: In e-mail messaging, a technique for generating e-mail addresses for the purpose of sending spam. Common names are randomly assigned number combinations and then joined to a domain name to create e-mail addresses. The addresses are then sent spam. *See also* spam.

digital subscriber line: *See* DSL.

directory: For Internet searches, a Web site at which Web pages are catalogued in categories and subcategories. Along with search engines, directories are the primary means of searching the Internet. Yahoo! Search Directory and the Open Directory Project are examples of directories. *See also* search engine.

discussion group: *See* newsgroup.

DMZ (demilitarized zone): A part of a computer not protected by a firewall.

domain name: The part of a Web address that refers to the Web server where a Web page and its attendant files are stored. *See also* Web address.

domain name server: A computer that provides computers with IP addresses. *See also* IP address.

download: To transfer a copy of a file or program from a site on the Internet to a personal computer. *See also* upload.

DSL (digital subscriber line): Digital technology that provides high-speed transmissions over the telephone lines.

e-commerce: Commercial transactions — buying and selling — on the Internet.

e-mail: Electronic messages sent over the Internet or a network.

e-mail bomb: To send hundreds or thousands of e-mail messages to the same e-mail address, tying up the address and rendering it unusable.

e-mail discussion list: *See* mailing list.

e-mail newsletter: *See* mailing list.

e-mail spoofing: Forging an e-mail return address to make it appear as though an e-mail message was sent from someone besides the real sender.

emoticon: In instant messages, e-mail messages, and chat rooms, a bundle of characters that form a little picture meant to convey the writer's emotional state. Emoticons mimic the facial expressions that accompany real conversations. For example, tilt your head sideways and watch this emoticon wink at you: ; -). Stands for "emotion icon." Also called a smiley.

exact-phrase searching: *See* phrase searching.

excessive multi-posting (EMP): *See* spam.

false drop: In Internet searches, a search result that is returned erroneously. Usually, false drops occur because words can have more than one meaning. For example, a search for information about porcelain with the keyword *china* can return false drops that have to do with the country of China.

FAQs (frequently asked questions): On a Web site, a page on which common questions about the site are answered. Rhymes with *backs*.

feed reader: *See* aggregator.

filtering software: Software designed to keep inappropriate material from appearing in a browser window. Also called blocking software.

firewall: Software or hardware that serves as a gateway between a computer or network and the Internet. The firewall protects the computer or network from unauthorized access.

flame: To bark childish insults at an anonymous stranger in a newsgroup or message board. Two parties flaming each other is called a *flame war*.

freeware: Software programs that can be downloaded for free over the Internet.

ftp (file transfer protocol): The protocol, or rule, that governs how files are sent over the Internet.

ftp site: A Web site that can receive Web pages for display on the Internet. Also a Web site with files that can be downloaded.

gateway: A computer that connects separate networks that use different protocols.

Google-bombing: Taking advantage of a search engine's method of obtaining search results to artificially raise a Web page's ranking in the search results list. The name comes from the Google search engine's practice of judging a Web page's relevancy according to how many Web pages are linked to it. By purposefully linking many Web pages to a single page, pranksters can manipulate the Google search results to move a Web page higher in the search results list.

Googlewhacking: A game in which players, using the Google search engine, enter two or more keywords in searches with the aim of producing search results with only one Web page on the search results list.

header: In an e-mail message, the sender's and receiver's addresses, the message date, and the message subject.

hit: A visit to a Web site.

hit counter: A device on a Web page that registers how many people have visited the Web page. Also called a Web counter.

home page: The Web page that opens in your browser when you start your browser or click the Home button. Also the introductory page of a Web site.

hotspot: A location where anybody with a computer equipped for Wi-Fi can go online wirelessly. *See also* Wi-Fi.

HTML: *See* hypertext markup language.

http: *See* hypertext transfer protocol.

http server: *See* Web server.

hyperlink: An electronic link between two Web pages or two different places on the same Web page. When you click a hyperlink, you go directly to another Web page or another place on the same page. You can tell when your pointer has moved over a hyperlink because the pointer changes into a gloved hand.

hypertext markup language (HTML): The formatting codes that browsers read to display Web pages on the Internet or on an intranet.

hypertext transfer protocol (http): A protocol by which computers are able to communicate with and send files to one another.

IM: *See* instant messaging.

IMAP (Internet mail access protocol): A protocol by which an e-mail program accesses and downloads e-mail stored on an incoming mail server.

incoming mail server: A computer maintained by an Internet service provider (ISP) where mail is kept until the person to whom it is addressed logs on to the server and collects his or her mail. *See also* outgoing mail server.

instant messaging (IM): Exchanging text messages by way of AOL Instant Messenger, ICQ, Yahoo! Messenger, or another such service.

Internet: The "network of networks" that links computers. Web pages are displayed on the Internet, and e-mail can be sent across the Internet. The term is an abbreviation of *inter-network*. Sometimes called *the Net*.

Internet Relay Chat: *See* IRC.

Internet service provider (ISP): A company that provides customers access to the Internet and e-mail services. Some ISPs also allow customers to post Web pages.

intranet: A private network, usually maintained by a company or institution, to which only employees or members have access. Web sites and Web pages can be posted on intranets as well as the Internet.

invisible Web: Refers to private databases that are connected to the Internet but have not been mapped and indexed by search engines.

IP (Internet protocol) address: The 32-bit binary number that identifies each computer connected to the Internet. In the case of Web sites, each site is associated with an IP address.

IRC (Internet Relay Chat): An Internet chat network by which people who have joined different channels — that is, chat rooms — can type messages to one another.

ISP: *See* Internet service provider.

Java: A platform-neutral programming language useful for programming applications for the World Wide Web.

Java applet: A small software program written in the Java computer language that is designed to run on a Web browser.

keylogger: A spyware program that surreptitiously monitors keystrokes in a log file with the goal of capturing credit card numbers, bank account numbers, and other such information. *See also* spyware.

keyword: For the purpose of searching the Internet with a search engine, a word that describes what information is needed. If the keyword is found on a Web page, the Web page is named in the results of the search.

keyword loading: Deliberately placing topical words in a Web page's title, text headers, and page code to make the page come up more often in Internet searches. *See also* cloaking, link loading, *and* spider.

link: *See* hyperlink.

link loading: Including many hyperlinks on a Web page to make it more accessible to spiders, the automated programs that index Web pages on behalf of search engines. Link loading is a technique for making a Web page appear more often in Internet searches. *See also* cloaking, keyword loading, *and* spider.

list: *See* mailing list.

list manager: The person in charge of managing a mailing list.

LISTSERV: Computer software, made by L-SOFT International, for managing mailing lists. *See also* list server.

list server: A computer program that manages mailing lists automatically. Popular programs include LISTSERV, Majordomo, ListProc, Mailserv, and MailMan. Also called a mailing list manager.

lurk: To eavesdrop but not participate in an online chat room or message board. One who lurks is called a lurker.

mailing list: A list of names and e-mail addresses organized for the purpose of exchanging information about a certain topic. A message sent to the mailing list is immediately relayed to all e-mail addresses on the list. In this way, people with a common interest can trade ideas with one another. Also called an e-mail discussion list.

mailing list manager: *See* list server.

Majordomo: Computer software for managing mailing lists.

malware: Adware, spyware, and other malicious types of software.

message board: A Web page where people can post questions or reply to questions. Also called a discussion board, online forum, and Web forum.

meta-search engine: A search engine that gathers results from other search engines and presents the search results in one place. Using a meta-search engine, you can search using several different search engines simultaneously.

MIME (multipurpose Internet mail extension): In e-mail messaging, a standard that permits e-mail messages to include pictures, formatted text, and other sophisticated stuff. *See also* uuencode.

modem: The hardware device by which computers can transmit data over the telephone lines. You need a modem to travel the Internet or send e-mail messages. The term stands for *modulator-demodulator.*

moderator: The person who oversees a message board or newsgroup to make sure that contributions stay on the topic and are relevant.

newbie: Someone who is new to using the Internet or has only begun frequenting an online message board or newsgroup.

news reader: *See* aggregator *and* newsreader.

news server: A networked computer through which personal computers connect to the Usenet. As you explore the Usenet, you download articles from news servers. *See also* newsgroup *and* Usenet.

newsgroup: A bulletin board on the Internet — or, more accurately, the Usenet — where people can post opinions on a certain topic. Each newsgroup is devoted to one topic. Also called a discussion group or user group.

newsreader: Software for subscribing to newsgroups, reading articles, and posting articles. Outlook Express, besides being an e-mail program, is a newsreader. (A news reader — two words — is another name for an aggregator.)

outgoing mail server: A computer maintained by an Internet service provider (ISP) that is responsible for sending your outgoing mail to addresses across the Internet. Also called the SMTP (simple mail transfer protocol) server. *See also* incoming mail server.

P2P: *See* peer-to-peer.

packet: A snippet of data sent over the Internet. Each packet includes its address of origin and destination address.

packet switching: A technique for sending data over the Internet in which the data are divided into smaller packets, sent by various routes over the Internet, and reassembled after its arrival. Packet switching permits data to travel faster.

patch: A fix-it file designed to correct a bug in a software program.

peer-to-peer (P2P): A technology for sharing files over the Internet without the need for central servers.

phisher: One who engages in phishing. *See* phishing.

phishing: Fraudulently soliciting credit card information, identifications, usernames, and passwords by means of realistic-looking Web pages or e-mail messages that appear to come from bona fide institutions or sellers. Comes from the expression "going on a fishing expedition," which means to vaguely and unhurriedly look into others' affairs with the hope of finding something damaging.

phrase searching: In Internet searches, to search for a string of words, or phrase. By convention, phrases are enclosed in quotation marks to distinguish them from keywords.

ping: When one computer sends a short message over the Internet to another computer to test whether the first computer gets a response.

plug-in: A companion program to a Web browser for handling special types of data or playing certain kinds of media such as video and audio.

podcasting: Recording an Internet radio program or other digital audio presentation and making the recording available for others to download to an iPod or other portable audio device.

POP (post office protocol): A protocol by which an e-mail program can access and collect e-mail stored on an incoming mail server.

pop-up window: A second browser window launched automatically from a Web page without the user clicking a hyperlink. Advanced browsers offer commands for preventing pop-up windows from appearing. Also called a pop-up.

port: A place where information goes into or out of a computer.

portal: *See* Web portal.

protocol: A computer standard or set of rules designed to permit computers to exchange data or connect to one another.

proximity searching: To search the Internet for Web pages in which two words — the keywords in the search — appear within a certain distance of one another. Also called adjacent searching.

Really Simple Syndication: *See* RSS.

relevance ranking: In the list of Web pages that results from an Internet search, how Web pages are ranked on the list. Pages judged to be more relevant to the keywords used in the search are ranked highest. Search engines use different algorithms to determine relevance ranking. *See also* algorithm and results list.

results list: In a search of the Internet using a search engine, the list of Web pages that appears as the result of the search. *See also* relevance ranking.

router: A hardware device that is responsible for sending electronic signals to the correct destination.

RSS (Really Simple Syndication): A protocol by which blogs and news Web sites can feed headlines and story summaries to aggregators. *See also* aggregator.

RSS aggregator: *See* aggregator.

RSS feed: Encoded information sent using the RSS protocol from a Web site or blog to an aggregator. RSS feeds allow aggregators to display headlines and story summaries. *See also* aggregator and RSS.

RSS news reader: *See* aggregator.

scraping: To create an RSS feed for a Web site without the permission of the Web site's owner. The RSS feed is called a scraped feed. *See also* RSS feed.

search engine: A tool for finding information on the Internet. To use a search engine, you go to the search engine's Web site and enter keywords. Web sites that match they keywords you entered appear in the search results. By clicking a Web-site name in the search results, you can go to the Web site. *See also* keyword *and* meta-search engine.

search operators: *See* Boolean operators.

serial port: The place on the computer where the modem is plugged in.

shareware: Software that is offered for evaluation at no cost. Users of shareware are usually asked to pay a registration fee. Most shareware programs cease operating after a trial period if the registration fee is not paid.

short messaging services (SMS): The text messages that cell phone users can send and receive by way of instant-messaging services to which they subscribe. *See also* instant messaging.

signature: In an e-mail message, a saying, address, or slogan found at the bottom of the message.

smiley: *See* emoticon.

SMS: *See* short messaging services.

SMTP (simple mail transfer protocol): The protocol by which e-mail is sent from an Internet- or network-connected computer to an incoming mail server. This server holds the mail until the person to whom it is addressed collects it.

social bookmarking: To share bookmarks with others over the Internet. *See also* bookmark.

spam: Unsolicited e-mail, usually in the form of advertisements. Spam is junk mail sent over the Internet. *See also* spim *and* spit.

spammer: One who sends spam e-mail advertisements.

specialty search engine: A search engine designed for looking into one area of the Internet — online travel booking, science, news, or health, for example. Also called a vertical search engine. *See also* search engine.

spider: An automated program for indexing and describing what is on Web pages. Information that spiders gather is stored in a database. When you use a search engine to search the Internet, you look in a database with information gathered by spiders. Also called a bot or a crawler.

spim: Spam, or junk mail, received by way of an instant-messaging (IM) service.

spit: Spam, or junk mail, received by way of an Internet telephone connection.

spyware: Software loaded surreptitiously on a computer that gathers information about a user without his or her knowledge or permission and transmits the information back to a source. Spyware programs are sometimes hidden inside freeware and shareware programs that users download over the Internet. *See also* adware *and* keylogger.

stemming: In Internet searches, reducing a keyword to its root form and using the root form for the search instead of the keyword. For example, a search with the keyword *production* also searches for *product* and *productive* on Web pages. Stemming results in a more thorough Internet search. Not all search engines are capable of stemming.

streaming: In regard to audio or video delivered over the Internet, instead of downloading a file to listen to audio or watch video, the audio or video file is played as it arrives in a media player or other program for playing media. Streaming permits long files to start playing before they are downloaded.

thread: In a newsgroup or message board, the initial post and all the posts made in response to it.

time bomb: A virus programmed to be dormant until a certain time, when it activates itself to cause damage.

top-level domain: In an e-mail address, the two- or three-letter designation at the end of the address that identifies the address type, in the case of a three-letter designation, or the country where the person who has the address resides, in the case of a two-letter designation.

Trojan horse: A virus that masquerades as one kind of program but is really another. *See also* virus *and* worm.

troll: On a message board or newsgroup, someone who posts inflammatory comments to bait others into responding.

uniform resource locator (URL): *See* Web address.

unsolicited bulk e-mail (UBE): *See* spam.

unsolicited commercial e-mail (UCE): *See* spam.

upload: To send Web pages across the Internet to an Internet service provider so that the Web pages can be displayed on the Internet. Also to send a file to an ftp site where others can download it.

URL: *See* Web address.

Usenet: A collection of newsgroups, each devoted to a particular topic, to which people can post messages. A part of the Internet, the Usenet is a decentralized network with the messages stored on many different servers.

user group: *See* newsgroup.

username: In an e-mail address, the name to the left of the at sign (@) that identifies the person to whom e-mail messages are sent. To the right of the at sign is the domain name and the top-level domain.

uuencode: In e-mail messaging, when a message is converted from binary to ASCII format — when it is stripped of its formats — so that it can be sent across the Internet to an unsophisticated e-mail program. Stands for *Unix-to-Unix encoding. See also* MIME.

vertical search engine: *See* specialty search engine.

virus: A self-replicating program designed to do harm to computers. *See also* Trojan horse *and* worm.

virus cleaning: Removing viruses from a file so that the file can be opened safely.

virus scanning: Checking files to see whether they contain known viruses.

Vlog: A blog that offers videos rather than text. *See also* blog.

voice over Internet protocol: *See* VoIP.

VoIP (Voice over Internet Protocol): A protocol by which voice communications are transmitted over the Internet in a manner similar to telephone communications.

vortal: A Web portal that serves a particular industry. The term is short for *vertical portal. See also* Web portal.

warchalking: Marking the location of an open wireless connection — a hotspot — to the Internet on the sidewalk or wall with chalk. *See* hotspot.

watermark: In a music or video file, a hidden marker that identifies the owner of the file's copyright.

Web: *See* World Wide Web.

Web address: The location of a Web page on the Internet. The address consists of the domain name, folder name, and filename. Each Web page has a particular Web address. Also called a uniform resource locator (URL).

Web-based: Refers to activities that take place on a Web page on the Internet rather than on a personal computer.

Web-based e-mail service: An e-mailing service in which mail is composed, stored, sent from, and received to a computer on the Internet, not a home or office computer. To handle the mail, you use a Web browser, not an e-mail software program. Yahoo! Mail and Hotmail are examples of Web-based e-mail services.

Web beacon: A signal sent from an e-mail message to a Web server telling the Web server to deliver images for the body of an e-mail message. Spammers use Web beacons to determine whether e-mail addresses are active and are therefore capable of receiving spam.

Web browser: A computer program that connects to Web sites and displays Web pages.

Web counter: *See* hit counter.

Web log: *See* blog.

Web portal: A Web site that offers many different services — news, Internet searching, e-mail, and others. Yahoo! is an example of a Web portal.

Web server: Software that provides HTML documents and associated files to Web browsers when requested to do so. Also called an HTTP server.

Web site: A collection of Web pages, devoted to one topic, located on the same Web server.

Webcam: A mounted camera that broadcasts pictures to the Internet at regular intervals. Also called a cam.

Webmaster: The person responsible for maintaining a Web site. By convention, the Internet address of the Webmaster can be found on the home page of a Web site.

Wi-Fi: A wireless local area network. Stands for *wireless fidelity*.

wiki: Software that allows for collaborative writing at a Web site or blog. *Wiki* is a Hawaiian word that means "quickly."

wireless: Using radio signals rather than cables.

World Wide Web: All the information and entertainment resources available on the Internet — Web pages, audio files, video files, and computer programs. Also called *the Web*.

worm: A virus that quickly makes copies of itself on many computers. *See also* Trojan horse *and* virus.

Index

Numerics & Symbols

Notes